TOTALED

"Shai Agassi had a huge vision: a global fleet of electric cars with hot-swappable batteries that could end our dependence on oil and save the planet. His passion, charisma and confidence persuaded governments, billionaires, celebrities and journalists (including me) to join his cult of hope. Five years and a billion dollars later, the company was a smoking heap. Brian Blum's deeply researched account is like playing a car-wreck video in slow motion: You can watch every stroke of bad luck, bad timing, and bad blood reduce a once-thrilling idea to dust."

— **David Pogue**, Yahoo Finance, former New York Times tech columnist

"Brian Blum's got the wheel and you get to ride shotgun. And you'd better hang on: this fast-paced, action-packed journey presents a side of the startup world that few ever get to see—much less survive. Blum's breezy style, muscular prose and impeccable research are a rare combination for any business book, but his eye for detail, character development and story are nothing short of genre bending. Blum makes it look easy, but don't be fooled: *TOTALED* is a literary achievement in the best sense of the word. Can't wait for the movie."

— **Gina Smith**, author of *iWoz: Computer Geek to Cult Icon: How I Invented the Personal Computer, Co-Founded Apple, and Had Fun Doing It* and former ABC News tech correspondent

"*TOTALED* tells an amazing true story that reads like fiction. Shai Agassi is an endlessly fascinating, larger-than-life figure, and Brian Blum's *TOTALED* ferrets out every colorful detail. In the process, the book gives us vivid living history from the early days of today's electric vehicle revolution."

— **Jim Motavalli**, author of *High Voltage* and *Forward Drive*, columnist for Car Talk at NPR and longtime contributor to The New York Times

"Part thrilling roller coaster, part slow-motion crash, Brian Blum's *TOTALED* is a fascinating history of Better Place's rise and fall. A treasury of lessons for entrepreneurs, managers, and board members alike, this book is required reading for ambitious innovators everywhere."

> — **Dr. Ron Adner**, author of *The Wide Lens: What Successful Innovators See that Others Miss* and Professor of Strategy and Entrepreneurship, Tuck School of Business, Dartmouth College

"The mystery of what really crashed electric car startup Better Place is finally unraveled. Brian Blum's *TOTALED* tracks the story—from Tel Aviv to Copenhagen, Palo Alto to Beijing. It's an account as fascinating as those that unfolded simultaneously at Fisker, Tesla and even GM. No one said getting into the 21st century would be a no-brainer—and with stories like this one, it's easy to see why it's already been such an epic ride."

> — **Chris Paine**, director of *Who Killed the Electric Car* and *Revenge of the Electric Car*

"Brian Blum writes about a watershed event in the development of next-generation transportation: the rise and fall of Better Place. There are deep lessons to be learned from this consummate insider who writes more like an author of detective thrillers than business books."

> — **Jon Medved**, venture capitalist and CEO, OurCrowd

"Brian Blum takes us on the wild ride that is the spectacular rise and fall of the most audacious startup of the last decade. Fueled by a grand vision, Better Place careens around the global course of a newly developing market. Brian Blum tells a story of unfettered ambition, unchecked hubris, bad luck and worse timing with the skill and dexterity of a professional driver on a rainy course."

> — **Chris Shipley**, executive producer, DEMO conference

"Eloquent, sharp, insightful and entertaining, Brian Blum's autopsy of a lavishly financed venture's collapse is a must-read for inventors, investors, economists and anyone curious about the Israeli start-up scene's culture of adventure, inspiration and risk."

> — **Amotz Asa-El**, commentator, Dow Jones MarketWatch

"Before there was the Leaf, the Volt, the Bolt and even the Tesla, there was Better Place—the first electric car startup. Using his deep reporting and research skills, Brian Blum brilliantly chronicles the fascinating story of this pioneering company. He makes us understand how difficult disruption is. Few know the real obstacles Better Place encountered. If you love cars and are interested in change, you will be captivated reading this book."

— **Sandy Schwartz**, president, Cox Automotive

"The spirit of every environmentalist was lifted when we heard about Shai Agassi's grand plan to wean the world off oil. But the resulting five years dashed those hopes, washed away by a well of power, dominance and Middle Eastern testosterone, as thick as the crude oil Agassi's company intended to displace. Brian Blum documents this remarkable meltdown from transformative beginning to sputtering end. Without his voice, the Better Place story might have remained untold—or been claimed by another company as its own. *TOTALED* is a riveting narrative that had me glued to each page."

— **Karin Kloosterman**, founder, Green Prophet

"A world-changing vision, a charismatic and talented CEO, massive funding— what could go wrong? A lot, of course, and Brian Blum's *TOTALED* takes us on the journey of Better Place, the electric car infrastructure startup that seemed to have it all. From its early days to its final closing, Blum describes in fascinating detail the players, the technology, and the missteps that ultimately brought the company down. The story has many strands, and Blum keeps the narrative clear and compelling. This is a book with important lessons for startups of all kinds."

— **Jeffrey S. Rosenschein**, co-creator of The Hebrew University of Jerusalem entrepreneurship course; Sam and Will Strauss Professor of Computer Science

"*TOTALED* is a fascinating case study and cautionary tale of the rise and fall of a 'change the world' entrepreneur. It can inoculate you against being taken in by charismatic visionaries."

— **Michael Maccoby**, author of *Narcissistic Leaders: Who Succeeds and Who Fails* and *Strategic Intelligence: Conceptual Tools for Leading Change*

To Sue & Steve —
May your Fallbrook
journeys be electrifying
Brian

TOTALED

THE **BILLION-DOLLAR CRASH**
OF THE **STARTUP** THAT **TOOK ON**
BIG AUTO, BIG OIL AND THE **WORLD**

BRIAN BLUM

BLUE
PEPPER
PRESS

Publishers Cataloging-in-Publication Data
Names: Blum, Brian.
Title: Totaled : the billion-dollar crash of the startup that took on
big auto, big oil and the world / Brian Blum.
Description: First edition. | Sherman Oaks, CA : Blue Pepper Press, [2017]
| Includes bibliographical references.
Identifiers: LCCN 2017908600 | ISBN 978-0-9830428-1-5
| ISBN 978-0-9830428-2-2 (ebook)
Subjects: LCSH: Better Place (Firm) | Agassi, Shai, 1968- | Battery charger industry.
| New business enterprises--Management. | Small business--Management. |
Entrepreneurship. | Leadership.
Classification: LCC HD9697.B324 B48 2017 (print) | LCC HD9697.B324 (ebook)
| DDC 381.4562131242--dc23
Book design by Melinda Martin
Cover design by Daniel Wolfsong
Printed in the United States of America
www.brianblum.com

To Jody, who loved her Fluence Z.E.

CONTENTS

CAST OF CHARACTERS

Yosef Abramowitz: co-founder of the Arava Power Company.

Dafna Agassi: vice president of marketing at Better Place; Shai Agassi's sister.

Reuven Agassi: Shai Agassi's father; business partner for Quicksoft and TopTier.

Shai Agassi: founder and CEO of Better Place.

Tal Agassi: vice president of global infrastructure, deployment and operations at Better Place; Shai Agassi's brother.

Zohar Bali: vice president of sales at Better Place.

Tal Bar: "switcher" at Better Place.

Robby Bearman: electric vehicle-to-grid integration lead at Better Place.

Dubi Ben-Gedalyahu: reporter for the Israeli business publication Globes.

Anthony Bernbaum: head of global special opportunities at HSBC, which invested in Better Place's Series B round.

Larry Burns: vice president of research and development and strategic planning at General Motors.

Daniel Campbell: head of telematics, web and mobile product management at Better Place. Expert in all things OSCAR.

Lilach Gon Carfas: marketing professional at Better Place who managed the interface between the Visitor Center and Better Place's corporate headquarters.

Tami Choteveli: management consultant; Shai Agassi's girlfriend.

Antony Cohen: chief financial officer at Better Place Australia.

Dan Cohen: chief of staff at Better Place.

Motty Cohen: head of innovation at Better Place.

Dimitri Dadiomov: Stanford graduate student who joined Better Place to work in product management and global business development.

Macgregor Duncan: vice president of global corporate development at Better Place.

Alan Finkel: chief technology officer at Better Place Australia.

Kiyotaka Fujii: president of Better Place Japan.

Quin Garcia: self-avowed "car guy," who built the first electric car for Better Place, as part of the company's Automotive Alliances group.

Alan Gelman: Better Place's second chief financial officer.

Carlos Ghosn: chairman and CEO of the Renault-Nissan Alliance, which manufactured Better Place's only electric car, the Fluence Z.E.

Nir Gilad: CEO of Israel Corporation and Idan Ofer's business partner.

Brian Goldstein: director of Better Place Hawaii.

Sidney Goodman: vice president of automotive alliances at Better Place.

Mike Granoff: president of Maniv Energy Capital and head of oil independence policies at Better Place.

Johnny Hansen: CEO of Better Place Denmark.

Yoav Heichal: chief engineer at Better Place.

Barak Hershkovitz: CEO of Better Place Labs and CTO of Better Place.

Eitan Hon: chief operating officer of Better Place Israel.

Yishai Horn: head of marketing strategy at Better Place.

Jeff Johnson: director of corporate development at Better Place.

Debbie Kaye: Shai Agassi's personal assistant.

Moshe "Kaplan" Kaplinsky: CEO of Better Place Israel and a former deputy chief of general staff in the Israel Defense Forces.

Ben Keneally: Better Place Australia's head of marketing and strategy.

David Kennedy: Better Place's general counsel and corporate secretary.

Mike Lindheim: worked in global infrastructure deployment at Better Place.

Bob Lutz: vice chairman of global product development at General Motors.

Hugh McDermott: vice president of global utilities and energy at Better Place.

Julie Mullins: director of communications at Better Place.

Amit Nisenbaum: head of strategic alliances at Better Place.

Idan Ofer: chairman of the Israel Corporation and the first investor in Better Place.

Ehud Olmert: former prime minister, who agreed to let Israel be Better Place's "beta country."

Joe Paluska: vice president of global communications and policy at Better Place.

Ziva Patir: vice president of policy, standards and sustainability at Better Place. Former CEO of the Standards Institute of Israel.

Patrick Pelata: chief operating officer of Renault.

Aliza Peleg: chief operating officer of Better Place's U.S. headquarters.

Shimon Peres: former president of Israel, who challenged Shai Agassi by asking "now what are you going to do?"

Guy Pross: director of governmental relations at Better Place Australia.

Emek Sadot: senior director for battery, electric vehicle charging systems and the smart grid at Better Place.

Alan Salzman: CEO of VantagePoint Capital Partners, which first invested in Better Place's Series A round.

David Shlachter: worked in global marketing at Better Place.

Lawrence Seeff: head of global alliances at Better Place.

Efi Shahak: head of the Association for the Advancement of Electric Transport in Israel, a non-profit organization of Better Place drivers.

Rebecca Shliselberg: global network planner at Better Place.

Shelly Silverstein: director of human resources at Better Place Israel.

Saul Singer: co-author of the book that coined the term "Start-up Nation."

Charles Stonehill: chief financial officer at Better Place.

Carlos Tavares: replaced Patrick Pelata as chief operating officer of Renault.

Matthieu Tenenbaum: deputy program director in charge of the electric car program at Renault.

Alison Terry: head of automotive and corporate affairs at Better Place Australia and a 20-year veteran of General Motors.

Brian Thomas: blogger at IsraellyCool and a Renault Fluence Z.E. driver.

Evan Thornley: CEO of Better Place Australia.

Ariel Tikotsky: knowledge management manager at Better Place.

Osnat Tirosh: head of global human resources at Better Place.

Susanne Tolstrup: director of communications at Better Place Denmark.

Carlo Tursi: director of corporate development at Better Place.

Guy Tzur: battery switch station research and development manager at Better Place.

Alex Umansky: helped lead investment in Better Place from two firms: Morgan Stanley and Baron Capital.

Daniel Weinstock: charging grid manager at Better Place.

Daniel Yergin: president of Cambridge Energy Research Associates.

Andrey Zarur: Young Global Leader who co-developed the plan that would become Better Place.

Geoff Zippel: head of deployment at Better Place Australia.

"So how would you run a whole country without oil? That's the question that sort of hit me in the middle of a Davos afternoon about four years ago. And it never left my brain."

—Shai Agassi, founder and CEO, Better Place
on the TED stage, 2009

INTRODUCTION

"For a moment, suspend your disbelief."

This was Shai Agassi's signature opening statement. He used it when talking to CEOs and students, to those in corporate conference rooms and in the corridors of power, to his devoted employees and to the more than a million people who would watch and share his viral video presentation.

Today, he was saying it to one of the wealthiest men in Israel, at the start of a polished speech that would change the destinies of everyone in the room.

Agassi was—and still remains—one of the smoothest-talking, charismatic entrepreneurs the high-tech world has ever seen. Like his idol, Apple co-founder Steve Jobs, Agassi—a poker-playing Israeli boy wonder—is never at a loss for words.

After just a few minutes, he can turn even the most skeptical into a believer—and for Agassi, who treated business and negotiations like a binary game of high-stakes cards, there were only the believing faithful and those yet to be converted.

Agassi was in the Tel Aviv office of Idan Ofer, chairman of the Israel Corporation, Israel's largest publicly listed company, and one of the richest men in Israel, at the time worth nearly $4 billion. Also in the room was Mike Granoff, who headed up Maniv Energy Capital, a small venture capital firm, and who was responsible for arranging the meeting. Agassi would have 45 minutes to pitch Ofer on a plan for a business that, if successfully executed, would quite literally make the world a better place.

It was June 12, 2007. For the past two years, as a member of the Forum of Young Global Leaders at the World Economic Forum in Davos, Agassi and another young up-and-comer, Andrey Zarur, had been working on an idea to address the world's reliance on oil. The key, they concluded in an 18-page proposal, was reducing and eventually eliminating the number of gasoline-powered cars on the road. Automobiles were the top "use-case" for oil dependence, they determined.

Agassi and Zarur had explored a range of technology options, from hydrogen fuel cells to compressed air, and had determined that electric battery-powered vehicles were the best path to their envisioned future.

At the same time, they were acutely aware of how electric cars had been a non-starter in the past. This was largely because of what's known as "range anxiety," the very real fear that you could run out of juice before arriving at your destination. Whereas gasoline-powered cars can travel hundreds of miles between fill-ups, the electric car of 2007 could go no farther than about 70 miles between charges.

Agassi and Zarur's solution to addressing range anxiety had a number of moving parts.

For relatively quick refills, electric "charge spots" would be available in every conceivable location—at home, at the office, in public parking lots and at the curb.

For longer journeys, the solution was more radical: Don't recharge the battery. Change it.

That wouldn't be as simple as changing the battery in a flashlight or in a radio. The battery for an electric car at the time weighed 500 pounds. But Agassi and Zarur designed a way to make a battery swap as easy—and as fast—as a stop at a gas station.

Robots.

Designed to look and operate much like a contemporary car wash, battery switch stations would have a robot "pit crew." Drivers would pull in onto a platform, and the vehicle would gently be lifted far enough to allow a robotic arm to slide underneath, smoothly remove the spent battery and replace it with a new one—all in less time than it takes to get a tank of gas.

The battery switch stations would be part of a nationwide network, with each station placed in sufficient range to keep drivers covered.

The other factor that had kept consumers away from electric cars, Agassi explained, was price. A battery big enough to last even 70 miles pushed the cost of an electric car to nearly double that of a gasoline-powered one.

Agassi and Zarur had a solution for that, too—and it was even more innovative. The car and the battery would be separated—financially, physically and conceptually. Customers would purchase the car itself, but the battery would be owned by a service provider, which would then charge a monthly subscription fee to cover refills from plug-in charge spots and batteries swapped at a switch station. It was a model not unlike a cell-phone plan.

Paying for both a car and its expensive battery, Agassi reasoned, made no sense; it was akin to getting a gasoline-powered car with enough fuel inside to run it for several years. Pay as you go, by contrast, made more sense for everyone involved and would dramatically reduce the price.

And when upgrades—such as next-generation batteries with greater capacity—became available, the car owner would receive these at no extra cost. It was the same way things often worked in the high-tech software industry, where Agassi had spent most of his professional life up to this point.

As Agassi laid out his vision to Ofer, the match was neither obvious nor natural.

Ofer's Israel Corporation held stakes in a dozen companies, including Israel Chemicals, which extracts potash from the Dead Sea; offshore ultra-deepwater drilling company Pacific Drilling; and Oil Refineries, Ltd., Israel's biggest petrochemical company.

Agassi's grand green scheme could very well obviate a sizable chunk of Ofer's profits.

The Tel Aviv early summer humidity was already creeping up, but the skies were perfectly clear, affording a breathtaking view from Ofer's luxurious suite on the 25th floor of the Millennium Tower over the entirety of the Tel Aviv metropolis, home to nearly half of Israel's population, and providing Agassi with a seamless segue.

Agassi motioned to the teeming traffic below—a visceral bumper-to-bumper data point testifying to the soundness of his environmentally, economically and geopolitically audacious plan. In order to prove his concept, he said, he needed more than a "beta site." In the high-tech world, a "beta" often refers to a pre-final release version of a website or software, one users can try out knowing there are still kinks to be excised.

Agassi needed an entire beta country.

Israel would be perfect.

A virtual island, surrounded by enemies with closed borders, the whole of Israel could be covered by only a few dozen battery switch stations. Add to that Israel's high gasoline prices and its total reliance on politically sensitive imported oil, and the picture was as compelling as it was complete.

Ofer listened politely and asked a few questions, but then indicated it was time to go. Mike Granoff pulled a copy of the nascent company's business plan out of his briefcase. It was labeled "Project Better Place."

Ofer promised he'd read it that night—he was flying to China to finish another car deal in which the Israel Corp. was investing.

With Granoff leading the way, the three headed toward the elevators and made the quick 25-floor trip down.

As the doors opened into the lobby, Granoff—who had another group of investors waiting to meet Agassi at a coffee shop around the corner—said a hasty goodbye and went on ahead.

In the seconds after Granoff had left them alone, Ofer pulled Agassi close and whispered that he was "in"—for $100 million.

It was one of the most successful (and nearly literal) "elevator pitches" in high-tech history.

The $100 million would come from the Israel Corp. Ofer would add an additional $30 million of his own money. Granoff helped bring in another $70 million—an unprecedented Series A amount for a company that had at that point no products, no staff and no offices.

In 2007, when Better Place formally launched, Wired magazine called it the fifth-largest startup in history.

And some five-and-a-half years later, when it declared bankruptcy, Better Place held the unenviable distinction of being perhaps the most spectacularly failed technology startup of the 21st century.

1

THE EARLY DAYS

Better Place was not the first firm that Shai Agassi took from nearly nothing to a multimillion-dollar global status. Agassi had sold another company, TopTier—which he had started with his father, Reuven—to Germany's SAP for $400 million in cash in 2001.

Reuven Agassi immigrated to Israel from the southern Iraqi city of Basra. It was shortly after Israel had achieved independence. He was 9 years old at the time. Reuven's father had been an accountant for the Basra Port Authority, but when the state of Israel was declared on May 14, 1948, "the Iraqi government fired all its Jewish employees, confiscated Jewish property and arbitrarily arrested members of the community," Reuven explained. "In Baghdad, the government even carried out public hangings. We were very scared for our lives."

With nowhere else to go, the Agassis joined a flood of 150,000 Iraqi refugees arriving in Israel in 1950.

Reuven Agassi eventually was drafted into the Israel Defense Forces, where he became a communications officer. The job proved valuable for another reason: That's where he met Paula, an immigrant from Morocco who served as a wireless communicator. The two would soon marry.

Like most immigrants to Israel who had been forced to flee their homes, the young Agassis started out with nearly nothing. Fortunately, the army had a program where the state would pay for education for those who pursued a long-term military career. Reuven Agassi received a bachelor's degree in engineering from the Technion, Israel's leading technology institution, in Haifa. He continued in the army as a career officer for the next 16 years.

Shai Agassi was born on April 19, 1968, while his father was still in the army. When Reuven retired from the military in 1981, he landed a job with the Israeli company Tadiran, exporting communication equipment to South America. The Agassi family moved to Argentina. Shai, then 13, along with his younger siblings, brother, Tal, and sister, Dafna, was enrolled in English language schools there.

"I got exposed to American culture and to my first Apple II computer in the American high school of Buenos Aires," Agassi recalled, in a 2007 blog post. Agassi persuaded his father—who recognized a technical talent in his son early on—to buy him that Apple II in exchange for 10 percent of his "lifetime profits" from writing software.

Agassi graduated from the Lincoln International School in Buenos Aires at 15 and returned to Israel to study computer science at his father's alma mater. Before he had finished his degree, however, he was hit by a truck while trying to cross an expressway on foot. ("I made it four lanes, but the fifth was the killer," Agassi once quipped.). He was hospitalized with a broken leg for several months.

The accident became a pivotal event for Agassi.

"He lay for months in the hospital," Udi Ziv, his roommate at the Technion, recalled. "It's rare that someone gets that time to think, and I think it gave him a vision that everything is really fragile and perhaps drove him to larger and more meaningful things."

Agassi's complete recovery took nearly a year, during which time he was able to complete his bachelor's degree. Because of his injury, however, Agassi was judged not fit for a combat unit for his compulsory military service. That would turn out to be another blessing: He was taken instead into the Intelligence Corps, focusing on the computers he loved so much.

Upon his release from the army, Agassi was ready to start his first company.

Launching a business of your own might not seem like a logical next step. Don't most young software whizzes start their careers by working for an established firm?

But Israel is not like everywhere else.

Israel has earned the nickname "Startup Nation." Coined by Saul Singer and Dan Senor, authors of a best-selling 2009 book of the same name, it describes the remarkable development of a thriving tech scene second only to Silicon Valley's.

Israel has more companies listed on the NASDAQ stock exchange than does India, Japan and Korea combined, has more venture capital investment per capita than anywhere else in the world, and is No. 1 in the rate of per capita R&D spending. The results of this high-tech culture include global market leaders such as Teva Pharmaceuticals, the world's largest maker of generic drugs, and security software powerhouse Check Point Software Technologies.

The question that the book "Start-up Nation" sets out to answer is, "How is it that Israel—a country of [then] 7.1 million people, only 60 years old, surrounded by enemies, in a constant state of war since its founding, with no natural resources—produces more start-up companies than large, peaceful and stable nations like Japan, China, India, Korea, Canada and the United Kingdom?"

It's not just startups.

Just about every major tech company—Intel, Microsoft, Google, Cisco, Motorola, Apple, eBay, PayPal, Facebook—has an office in Israel. As far back as 1979, Intel entrusted its Israeli team to develop the 8088 chip. That was the chip selected by IBM to power the very first personal computer. The subsequent 386 chip was also an Israeli product.

Given that milieu, by choosing to start his own company, Agassi wouldn't be doing anything at all out of the ordinary in tech-savvy Israel.

But he needed a partner. He found one in his father.

Agassi wrote on his blog that he convinced Reuven Agassi "to do the unthinkable—to leave the security of a technology giant to jump in the uncharted waters of a startup."

Together, in 1991, the two started Quicksoft, which developed and distributed video, animation and web design software in Israel. In 1995, Quicksoft landed a deal with Apple to develop an educational online portal, and Shai Agassi, along with seven of his engineers, moved to California.

The team got busy coding, but within a year, Apple canceled the project.

"Someone at Apple decided that our choice of underlying technology stood very little chance of significant market penetration by the end of the century. You may have heard of the technology my team recommended—it was called the Internet," Agassi wrote on LinkedIn as part of a series called "My Best Career Mistake."

Agassi explained why "betting on Apple" was his "best career mistake." It created a sense of urgency—he and seven engineers were a 24-hour flight away from their home base in Israel, and the company's biggest contract had just gone bust.

"We huddled and concluded that the lesson from this failure at Apple was to diversify our customer portfolio," Agassi wrote.

Within three months, Quicksoft had signed on five new long-term clients. But the company's luck wouldn't last long. In the course of a single devastating week, one company after the next called to back out.

By Friday, all five companies were gone.

There was one final call—this one from Israel, from Reuven Agassi.

We have only two more weeks of cash in the bank, the senior Agassi told his son.

Shai Agassi begged his father for more time.

Two weeks, Reuven said. That was it.

Agassi and his team in Silicon Valley went into hyper-brainstorming mode. They had built educational portal software that Apple didn't want. Could it be used for anything else? How about for businesses?

Yahoo was already a success as a consumer portal. Could the Quicksoft technology become a kind of Yahoo for business, Agassi wondered?

The team put together a prototype for a product. It was an answer, Agassi wrote, "for visionary corporate CIOs trying to figure out how the Internet could be used inside their IT shops."

Agassi called a friend at Apple who called another few friends and, before his father's deadline had expired, Agassi had assembled a team of 14 angel investors, which injected $800,000 into the company.

Quicksoft's corporate portal division was renamed TopTier. It built "enterprise information portals" that give a company's employees easy access to a wide variety of information from throughout the organization—from online applications and databases to websites and documents.

In 1998, Agassi sold 56 percent of TopTier to the Holland-based Vanenburg Fund, run by the brothers Jan and Paul Baan, at a valuation of $110 million—not bad for a company that two years prior had been nearly broke.

With funding in the bank and a technology that was proving increasingly popular, TopTier took off. By 2000, the company was generating $20 million in annual revenue. Headcount grew to 200 in both the United States and in Israel, where the company's R&D office was based.

One of its key clients was SAP.

SAP had the deep pockets and the connections to take TopTier and Agassi to places he'd never dreamed of. With 13,000 employees, SAP was one of the largest technology companies in Europe.

SAP's acquisition of TopTier in 2001 put Agassi squarely on the high-tech success map.

An analyst report by AMR Research called the TopTier acquisition "unprecedented for SAP" and its $400 million cash price tag "exceptional, since it is 20 times TopTier's annual sales."

Agassi did well in the deal too—he held 8.8 percent of TopTier, worth about $35 million. Years later, when a reporter asked Agassi whether he was looking to get rich from Better Place, and Agassi replied that he was on a mission to get the world off oil, and he didn't need the money, he was probably telling the truth.

Agassi was put in charge of the entire portals business with a staff of 700.

A year later, he was invited to join SAP's Executive Board. He was only 33 at the time.

The following year, SAP Chairman Hasso Plattner relinquished his role guiding technology development at the company he co-founded and handed off day-to-day oversight of all the company's software development activities to Agassi.

"There was a huge sense of pride and excitement, that this little startup from Israel could do something that the great big SAP couldn't and a recognition that there was a real need for this capability," recalled a former TopTier staffer who was part of the move to SAP.

THE NEXT CEO OF SAP?

Hasso Plattner had, like Agassi, been a bit of a renegade when he started SAP, in 1972.

"Plattner built a corporate culture in his own image: engineering-focused, headstrong and determined to do it all without help," Steve Hamm wrote about him in BusinessWeek.

But by 2001, SAP had become "insular and slow to change its ways." And the go-it-alone credo that Plattner had nurtured was becoming a liability rather than a strategic advantage in the Internet age.

Plattner launched mySAP.com—a net-ready version of SAP's array of software—in late 1999 and with it, a very un-SAP-like openness to partnership. Buying TopTier was part of this policy.

Plattner adored Agassi's radical approach.

Wired magazine reporter Daniel Roth wrote that at Agassi's first executive board meeting at SAP, "Agassi suggested nearly a dozen heretical ideas. He said SAP should give away its hardware and software for free—just charge for IT support. He said SAP should make its database business open source to undermine [arch competitor] Oracle. The other board members laughed: The new kid was a cutup! But they stopped when SAP cofounder Hasso Plattner looked around the table and said, 'He's the only guy making sense here.'"

Agassi took his new role as corporate rabble-rouser to heart, and a rumor spread that Plattner had anointed him as imminent successor to CEO Henning Kagermann, who was due to step down in 2007.

Instead, Agassi found himself competing with SAP's head of marketing, Leo Apotheker, for Kagermann's spot. When Kagermann's contract was extended for another two years, Agassi was offered the position of co-CEO.

Agassi kept his cool publicly, but the loss hit him hard personally.

"It changed him forever," recalled Andrey Zarur, who since 2005 had been Agassi's partner at the Forum of Young Global Leaders in Davos. "I don't think he necessarily wanted the SAP job. He may even have turned it down if they'd offered it to him. But he was thoroughly hurt when he was told 'you'll be the CEO, but not now, not on your terms and with a co-CEO.'"

Agassi told the Harvard Business Review he had already made up his mind several months earlier when he had a "sliding doors" moment—"a moment when if you turned one way, your life and career would go in one direction, and if you turned another way, you would go off on a completely different track."

"The moment could have passed me by quite easily," Agassi continued. "I remember walking down the Champs-Élysées [in Paris], so that I could think. I paced it one way, imagining myself at fifty years old having decided to stay at SAP. I imagined not only that SAP had succeeded under my leadership but that we had beaten Microsoft—we were number one. Then I walked the other way, picturing myself at fifty but having left SAP and pursued my dream. I pictured the worst-case scenario—that Better Place had been a failure. At five o'clock in the morning, after walking all night, I said to myself: This is the sliding-doors moment, and there's no question which path I should take. I'd rather fail at Better Place than succeed at SAP because no other job could compare to trying to save the world."

Agassi resigned from SAP on March 27, 2007.

"I've never seen someone as skilled as Shai at selling abstract concepts," Nimish Mehta, then senior vice president at SAP, told The Wall Street Journal at Agassi's departure.

Agassi was about to get the chance to sell his biggest concept yet.

THE WORLD SERIES OF POKER

Few people knew that during the time TopTier was racking up success after success and the SAP deal was being formulated, Shai Agassi had quietly begun playing competitive poker in Las Vegas. Through engaging in professional cards, Agassi honed the art of the bluff and a confidence to cope with whatever hand he was dealt.

Agassi's first reported earnings were at an event called "The Speedway of Poker" on August 26, 2000. There were 75 entrants and Agassi came in 10th. It wasn't a big win—he took home only $125—but he did better at his next reported competition, the 35th annual World Series of Poker's "No-Limit Hold'em," where he won $3,600 on May 18, 2004 at Binion's Casino.

At that event, he placed well ahead of several celebrity players, including film stars Ben Affleck and Toby McGuire.

In 2008, at another World Series of Poker event, he won $3,964.

Agassi didn't hide his poker exploits, but he didn't advertise them, either. Lindsey Held, a member of SAP's public relations team, was surprised when she learned about his hobby.

"Shai is very private," she explained. "All we knew was that he enjoys reading and spending time with his family." Agassi's wife, Nili, insisted that he donate all his poker winnings to charities for children and health causes.

Despite his earnings, Agassi played down his skills.

"I'd say that my poker game is uneducated … I'm not really very good," he told Investor's Business Daily in 2005.

But to his confidants, Agassi was more sure of himself.

"The way he talked about it, it was just so easy, like it was second nature to him," recalled Macgregor Duncan, one of Better Place's early finance executives. "The ability to see and read those others at the table were the same skills he would use later to convince people to join his mission."

Agassi himself said there are clear lessons one can take from playing poker.

On the one hand, "in business, you can't bluff too much or you'll get caught," he explained. On the other, the goals of both business and poker are similar: to understand your opponents and lure them into your positions of strength.

"Poker helps develop that level of awareness of the people in front of you," Agassi added. And "it's not about winning every hand, but about winning the last battle."

2

A MODERN DAY MOON SHOT

The 238 invitees to the Forum of Young Global Leaders in Davos, Switzerland, read like a who's who of some of the most prominent superstars in politics, science and technology today.

Among the attendees were Google founders Sergey Brin and Larry Page; Gavin Newsom, then mayor of San Francisco; Jack Ma, CEO of the Chinese e-commerce leader Alibaba; Loic Le Meur, the driving force behind the prestigious European tech conference LeWeb; Marc Beniof, chairman and CEO of Salesforce, a world leader in software-as-a-service; Brandon Burgess, who orchestrated NBC's acquisition of Universal Entertainment; venture capitalist Steve Jurveston; and Samantha Power, who would later be appointed U.S. ambassador to the United Nations.

Shai Agassi's road to what would become Better Place began in Davos, too.

It was 2005—several years before his abrupt departure from SAP. Agassi, 37, had been invited to join the first cohort of the highly selective Forum of Young Global Leaders, part of the World Economic Forum.

According the YGL's guidelines, members must have "achieved their success young—under the age of 40—and have shown a commitment to making a positive impact on society" before starting the six-year program.

The Forum of Young Global Leaders was started by German-born Klaus Schwab, a professor of business policy at the University of Geneva, who envisioned that corporate leaders might be in a position to do good in the world—to bring peace, reduce pollution, fight disease.

Each Young Global Leader was asked to pick a topic to tackle. The theme was "how do you make the world a better place by 2020?"

"It was intended as a conversation starter, but I took it seriously," Agassi told the Harvard Business Review in 2009.

Groups were formed to look at issues regarding health, the environment, aging, poverty, the media and more.

"There were no assignments; everything was self-selection," recalled Andrey Zarur, then CEO of BioProcessors, a Boston-based venture capital–backed biotechnology company that was building a platform for developing therapeutic drugs.

Zarur describes Schwab as "completely uncharismatic, as nerdy as they come, but who had this weird way of inspiring people. He told this group of young overachievers that they were wasting their time, that what they were doing in their day jobs was not sufficient, and it was up to them to change the world. No one from the older generation could do it, he said. They had too many vested interests. And every single last one of us drank the Kool-Aid. We all believed him."

Zarur's main area of interest was health care. But a fellow YGL member insisted Zarur sit down with Agassi.

"He's a bigwig at SAP, and he has all these crazy ideas about making Israel independent of oil," Zarur's colleague said.

Zarur and Agassi met at the Davos Schweizerhof, a 4-star hotel with a cozy piano bar and a large outdoor garden. It was January 2006, so the two skipped the deck chairs and stayed warm by the fire.

Agassi had been living in the United States for a decade, but his connection to Israel remained strong. He had become fascinated by the idea that tiny Israel could somehow be weaned off oil and serve as the proverbial "light unto the nations" by implementing a carbon-free economy.

Zarur had done his share of thinking about climate change as well: As part of his PhD thesis—which covered energy issues and life sciences in equal parts—he had investigated various technologies for reducing greenhouse gases.

Agassi was under the impression that "there was a whole bunch of radical science that had yet to be discovered," Zarur recalled. "But that wasn't true. It's just policy and business. The key is how can you apply economies of scale to renewable energy."

Over the course of the next few hours, the two clicked, reveling in a stream of synchronized thinking, shared stories and a love for big numbers and bigger dreams, all the while hatching plans that would live up to Schwab's exhortations.

"Shai came out of our meeting with a different mission," Zarur said. "If before, he thought he was going to leave what he was doing at some point down the road and fund NASA-type blue-sky technologies and new discoveries, now he had a call to action. He got very excited.

"Shai was gifted with an unparalleled intelligence," Zarur continued. "I mean, the guy is extraordinarily smart. I am very smart too, and I always feel like I'm the smartest guy in the room. But when I was with him, I felt like my brain was a 1973 VW, while he was driving a Porsche.

"He also has something else most of us nerds don't have—and that's a lot of charisma and personality. His thinking was, if you're gifted with certain abilities, it's your responsibility to do something with them. He was very noble about it—he believed he was building something for his children and their children."

For the rest of that weekend in Davos, Agassi and Zarur got down to details.

When it came to hydrocarbon production, what were the main culprits in Israel?

There were a few oil refineries in the country, plus the Dead Sea Works, the world's fourth-largest producer and supplier of potash products—mined and manufactured salts containing potassium, along with various other chemicals and industrial salts. But cleaning that up wouldn't be sufficient.

"The only place we could really move the needle was cars," Zarur said.

Research backed up that contention.

The holiday of Yom Kippur is marked by Jews in Israel by a complete and total cessation of vehicular traffic. Even in mostly secular Tel Aviv, where fasting and synagogue do not play a major role, driving is considered a social taboo, so much so that the city's major freeway—the Ayalon—is filled with children riding their bikes up and down its eight blissfully car-free lanes.

Dr. Ilan Levy, a professor at the Technion (the Agassi family's alma mater), looked at pollution levels in Tel Aviv on Yom Kippur over a 15-year period. He found that the levels of nitrogen oxide (the building block of smog) drop by 83 percent to 98 percent in the Tel Aviv area over Yom Kippur. Ozone levels and nitrogen dioxide levels fall as well.

If replicated on other days of the year, the Yom Kippur effect could make a substantial impact on the environment, Levy wrote. "A change in vehicle fleet to low-emission vehicles will have a major impact on both primary and secondary pollution levels over large regions."

It was not just paring down pollution that intrigued Agassi and Zarur.

"Reducing oil consumption was also a national security issue," Zarur said, especially given that many of Israel's enemies financed their economies and, in some cases, terror operations, from petroleum.

The next step was to determine what it would mean to replace gasoline-powered cars with clean vehicles.

"Electric cars were just one of ten different things we looked at," Zarur said. "We analyzed all the different technologies that existed. We projected them into the future. Would they get more expensive or cheaper? Which made the most sense?"

Agassi brought the high-level vision; Zarur was the numbers guy.

"I created a fairly sophisticated Excel model that included all kinds of public sources of information, such as the price of gas, compressed air, zinc, electricity, the price of batteries, connectors, power plants, predictions about the sources of energy available in different geographies, the cost of hybrid cars down the road," Zarur said. "Shai wanted the biggest bang for the buck. He didn't have a preference for one technology over another."

Before they settled on electric vehicles, they briefly considered hydrogen. After all, General Motors had spent years focusing on hydrogen fuel cells, as had BMW.

"We also looked at things that would make you laugh," Zarur recalled. "Air cars, slot cars on electric rails, biofuels, everything."

At one point, they wondered if they could build highways with the power to charge cars in motion.

But the math kept pointing to electric cars.

"The curve in my model showed that over time, the most cost-effective technology was electric," Zarur said. "They were cheaper than hybrids, which are cheaper than gas, which are cheaper than hydrogen and compressed air. What's so powerful about math is that it's not magic. We could sit down with the guys from BMW and show them the model. Projecting out to 2010, to 2020, the gap between electric vehicles and all other technology widened significantly."

Once the decision had been made, Agassi and Zarur pushed forward with a zealous intensity. They had to get rid of gasoline-powered cars.

"Not just some cars and not just substituting hybrids or flex fuels. No half measures. The internal combustion engine had to be retired," Wired magazine wrote about Agassi and Zarur's thinking in those thrilling Davos days.

A SHORT HISTORY OF ELECTRIC CARS

Electric cars have been heralded as the vehicle of the future for more than 100 years.

While the very first electric vehicle was invented in 1828 by the Hungarian Anyos Jedlik, the first practical cars would not become available until 1859, with the invention of the lead-acid battery by French physicist Gaston Plante, improved in 1881 by Camille Faure.

The first production electric car arrived initially in London in 1884, built by the English inventor Thomas Parker. A similar car in the United States was developed in 1890, by William Morrison of Des Moines, Iowa. The six-passenger wagon could zip along at the staggering speed of 14 miles per hour, with a maximum range of 40 miles.

Meanwhile, a small fleet of electric taxis took to the streets in both New York and London, where they were nicknamed "Hummingbirds" due to the whirring noise they made.

In New York City in the spring of 1897, the Electric Carriage & Wagon Company introduced a dozen electric taxicabs intended to compete with the existing horse-drawn taxi infrastructure.

The fleet expanded to over 100 electric vehicles, and the EC&WC was renamed the Electric Vehicle Company (EVC), which spread out to a half-dozen of the largest cities in the United States, with sales agents as far afield as Mexico City and Paris.

Regional operating companies were established, and EVC distributed some 2,000 electric vehicles to them. But by 1907, just 10 years after its launch, the company was beset by a myriad of managerial mishaps. Production delays and warehouse fires led to shareholder lawsuits and blistering public attacks. The company eventually declared bankruptcy.

But the real tipping point was the gasoline-powered car, which could soon go much further and required much less time to refill than an electric vehicle did to recharge.

Still, in the early part of the 20th century, there was a point when electric cars looked like they might have a chance—at least on paper.

In a survey done in 1912, 38 percent of all American automobiles were powered by electricity, versus 22 percent by gas. (The largest power system for mass-market cars at that point actually was steam.) A total of 33,842 electric cars were registered in the United States, made by some 20 different manufacturers.

Electric cars had a number of key advantages, as well: no vibration, no smell, no noise; no hand crank required to start the engine; no gears. (Steam cars were gear-free, too, but were eventually retired when their long start-up times—up to 45 minutes on cold mornings—made them a poor third choice.)

It wasn't range or speed, however, which ultimately doomed the electric car. It was the electric self-starter, invented by Charles Kettering in 1912. This eliminated the hand crank in internal combustion engine cars, making these newfangled vehicles more amenable to the less brawny.

When Henry Ford introduced assembly-line production of the Model T in 1908, the price of his gasoline-powered cars plummeted. By 1912, one of Ford's gasoline cars sold for half the price of an electric car.

While Better Place would come to popularize the concept of battery switching in the modern age, this concept was not entirely new, either. It was first put into practice by the Hartford Electric Light Company in 1910, for electric trucks.

Owners would purchase their vehicle from General Electric's GVC subsidiary, but without a battery, which came from the Hartford Electric utility. As with the model Better Place would eventually offer, GVC electric truck owners in 1910 paid a variable per-mile charge and a monthly service fee to Hartford Electric to cover maintenance and battery exchanges.

The service operated for 14 years. A similar service, with separate car and battery ownership, was opened in Chicago, in 1917.

THE BLUEPRINT

Members of two student groups at Stanford University—the Energy Club and the Entrepreneurship Club—received an email in November 2006. It stated that the president of the product and technology group at SAP would be coming to speak on the future of scalable oil-free transportation. All were welcome.

About 40 people attended. One of those was Dimitri Dadiomov, an energy science and technology major at Stanford.

Dadiomov had never heard of Shai Agassi, nor was he expecting much from the talk.

"I'm imagining this software executive in a suit, working for a big German company. Already I'm thinking, what can he say that's going to be interesting?" Dadiomov recalled.

As Dadiomov would discover in the course of the hour-long talk, Agassi was far more than a staid suit and had by this point been working with Zarur tirelessly for months—nights, weekends and on transcontinental flights—on their idea to reduce oil dependence.

Agassi and Zarur needed help to flesh out the details. And where better to recruit smart, enthusiastic (and inexpensive) labor than the university Agassi admits he applied to—and was rejected from—in 1990.

Of the students who attended Agassi's lecture, eight, including Dadiomov, were convinced that Agassi and Zarur were on to something and agreed to continue working with the charismatic Israeli and his business partner.

Agassi spent many hours with the group, popping over from his office at SAP, conveniently located just down the street, in Palo Alto.

The result was an 18-page document dubbed "Transforming Global Transportation: Fuel independence at country level as a business opportunity. A modern day moonshot."

The latter reference was deliberate.

A moonshot, in a technology context, refers to "an ambitious, exploratory and ground-breaking project undertaken without any expectation of near-term profitability or benefit."

The paper placed Agassi's proposition alongside other history-altering events: Thomas Edison's light bulb, James Watt's steam engine and the Apollo space program, which landed the first human on the moon in 1969.

Every social transformation requires "the bravery of Churchill, the vision of JFK, the determination of Reagan, the rare ability to galvanize a country or the world to take the right step for a greater cause," Agassi and Zarur wrote in the preface to their paper. "We are standing on the verge of such an event, when a technical revolution will meet political determination and make a difference in this world."

By the time the visionary plan was released, in December 2007, it had been labored over and revised six times. It also carried fewer names—Agassi and Zarur were the only ones to appear as authors, with all the young collaborators stripped out, not even mentioned in the acknowledgments.

The resulting paper was nevertheless inspiring in its grandiosity.

"We are staring at a huge business opportunity where we could reinvent the automotive industry," the document began. "We are at a juncture when a leader needs to step up and change the destructive path our planet has taken in the age of global climate change. It is time to transform transportation out of its oil dependency, out of fossil fuels and into electricity."

While most of the details focused on the Israeli market, the model would still be relevant to other countries.

Israel had some 2 million cars at the time, of which 1.6 million were passenger cars. Eighty percent of drivers commute on average 30 miles a day, "which is well managed within the current electric vehicle range of 50 miles for lithium-ion batteries," the paper read.

Because cars would primarily be charged overnight through a driver's home charge spot, even the optimal scenario, where Israel's entire vehicle fleet had been converted to all-electric, still wouldn't overtax the country's electrical grid.

The math goes like this: All those cars would need 6,000 megawatts of electrical power, in order to charge over a 10-hour period. (A typical coal plant offers about 600 megawatts, and the Three Mile Island nuclear facility in the United States has a capacity of 800 megawatts.)

Israel's existing infrastructure already had the capacity to generate 8,000 megawatts at peak hours; overnight, the country typically consumed just 2,000 megawatts. So there was plenty of power to go around. No new power plants would need to be added to Israel's current 55.

And this was based on the wildly optimistic assumption that everyone in the country, all 2 million vehicle owners, would give up their gasoline-powered cars in the coming years. (An earlier draft of the paper anticipated sales of "just" 100,000 vehicles a year.)

Other countries reviewed by Agassi and the team sported similar electric profiles; in most, the grid at off-peak hours was usually at only 25 percent consumption.

The savings on a countrywide level could be significant as well.

Two million electric cars on the road in Israel would replace some 20 million barrels of oil a year. With 2007 prices predicted at $80 per barrel, that was a savings in the cost of purchasing pre-refined crude oil of close to $2 billion every year.

When it came to consumer costs, however, electric cars didn't seem like such a bargain.

In 2007 numbers, a Honda Civic came with a sticker price of $15,000. A Prius hybrid cost $20,000 and an equivalent electric car $23,000. Fuel costs for the Honda would be $10,000 over the life of the car, versus $7,500 for the Prius and $7,000 for the electric vehicle.

But that was at peak electricity costs.

When off-peak nighttime rates are used, electricity costs "should be cut in half," the document predicted.

Further savings could be realized by removing the cost of the battery from the purchase price of the car. That was the model Better Place would adopt, treating the batteries as a "consumable energy source," comparable to that of fuel for a gasoline-powered car.

Ultimately, as battery technology improved, an electric car should be "cost-competitive with a [gasoline-powered] vehicle within two years [and will have] a 13 percent cost advantage within five years."

Beyond the consumer value proposition, investing in electric would spur battery research and production, innovation in electric engines, improved regenerative braking, lighter materials, transportation software inside the car and on smart roads, and distributed charging stations and mobile charging devices, the paper claimed.

There would be spillover advances in wind power, tidal power, wave power and nuclear power generation.

Moreover, "the first countries to take on such a bold project will enjoy a tremendous long-term branding effect" that will give their leaders the credibility "to drive follow-up social improvements" internally and to attract "the next generation of scientists into local research centers." It would, in addition, provide legitimacy for countries in their "drive for other positive political agendas."

Indeed, the entire world would look with envy to what Israel had created.

"Other green developments will undoubtedly want to borrow blueprints or components from the success story as they implement similar solutions in their countries." The result would be "transformative ... creating a gravitational effect for future innovations."

The paper concluded with a call to action for "global cooperation" that would result in "3-4 countries scaling from 200,000 cars to 20 million cars in consecutive increments."

The top choices were all islands of sorts: the United Kingdom, with 25 million cars, a large economy without local oil, strong environmental awareness and great renewable energy sources; the city-state of Singapore, with one million cars, no oil sources and an "unrivaled ability to drive policy changes"; Iceland, with 150,000 cars and "abundant excess electrical power" particularly from geo-thermal; and of course Israel, a "virtual island when it comes to transportation, as no cars come and go" from the country plus "strong technical innovation and a strong social need to reduce global oil dependency."

Andrey Zarur was never 100 percent comfortable with some of the document's lofty ambitions.

"Shai never intended to say that he was JFK, putting a man on the moon," Zarur said. "His point was that the only way we can solve the problem of oil independence is by taking big shots—moonshots. Incremental little steps won't do it."

Nevertheless, the paper provided the inspiration and some of the nuts and bolts that would launch and ultimately guide Better Place on its journey. It would be trotted out frequently—with investors, with potential employees, with third-party partners. It would prove irresistible, becoming ubiquitous in Better Place lore and required reading for new hires.

There was just one problem.

It was never intended to be a business plan.

The paper "was only meant as an exercise," Zarur insisted. "Shai wanted to leave it as his legacy to the governments of the world. It was his mission."

But an operational plan is what it eventually became, Zarur said. "Almost word for word."

And the time had come to show it off.

SABAN FORUM

Energy consultant Daniel Yergin stood for pretty much the opposite of everything Shai Agassi had been developing in his visionary plan.

The president of Cambridge Energy Research Associates, Yergin posited that the world had enough oil to last for decades, and that dire predictions about the imminent approach of "peak oil"—the point at which all of the known resources have been found and oil production begins a precipitous drop—were unfounded.

In contrast to Agassi, who saw energy independence as an immediate economic imperative, Yergin saw no reason to panic. In the magazine Foreign Affairs, in 2006, he wrote: "Global output has actually increased by 60 percent since the 1970s, the last time the world was supposedly running out of oil." His research group predicted that "net productive capacity could increase by as much as 20 to 25 percent over the next decade."

"There will be a large unprecedented buildup of oil supply in the next few years," Yergin added, in The Washington Post.

Yergin delivered this prognosis in front of a crowd of international leaders at 10:30 on the morning of December 10, 2006, in the ballroom of the Ritz-Carlton in Washington D.C., where he had been invited to speak at the third annual Saban Forum, a high-powered gathering established by billionaire Israeli Haim Saban, who had launched his American career by bringing the "Mighty Morphin Power Rangers" to American television.

Yergin spoke on a panel entitled "Energy Independence or Security?"

Immediately following him was Shai Agassi.

As Agassi looked up and down the long rectangular table in the ballroom where 60 of the world's smartest and most powerful men and women had been assembled, he was quietly nervous. This was to be the first time he would present his arguments publicly.

Among the participants seated near him: former U.S. president Bill Clinton; former Israeli prime minister, Nobel Peace Prize–winner and future Israeli president Shimon Peres; U.S. Supreme Court Justice Stephen Breyer; and two past directors of the CIA.

At just 38 years old, Agassi was the youngest invitee.

When Agassi's turn came to speak, he started with an uncharacteristic stammer. Agassi disagreed with Yergin, he told the other participants. Getting the world off oil was not something that could wait.

With that, Agassi launched into the speech of a lifetime.

As he pushed through, point by point, describing the reasons why electric cars were the future and the extent of the charging infrastructure that would be needed, his hesitancy vanished and his trademark grin took over.

Wired magazine's Daniel Roth was reporting on the Forum that day. He described the mesmerizing effect Agassi had on the crowd.

"As he talked, he read the body language of the audience—they were leaning forward, they were nodding—and he fed off it, layering on details. A country like Israel, he told them, could get off oil by simply adopting his new business model. No technological breakthroughs were necessary. No new inventions. It was as if he'd discovered a trapdoor beneath both the gasoline industry and the auto industry, a combined $3 trillion market. It sounded easy and unavoidable. Even Daniel Yergin was amazed. Shai Agassi had stolen the show."

In the middle of Agassi's presentation, Shimon Peres interrupted him.

"Do you have this written down anywhere?" he intoned in his well-known, gravelly voice.

Agassi briefly stepped down from the dais and handed Peres a copy of the paper he and Andrey Zarur had only recently completed.

"You are my witnesses," he told the audience. "The government of Israel has now received my plan!"

After Agassi's presentation, another international statesman, Bill Clinton, approached him.

"You're solving the right problem at the wrong time," Clinton told Agassi.

Referring to the part of Agassi's plan to sell brand-new electric cars though automotive dealers, Clinton continued: "The average Joe doesn't go to a dealership; he buys a nine-year-old used car and drives it into the ground, and then he buys another nine-year-old car. You need to figure out how to get the average Joe into an electric car for free and still make money."

Agassi pondered Clinton's friendly advice. How could you give away a car and still make money? Never one to shy away from a conversation, even with one of the most powerful men in the world, Agassi shot back.

"And how exactly should I do that?" he asked.

"You're the smart guy," Clinton said with a smile. "You figure it out."

SHIMON PERES

A week after the conference, Agassi was lying in bed when his phone rang. It was Shimon Peres.

Agassi sat up. At first he assumed it must be a joke, but the rumbling voice on the other end of the line was unmistakable.

Peres said he couldn't stop thinking about Agassi's presentation at the Saban Forum.

"Nice speech," he told Agassi. "Now what are you going to do?"

"What do you mean?" Agassi asked.

"You spoke so beautifully," Peres replied. "You have to make this a reality. Otherwise it will remain a speech."

Peres paused for a moment.

"Can you really do it?" he challenged Agassi. "Is there anything more important than getting the world off oil? Who will do it if you don't?"

Peres's call was an unexpected reality check for Agassi, whose speech at the Saban Forum in Washington was still in the realm of "thought experiment." Even after attracting the attention of superstars like Shimon Peres and Bill Clinton, Agassi said he had been until that point "merely solving a puzzle."

If anything, "I wasn't thinking about it as a company, but more as an arm of government," he wrote in a Better Place internal publication.

But Peres was thinking bigger.

"[Government] agencies don't do things. Entrepreneurs do," he said to Agassi. "You have to start a company. Otherwise this is just an idea. You have a good job [at SAP], but this is a better job, because you can save the world."

The final kicker: "What can I do to help?" Peres asked.

Shimon Peres wasn't always interested in the environment. He started his 60-year career in politics as the deputy director general of the Israeli Ministry of Defense. He was considered a hawk, and he had helped build Israel's first (and only) nuclear reactor in Dimona. But by 1993, he had moved to the left as he became one of the architects of the Oslo Peace Accords, for which he shared a Nobel Peace Prize with Yitzhak Rabin and Yasser Arafat.

In 2007, Peres was elected president, a mostly ceremonial position, and he turned his attention to all things green.

"Oil is the greatest problem of all time—the great polluter and promoter of terror. We should get rid of it," he said once in an interview with BusinessWeek.

Peres was equally interested in pushing the solar option.

"Why should we hang on oil when we can hang on the sun? The sun is much more permanent, more democratic, and there's plenty of it," he told Wired magazine. "Israel is going to be a green country. That's our ambition ... to do it as soon as possible."

Israel was the ideal size for a company like Better Place, Peres felt.

"When you are small, you can be really daring," he said. "Israel can't become a major industrial country, but it can become a daring world laboratory and a pilot plant for new ideas, like the electric car."

Ultimately, he concluded, nature was "impatient. You cannot say: I'm going to negotiate pollution for ten or twenty years. Pollution won't wait for you. Pollution is not a political force. It's a force of nature."

Shai Agassi flew to Israel at the end of December 2006. For the next week and a half, Peres organized a whirlwind tour of more than 50 governmental meetings for Agassi.

"Each morning we would meet at [Peres's] office and I would debrief him on the previous day's meetings," Agassi explained. Peres would then "get on the phone and begin scheduling the next day's meetings. These are appointments I could never have gotten without Peres."

Agassi sat with Israel's top leaders in industry and government. Key among those was a meeting with the prime minister, Ehud Olmert.

Olmert was surprisingly supportive. But he was also realistic. He set two conditions that were tough, but sensible. They would indelibly shape the new company's trajectory and decisions going forward.

"You don't know anything about cars, and I don't know anything about cars, either," Olmert told Agassi. "So if we are going to do this, you need to bring in a top five automaker that says they are going to build the car for your network."

The second condition: "The Israeli government is not a venture capitalist," Olmert said. "You need to raise at least two hundred million dollars on your own. But if you do both of these, I'll let you experiment on our country."

When he heard Olmert's figure, Andrey Zarur was shocked.

"We only intended to raise five or ten million dollars in seed capital," Zarur said. "The idea was we'd later raise another fifty to 100 million, only after we'd proved things."

Still, if Agassi could deliver on those two conditions, Olmert promised he would put pressure on the right government ministries to reduce taxes on electric cars.

That would translate into some serious savings for customers.

Under Olmert's proposed tax scheme, the bruising 78 percent import tax Israel levied on gas-guzzling cars would drop to just 8 percent for 100 percent electric vehicles for four years.

The tax would rise sharply afterward, but Agassi said he wasn't worried. The threat of the tax returning to its original rate would only serve as further incentive for early adopters.

The Finance Ministry was less sanguine: The revenue losses could add up to $700 million over five years, it claimed.

The number crunchers needed to see the big picture, Agassi countered. The potential hit to tax revenues was nothing compared with what foreign oil costs the economy.

Olmert's plan prevailed. Electric cars eventually would receive the promised tax reduction.

THE AUTOMAKERS

Shimon Peres didn't stop with setting up meetings in Israel. He also sent letters to the CEOs of the five biggest automakers in the world, inviting them to sit down with him and Agassi.

In January 2007, Peres and Agassi flew together to Davos to meet the automakers. Three of the automotive CEOs didn't even bother to reply to Peres's letter. Of the two who showed up, Toyota was the first to arrive.

The executive announced that he'd read Agassi and Zarur's paper, and then proceeded to thoroughly trash the idea. Not only did he call the proposal "crazy," he spent most of the meeting trying to talk Peres out of pushing it any further. Hybrids like the Prius were the future, at least in the interim, the executive insisted. Electric cars were nothing more than science fiction.

"But I'll tell you what," the executive concluded with a flourish. "How about we give you guys a big discount on bringing our hybrids to Israel?"

Agassi was horrified.

"I had completely embarrassed this international statesman," he recalled, referring to Peres. "I made him look like he did not know what he was talking about."

Peres was nonplussed. If anything, he was more charged up than before.

"Can't you tell?" he said to Agassi. "They're really nervous about what you have to say."

Bring on the next one.

Carlos Ghosn was the CEO of Renault and, since 1999, of the Japanese car manufacturer Nissan, which he had bought and, in scarcely more than two years, turned around, from a company hemorrhaging cash into one making a profit.

Ghosn was considered a hero in Japan—there was even a *manga* comic book chronicling his life and business acumen—and a forward thinker in France, where Renault is based. Born in Brazil to Lebanese parents, his last name rhymes with "bone"; the "s" is silent. Forbes magazine called Ghosn "the hardest-working man in the brutally competitive global car business." Japanese media nicknamed him "Seven-Eleven" after his daily work schedule, which starts early in the morning and ends late at night.

Ghosn listened politely to Peres's impassioned speech about Agassi's plan for all of about five minutes.

Ghosn stopped Peres.

"Look," he said, as Agassi got ready for another rejoinder. "I read Shai's paper, and he is absolutely right. We are exactly on the same page. We think the future is electric. We have the car, and we think we have the battery."

Agassi and Peres were flabbergasted. They'd steeled themselves for a typically French dressing down. At best, they figured they might get another lecture on why hybrids were the way to go.

Peres couldn't control himself.

"So what do you think of hybrids?" he asked Ghosn.

"I think they make no sense," Ghosn shot back. "A hybrid is like a mermaid: If you want a fish, you get a woman. If you want a woman, you get a fish."

The three men erupted in laughter. Agassi knew he had his carmaker.

Agassi and Ghosn delved further into the nitty-gritty. Emboldened by the surprising turn of events, Agassi went so far as to propose that Renault actually manufacture its electric cars in Israel. After all, Intel had fabrication plants in the Holy Land, where it produced some of its most sophisticated PC computer chips.

Ghosn responded that he'd consider it, but that it would only be viable with a commitment to at least 50,000 cars a year.

Why not make it 100,000? Peres jumped in, throwing out a number that didn't appear in any spreadsheet. Ghosn nodded his approval—and that number would become the benchmark upon which Agassi's future company would be judged.

Although Agassi and Peres didn't know it when they invited him to Davos, Ghosn's enthusiasm was part of a long-term play to differentiate Renault, the world's fourth-largest carmaker, from its competitors in the clean-vehicle arena.

As Ghosn saw it, Toyota had its Prius hybrid, GM had been pursuing hydrogen fuel cells for years, and Ford was talking up biofuels. Tesla was just getting started but could conceivably evolve into a threat.

And what did Renault have at the time? A tiny electric Nissan that maybe Renault could sell to government facilities such as post offices or to childless consumers who never drove more than 60 miles from home and didn't need such luxuries as a back seat.

Agassi had laid out a direction that Ghosn imagined could help Renault leapfrog the others, while demonstrating innovation and bold leadership.

Ghosn was not a visionary. He was a capitalist through and through.

In Chris Paine's documentary, "The Revenge of the Electric Car," Wall Street Journal automotive reporter Dan Neil described Ghosn as someone who measures success purely "in dollars and cents. Ghosn doesn't get up in the morning unless there's money in it."

Regarding electric cars, Ghosn said in a meeting captured in the documentary, "We're the only ones on the offensive. Everyone else is on the defensive."

While Renault was the only carmaker that day to respond positively, Shimon Peres had no doubt that the concept would catch on with other manufacturers.

"I never worried about it. My great advantage is that I'm ignorant," he recalled. "My own mentor was David Ben-Gurion," Israel's first prime minister. "He used to say all experts are experts for things that did happen. There are no experts for things that may happen."

With Ghosn and Renault on board, Agassi now needed to fulfill Israeli Prime Minister Ehud Olmert's other condition: to raise the initial seed round. If he could, the vision that Shimon Peres had so remarkably believed in might actually become something more than just the schemes of two Young Global Leaders and a clutch of unpaid student interns.

3

BUILDING A BETTER PLACE

Mike Granoff was sitting in the lounge of the David Citadel Hotel in Jerusalem in late January 2007, flipping through The Jerusalem Post, when he noticed a column of short news briefs on the left-hand side of the newspaper's first section. The headline: "Peres returns from Davos."

Granoff skimmed the article. One line caught his eye.

"Israel would be a great test bed for electric cars," Peres had said while attending the World Economic Forum the previous week.

Granoff was a marathon runner. He took a similar long-term approach to investments. He had established Maniv Energy Capital in 2005 to explore opportunities in new energy technology. Granoff was part of the team that founded Securing America's Future Energy (SAFE), a Washington D.C.–based group that works to address "the economic and national security threats posed by America's dependence on oil."

Most recently, he had helped raise some of the initial capital for Israel Cleantech Ventures (now ICV). It was to be the first fund focused exclusively on clean technology in Israel, and it fit Granoff's personal connection to the Jewish State: For some time, he had been splitting his time between the United States, where he and his family lived, and Israel.

As part of Maniv's mission, Granoff had been looking "to fund a company with ambitions to scale electric cars," he said. The blurb about Peres was the first time he'd thought there could be an overlap between his interests in energy and his commitment to Israel.

"Before this, I had never associated Israel with anything to do with cars," he said.

Israel is a very small country, and everyone seems to know everyone else. It didn't take Granoff more than a couple of phone calls before he got the name of someone in Peres's office. He fired off an email with his vehicle electrification research, asking if they could meet.

"Within an hour, I got a message asking if I could come for breakfast with Peres the very next morning," Granoff recalled.

The two met in Peres's office, where the president described a grand plan to make Israel the leader in electric cars.

"It was all very exciting to me, but I also knew Shimon Peres," Granoff recalled.

In his reinvention as Israel's elder statesman for innovation, Peres had gained a reputation as a dreamer.

"People used to say he's had a hundred great ideas for Israel. Ten of them have literally saved the country, and the other ninety have never been heard from again," Granoff said. "So I had to ask, why is this idea going to be one of the ten percent that actually works?"

And even if it did work, Granoff said to Peres, "You're not going to do this yourself and the government's not going to get involved. So who is?"

"Shai Agassi," Peres replied.

Granoff had never heard of Agassi, but after he left the meeting with Peres, he Googled him and was impressed by what he read: Head of products at SAP. Sold his previous startup for $400 million. Successful Israeli entrepreneur.

Still, it didn't make any sense.

"Here's this guy, he's number two at one of the world's largest software companies, obviously he wants to be number one," Granoff thought to himself. "Why was he getting distracted with a project like the one Peres was describing? So I kept it in my head but kind of put it off to the side."

That is, until Granoff read an article on the front page of The Wall Street Journal two months later that described the sudden departure of SAP's young wunderkind "to pursue interests in alternative energy and climate change."

Granoff called back Peres.

"OK, I'll take his contact information now," he told Peres's secretary.

Granoff emailed the newly unemployed Agassi, and they agreed to meet. Granoff was impressed and immediately thought of some potential investors Agassi ought to meet.

One of those was Idan Ofer, who—following that fateful "elevator pitch" in June 2007—was to become the first investor and chairman of the board of Agassi's new company.

Ofer had inherited his business acumen—along with much of his wealth—from his father, shipping magnate Sammy. Within several years, Idan Ofer would rocket to the top spot as Israel's wealthiest man, with a reported net worth in 2013 of $6.5 billion. Short and powerful, with close-cropped hair and a square jaw, Ofer projected the confidence of a wrestler ready to pin his opponents on the way to financial domination. (Ofer actually played rugby and squash in high school.)

Ofer believed in both Agassi and the "CO2 story," as he later told The New York Times. "Climate change is real. The CO2 equation has gone haywire. And coming from the oil business, I know that oil is becoming more and more difficult to find. I mean, this planet, how much oil can you have?"

Ofer was, in fact, ready to blow up his own business interests.

"Even if this ends up destroying—for lack of a better word—my refinery business, that will be small money compared to what this will be," he said. "When you play chess, you give up something to get something else."

With Ofer on board, Granoff took Agassi on a road show through the Big Apple.

"Suspend your disbelief," Agassi repeated over and over, in boardrooms across New York.

In the midst of the presentations, Agassi flew to California to meet with VantagePoint Capital Partners. Agassi had secured the introduction through his SAP Silicon Valley network.

Alan Salzman was VantagePoint's CEO. He co-founded the fund in 1996 and had been bullish on clean tech since investing in rival electric carmaker Tesla in 2006.

With his piercing blue eyes, square jaw, cautious smile and a head of mostly receding, formerly blond hair, Salzman couldn't be more different in appearance than Agassi, with his impish grin and prom-date good looks. But Salzman's blunt, take-no-prisoners way of speaking would have seemed at home in front of many an Israeli whiteboard.

"Our approach to clean tech is to invest in accelerating the inevitable," Salzman told the magazine VentureBeat. "After we invested in Tesla, we thought long and hard about the missing links needed to make electric vehicles broadly popular. Better Place is about providing the systems and environment to make owning an electric vehicle a seamless, simple experience. Basically, Better Place is to Tesla what iTunes was to MP3 players."

Shai Agassi put the comparison differently.

"If you think of Tesla as the iPhone, we're the AT&T," he told The New York Times' John Markoff.

Salzman also described his passion for electric vehicles to Forbes magazine.

"Every car in the world is going to become electric, and not someday 100 years from now, but in the next 20 years. The reason is that the combustion engine is antiquated and inefficient. It was popularized in the 1920s. Ask yourself where in industry do we still use combustion engines, and you'd be hard pressed to find a spot. Electric motors are cheap, reliable and efficient. [They] outperform any combustion engine car ... and produce zero emissions. Why in the world would anybody want the slow, smoggy, expensive version?"

To David Pogue on the "CBS Sunday Morning" TV show, he said about Better Place, "I think it's one of those seminal companies that is going to change how the world functions."

Salzman told Clive Thompson at The New York Times why Agassi was the right man to be heading such a company. "Electric vehicles are software-driven vehicles. You need a software industry guy [like Agassi]. He's the Steve Jobs of clean energy."

Agassi was "a visionary, technologist and businessman," Salzman wrote in Time magazine. Working with him was "exhilarating, exhausting, challenging and gratifying."

As to the size of the investment, "If you're going elephant-hunting, you need an elephant gun," he quipped to The Wall Street Journal.

Over the course of the summer of 2007, Ofer's and Salzman's teams conducted their due diligence on Project Better Place, while Agassi and Granoff continued to pound the pavement.

As the buzz built, Granoff brought investors through his own Maniv operation, including former World Bank president James Wolfensohn and Seagram's head and philanthropist Edgar Bronfman Sr.

The Israeli venture capital firm Pitango was interested too, but there was a conflict of interest—the fund was co-founded by Chemi Peres, Shimon's son.

Pitango instead introduced Agassi to Morgan Stanley, which took Pitango's place in the round.

The result stunned the tech world—at $200 million, it was one of the largest Series A rounds in history.

QUIN GARCIA

Quin Garcia had never been to Israel before. A California native, he'd never even considered a vacation there.

But on his unexpected arrival in October, 2007, as one of the first employees of the yet-to-be-launched Better Place, Garcia was given an intense challenge that he still marvels over.

"I was told we needed to build a prototype electric car in six weeks," he said. "We needed to show the car to the president, the prime minister and the CEO of Renault by mid-December."

Garcia was a self-avowed "car guy." He loved getting his hands dirty taking apart and building old muscle cars, race cars, aging gas guzzlers. He had met Shai Agassi six months earlier when the latter gave a second talk at Stanford University, where Garcia was completing his master's degree, conducting research related to electric and autonomous cars.

Agassi's talk, entitled "The Physics of Startups," promised to "draw parallels between the principles of business and the laws of physics [emphasizing] the importance of acting on an idea before it's adopted by the mainstream and navigating the inevitable uncertainties that can result in success or failure."

Garcia was taken by Agassi's bold vision and by his charisma. He approached Agassi after the lecture and the two clicked.

Garcia had been mulling ideas of what to do after he graduated. Maybe he'd go for a PhD. Maybe he'd start his own company.

Agassi had another idea for the young man.

Garcia set up operations at an auto body shop called 4x4 Projects located in Kfar Saba, a middle-class suburb north of Tel Aviv.

4x4 was located in a mustard-yellow warehouse on a side street in the cluttered Kfar Saba industrial zone. Inside, high up on a lift, there was a white Jeep Wrangler outfitted with supersize off-road wheels, like a monster dune buggy. In a corner sat a silver BMW 318i with a brand new Corvette V-8 engine. A green Hummer was parked out back.

Better Place had provided Garcia with a 2005 Renault Mégane, a five-seat family sedan, to transform into an electric car. With no time to waste, "we basically ripped out the engine, ripped out the fuel tank and put in this electric motor we'd brought over from California," Garcia recalled. "We adapted the transmission and popped a huge battery from Germany in the trunk. I was in the trenches, seven days a week, for that period. I didn't get to enjoy too much of the Tel Aviv nightlife."

But at the end of the six-week period, the car worked—and it included a very early version of the car's energy management system, then dubbed AutOS (pronounced "autos").

"You could get a hundred and twenty kilometers of range, as long as you babied it," Garcia said.

Garcia hadn't had a chance to properly test the car before Idan Ofer demanded a test drive. With Agassi in tow, Garcia took the tricked-out Mégane to a driver's education school in Tel Aviv.

"The wedding hall where Shai got married was right next door," Garcia recalled.

As Ofer hopped in, Garcia warned him, "'OK, Idan, take it easy.' But then I see him just goose it and he starts flying. I think, oh, this isn't going to end well. He takes a sharp corner, he's still gunning it, and I hear this big old bang. And then clunk, clunk, clunk."

The car stopped and Garcia came running over along with other horrified onlookers.

Ofer stepped out very nonchalantly, as if to say, *no big deal* and *that was really cool.* Garcia popped open the hood and spotted the problem immediately.

"He'd snapped one of the axles," Garcia said.

An electric motor has much more torque and "is a lot more powerful than a regular gas engine. We were able to spin that for some positive PR," Garcia laughed.

Garcia promptly bought an upgraded, heavy-duty axle. The car was ready for its debut with Peres, Olmert and Ghosn.

LAUNCH NO. 1

Better Place launched to the world at a press conference on October 29, 2007, held at the tony Essex House on Central Park South in Manhattan. The Series A financing had closed just three days before.

The timing seemed quick to Mike Granoff.

"I wasn't sure why we were launching so early," he recalled. "And I was a little surprised that it was so lavish."

Joe Paluska, head of the technology practice at PR firm Hill+Knowlton, had been engaged to do public relations for the announcement. Paluska would leave Hill+Knowlton a few months later to take the role of VP global communications and policy at Better Place.

Idan Ofer, Alan Salzman and Shai Agassi all spoke. Granoff punched the buttons to swipe through the slides on Agassi's MacBook Pro laptop.

A snazzy 3-D animation had been created ("literally overnight," according to Agassi, in keeping with the overall rapid decision making). It showed cars pulling into a switch station and being charged in public parking lots.

Agassi was up first.

"Our global economy urgently needs an environmentally clean and sustainable approach to energy and transportation," Agassi said. "We have crossed an historic threshold where electricity and batteries provide a cheaper alternative for consumers. Existing technology, coupled with the right business model and a scalable infrastructure, can provide an immediate solution and significantly decrease carbon emissions."

"The tailpipe problem has always been the most challenging wedge of the climate change problem," Ofer added. "Under Shai's leadership, this project has the promise to stimulate the largest blue-ocean economic opportunity in the history of capitalism, with our children as its greatest beneficiary."

The press launch received mixed reviews from other car manufacturers— they saw the electric car startup as less a partner and more an unwelcome competitor.

Former General Motors executive Steve Girsky said Better Place was facing a classic chicken-and-egg problem.

"The car companies won't build cars for this until they see a commitment on infrastructure, but [Better Place] can't build the infrastructure until the car companies build cars," he said.

Girsky nevertheless gave Better Place credit for generating a "lot of momentum."

Tony Posawatz, vehicle line director for the Chevrolet Volt plug-in "range extender" vehicle, which was under development at GM at the time, didn't dismiss Better Place out of hand.

"By removing the battery cost from the vehicle price, the customer derives much value," he said.

Tesla VP of sales and marketing Darryl Siry said he welcomed the new company—provided, of course, Tesla vehicles could be charged with Better Place's infrastructure. As for battery swap, Siry said that while it was very technically challenging, if Better Place could figure out how to do it, "it would be very compelling."

Notably absent from the launch was Renault. Although internally, Better Place knew Renault was on board, the news hadn't been made public yet.

The company's only comment was an oblique one from spokesperson Frederique Le Greves.

"It's definitely a technology that we're very interested in, and we're investing to develop that technology, but how we're going to sell and lease it is still something we're looking at and not something we've taken a decision on," he said.

LAUNCH NO. 2

Winters in Jerusalem can be cold. Any conception of Israel as a blooming desert doesn't apply in the country's capital on a hill, 2,500 feet above sea level. Rain is frequent, with snow visiting once or twice a year.

A large tent was erected outside the prime minister's office. A banner proclaiming in Hebrew "Making peace between transport and the environment" fluttered lightly in the background, as Better Place launched its Israeli operations on January 21, 2008, just under three months after it had debuted in New York.

The Israeli announcement was in many ways the "real" one, as this was where both R&D and first deployment would take place. A delegation of international and local reporters was in position, notepads, laptops and cameras at the ready.

Renault CEO Carlos Ghosn spoke first.

"We have for the first time in history created the conditions to mass-market electric vehicles in a country, Israel," he said to the snapping cameras. The Fluence Z.E., as the car would be called (Z.E. stood for "Zero Emissions") would be "a one hundred percent fuel-free car, which will contribute to the relief from expensive oil dependency, with zero carbon dioxide emissions, zero particles pollution and zero noise. The electric vehicle will be the most environmentally friendly mass-produced car on the market."

"In order to bring about a dramatic change, sometimes we need a boy like in the fairy tales to say, 'Look, the emperor has no clothes,'" Prime Minister Olmert said, beaming down from the podium at Agassi. "We can all see that for ourselves, so how come we haven't said so? And this boy comes along and puts things in motion to bring about change. And the boy in this story—and he really is a boy, practically, but he has achieved more than many adults have—is, of course, Shai Agassi."

Shai Agassi acknowledged the significance of the day and the leaders surrounding him.

"It is a rather humbling moment for a founder of a small startup to share a stage with the prime minister of his own country and one of the legendary CEOs of our times, Carlos Ghosn," he said. "But these are not typical times. These are times where we are running out of oil in the ground and we are running out of air. The oil we burn harms the atmosphere that controls the climate of our planet. We have reached times where in some parts of our world children cannot see the sky. Finally, we are running out of our most precious commodity of all—we are running out of time.

"Mr. Prime Minister, a year ago, when I shared this vision with you, you set ground rules that were very clear. Find the money to fund this vision, outside the government. And find one of the world's greatest car companies that will build this great electric car. I thank you for challenging me. You have brought us all to this moment.

"President Shimon Peres [once] asked me, 'What could be more important than solving this for your country and the world?' He has been an ongoing mentor in this project and is my personal inspiration for what the will of one man can do for this country of ours.

"But most importantly, I am inspired in this by my two boys. I think about the world that they will inherit from us. And I worry. If we pass to them an unlivable planet, we have sinned them. Our way of living, our freedoms, our kids' future all depend on solving this problem using only the science and technology we have in our hands today, because we don't have time for a science experiment.

"The prophet Jeremiah says that 'The fathers have eaten sour grapes, and the children's teeth are set on edge.' Let this proverb not happen in our generation."

Agassi was less diplomatic the next day.

When asked by reporters Doreen Avigad and Noa Paraq from the Israeli business newspaper Globes what he would say to arguments "that your electric car venture is unviable," Agassi responded flippantly that they were giving him an unwitting compliment.

"It means that I'm a magician. That I was able to raise two hundred million dollars without a business plan," he said. "Obviously that isn't the case. Enterprises like the Israel Corp. and Morgan Stanley don't put in money without seeing a business plan, and this was one of the strongest business plans [they had] ever seen."

Globes was just one of 94 publications and websites that covered the Israeli launch. The New York Times, Time and BusinessWeek in the United States; Le Monde, the International Herald Tribune and Der Standard in Europe; and The Jerusalem Post in Israel all ran articles.

There was reporting in Austria and Spain, and an Associated Press article appeared in 12 more publications. CNET, Wired, Engadget, Autoblog and Edmunds all published pieces.

Agassi told The New York Times' Steven Erlanger that there would already be a few thousand electric cars on Israeli roads within a year and 100,000 by the end of 2010. And these cars would be cheap.

"You'll be able to get a nice, high-end [electric] car at a price roughly half that of the gasoline model today," Agassi said.

Steve Hamm wrote in BusinessWeek that Better Place's backers hoped that "once the program is running smoothly, the total costs of owning one of these cars will be as much as 50 percent less than for owning a comparable gasoline-powered car," although he reserved judgment on whether the system would "succeed on a grand scale."

Agassi explained in an interview with the Harvard Business Review why there was no alternative to unequivocal, smashing success for Better Place.

"If the world is to end its oil addiction," Agassi said, "hundreds of millions of electric cars must be put on the road in the next five to eight years—if it's just ten million, twenty million, thirty million cars, we're dead. Cars are not a niche market, and climate change will not wait for us to invent the perfect car, battery or business model."

The stakes were too high for ego to get involved, Agassi added.

"I am willing to lose my 'wunderkind' status," he wrote earlier on his personal blog. "I'm not looking for Nobels, and I am even willing never to raise money again—if we can get this plan to work. The race is bigger than one person."

4

HIRING THE TEAM

"The challenge isn't the batteries, and it isn't the cars," Sidney Goodman said, explaining his mission at Better Place. "It's the coalition you need to make it happen. It's a huge integration project."

While Goodman was referring to his specific job description as vice president of automotive alliances, he could just as easily have been talking about the task of staffing Better Place.

With the Series A in the bank and the company formally launched on two continents, Shai Agassi needed to hire a team with a wide variety of expertise—from building the hardware and software itself to making the deals that would bring affordable electric cars to drivers around the world. And he needed to do it fast.

He turned first to past work colleagues, friends and even family.

Originally from South Africa, Sidney Goodman had been with Agassi since the TopTier days, where he managed the consulting services division. He stuck with his boss when SAP acquired TopTier.

Agassi trusted Goodman even with tasks for which Goodman had little experience. It was nevertheless surprising, at least to outsiders, that Goodman—with a business development background entirely in the software industry, a bachelor's degree specializing in management and information systems from the College of Management in Israel and zero experience with cars—was given one of the most important jobs in the company.

It would be Goodman's job to not only manage the relationship with Renault but also to find new auto manufacturers to build battery-switchable electric cars.

Agassi's second TopTier hire was his younger brother, Tal, who was made head of global infrastructure, in charge of building the battery switch stations, charge spots and the entire electric grid.

As was Goodman's, Tal Agassi's background was all about software.

"Tal was a very intelligent guy, but because he had no experience building out a physical network, most of the time he just didn't get it," recalled Geoff Zippel, who would become head of deployment for one of Better Place's divisions.

Agassi hiring his brother raised many eyebrows.

"It's great to say 'I can do anything,' but Tal had spent his whole career in software and here he had responsibility for big industrial things that have real costs and touch the electrical grid," one Better Place staffer said. "It's not the same as building a cool app for the phone."

"Tal was an earnest employee, well liked, who tried his hardest, but was continually in over his head," said another.

The family connection didn't stop with Tal, though.

Shai Agassi also hired his sister, Dafna, to head up marketing. And Agassi's father, Reuven, frequently sat in on meetings in the company's early days.

Not all of Agassi's TopTier/SAP hires met a critical reception, however.

Barak Hershkovitz didn't have a software or a hardware background—he had originally trained to be an ophthalmologist—but he was widely respected as a self-taught programmer, an effective manager and a hard-nosed realist. Agassi hired Hershkovitz—who had served with Agassi in the army and then dropped out of medical school prior to starting his residency to join SAP and write computer code—to be Better Place's chief technology officer.

Hershkovitz saw his high-tech career as a natural fit with his former physician ambitions. In an interview with the Israeli journal Computerworld, he commented, "here I also save lives."

Hershkovitz recounted a challenge given to him from one of his instructors at medical school.

"He told me to do a calculation comparing the number of patients affected by lung disease with the effect of contamination by cars."

Hershkovitz did. The internal combustion engine, he concluded, causes "catastrophic damage to health."

"My supreme goal is to get off oil, not just to make Better Place profitable," he told The Jerusalem Report's Matthew Kalman. This is "not a small enhancement. It's a revolution."

Hershkovitz was well liked at Better Place.

"Barak knew how to design a product and had a holistic understanding of what Better Place should be delivering and how everything interacts. He was a big-picture guy and very customer focused," recalled Ariel Tikotsky, who headed up knowledge management systems at Better Place.

For Emek Sadot, who would become the company's senior director for battery, electric vehicle charging systems and the smart grid, one of Hershkovitz's most important qualities was that he "didn't yell. He was very smart, a pleasant guy."

PROTEXIA

Shai Agassi's penchant to hire people with whom he had a personal connection was the result of a simple and widespread Israeli principle: *protexia*.

A Hebraicized version of "protection," the term can be defined as "not what you know but who you know."

Adam Corre, who runs the Street Hebrew website, describes *protexia* this way: "Israel is like one big family, [so] people tend to look after their own and help others out. Most Israelis have an aunt in City Hall, an uncle on the police force or a cousin in the bank. [If] you go for a job interview and end up getting the job because the interviewer was in the same unit as your dad in the army, that's *protexia.*"

Protexia is not necessarily a bad thing.

The founding team of Check Point, which specializes in network security and is one of Israel's biggest high-tech success stories, was composed primarily of members of the same army intelligence unit.

Think of *protexia* more in terms of developing and using your personal network to leverage your job search.

"Israel is geographically smaller and there's a lot less transitory behavior here than, say, in the United States," explained Bob Rosenschein, the American-Israeli serial entrepreneur who founded Answers.com and sold it for $127 million.

As a result, *protexia* is not just natural but inevitable. It's like hiring your entire team from your first-level connections on LinkedIn.

Protexia extends its tentacles everywhere in Israel, and not just when you're looking for a job.

A patient who needs a medical procedure performed quickly will scour his or her personal network to check which doctors, nurses or administrators might help get a specialist in the loop now—and not in another six months.

A 17-year-old music student hoping to find a way into the highly selective IDF orchestra will have a better chance if he can find someone on the inside to vouch for him.

Protexia can get you better seats at a performance or a faster table at that hot new restaurant.

Of course, there is nepotism too in Israel. But in general, *protexia* is benign and often quite helpful.

The connections Israelis have from the army, school and previous jobs can be "an important source of talent," Rosenschein explained. "It's not so much *protexia* as people bringing people. As long as it doesn't affect the final hiring decision, it's fine. Ultimately, *protexia* means taking a shortcut. But shortcuts are not always bad."

So when it came time for Shai Agassi to staff up Better Place, it would have been considered entirely normal and logical to turn first to people he knew and trusted. Never mind if their professional experience didn't always match up.

KAPLAN

Agassi's last early hire came from the Israeli army, although the two had never served together.

Moshe Kaplinsky was brought on board to head up the Israeli operating company. It was known colloquially as "OpCo" to differentiate it from the global division, which would be called "TopCo."

Kaplinsky—who went by the more internationally pronounceable nickname "Kaplan"—was a major general in the IDF, where he had ended his tour of duty as deputy chief of the general staff. His name was on a short list to become IDF chief of staff at the beginning of 2007, but he didn't get the promotion. He joined Better Place just a month after his retirement, following 31 years in uniform.

"I came to this project mainly because of a deep understanding of Israel's dependence on oil," the burly army man told the Financial Times.

To the Israeli business newspaper Globes, he added, "I came because of Shai's enthusiasm."

Kaplan was drawn into troubleshooting the kind of "extreme scenarios" he had been confronted with in the army. In the case of Better Place, this might be how the network would cope if a major event—military or otherwise—caused a sudden surge in demand on the electrical grid.

Kaplan was not only an army man. He was *Golani*.

The Golani brigade is one of the most prestigious in the Israel Defense Forces. Named for the Golan Heights, the brigade's graduates have gone on to some of the highest positions in the military (three of its commanders, Mordechai Gur, Gabi Ashkenazi and Gadi Eizenkot, became IDF chiefs of staff). Say you were Golani in casual conversation in Israel, and you immediately command respect.

Once, Kaplan met a new Better Place employee who had served in a different unit—the paratroopers. Upon learning this, Kaplan responded with a good-natured dig, "Well, no one's perfect."

Golani soldiers are considered "the salt of the earth," Shelly Silverstein, Kaplan's director of human resources, explained. Kaplan's preferred hot beverage was a simple cup of black coffee with two sugars.

"Like we used to make on the bonfire during boot camp," Kaplan would say.

There were downsides to this surfeit of admirable experience, however.

"There was a gap of cultures in the company," recalled Dan Cohen, who would soon be hired as Agassi's "chief of staff" (a term which itself comes from the army). "The U.S. team had a Silicon Valley culture of innovation, of out-of-the-box thinking. It was an open environment, very much opposed to the hierarchical style that Kaplan brought from the military."

Still, Kaplan didn't simply "give orders, and say 'Do it and leave me alone,'" recalled Eitan Hon, the Israeli OpCo's chief operating officer. "Kaplan's way was to have lots of discussion, to take input from his team, from all levels, not only managers, and to create an environment where all ideas are welcome. But then, once a decision is taken, you execute on it and you deviate as little as possible. Once we had a target and a mission, there was no question that we'll do all we can to achieve it. He wouldn't give up on anything—even it was a bad idea coming from upper management."

Kaplan's hire surprised Mike Granoff.

"The one thing Shai always told me was that he didn't want a general," Granoff said. "Kaplan didn't know anything about running a startup or staying within a budget. But that was OK with Shai, because he didn't see Better Place as a startup. Better Place was going to be enormous and Kaplan could get things done. We used to joke he could take the hill, and then send you the bill."

THE ROLE OF THE ARMY

A senior military man (and they're almost all men) leading a high-tech startup might seem oxymoronic in much of the Western world. In Israel, such a move is practically a rite of passage.

A former chief of staff or high-ranking official from the Israel Defense Forces can expect to be offered any number of CEO or board member positions at leading high-tech and industrial corporations.

The thinking goes that learning to make tough decisions under intense life-or-death pressure is the hands-on, field equivalent of an MBA.

Former IDF chief of staff Dan Halutz, for example, was hired directly out of the army to manage Kamor Motors, which imports BMW cars to Israel, and was concurrently appointed chairman of the board of Starling Advanced Communications, which makes satellite-based communication systems.

You don't have to be a former chief of staff to make your mark in the Startup Nation. Dan Senor, co-author of the book of the same name, told the Freakonomics website how army service impacts the high-tech scene in Israel.

"Certain units have become technology boot camps, where 18- to 22-year-olds get thrown projects and missions that would make the heads spin of their counterparts in universities or the private sector anywhere else in the world," Senor said. "The Israelis come out of the military not just with hands-on exposure to next-gen technology, but with training in teamwork, mission orientation, leadership, and a desire to continue serving their country by contributing to its tech sector—a source of pride for just about every Israeli."

One of the most fabled of the IDF tech units is 8200, Israel's equivalent to the National Security Agency (NSA) in the United States or Britain's Government Communications Headquarters. With a focus on intelligence gathering and in-house hacking, 8200 is the army's leading developer of both cybersecurity defense and attack systems.

Israeli venture capitalist Izhar Shay explained that "IDF service in 8200 ... is without a doubt an important training ground for future entrepreneurs. In many cases, it gives them a boost in the difficult contest of getting investors' attention."

Indeed, just saying you served in 8200 can open otherwise recalcitrant doors.

"There are job offers on the Internet and want ads that specifically say 'meant for 8200 alumni,'" Forbes reported. "It doesn't really matter what you did in the unit—you've already benefited. It simply raises your shares in the civilian market."

In 2011, 8200 alumni went a step further and set up a five-month intensive high-tech accelerator that has launched some 78 startups and raised over $250 million, with four exits already.

Startup Nation leaders come from all corners of the military, not just 8200.

Israel's compulsory service "produces a maturity not seen in Israelis' foreign peers who spend that time in university," Senor told Freakonomics. While "perspective typically comes with age ... in Israel you get [it] at a young age, because so many transformational experiences are jammed into Israelis ... in their late teens and early 20s."

THE ONLY HOLD OUT

Andrey Zarur, Agassi's partner from Davos and co-author of the blueprint that had launched the company, declined Agassi's offer to join Better Place full time.

It wasn't anything against Agassi or the company, Zarur explained.

During the time they had been working together defining the problem and the electric opportunity, Agassi was still at SAP and hadn't committed to leaving and starting Better Place.

Zarur, meanwhile, had received a job offer from a Boston-based venture capital firm and had a new baby at home.

"They want me to make a ten-year investment to them," Zarur told Agassi. "Dude, what are you going to do with this?"

"I don't know," Agassi responded. "I'm getting all these signals from Hasso Plattner, he's introducing me to Bill Gates. I think he might ask me to become the next CEO of SAP."

Zarur felt he had no choice: He took the job on the table.

A few months later, Agassi finally left SAP. One of his first calls was to Zarur.

"I'm going to do it," he said. "Let's turn our vision into a real business plan, raise money, and I will lead it."

"We've got a problem, my friend," Zarur told Agassi. "I've made my commitment, and it's to someone else. You know how I was raised. I'm a good Catholic boy, I don't lie, I don't cheat or betray and I never go back on my word. And I gave my word that I would be with this new firm for the next ten years."

Agassi was furious.

"We got into a big fight," Zarur recalled.

But Zarur didn't back down.

"Look, I'm totally bummed, too," he told Agassi. "But, dude, this is who I am."

5

NUTS, BOLTS AND ROBOTS

Tal Agassi was standing in front of three gray-and-blue foam mock-ups of Better Place charge spots. This is where most electric car owners would interact with the company—when they plugged their cars in at night, at home, at the office or at a charge spot in a public parking or shopping mall lot.

Two dozen engineers and executives had assembled to review the mock-ups in Better Place's spanking new offices in Kiryat Atidim, a high-tech hub of mostly squat buildings punctuated by the occasional skyscraper forming a makeshift "campus" on the northern outskirts of Tel Aviv. Some of the team had flown in all the way from Palo Alto, where Better Place had opened its official U.S. headquarters.

For many, it was the first time they had met each other.

Fresh chilled watermelon was served, but the atmosphere quickly heated up.

Wired magazine's Daniel Roth had traveled to Israel to profile Better Place. He described the three mock-ups.

"The first looks like a giant Pez dispenser with a skinny trunk leading up to a cantilevered box that houses the charging equipment," he wrote. "The second has a fat base and a skinny body that zigs in the middle, like a svelte E.T. The last one is waist-high, smaller than the others, and resembles a stunted drive-through squawk box."

A lot was riding on the decisions that would be made that sunny day in May 2008.

Better Place's business plan called for charge spots to be installed in 500,000 of the three to four million parking spots around the country, so that "people feel like they can charge their cars whenever they need to," Time magazine reported.

Getting the look and feel right for a large physical device like a charge spot was not the same challenge as building a website—something you can roll out in stages, making changes big and small almost any time, or doing A/B testing to home in on the most attractive color palette.

NewDealDesign in San Francisco had collaborated with an Israeli industrial design firm called Nekuda (Hebrew for "point") to design the charge spots. They were working under stringent requirements: In addition to carrying a charge flawlessly, the charge spots had to withstand being banged by drivers with questionable spatial intelligence, vandalized by thieves and baked by Israel's blazing summers.

The user interface had to be seamless as well. The public charge spots would open automatically with the swipe of a member's smart card. LED lights created a non-verbal feedback loop to indicate whether the charge spot was ready to use or already charging.

Tal Agassi looked around the room. He wore a tight-fitting button-down shirt that day, which was meant to project two images simultaneously—corporate professionalism (it was not a T-shirt) and hipster pretensions (it was tight). His hair, as always, was heavily gelled; little spikes protruded here and there.

He called for a vote.

The third option won unanimous approval. It was the most practical: It could be freestanding or mounted to a wall, making it more flexible for retail centers.

Shai Agassi had been listening quietly. Now he jumped in, shaking his head.

As beautiful as the selected design is, it simply won't work, he said.

"Our customer goes to park her car," Agassi said. "She pulls in, then she's squeezing between two cars to drag out this big cable and walk it back to her car. She'll be wearing her nice work clothes and getting them dirty."

Agassi closed his eyes.

"Guys, we've just lost half the market. You need to make life simple for people."

At the front of the room, Tal Agassi looked stunned. Two other Agassis were in the room too. Father Reuven remained quiet, but sister Dafna pushed back.

"It's not a lot to ask people to pull into a parking lot a certain way," she said.

Tal had an idea.

"We can have a hydraulic arm holding the cable," he suggested.

The idea was not received lightly.

"The cost of adding an arm to the hundreds of thousands of charge spots we're planning will destroy our business model," one person said.

"Forget the money," added another. "Redesigning these things will push us way behind our deadlines."

Shai Agassi wasn't sold either.

"It will break in three months," he muttered quietly to himself.

"Let's move on," he added audibly, but it was too late—the topic of the cable and arm kept rising, like a cybernetic-controlled tentacle from some gas-guzzling octopus. Each proposed new solution created another set of problems. Voices were raised; everyone began talking over each other.

Shai Agassi stopped the debate.

"Maybe the arm isn't so wrong. This is 'think different,'" Agassi said, invoking one of Apple's many iconic ad campaigns, and reversing his decision from just a few moments earlier.

"What would we actually need to make this happen? Two servos, two degrees of movement for the arm?"

He had warmed to the idea; it was crazy no more. Now it was essential!

Agassi laid out the new driver experience: "He goes into a spot and the spot connects itself. In 2008, we put the cable in the unit. In 2010, we use an arm. In 2012, there's a smart arm that connects automatically."

Agassi had already begun calculating the costs in his head. The home unit would come ready with the original pull-out cable idea. Customers could pay to get the auto connect.

"It will cost two hundred and fifty dollars to build, and we'll sell it for five hundred," Agassi exclaimed.

The idea that had only minutes earlier been so far out of the box as to engender a small riot of backroom bickering was now part of the Better Place business plan.

Tal Agassi did his best to hide his frustration about how the discussion on the charge spots had gone. Maybe his brother was right, but Tal's team had been working with NewDealDesign for months on the three original mock-ups. Now he had the unnerving task of calling up Gadi Amit, NewDeal's Israeli expatriate CEO in San Francisco, and telling him they needed to add smart arms—and that they had to be ready for the next engineering meeting, in just 90 days.

The discussion was mostly academic; the robotic arm would never be built, as the costs for building and installing the charge spots as they were originally conceived would quickly balloon.

Engineer Emek Sadot recalled the evolution of the charge spots' cost.

"Originally we thought they would cost fifty to a hundred dollars each," he said.

That's what was in the business plan.

"But then we started to add functionality," he continued. "We wanted it to communicate back [to Better Place headquarters], so it needed a wireless modem, memory on board and a computer processing unit to accommodate the communication needs. Then we needed a meter built into the charge spot [to keep track of how much electricity was being used]. It all adds up. By the time we were done, an individual home charge spot was seven hundred and fifty dollars without the cable, which was another one-fifty, so nine hundred dollars total."

The charge spot development team at Better Place was the best in the business, Sadot insisted. "They did their utmost to make the best product with the best quality. These are just the prices they came up with."

The charge spots were designed before there were any cars or customers.

"We didn't have anyone to give us feedback," Sadot said. "On the one hand, it was a shorter loop; it helped us move faster. On the flip side, we were making decisions that might not be appropriate."

The resulting prices "generated a lot of heat in the company," Sadot added. "There was resistance and frustration."

A furious request came from Israeli OpCo head Moshe Kaplinsky, demanding immediate options for making the charge spots cheaper.

"We came up with a cost-reduction plan, a menu," Sadot explained. "If we want a charge spot without a cable, we could save a hundred and fifty dollars, but then the car owner has to buy it on his own, which impacts on the user experience. If we build it without the meter, we'll save a hundred dollars there, but then we will lose the ability to do smart charging. We could change the design, make it more like a plain cabinet, but the marketing guys said, 'Over my dead body will we make the charge spots so ugly.'"

Ultimately the charge spots stayed exactly as they had been originally designed.

"Maybe we saved five percent using less-expensive components," Sadot added.

In two years, GE would unveil the WattStation, which remains a popular off-the-shelf charge spot used by DIYers in their home garages.

"But in order to have a charge spot ready, tested and bulletproof by 2011, which was when we planned to launch, we needed to start years before that," Sadot said. "And at that point, no other companies were building charge spots."

Always thinking big, Agassi toyed with the idea of becoming "a charge spot plant," Sadot recalled. "Shai thought we could build hundreds of thousands of charge spots for every electric car out there, not just Better Place. He thought it might be a means of penetrating the U.S. market."

While that never happened, it highlighted the dynamic of how ideas flowed within Better Place, going from wacky to wonderful, flirting on the edges of the possible, sometimes soaring, other times drifting quietly away.

"Shai's got two big traits," Better Place's U.S. chief operating officer Aliza Peleg told reporter Daniel Roth after the charge spot design meeting in 2008. "By the time he's thought of something, to him it's been completed, it's been achieved. The other trait is that by the time you've understood what he's thinking, he's already somewhere else. You're in catch-up mode, 24/7."

STANDARDS

Tal Agassi would fight another battle that week, this time with Better Place's standardization guru, Ziva Patir.

Tal wanted Better Place to develop its own cable to connect the charge spot and the car, complete with the plugs on both ends. And he wanted every other car maker to use that cable.

Emek Sadot described Agassi's desire as "like going to Coca-Cola and telling them every bottle should come with my straw."

"Better Place wanted to impose its own proprietary standard on the industry," Patir said. "Tal didn't understand that the industry will come up with its own."

Patir ought to know. At 57, she was the oldest employee at Better Place, having spent the previous 31 years—her entire career—at the Standards Institute of Israel, or SII, where she eventually climbed the ladder to the CEO position, the first woman to do so.

Patir also held the chair of the technical management board of the worldwide International Organization for Standardization.

When it came to international standards, there was probably no one better in the country—and few in the world—to help guide Better Place through the bureaucratic morass it would soon face.

Patir retired from the SII in November 2007 and met Shai Agassi a few days later at a hotel in Jerusalem, following a conference where Agassi had been speaking.

"It was the strangest interview," Patir recalled. "For a solid hour, he told me the story of Better Place. He didn't ask a single question about me."

At the end of the interview, Agassi said to Patir, "I suggest you write your employment agreement and join me on Monday."

Unlike Tal Agassi's fiat from above approach, Patir's method for creating the right cable and socket was to help guide a bickering industry towards a standard—one that Better Place, of course, would have a major role in creating.

It wasn't easy: The German automotive giant Daimler was behind one standard. The Japanese automotive parts supplier Yazaki had another.

Without a standard, crazy situations had cropped up.

"There was this guy in Switzerland with an electric car who was driving hundreds of kilometers between his home and Germany," Patir recalled. "But there were no charge spots then. How would he do it? He'd look for a crane that would have a lot of electricity flowing through it, and he would connect to it. He wouldn't ask permission. And then he'd go on to the next crane."

It was terribly unsafe.

"You cannot charge your car from a normal socket like that," Patir grimaced. "The voltage and amperage are too high. It's not like a computer or a shaver that you can plug into the wall."

Tal Agassi's mandate to create something unique to Better Place, something that could become an industry standard, came from the top.

"At the end of the day, Shai's presence was everywhere," Patir recalled.

"We all admired his vision, and we were influenced by that. But it did keep people from questioning at times."

Patir recalled how Agassi wanted Better Place to model itself after Apple.

"One of Shai's mantras in the early days was: Are we Apple, or are we HP?" Patir said. "Before I came to Better Place, I felt that HP was a good company, but Shai told us that Apple was the ideal, and that everything should be designed as Apple would design it."

Ultimately, Patir prevailed, and Better Place accepted the evolving industry standards.

No one has tapped into a crane since.

THE BATTERY SWITCH STATION

If the charge spots were the day-to-day charging apparatus for Better Place's customers, the battery switch stations were the "backup system," a psychological boost that enabled drivers to push past "range anxiety"—to feel they could travel unlimited distances in their electric cars because they could always swap batteries if they were running low—even if, in general practice, 90 percent of charging would be done at home or at work.

The switch stations were to become the public face of the company. And why not? They were sexy and oh so futuristic: a network of filling stations run entirely by robots.

Agassi preferred another metaphor.

"Ever been to a carwash?" he asked, while on stage during an appearance at the NDN think tank's "Moment of Transportation" conference in Washington, D.C., in March 2008.

"A carwash has lots of moving arms. Now, if I wanted to scare you, we'd call them robots. They move in all kinds of directions, they have shampoo, they have wax. Stuff is coming in. A battery switch station, on the other hand, has only one arm. It only goes up and down. It comes underneath your car, like you're sitting in a carwash. The empty battery goes out and a full battery goes in."

Better Place's battery switch stations would be a wonder of automation.

As the car approaches, the station identifies it through a cellular connection to Better Place's central Network Operating System, a room filled with enormous screens and technicians hunched over computer terminals, resembling the iconic Mission Control Center of the NASA moon launches.

After the identification is complete, a swinging gate at the entrance to the switch station automatically opens. Large, color LCD signs guide the driver to pull the car up to a stopping point, then to switch the vehicle into neutral and turn off the engine.

Hydraulic clamps grab the car and move it slowly forward while the platform rises slightly. It's all very graceful. While the driver must stay with the car, passengers can get out and watch the process from a glassed-in observation deck.

Once the car is in exactly the right spot, a mechanism gives the underside of the car a quick wash, to avoid dirt contaminating the battery and to make sure none of the parts have gotten rusty.

At this point the real magic begins.

Beneath the back half of the car, a secret door slides open, revealing a deep well.

The first robot sidles up to the car from the right, rises up and twists open four screws. The car's 500-pound battery drops slightly from its location between the rear passenger seat and the trunk onto the robot's sturdy serving tray. The battery is then whisked into the bowels of the station, where up to 16 other batteries are being cooled to ensure that, when they're charged under these optimal conditions, any degradation will be kept to the absolute minimum.

On the other side of the observation deck, a window allows drivers to peer down several stories into the ground, where the interior of the station is laid out like a giant jukebox—except one filled with batteries, not vinyl records.

The spent battery goes into one bay, while a second robot plucks a fresh battery from its resting spot and sends it along a conveyer belt until it is ready to be inserted into the car. Up it goes, jiggling gently until snugly in place. The screws are returned, the hidden well is sealed and the car is lowered back to ground level.

Once the clamps are released, the LCD screen, which has been providing progress reports the entire time, changes to green, indicating it's time to put the car back in drive and head on your way.

The biggest difference between a battery swap and a carwash: If you stay with your car, you can't listen to the radio. After all, during the switch, your car has no battery!

———

Better Place's switch stations would be fast, Agassi predicted—faster than a carwash and certainly faster than plugging your car into the charge spot on the wall.

"We're not dealing with electrons moving in and out, we're dealing with mechanics moving in and out," he told the NDN audience.

The first switch station to be prototyped took one minute and 13 seconds to swap a battery.

"If we can't do this in less time than it takes to fill your gasoline tank," Agassi told New York Times reporter Clive Thompson, "we don't have a company."

Agassi went farther in his NDN talk, calling the Better Place system a "social contract."

"Technologists will tell you that, until you have a battery that charges up three hundred miles in three minutes or less, like you can do with gas, people won't buy it," he explained. "We think the social contract is a bit different. We think people are not going to be willing to stop more than fifty times a year for more than five minutes [for a fill-up]. So if you can guarantee me [I'll have to stop] less than fifty times a year—less than my current once a week fill-up model—and guarantee that it won't take more than five minutes, I'm good. We do that; we guarantee that in our contract."

Moreover, how often do you drive more than 100 miles non-stop? Agassi mused. "So we're actually giving you a better contract. You'll stop less than 50 times a year, because most of the time, you drive to work and an hour later it will be topped off magically."

No one goes out to the movies or dinner for less than an hour, he added, so as long as there's a plug nearby, your filling experience is far superior than with a gasoline-powered car.

YOKOHAMA

Better Place built its first battery switch station not at home in Israel or in the United States, but in faraway Japan.

Better Place won a government competition sponsored by the Japanese

Ministry of the Environment to build a prototype battery switch station in Yokohama, an hour's drive from Tokyo.

The Japanese government wanted to prove that electric cars were viable and had set a goal of having electric-powered cars account for 50 percent of the cars sold in Japan by 2020.

Nissan was pressing forward with the Leaf, which would, seven years later, become the best-selling 100 percent electric vehicle in the world. There were others, too: Subaru had a car called the Stella and Mitsubishi was pushing the i-MiEV.

But that old gremlin, range anxiety, was damping down sales. The Japanese were asking for innovative ideas on how electric cars could travel farther.

The first thing to build was the car itself, because the existing electric vehicle models in Japan were not switchable.

So Quin Garcia, who had cobbled together the first electric prototype in Israel just a few months earlier, was dispatched to the Land of the Rising Sun to work his magic again.

The vehicle chosen for the trial was a Nissan Qashqai, a crossover SUV. Garcia opted for what's called a "pancake" battery, mounted on the bottom of the car, rather than in the trunk as the Renault design would be.

"It's much easier from an engineering perspective," Garcia said. "You just push it up into the bottom of the car. You don't have to line it up perfectly in a long deep cavern, as in a trunk-mounted design."

Better Place chief engineer Yoav Heichal was Garcia's counterpart in bringing the battery-switch technology to Japan.

"We were tasked with building both the car and the station in Japan, so we could do whatever we wanted," he said. There were no troublesome third parties to worry about.

Heichal and Garcia traveled back and forth to Japan every two months.

"Everything we wanted them to do, they did," Heichal recalled fondly. "The Japanese are very efficient, practical, logical and disciplined. If their boss told them to do something, they'd do it. They wouldn't argue or ask questions."

It was a subtle commentary on the corporate culture of Israel, where every question could and would be challenged.

SWITCH WILL NEVER WORK

Not everyone within Better Place backed the battery switch station concept.

Danny Weinstock should have been a believer—it was his job as charging grid manager—but looking back, he admitted the company's tireless focus on switch "never made sense" to him.

Weinstock, who previously worked at the Israeli Energy Ministry, was concerned about the high cost of maintenance.

"When you come from low-tech like me," he said, "everyone knows that if you have something that's moving, there's going to be costs involved for maintenance. But Better Place never took that into account. There were all these moving parts that needed to be very accurate, with optical sensors and the like."

Car manufacturers are conservative, Weinstock warned. "Shai thought he could change the whole industry, to force everyone to take the battery in and out. But it was against their nature."

Shmuel Harlap, chairman of Israel's Mercedes importer Colmobile, felt Better Place's solution was actually moving backwards.

They're setting up "the world's biggest puncture repair shop," he said, likening the battery-switch process to that of fixing a flat tire by swapping in a new one rather than by making a better, puncture-proof tire.

"It's a solution that belongs in the nineteenth century," he said disdainfully.

Sue Cischke, group vice president for sustainability, environment and safety engineering at Ford, was doubtful Better Place could convince all carmakers to agree to design their cars around one standard-size battery bay.

"The chemistry is still changing, and it's still a developing technology rather than a mature technology," she told The New York Times. Given that cars can take years to design, making the wrong call on a standardized battery could be economically fatal for a carmaker, she added.

Better Place's Sidney Goodman said he wasn't worried.

Even though there would one day be many different makes and models of electric cars on the road, they'd use batteries from a relatively small number of manufacturers, Goodman explained to Wired. And even if some automakers didn't sign on to the switching strategy, their cars would still work with Better Place's charge spots.

Others weren't convinced.

Bill Reinert, national manager for Toyota Motor Sales' Advanced Technology Vehicle Group, pointed out that "an electric vehicle battery pack needs to be weather-tight to keep water out, and ... battery pack seals are not traditionally designed to be taken on and off all the time."

Ford's Cischke was worried that if there was an issue with the battery exchange, and the consumer has a bad experience, "then they will blame Ford, not necessarily Better Place."

Other ideas were toyed with. In an earlier version of Agassi and Zarur's blueprint, they had proposed the option for a driver to rent "a trailer with a compact generator to recharge the battery pack during extended driving" as well as the possibility of a "gasoline-electric hybrid design which could use a small (1 liter) onboard engine powered by biofuels."

What could Better Place have done instead?

Danny Weinstock was a big fan of fast charge—the system adopted by most electric cars today—where you stop and plug in for 40 minutes and get an 80 percent charge. Like the battery switch station, it was a psychological trick that allowed drivers to feel they wouldn't get stranded, even though they would rarely use it.

"Shai always considered himself an average person, and if he wouldn't wait, no one would," Weinstock said. "I told him, you're not average. Other people aren't flying 200,000 miles a year. Not everyone is as busy as you. So what if a driver has to wait while the car is charging? Give him a croissant. It's a marketing issue."

Fast charging also got around Weinstock's concerns about maintenance costs.

"Fast charging is just electricity; there are no moving parts," Weinstock said.

Fast charging is no panacea. It can degrade the battery much more quickly if done too often or not in super-cooled conditions (as in a Better Place switch station). But if car owners only plugged in for a fast charge a few times a year as a backup, as Weinstock surmised, it would hardly make a difference. That's how Tesla views fast charging—it's done so infrequently it's a non-issue. Most charging, like with Better Place, is done at home overnight.

Sue Cischke admitted that Better Place had "really energized people with thinking outside the box. But I don't think that's the answer that we're looking at."

In many ways, the debate was reminiscent of the Betamax vs. VHS wars of the 1980s. Even though Sony's Betamax was arguably the superior video technology, consumers chose VHS—and Betamax tapes have been relegated to a footnote in a tech museum.

Would that be the fate of battery switch as well?

THE REAL COST

Even if the industry were able to put aside its misgivings about the value or viability of battery switch, there was another, much bigger problem, and this one was all internal: cost.

Better Place had hired Mike Lindheim, an electrical contractor in California, to estimate how much it would cost to build a switch station. With a background in electrical design and engineering, he ran his own construction business in the Bay Area, building industrial facilities for clients such as Oracle.

Lindheim put together a detailed spreadsheet, broken down by categories. He solicited quotes from different contractors for electricity, plumbing and digging, eventually resulting in 50 line items.

The price: $3 million per station covering everything related to construction. That didn't include the costs for land acquisition. The robot alone was $900,000.

While the prices Lindheim came up with were for Northern California, "when you look at the whole scheme of things, it's not that much different than other places in the world," he said.

But $3 million was not the number Shai Agassi wanted to hear.

Agassi had a different cost in mind: $500,000 per station. That's what he told the company's investors.

Where did it come from?

"It didn't come from anywhere," Lindheim said. "It was just thrown out at some point."

Andrey Zarur disagreed.

"I have the original spreadsheet. I wrote down a range of prices between $500,000 and $700,000. That number came from quotes and conversations we had with people at Siemens and ABB [Swiss transportation and infrastructure provider ASEA Brown Boveri], pricing it from the ground up, including labor."

Better Place's financials were built on the $500,000 figure. And now there was a discrepancy—a big one.

Agassi and his team—brother Tal and Barak Hershkovitz primarily—argued about the price on a conference call from Copenhagen in early 2008.

"We have to cut it down to $1.5 million at the most," they told Lindheim. "Your price is too high because we haven't given you enough information yet."

Lindheim pushed back.

"The numbers don't lie," he said.

Could the price come down?

Perhaps, but it would require significant redesign and sourcing the equipment from, say, China.

Maybe once the company gained experience, costs would be lower?

Even that thinking was flawed, Lindheim said.

"Tal and Shai didn't understand the intricacies of a construction project," he explained. "Shai would say—we just need this machine that goes boom, boom, boom. But when you're building infrastructure, variability is the key. You could have two identical buildings right next to each other, and there would be differences. Every battery switch station had its own conditions—soil, ground water, municipal codes and rules—this is what threw them for a loop.

"Shai came from software, where the marginal costs for the next release are low, because it's just printing another disk or sending it through the cloud. Variability is what stopped the price from getting lower."

Still, despite Lindheim's expert opinion, the $500,000 number stayed on Better Place's spreadsheets.

"In every company meeting when Shai would speak, there would be three to four people in the audience who knew he wasn't getting it exactly right," Lindheim said. "I always hoped Shai would see the light."

OSCAR

Sitting in the dashboard's pride of place, replacing the large color LCD entertainment system control screen, was OSCAR. But unlike his Sesame Street counterpart, Better Place's OSCAR was no grouch.

A playful acronym standing for "Operating System for Cars" (replacing the equally cutesy AutOS), OSCAR would be the main driver interface for Better Place's electric vehicles. Its primary function was to tell you how much power your car's battery has left and where the nearest recharging option is. OSCAR would also give drivers turn-by-turn vocalized instructions on how to reach any destination, making it a full-fledged in-car GPS system.

OSCAR was an irreducible component of the trifecta of technology that Better Place needed to build (the charge spots and battery switch stations being the other two).

Barak Hershkovitz described how OSCAR would work.

"If I want to drive from here to Jerusalem, all I have to do is put the address inside the car," he explained. "Once you put the destination inside OSCAR, it will not just build a route plan, like any GPS system. It will do a very accurate range calculation of what will be the exact state of charge of the battery when we get to our destination."

OSCAR learns each driver's habits and adjusts its calculation of electricity consumption accordingly. It takes into account various factors including the weather, how many people are in the car, whether there are bicycles on the roof creating extra drag and whether the journey is uphill or downhill.

"We will know how you drive, how your specific battery behaves, how your specific car behaves, and we will have a very accurate statistical model that will predict the range when you arrive. The longer you drive the car, the smarter the system becomes," Hershkovitz said. "It knows everything about the car, it knows everything about the battery … when you go for a battery switch, OSCAR already communicates with the switch station. He senses that you are coming … he will tell you at each step where you are in the process."

To do all this, OSCAR needed to sit on top of a system of maps.

Better Place could have built its own. But GPS systems are highly specialized work that take years to perfect. Just look at what happened when Apple tried to compete with Google Maps on the iPhone—the initial rollout was so error-strewn that Apple CEO Tim Cook had to write a letter of apology to customers. In it, he suggested users try, at least temporarily, an alternative mapping app.

One of the apps Cook suggested was the Israeli company Waze.

Waze's secret sauce is that it generates real-time traffic maps based on data from drivers who keep the Waze app open while cruising the country's highways. As long as it is turned on, the app requires no user interaction whatsoever; it can measure how fast the car is moving in order to calculate when a traffic jam is arising.

Users can also proactively report accidents, tapping the screen to note speed traps and road conditions, winning points and feeling like overall good social road warriors. Waze adjusts accordingly, with updates and alternative routes.

In 2008, Waze had just raised an initial seed round of $12 million. Its maps were still incomplete, limited mostly to Israel; its software still sketchy and unreliable.

Still, partnering with an existing GPS service like Waze made more sense than going DIY.

Barak Hershkovitz invited Waze's senior team for a meeting.

"We like what you're doing," Hershkovitz said. "Could you build this for OSCAR?"

The Waze guys had done their homework.

"We can do it, yes," replied the company's chief engineer. "We'll have to do some minor adjustments to our software, though. Not a lot. It will cost you about sixty thousand dollars."

Hershkovitz looked at his colleagues across the table impassively.

"You don't understand," he said. "Working with Better Place is not just a job. It's joining a revolution. We are giving you the *right* to join this revolution."

He leaned forward and added the kicker.

"In exchange, we'd like you to do it all for free."

"This was a common approach by Barak and Shai," explained Motty Cohen, who held the title "head of innovation" at Better Place. The company was so special, the thinking went, that third parties should be lining up and paying Better Place just to get in the door, to help change the world (and presumably to make a lot of money along the road).

The Waze guys, however, were not moved. They were still a small company; every minute of development time counted. Working with Better Place might indeed be prestigious, but when salaries needed to be paid, it was neither prudent nor a relevant option.

The meeting ended without a deal.

Years later, when Waze had become a global success story, Hershkovitz approached the company again.

"We'll put two of our best engineers at your facility if you're willing to collaborate now," Hershkovitz said.

But Waze turned Better Place down again.

"We don't have time for it anymore," their chief engineer said.

The company had by that point spread around the world, and 50 million drivers were now using Waze to navigate big American cities and out-of-the-way locales alike. One fan even reported Waze accurately predicting traffic on the eponymous Monkey Forest Road in Ubud, Bali. (Bumper-to-bumper with chimpanzees?)

Moreover, Waze was already in secret talks to sell to Google. And in 2013, a deal was struck: The search engine giant acquired Waze for a stunning $1.1 billion.

With Waze not interested, Hershkovitz turned to another mapping company: iGo, which made a popular GPS device that came either integrated into the car or could be purchased as an add-on. It was especially popular with rental car companies, where it represented a nice chunk of upsell income.

iGo was founded and run by two Israelis, so there was a local connection, but development was located primarily in Budapest, Hungary. While iGo had none of the sexy social traffic features that were to make Waze the darling of the turn-by-turn-directions world, it had one thing going for it that Waze couldn't provide: It could be downloaded onto a device—in its entirety.

Daniel Campbell, Better Place's head of telematics, web and mobile product management, explained why that's important.

"Because Waze relied on remote maps, if you didn't have cellular coverage, you were out of navigation," he said. "It might look straightforward to navigate with Waze in Israel, but if you're driving in Germany or Denmark, you don't always have full cellular coverage. Waze's software at the time was not considered automotive-grade."

But iGo's offline advantage was also a limitation.

Because the maps lived on the car itself, they were constantly going out of date. And because iGo didn't have an over-the-air update system like Waze, you'd need to go back to your dealer to get the latest version.

"Ninety-five percent of drivers never update their maps," Campbell said.

In most cases around the world, changes for road infrastructure are anticipated, Campbell added, "so even if you got a map that's from half a year ago, it can hold the content of things that are way ahead. Israel, on the other hand, is a mess."

Better Place's engineers ultimately figured out a way to do over-the-air updates through OSCAR using iGo maps. But none of it came cheap.

And the hardware couldn't be updated at all. That's because car specifications must be frozen 18 to 24 months in advance; nothing new can be introduced while the cars are being road-tested. By the time the first Better Place customers would take delivery on their cars, "the solution they got would already be two years old," Campbell said.

When all was said and done, the total budget within Better Place to build OSCAR, based on a dedicated team of 30 employees working for three years and earning approximately $100,000 each, was some $60 million.

WINDMILL COUNTRY

Travel the countryside in Scandinavia and, in addition to lovely rolling hills and deep waterways, you will see windmills. Thousands upon thousands of them, twirling away, generating electricity in mind-boggling abundance.

Denmark in particular has been so proactive with building a network of windmills that it has a highly unique problem: All those windmills are generating too much electricity.

In 2008, around 18 percent of Denmark's total energy came from the wind. The wind doesn't differentiate between day and night—if anything, it's stronger in the evening as the wind picks up when the air cools down—but electricity use does.

When the country has gone to sleep and the lights and appliances and air conditioners are switched off, wind-generated electricity is still pouring into the grid—so much so that Denmark has to export some of its nighttime energy to neighboring countries.

The situation in 2008 was even more absurd: Denmark actually had to pay Germany to take its excess electricity.

Enter Better Place with a deceptively simple yet brilliant idea: Let us build a network of battery-powered cars and switch stations that will allow Denmark to store that excess power within the country's borders—inside the cars themselves.

The country's major utility, DONG (it stands for "Denmark Oil and Natural Gas") was intrigued, both for the potential cost savings and to address another problem it had.

Like Idan Ofer in Israel with his oil, coal and Dead Sea Works, DONG's corporate image was also suffering as a major generator of pollution. A partnership with an innovative electric car company with environmentally friendly aspirations could be just the greenery needed to hide some of the grime.

That direction is reflected in how DONG describes itself.

"Since DONG Energy was formed, in 2006, we have transformed from one of the most coal-intensive utilities in Europe to a global leader in renewable energy. We are the world leader in deploying offshore wind, helping to reduce carbon emissions and harvest Europe's own energy resources."

DONG agreed to partner with Better Place to establish the company's second countrywide operation. In December 2007, DONG and local investors put around $25 million into Better Place, ensuring that the new Danish outpost would have a bit of independence and wouldn't be a direct financial drain on the main company.

Denmark was ideal in Better Place's eyes. The UPI news service described it as "a small [nation] with a well-connected road system and a lot of green idealism." The government had set a goal of becoming entirely fossil-fuel-free by 2050.

And while Denmark isn't quite an isolated "island," as Agassi's and Zarur's original document had called for (nearby Iceland was its recommendation), the country is compact, with most of the population living within a relatively short driving distance of the capital, Copenhagen. All of Denmark could be covered with just a couple-dozen battery switch stations.

Denmark is also cold, the opposite of hot and humid Israel, which would allow Better Place to demonstrate that its technology would work in all kinds of weather.

From a financial perspective, the Danish government had recently put in place a highly favorable tax scheme for owners of electric vehicles. Although gasoline-powered vehicles faced a crippling 180 percent tax levy, electric cars would be taxed at zero percent.

And—good news for Better Place—Renault was firmly established in the country.

To launch Better Place Denmark, Shai Agassi spoke at the closing event of the Copenhagen Climate Council. Present were the deputy prime minister of Denmark, Bendt Bendtsen, and DONG CEO Anders Eldrup.

"How do you run all cars in Denmark without gasoline?" Agassi asked on March 29, 2008, immediately jumping to the Better Place answer: through "the creation of a virtual oil field—one that will never run dry and will not kill us in the process."

Better Place would "leverage the batteries as a distributed storage device for electricity," he added, one that "can make wind and other intermittent electricity sources a convenient source of energy."

DONG wanted more than just a virtual oil field. It hoped to use Better Place to create "virtual power plants."

The thinking went like this: If Better Place could control the amount of electricity that was flowing into its cars, dialing that ever so slightly down when overall demand was particularly high, the incremental savings to DONG could equal the output of a new power plant that the utility would not have to build.

Hugh McDermott was Better Place's vice president of global utilities and energy. It was his job to figure out how to turn DONG's desires into workable technology.

"Let's say that we'll have ten thousand or one hundred thousand cars in a country at the end of the decade," McDermott explained. "If they're all plugged in, that's equivalent to one physical power plant. But they don't all have to be charging at the same level at the same time. Better Place could, for example, cut the charging load for up to one-hour maximum, up to ten to twenty times per year, when the electrical grid gets stressed."

Or, in a less extreme example, Better Place could allow its utility partners to simply "turn down the throttle on a gas-fired power plant," McDermott said. If they know in advance that 50,000 cars will need 40 percent less power at 2 p.m., the power plants don't have to work as hard—another way of saving money.

Think of it like the dimmer on a light switch, operated by software algorithms rather than human hands.

"If you reduce it by ten percent for an hour, no consumer is going to notice. If you turn it down ten percent for three hours, maybe someone notices. But if it's a big battery—the kind that are coming down the road [like in a Tesla], no one will detect it."

The main thing is that to the grid, "it looks just like a real power plant going up and down," McDermott added. "I can use my network of plugged-in cars—my virtual power plant—to reduce emissions at a real-world power plant."

The technology to enable the management of these virtual power plants was known as "the smart grid." It was a long-term futuristic function no less critical than the company's more visible components: the battery switch stations, the charge spots, OSCAR and the car itself.

Better Place's smart grid, which was envisioned not just for regions like Denmark that are rich in renewable energy but also for "regular" countries like Israel, ensured that if every single electric car were plugged in to charge at once, the electrical system wouldn't crash under the massively increased demand.

Instead, the smart grid would monitor who was charging at what time and match that with historical data and driving patterns to determine how much each car would need. The smart grid gave complete control over every plug-in point.

If, for example, demand for electricity across a country was particularly high on a hot summer afternoon at 4, the smart grid could determine that driver X, who was plugged in at his office parking lot, normally needed a battery charged to just 70 percent for his or her commute home, while driver Y needed a full 100 percent for the ride.

Using the modem and wireless communication built into Tal Agassi's charge spots, the smart grid could dynamically adjust the amount of electricity each car would receive according to its most likely needs.

Hugh McDermott called it "a great big shock absorber for the grid."

If drivers had a change from their regular plans—for example, they were driving not home but instead to a wedding far out of town, beyond their usual range—they could notify Better Place, which would dial that owner's car back up to full charging. Worse comes to worst, they'd have to use a switch station on the way.

Preventing potential grid blow-outs was also one of the reasons Agassi was opposed to fast charging—there was no way to properly know in advance who was going to need charging, and the electricity required for a fast charge was that much greater.

"Better Place came up with the idea of smart charging," explained charging system manager Emek Sadot. "But the relationship with DONG took it to an entirely new domain."

For example, DONG wanted the ability to *remove* electricity from a driver's battery.

The principle was the same: If the national electricity grid was getting overloaded on a particularly hot day and the power plants couldn't keep up, Better Place could discharge the batteries in its customers' cars temporarily, return the electricity to the grid, then put it back in the car an hour or two later. This would, of course, be based on the knowledge Better Place had of when a customer would be leaving work and how much juice was needed to get home.

Better Place had even grander plans: When the batteries in drivers' cars had degraded (through repeated charging) to a no-longer-acceptable level, at the next battery switch those batteries could be "retired" and moved to a warehouse, where they would continue to store excess energy at night— just not for powering cars.

It's a model that Tesla has adopted today with its Powerwall—a large battery meant for mounting in a customer's garage, and ideally paired with solar panels installed by Tesla sister company SolarCity, to store off-grid energy.

Ultimately, a utility company like DONG could use the data coming from Better Place's insight into drivers' charging requirements to plan out its future requirements.

"Utilities do ten- to twenty-year forecasts of energy usage, because that's how long it takes to build a power plant," McDermott said. Usually, they overbuild.

"Their whole business is built on probabilities," he added. "They have to build extra stuff in case things break, for downed power lines or other unforeseen events. If they had better control over their load, the equation changes."

The smart grid was super smart for Better Place and its utilities, and smart enough for the drivers.

"There's always a tension between minimizing costs and maximizing service," Sadot said. "The driver plugs in the cable; he wants his car to be at full capacity. Smart charging by definition does not do that. The customer wants maximum service; the company wants minimum costs. You need to find a balance. That's what our system did—it found a way to charge in the most efficient way to best serve the customer, while at the same time reducing costs for the providers."

6

TAILPIPES NOT INVITED

G eneral Motors was in trouble.

By the end of 2007, the Great Recession had kicked in. Tightening credit made it difficult for buyers to finance any prospective purchases, including new cars. GM was looking at liabilities of close to $200 billion compared with assets of under $100 billion. The company that had for nearly a century helped to define auto making in America seemed both figuratively and literally to be coming to the end of the assembly line.

Some of GM's problems had already been forecast—heavy union and health care obligations, for instance, were adding an estimated $1,400 to the cost of every car. Others hit the company by surprise. Oil prices soared; as gas topped $4 a gallon in the United States, consumers turned away from the SUVs and mammoth pickups that had become GM's bread and butter and its first-line strategy to differentiate itself from the smaller and snappier Japanese imports.

GM's chief financial officer at the time, Fritz Henderson, tried valiantly to raise funds. A plan to generate $3 billion through a sale of bonds or shares that began in early 2008 imploded when Lehman Brothers collapsed later that year.

It was a short path to the following year's shocking, if inevitable, declaration of bankruptcy and subsequent government bailout.

Although the full extent of GM's problems would not become water-cooler chatter for several months to come, when Shai Agassi and a small team of Better Place executives arrived at GM's Detroit headquarters on May 6, 2008, they could sense the distress—and they smelled opportunity. If a company as storied as GM couldn't make its business work, Agassi reasoned, the timing could not have been better for a new model; something fresh, revolutionary ... and electric.

It didn't hurt that the one shining star in GM's product portfolio was a peculiar yet promising plug-in hybrid. The Chevrolet Volt wasn't an all-electric car like the Renault Fluence Z.E. Still, it was closer to Agassi's vision than were traditional hybrids such as the Toyota Prius.

The Volt had made its debut in Detroit at the 2007 North American International Auto Show. The car's key differentiator is what's known as a "range extender." Unlike the Prius, which alternates constantly between its small electric and larger gasoline engines—essentially only improving gasoline mileage—the Volt runs strictly on electricity until the battery is depleted; only then does its gasoline engine kick in to power an electric generator, extending the range as needed.

The Volt's internal combustion engine isn't attached to the car's drive train; it recharges the battery directly. The Volt can run for about 40 miles before the internal combustion engine powers up, a distance greater than the typical commute for 80 percent of U.S. workers and certainly sufficient for casual use around town running errands. These features were more than enough to make the Volt a suitable stand-in for an "all-electric" car.

That was good—but not good enough—for Agassi. His goal for the meeting with GM: to convince the company to build a completely new version of the Volt with a switchable battery that could operate using Better Place's infrastructure.

A deal with GM would bring Better Place solidly into the U.S. market, lending the critical cache of the General Motors name. Despite GM's impending woes, it was of infinitely more value than Better Place's only other automotive partner, Renault, which didn't sell cars in North America at all.

It would be by far the most significant and high-level meeting in Better Place's short history.

BOB LUTZ

The possibility of forging a relationship with GM began in February 2008, when Mike Granoff saw a Newsweek article featuring Bob Lutz, GM's vice chairman of global product development. Lutz told Newsweek that "the electrification of the automobile is inevitable … I believe strongly that this country has to get off oil."

As a top GM executive with nearly 50 years in the auto industry, Lutz would have hardly seemed an electric vehicle champion.

The Swiss-born Lutz started with a brief stint at GM Europe before coming to stateside GM's cross-town competitors Ford and Chrysler, moving to GM in 2001. His babies included such gas guzzlers as the Dodge Viper muscle car and the 1,000-horsepower Cadillac Sixteen, as well as a host of other vehicles: the Pontiac GTO, the Chevy Malibu and the Buick Lacrosse.

On top of that, Lutz was also an outspoken critic of the environmental argument for electric cars.

As recently as January 2008, in a closed-door session with several journalists, he had called climate change "a total crock of shit," a claim he defended in subsequent interviews.

He qualified his opposition by adding, "I'm a skeptic, not a denier. Having said that, my opinion doesn't matter."

Indeed, when Lutz began quietly spearheading the Volt project under the radar at GM, the motivation was more business than ideological.

"We saw Toyota getting highly beneficial rub-off from their Prius success, which permitted them to cloak themselves in the mantle of total greenness," Lutz told Newsweek. "This was starting to hurt because it was one reason for [the] sudden surge in Toyota's market share."

Lutz's skunkworks approach to getting the Volt built in its early days was in part an attempt to appease GM's engineers, who were reluctant at first to even consider an electric-powered car. After all, the company had poured billions of dollars and years of work into hydrogen fuel cells as GM's post-oil play. They didn't believe a car could be run on lithium ion batteries, the same type that power smaller electronic gadgets like laptops and cell phones.

And GM was still smarting from the public beating it had taken 10 years before, when it took its first foray into electric vehicles.

THE EV1

In 1996, GM introduced the first modern electric car, dubbed the EV1. (It was originally given the unfortunate name "Impact," but that was quickly changed.) GM was responding to the Zero Emissions Vehicle mandate passed by the California Air Resources Board in 1990, which required the seven major automobile suppliers in the United States to offer electric vehicles if they wanted to continue selling gasoline-powered vehicles in California.

The EV1 was a sleek state-of-the-art car, with many of the same features found on today's electric vehicles: a range of 100 to 140 miles on an eight-hour recharge, full torque capacity without the need to shift gears, keyless entry and ignition, acceleration from 0 to 50 miles per hour in just six seconds, a home recharger and strategically located public charging spots. All told, GM spent close to $1 billion to design, produce and market the car.

The EV1 was universally adored by its owners, who included high-profile celebrities like Mel Gibson and Tom Hanks.

But just a few years after its launch, citing ostensible "lack of demand," GM moved in aggressively to kill the project. During the car's three-year run, GM sold just 1,117 EV1s.

By 2002, GM had bought back or taken possession of every vehicle it had produced, and, beyond that, had crushed and demolished them all. The shocking latter process is captured on film in director Chris Paine's 2006 documentary, "Who Killed the Electric Car?" (Perhaps anticipating such a sour ending, drivers were allowed only to lease, not buy, the vehicles, making GM's total recall possible.)

Forty cars were saved for museums, but with their electric powertrains deactivated, and subject to an agreement that the cars were never to be driven on the road again. A single intact EV1 was donated to the Smithsonian Institution.

Why had GM refused to let any of its EV1s remain on the roads? The question has been the source of frequent speculation and conspiracy theories among early electric car enthusiasts. Paine's movie remains a popular download, and GM became public enemy No. 1 to much of the green community.

Given that history, what made GM under Lutz embrace electric cars again? Lutz said it was strictly business; the launch of Tesla did it.

"That tore it for me," he explained in 2007. "If some Silicon Valley start-up can solve this equation, no one is going to tell me anymore that [a car run on lithium ion batteries] is unfeasible."

Lutz made one more statement that surely caught the eye of Shai Agassi.

Referring to the Volt in 2008, he declared, "This is like JFK's call for the moonshot."

Just two years earlier, Agassi had framed his own vision for electric cars using pretty much the same wording.

A challenge had been thrown down.

When Mike Granoff saw Lutz's statements on the inevitability of electrification in Newsweek, "I read that and I thought, oh my God, this is it. We're home free," Granoff recalled. "It's like seeing the kosher certification on a label. Bob Lutz—Mr. Detroit, Mr. Gas Guzzler—just gave us the seal of approval."

Granoff came up with a ploy to get Lutz's attention.

"I had a friend, Richard Demb, in New Jersey, whose company made gourmet popcorn," he said. "So I said to Richard, I want the biggest tin you've got, and I want you to send it to Bob Lutz in Detroit with a note reading 'Loved the quote, I couldn't agree more, let's meet.'"

The trick worked, and Lutz set up a meeting.

THE RENAISSANCE CENTER

The headquarters of General Motors in downtown Detroit sprawls across 14 acres. Opened in 1977 and purchased by GM in 1996 to house 5,000 of its key executives, the Renaissance Center is more a small city than a typical Silicon Valley–style laid-back corporate campus.

It consists of seven skyscrapers—four with 39 stories each and two at 21 stories, surrounding the seventh, the stunning cylindrical Detroit Marriott. At 73 stories, it's the tallest building in Michigan and one of the tallest hotel buildings in North America.

The meeting between GM and Better Place was in a setting intended to be intimidating: Tower 300 on the 30th floor, in conference room A21. But that effort would prove to be wasted on Agassi. He entered the assigned meeting room brimming with his usual bravado, confident and ready to rumble.

At Agassi's side were two of his top lieutenants: Mike Granoff, here wearing his hat as head of oil independence policies for Better Place, and Sidney Goodman, leader of the automotive alliances group at Better Place, who had been tasked with finding a second carmaker after Renault.

The Better Place team arrived first and sat down on one side of a long wooden table that exuded history and demanded respect. Administrative assistant Sandy McElroy, a GM lifer who has been with the company since 1976, brought in hot and cold drinks and laid out a few snacks.

The GM guys arrived soon after and took up positions on the opposite side of the table.

There were 10 of them, each with a pedigree more impressive than the next, representing a healthy sprinkling of relevant GM departments: product development, energy and safety policy, corporate finance, strategy initiatives.

Notably, Bob Lutz was not among them.

In his place was Larry Burns, GM's vice president of research and development and strategic planning.

Burns was a good stand-in: a down-in-the-trenches guy who understood the technology intimately and was a strong champion of the Volt and of GM's move to electrification.

Agassi launched into his presentation. He laid out what Better Place was building and why existing automotive models were at a dead end. He described the relationship between auto manufacturers and oil companies as "abusive," with companies like Exxon Mobil earning all the profits while the carmakers got nothing (not a hard sell given the trouble carmakers were in at the time).

Agassi extolled the virtues of battery swap versus fast charge and how nimble companies without all of Detroit's baggage could turn things around and save the day. Better Place, he predicted, would sell 100,000 cars in just a few years, including tens of thousands in Israel in Year One alone. He explained how the Volt could be adapted to work with Better Place's battery-switch infrastructure.

The GM team nodded in agreement at Agassi's analysis of the raw deal American carmakers were getting at the hands of the oil companies, but they were skeptical of Agassi's predictions on the uptake of electric vehicles.

"It took the Toyota Prius 15 years to get to just 1.5 percent market share in the United States," said one of the GM leaders.

"The GM people were also not convinced that battery switch was the future and, in any case, the Volt was just not designed to work that way," Granoff recalled.

Better Place's switch stations and infrastructure were being crafted to work with Renault's rectangular battery, which could simply drop down and scoot out on a platter. But the Volt had a T-shaped battery.

"We could never really figure out how to make that work with our switching mechanism," Granoff said.

But at the conference table that day, Agassi persisted, thinking perhaps that he could sway the GM team if he just chose the right words.

"All you need to do is take the engine out, redesign the carriage and put in a flat battery," he said matter-of-factly.

It made perfect sense to Agassi.

Meanwhile, Granoff squirmed, and Goodman was silent. In Agassi's shadow, the latter would barely say a word the entire meeting.

VOLT ON THE TABLE

Larry Burns and his team at GM weren't rattled by Agassi's onslaught, though. Instead, Burns made a remarkable offer.

Would Better Place be interested in becoming the global infrastructure partner for the fixed-battery Volt?

Agassi didn't respond. Not right away, at least. Granoff was enthusiastic, nonetheless.

He told Agassi by phone afterward, "We've got to do this! Yes, we know there's no future in that model, but this is GM. We can develop the relationship. We can move them toward our vision. Who knows where it can go from here?"

Agassi dismissed the offer out of hand.

"Mike, you don't understand. That car, the Volt, it has a tailpipe," Agassi said. "It's a stupid car. They'll never build it. We don't do things halfway. If we do this, we do it right, we do it pure. We don't work with tailpipe cars, period."

Agassi wasn't necessarily wrong. It would have been a major step down compared with turning the Volt into a fully switchable vehicle. And it would have taken the new company far from its stated core mission. Essentially, it would have meant installing charge spots at homes and offices and managing the network—a small subset of the full Better Place offering.

Plus, it was a low-margin business, competing against other charge spot providers on a product that sold in the hundreds, not tens of thousands, of dollars per unit. Add in the need to set up and manage thousands of local electricians, technicians and support staff, and it might very well *cost* the company money.

"It's true that it would have been a low-margin business," said Dimitri Dadiomov, the Stanford graduate who subsequently joined the company to work in business development and product management. "But it's not like we were going to base an eventual multi-billion-dollar IPO [an initial public offering] on servicing infrastructure and charge spots. It would have been a division, and a valuable one to have."

"We don't work with cars that have a tailpipe" would become a mantra for Agassi and, by extension, for all of Better Place in the years to come. For Agassi, not deviating from the path of the 100 percent–electric switchable-battery car was as close to a religious belief that the secular CEO would ever profess. To the faithful, he was the *rebbe* who, by blessing dollar bills and handing them out to his students, could channel heaven and bend the laws of nature—or in this case, the wills of intransigent would-be partners.

THE PRICE OF OIL

If the group around the huge wooden conference table at GM in 2008 could have seen 2016's headlines, they might not have believed them.

"Oil prices tank."

"Price per barrel in free fall."

"Energy companies drag U.S. stocks lower as oil prices plunge."

And the numbers: as low as $30 a barrel.

Few had seen it coming, but by the middle of the second decade of the 2000s, it was normal to talk about the "death of oil." A massive boom in U.S. fracking, among other economic factors, had resulted in prices that hit other industries and global markets like dominos and sparked concern about another recession.

But Better Place's business proposition was built on the opposite assumption: that the price of oil would go up, steadily and irreversibly. The higher the price of a barrel of oil, and the lower the cost of electricity (which these days is generated nearly entirely by sources other than oil, with natural gas and renewables on the rise), the better the economics of driving electric became.

Agassi had predicted that the price of oil would spike to more than $100 a barrel before the end of 2007.

It hit $98 in November of that year and peaked the following July, just two months after the meeting at GM, at $147 a barrel.

Agassi was buoyed by the steady rise. The world was moving even faster than he had foreseen.

The New York Times' Thomas Friedman seemed to agree.

"What I find exciting about Better Place," he wrote, "is that it is building a car company off the new industrial platform of the 21st century, not the one from the 20th—the exact same way that Steve Jobs did to overturn the music business."

The meeting was nearing its conclusion. Agassi leaned forward for his final argument.

"Listen," he said quietly. "The gas bill on an annual basis for the average car in Europe today is higher than the value of the car itself."

What Agassi was getting at was that, with the cost of gasoline in Europe approaching $8 a gallon at the time, the combination of Better Place's monthly subscription fee for electricity and service and the cost to lease a car would be less than what a German or French or Belgian driver would pay for gas alone.

If the cost of batteries came down, as Better Place predicted? Even better.

Ron Adner, author of "The Wide Lens: A New Strategy for Innovation," devoted an entire chapter in his book to Better Place, among other things pointing out that, based on Agassi's math, "driving an electric vehicle is like getting your gasoline at 75 cents per gallon."

Compared with $8 a gallon for gasoline, there would be plenty of room to factor in the full price of a monthly lease and still come in for less.

Agassi's magic number was $500 per month, everything included. Who wouldn't want an electric car at that price?

"So, let me give this to you straight," Agassi told the GM guys. "Imagine it's 2012, it's Europe. How many of your $40,000 plug-in hybrid cars are you expecting to sell when I am giving cars away for free?"

It would not be the last time Agassi would make such a claim.

While communicating with a European carmaker about his plans for Denmark, Agassi sent a text message with a stark vision that was a variation on the same theme.

"I'll be offering $20,000 cars in a market where you're selling $60,000 cars," Agassi wrote. "How many have you planned to sell in 2011 in Denmark? Because I recommend you take them off your plan."

One of the GM executives pushed back.

"So, if it's free, why don't you just swap the car instead of the battery?" he demanded.

"That's a stupid question," Agassi barked.

The GM guys looked shocked by the suddenness of his attack.

Not missing a beat, Agassi continued spinning out his internal combustion nightmare scenario.

If Better Place was giving away cars, the "residual value" of a gasoline-powered vehicle at the end of its leasing agreement—that is, the amount for which GM's leasing department could resell a used company car to the public—would be gutted. The entire leasing and financing business, which GM's dealers depended on, would dry up.

"You won't be able to sell those cars at all. You're just a couple of years from falling off that cliff," Agassi said, apocalyptically.

The GM guys were silent, maybe taking it in, perhaps mentally dismissing it all outright. But Larry Burns muttered something under his breath that both Agassi and Granoff picked up on.

"He was saying 'disruption, disruption, disruption,'" Granoff remembered.

Even if a deal didn't come out of the meeting, "this was all the validation that Shai needed," Granoff said.

As the meeting ended and the Better Place team said their goodbyes and headed towards the elevator to take them back to the Renaissance Center's lobby, Agassi turned to Granoff.

"The next meeting we have," Agassi said, "it'll be at our headquarters."

"Why's that?" Granoff asked.

"Because we'll have the bigger market capitalization," Agassi replied without blinking.

Agassi's bold statement was right. Within a year, General Motors would declare bankruptcy, resulting in a corporate value of essentially zero. And Better Place would be on its way to a staggering valuation of $2.25 billion.

———

Afterward, though, Granoff was uncomfortable.

Agassi had been too aggressive, too assured, he felt. That brashness might work in brainstorming out-of-the-box solutions in Tel Aviv, but it had gone too far here in Detroit.

"Everything was said without regard to the fact that this was General Motors," Granoff recalled. "Never mind all the problems they had. This was one of the most legendary companies ever. And we walk in with a plan to turn their business upside down."

Nor was the free car idea supposed to be brought up. That wasn't ready for prime time; it was a thought experiment, a notion for *kibitzing* around the white board in Davos, not something that takes center stage in the Renaissance Center.

"It was a complete absurdity," Granoff said in hindsight.

In the days after the meeting, Granoff tried to play good cop. He sent a letter to the organizers that was dripping in politically correct, if backpedaling, sincerity:

> It was comforting to find that the leadership of one of the world's most legendary companies to be of like minds to us as to the urgency of moving transportation off of its dependence on oil. That urgency was reinforced as we drove to the airport and heard on the radio that oil had yet again reached a new high of $123 per barrel. Time is clearly not on our side.
>
> To the degree to which the conversation was spirited, I hope you understand that, just as you admirably have great passion about your company and your roadmap to reduce oil dependence, we have each abruptly made career changes in the last 18 months because of our conviction about a specific roadmap to that end. Happily, there is a great degree of overlap between each of our visions. We would never tell you to abandon the various strategies you have already adopted. We would just like you to consider the risk involved in not adopting our approach as one such strategy in your portfolio.
>
> You are clearly heirs to a great tradition of automotive innovation that has touched billions of lives. We know that you will continue in that great tradition to help us all give our children a future of affordable, clean and sustainable personal mobility.

———

It didn't make a difference.

General Motors formally turned down Better Place's switchable battery proposal for the Volt, in a letter sent a month later, on July 17, 2008.

"Based on our analysis ... we have decided to remain focused on our E-Flex EREV (Extended Range Electric Vehicle) system and related battery development activities at the present time," the letter stated succinctly. "We look forward to hearing more about Project Better Place's progress ... and wish you continued success in this important endeavor."

7

ELECTRIC LAND GRAB

E van Thornley was on vacation with his family in France, when his mobile phone started to take on a life of its own. It was 6 a.m., and he was woken up by "a firestorm of email and text" from back home.

Thornley was a relatively new entrant into Australian politics, with only two years on the job as a member of the Victorian parliament, but his political and business acumen had already made him a high flyer in Victorian Premier John Brumby's government. He had honed his jovial yet savvy public persona over years as a successful startup entrepreneur, first in Australia and then in Silicon Valley, taking on no less than Google itself in the battle for search-engine supremacy.

Everyone knew he'd eventually be tapped for a cabinet seat—it was just a question of when.

"When" came early in the morning of December 24, 2008. An Australian cabinet minister had been charged in a rape and, in the ensuing scandal, had been forced to resign from the government.

"I want you to take up his role as minister for industry and trade," Brumby told Thornley on the phone.

It was the opportunity of a lifetime.

"People wait twenty years to get offered such a position," Thornley recalled. "I'd only been in the government for two."

There was just one problem: Unbeknownst to anyone back home, Thornley was in discussions with Better Place to become CEO of its Australian division.

There had just been a few conversations so far, but Thornley knew that if he took on a government position in charge of industry, he could never take a job at Better Place down the road.

"It would have been completely politically and ethically untenable,"

Thornley said. "People would have said I used insider connections to get the job."

Thornley called Agassi.

"If you're serious, we need to talk," he told Agassi. "I've got to get on a plane back to Australia and make a decision in the next forty-eight hours."

That's when the labor caucus in Australia would next be meeting.

"Why don't you route your trip from France back to Melbourne the long way, through San Francisco?" Agassi suggested. "I'll meet you at the airport."

Better Place's interest in Australia was part of a zeitgeist that can best be described as a "land grab."

While a more typical trajectory for a startup like Better Place would be to focus on a single location, working on a small pilot to prove the concept before expanding, Agassi and his team pursued an approach that was at once deeply hopeful and on guard against unexpected market challenges.

On the one hand, belief in the Better Place concept saw Agassi take a "we can change the world all at once" approach.

On the other, there was fear that just as the first iPhone had jumpstarted an entire industry, leading to hungry (and well-funded) competitors, electric car copycats would quickly rise up as well.

But in this was opportunity. During the great California Gold Rush that began at Sutter's Mill in 1848, it was the infrastructure guys—the guys who sold the shovels—who emerged the biggest winners. Better Place sold "shovels" too: the electricity and the network to power the cars.

Within its first two years, Better Place had operations and offices in Australia, Denmark, Canada, Austria, Spain, France, Japan and the United States—in Hawaii, where the state's Renewable Energy Development Venture would kick in a grant of $500,000—all in addition to Israel, of course. China was soon to follow, as was the Netherlands. There were deep discussions with public officials in New York and in San Francisco.

All of this contributed to the Better Place buzz; the feeling that the company with its telegenic leader was unstoppable.

But it also took resources—of both cash and time. Even those who supported a multi-national approach would admit years later that it replaced focus with frustration; vision, with velocity for its own sake.

Thornley was able to rearrange his flights back to Australia. His revised itinerary included a three-hour layover in San Francisco. Agassi met him at a Japanese restaurant just outside the security check.

The conversation was not about salary or stock options—it was still too early for that. It was more to gauge whether Agassi and Better Place were serious about doing something in Australia.

The two talked for an hour and a half; Agassi with his laser seriousness, Thornley equally engaged, but with the everyman charm that had propelled his career so far.

Thornley finished the meal convinced.

"No one had turned down a cabinet position in one hundred-twenty years of Australian politics," Thornley said. "Everyone was expecting me to say yes. They just assumed I'd take it. To say no would be taken as a personal insult by every serving politician who'd waited years. But at the end of my conversation with Shai, I realized I wasn't willing to walk away from the Better Place opportunity."

Thornley left Agassi and walked through security on his way to his flight. He called the premier, but he wasn't available.

"I was sweating bullets," Thornley said. "I'm about to get on a fourteen-hour flight, and I know there will be all kinds of TV cameras and newspapers when I land at the other end. So I get one of Brumby's staffers and I say I need to talk to the premier *now*. A minute before the plane was about to leave, he calls me back and I tell him I won't be able to take the role. It was not the news he was expecting, but he took it extraordinarily graciously."

Thornley was greeted less graciously by people back home. One member of parliament told him that his behavior was a "f—ing disgrace."

"There were TV cameras parked outside my house, the media was staking out the airport," Thornley said. "I was the front page story in the Australian tabloids for five days in a row."

Because he didn't have a formal job offer from Better Place, just the verbal intention that Agassi was serious about opening an operation Down Under, Thornley couldn't tell anyone why he'd turned down the government post.

"Rumors flew that I was going to be a high-paid lobbyist for some French company," he said. "The assumption was I was doing this to get a lot of money. But you have to remember, I already *had* a lot of money."

Better Place hadn't picked Evan Thornley as its candidate to lead the company's Australian operations for his political connections.

Thornley had long been known in his home country as the Steve Jobs of Australia; a successful entrepreneur in a country without much of a startup culture.

In 1995, Thornley co-founded LookSmart, which at the time was one of the Internet's leading search engines.

To go up against Google, LookSmart signed a deal in 1998 with Microsoft to power the search engine on the MSN website. On the basis of that deal, LookSmart relocated to San Francisco and went public in 1999. The stock debuted at $12 a share and climbed to more than $70 per share by early 2000. Thornley became a multi-millionaire.

LookSmart ran into trouble in 2003 when Microsoft severed its relationship with the company while quietly launching MSNBot, which would eventually morph into the Bing search engine.

At the time of the break-up, Microsoft accounted for 64 percent of LookSmart's revenue. LookSmart's shares tumbled and the company never recovered. LookSmart is still in business and receives some 6 billion search queries monthly—but that's a fraction of Google's 100 billion a month.

Evan Thornley's star continued to shine in the tech world. Plus, he had a keen interest, both personal and professional, in all things Israeli.

Several years earlier he had visited Israel with a delegation organized by the Australia-Israel Chamber of Commerce, which helped Israeli companies make connections when they came to visit Australia.

"Any Israeli ministers who would travel to Australia, or any business or trade deals happening would go through us," explained Guy Pross, who headed up the Chamber's Melbourne office.

Better Place was one of the businesses that Pross hosted in Australia. When the company got serious about opening an office in Melbourne, Pross headed up the search for a local CEO.

At the same time, Thornley was chatting with David Carlick, then managing director and venture partner at VantagePoint, which had just invested in Better Place and knew of the company's interest in Australia.

"I'd be glad to help, give them a few tips," Thornley told Carlick.

"Two of the four guys on our list used to work for you," Carlick replied. "Why aren't you our candidate?"

Thornley brushed him off. "No, no, I'm trying to change the world through politics now!"

Still, Thornley was planning a trip to the United States to visit Civil War sites with his son.

It was a "non–bar mitzvah, bar mitzvah trip," Thornley joked. (Thornley was just at the beginning of a lengthy process to convert to Judaism.)

"Why don't you meet with Shai Agassi while you're over here?" Carlick asked.

Thornley did. Discussions continued until Thornley's fateful plane ride home.

Geographically, Australia was everything Israel was not: a sprawling continent with massive cities, filled with freestanding homes sporting two-car garages. That meant that most car owners could have a charge spot installed at home (unlike Israel, where the majority of the population lives in apartments).

If Israel was chosen for its oil dependence, closed borders and the ability to cover the entire country with a limited number of battery switch stations, Australia was a "stand-in" for the United States.

As do U.S. drivers, Australians favor large vehicles—SUVs, jeeps and trucks. And with so many homes owning two vehicles (again, unlike Israel, or Denmark for that matter), it would be easier to convince consumers to make at least one of those vehicles electric while keeping a "backup" gasoline-powered car on the other side of the garage.

Moreover, Australian car owners were used to driving long distances. Melbourne, for example, is the physical size of Los Angeles.

The economics of Better Place's switchable-battery network posited that the more you drove, the better the value.

"The best way to prove that was to target a country with plenty of … high-kilometer drives," Thornley told CNET Australia, after he'd taken the CEO job and had time to noodle on the numbers. "Because when you look at the lifetime cost of a car, much of it goes into the petrol tank, not for [purchasing] the vehicle itself."

Thornley laid out the financial logic for consumers to go electric in Australia.

"Australia spends around twenty to twenty-five billion dollars a year on petrol, depending on the oil price and the currency," he explained. "If we were able to convert the whole fleet [of cars] over, then the renewable energy costs to power that fleet would be around three to four billion dollars a year."

The predicted 115-mile range of the battery was perfect for tooling around Australia's three major cities, of Sydney, Melbourne and Brisbane. To drive between the metropolitan areas, Guy Pross, who was also interviewed by CNET, suggested that "we can electrify the Hume Highway between Sydney and Melbourne by putting in [just] twenty battery-switching stations."

Thornley had greater ambitions: He hoped to build up to 500 battery switch stations and millions of plug-in charge spots. Thornley predicted the cost at close to $1 billion.

"It's not a trivial amount, but it's not mind-boggling," he added.

Evan Thornley finally faced the Australian media on January 14, 2009, and revealed that he was not, in fact, abandoning politics for a high-paying lobbying job. The pundits were incredulous.

"They were saying, 'What—you're leaving a cabinet position for this? Electric vehicles? That's like flying saucers. No way, what's the real deal?'" he recalled. "It's hard to explain if you're not in that system, but it would be the equivalent of a kid working his way up through the minor leagues, finally getting a contract to play major league baseball after waiting fifteen years and at the moment of being the number one draft pick, he says, 'Nah, I'd rather be a Realtor.'"

But the press eventually bought it and the media caravans parked outside his house moved on.

"My story moved to page eleven," Thornley joked.

He now had two tasks in front of him: to raise money and staff up.

The staff came first.

Unlike Agassi's first picks, based on connections from previous companies, the army and family, Thornley wanted people with proven experience in the automotive industry.

Key to that was Alison Terry, who became head of automotive and corporate affairs at Better Place Australia.

Terry was a 20-year veteran and senior executive for General Motors' Australian operation, where she had served as the company's general counsel. Not surprisingly, she was critical of Better Place's negotiations with GM in Detroit.

"GM made a strategic call to develop the Volt with range-extension capability. That was the basket into which they chose to put their eggs, for better or worse," she explained. "For Better Place to try to turn that ship around was something that would always have been difficult."

The way Agassi conducted the discussions, Terry added, "was very uncommercial, that's the kindest word I can use. Why go into a negotiation effectively saying: We think everything you've done to this point is rubbish, and we want you to come over to our singular view of the world where the future is switchable?

"It's difficult to see why we weren't open to having a broader discussion with GM as an infrastructure provider, and then progress to fully electric at some point. Yes, it's true that it would have taken time and money away from the main business. But you don't necessarily make money on your first customer."

Thornley's team was rounded out by head of marketing Ben Keneally, who had worked at the Boston Consulting Group in the United States before returning to Australia; Antony Cohen, Better Place Australia's CFO, who jumped ship from KPMG where he had led that firm's energy consulting practice; and Geoff Zippel, who held the title of head of deployment.

With its executive team in place, Better Place Australia raised $25 million—peanuts compared to what Agassi had already raised. Still, Better Place Australia CFO Cohen, who led the fundraising team, was proud.

"That amount, from Australian investors, at a $230 million pre-money valuation, with just a PowerPoint deck, was unheard of for a company in this country," he beamed.

Not everything went smoothly. Like Terry, Thornley disagreed with a key Agassi tenet.

"I didn't want to go to war with the automotive industry about switch," he said. "I wanted to be able to go into every auto manufacturer and say 'I want to be your partner to sell more electric cars.' If they didn't want to do switch at first, over time, they'd realize it was a better solution. And we'd be in position to take them there."

Thornley and Agassi argued about this plenty of times, "both in public and private," Thornley recalled.

Thornley thought he'd eventually gain the upper hand.

"Even Shai said that switching was only ever meant to be a backup. The vast majority of charging would be through a charge spot with a plug. So why not give drivers an integrated network, with home charge spots, fast charge on the road and battery switch as well," he said.

Either way, Australia was up and running, and its team would play an increasingly important role as the company grew.

JAPAN

A year after Better Place won the tender from the Japanese government, the very first battery switch station opened to the public in Yokohama, on May 13, 2009. Some 5,000 people visited in the first months of its operation. Robots worked their magic just as Agassi had described—one removed the depleted battery via a cyber-controlled conveyer belt while a second robot shuttled in a fully charged battery.

As promised, the station looked and acted just like a high-tech car wash. A white Nissan Qashqai with the words *Better Place* written across its rear left (a small blue Better Place logo balanced the text from the right) drove onto the grounds of the small station, with its white canvas roof. The whole affair had a bit of a circus big-top feel.

The Qashqai circled around the back before entering the station to roll on top of the charging platform, which was raised so audience members assembled for the demo could see what was happening underneath, before the Qashqai continued on its way.

For good measure, photovoltaic solar panels provided by Japanese manufacturer Sharp were positioned across the top of the switch stations, "creating a truly zero-emission solution," according to a Better Place press release.

Better Place had invited an international coterie of reporters and automotive bloggers to the event. The Danish and Israeli ambassadors to Japan were there, as were most of Better Place's key executives. The entire event was webcast live.

Shai Agassi gave a variation on his standard *shpiel*.

"Today marks a major milestone," he exclaimed. "For nearly a century, the automotive industry has been inextricably tied to oil. Today, we are demonstrating a new path forward."

Better Place Israel general manager Moshe Kaplinsky called it "a great achievement for Better Place and for Israel."

Kiyotaka Fujii was head of Better Place operations for Asia Pacific and the newly minted president of Better Place Japan. A former SAP-er, Fujii had been the point man for the software giant's operations in Japan for six years and pre-dated Agassi at the company. With his smooth English, salt-and-pepper hair and movie-star good looks, he was well-placed to make the connections Better Place needed.

Given that Better Place Japan was the first location on the globe where battery switch would be demonstrated, it was somewhat surprising that Fujii was, like Evan Thornley in Australia, not a confirmed believer in Agassi's "switch or else" mantra.

Flexibility is critical for startups, especially in their earliest stages, Fujii felt. But Better Place's steadfast adherence to a single solution at all costs sabotaged that.

"Better Place alienated a lot of people," Fujii said. "For Shai, switch or not switch became a religious war. It wasn't electric vehicles versus the internal combustion engine, but only about switch. If Shai could have convinced an auto manufacturer to build ten switchable cars as a trial, he'd spin it as if that company had decided to go switch all the way."

Agassi's approach confused potential car partners in Japan, who told Fujii that they didn't know if Agassi was promoting electric vehicles in general or just the Better Place solution.

"If you advocate only a certain way to promote electric vehicles, as was Shai's case, and you're wrong, it can backfire on the entire industry and create huge damage," Fujii said. "People would say—you guys are doing great things, but you may not be the only solution."

Like Danny Weinstock, Fujii felt fast charge was a better interim approach.

"I thought we should start from there and build a base, while working to improve the battery range," he said.

Fujii remembered a telling conversation with Nissan.

"One of the top guys at Nissan said, 'You know, we need a partner like you. We're not infrastructure guys, we're car guys. But there's a problem if you force us to build electric vehicles that require battery-switch only, and you don't support fixed-battery electric cars, because we don't know which way the market will go. So if you can service both methods, then we are real partners.'"

Agassi responded strongly, Fujii recalled.

"You guys don't understand this," Agassi said. "Fixed-battery cars are a dumb idea. It has to be switchable. This is the only way."

"So the partnership didn't happen," Fujii said. "I talked to Nissan's senior guys later. They said, 'If Shai is right, then the burden of proof is on his shoulders. You can't just tell us we're dumb.'"

Nissan's relationship with Renault didn't prove to be of any help.

"What we learned is that just because Renault has a deal with us doesn't mean Nissan is part of the deal or even interested in it," Better Place chief engineer Yoav Heichal explained. "Let's see how it goes with Renault, they said. If the technology picks up, then it will be easy to cascade to Nissan."

Fujii had another theory about what was going on, not only in Japan but with Better Place worldwide. Agassi was playing car companies off each other.

"Shai was convinced that there will be many car manufacturers lined up," Fujii said. "Why should he give a bigger stake to Nissan-Renault, when Daimler and GM will all be breathing down our necks? It was the whole poker mentality—making ourselves look bigger than we were, before we built anything of substance, to get leverage in negotiations. But the car companies are very conservative, and they talk to each other. Some young company who plays them off each other will eventually lose leverage."

Those two approaches—a single-minded focus in some aspects of the business and an aversion to commitment in others—make awkward bedfellows in any company. They would inevitably come to clash as Better Place moved forward.

BETTER PLACE'S FORREST GUMP

Amit Yudan was Better Place's equivalent of Forrest Gump. Like the character depicted by Tom Hanks in the movie of the same name, Yudan managed to show up in a remarkable number of significant places. In charge of European business development for Better Place, Yudan played a key role in Better Place's "open to anyone" approach (open, that is, provided they pledged loyalty to battery switch).

Yudan's first task was to replicate Better Place's Denmark success in Austria, where he was based. Over a period of two years, Yudan worked tirelessly to convince Verbund, Austria's largest power provider, to get on the electric bandwagon.

Like Denmark, Verbund needed something to do with its excess energy—not from wind power, though, but from water. More than 80 percent of the electricity Verbund generated in 2008 came from hydropower, much of it from the rivers that course through the Austrian Alps. Verbund is Europe's fourth-largest hydropower electricity producer.

"It took a lot of time to develop confidence with them," Yudan admitted. "But slowly, they became more comfortable with the potential of electric cars. They liked what Better Place was doing."

Yudan met with Verbund's CEO and even the Austrian finance minister. "We took them to Israel and Denmark to see what Better Place had done."

But when it came time to finalize the numbers, the two sides couldn't come to an agreement.

Verbund wanted a more or less even split. Better Place wanted it weighted more heavily in its own direction.

Better Place walked away.

The Austrian non-deal led to considerable friction within Better Place with some calling it a "big bang" and saying that "Shai Agassi blew it up."

The truth, Yudan said, was more akin to an intense but reasonable negotiation where the suitors were simply too far apart.

"It was the right decision from our end," said Dan Cohen, Agassi's chief of staff. "The Austrians wanted too much, and we couldn't come to terms." The split was amicable, he added.

Agassi didn't take the deal off the table entirely. As late as February 2012, he tweeted that Better Place "will come to Austria as soon as the government wants us to."

Meanwhile, Yudan had other irons heating up.

Germany, Europe's leading economy and right next door to Yudan's Austria, presented a special challenge.

As part of the process of getting Germany on board, Better Place had invited a minister from the German government to come to Israel for a test drive.

"We can't do this," the minister's chief of staff told Yudan. "It would be highly improper and even embarrassing for a German minister to be seen driving a French car."

Renault, Better Place's only car manufacturing partner was, of course, French, and the test car Quin Garcia had rigged up in Israel was the Renault Mégane.

Germans have a particularly tight connection with their automotive industry. Car manufacturers like BMW, Opel and Daimler, along with auto parts suppliers such as Continental and Bosch, account for 14 percent of the country's gross domestic product. Cars are Germany's top export, and Germany is the fourth-largest producer of cars in the world (after China, the United States, and Japan).

"It's OK, we can make this a private meeting," Yudan assured the German minister's worried chief of staff. "You don't have to publish a picture in the paper."

Reassured, the minister arrived—and was accompanied by a full team of German journalists.

Yudan was shocked.

"Come on, let's go for it," the minister said.

"But we heard from your chief of staff—" Yudan sputtered. "And all the media is here."

"Don't worry, it's no problem," the minister replied. "Just because I drive the car doesn't mean I'm going to invest in a French company!"

"The test drive went very well," Yudan recalled afterward. "He drove and was very satisfied. I guess it just goes to show that sometimes politicians are more open than the people they have trying to protect them."

But while the German minister seemed happy, Agassi was creating enemies elsewhere in Germany, particularly among the country's auto industry executives. His brash dismissal of anything non-electric or without a switchable battery, and his positioning of Better Place as an "equal partner" to storied brands such as Mercedes and Volkswagen—as he had done previously at General Motors—didn't go over well.

One particular meeting stood out, Ziva Patir recalled. It was held with "all the big shots of the German car industry."

"You will see that you don't understand what I'm talking about," Agassi lectured the group. "You'll all learn."

"They never forgave him for that," Patir said. "They were so furious."

Other times, Agassi simply didn't show up.

Once, Idan Ofer set up a meeting at the Frankfurt Auto Show with one of BMW's senior designers.

It wasn't easy to get, but "they took it seriously because of me," Ofer said. "So we flew to Munich to meet with them. You would have thought that Shai would have come to a meeting that I, as chairman of the company, arranged. But he said, no, I'll do it via video conference."

Ziva Patir got the full brunt of Europe's disdain for Agassi's attitude at an automotive show in Geneva. On stage was a speaker from BMW.

When asked a question about the future of electric cars and Shai Agassi's company, the speaker thundered, "I wouldn't invest $750 million in Better Place. I wouldn't even invest 75 cents."

Fast Company magazine quoted an unnamed Better Place executive who summed up Agassi's misadventures in Germany. "If we hadn't been such assholes, BMW would have agreed to do a swappable-battery car. Instead, they gave us the finger."

But when the German publication DW asked Agassi point blank, "What is the reason you were not successful in Germany?" Agassi replied, "I don't know, you need to ask them … we were, I think, misunderstood by some of the players in the market. We're great enablers, and we're great partners. If you ask Renault, they'll tell you how great a partner we are."

As he had with Austria, Agassi insisted he wasn't giving up on Germany.

"The question is only—when," he said in an interview with Financial Times Deutschland, before conceding that, "I have no idea which political power plays are ongoing behind the scenes."

"Shai correctly wanted to create a situation where the automakers would move quickly to electric," Amit Yudan said in defense of Agassi. But "the carmakers are used to a totally different ecosystem. Somebody from another industry trying to treat them as an equal partner [rather than with deference] is not in their DNA."

Better Place was spun "as being a very neat, easy solution," said Lawrence Seeff, head of global alliances at Better Place and Amit Yudan's boss. "The story was that all you have to do is put a battery switch station in the ground, get a car manufacturer to build you a battery-switchable car and you can solve your pollution issue."

That led to meetings in some far-flung locations.

Indeed, sometimes it seemed that wherever Better Place could get a meeting, someone from the business development team would take the opportunity and get on the plane.

"We had a guy who wanted to be our man in Chile," remembered Carlo Tursi, who worked as Better Place's director of corporate development. "He did a lot of work for us for free. He connected us to a bunch of different government officials and companies and even brought a delegation over to Israel. But nothing ever came of it."

Seeff remembered that there would be conversations with the Chile contact "once or twice a month. We were waiting to see if he could get someone in the government serious enough to be willing to invest. Santiago had a very strong need for electrification because of pollution."

Tursi had a folder in his laptop with all the countries that had contacted Better Place. There were inquiries from Southeast Asia, Eastern Europe, "even some in Africa," Tursi said. "You'd be surprised."

Dimitri Dadiomov was struck by what he characterized as a "random" meeting with the head of industrial research at a company in Taiwan.

"It was an island, after all, and they were completely dependent on outside oil," Dadiomov said. "Maybe there was something there."

A Better Place staffer from Palo Alto revealed that a group came to Israel from Bhutan.

"It took us months for someone to say no to the Bhutanese," the staffer said.

An inquiry was even made by the CEO of the strategic investment arm of the government of Bahrain.

"I like the Bahrainis," Agassi responded in a quick email. "They need our network."

A status update sent to Better Place management in those early days reported that business development staff had done an Asian blitz, visiting "Beijing, Singapore, Hong Kong and Tokyo all in four days." That same update mentioned contacts with interested parties in New Zealand, Mexico and Ukraine.

Agassi himself once boasted that "in the last six weeks, I've been in thirty countries. I have so many sins to pay on my climate bill!"

Still, Agassi admitted the company couldn't be everywhere.

In his interview with DW, Agassi said that, although Better Place had been in conversations "with, I think, fifty countries around the world ... there is a limit to how many we can do at any point in time."

Just the same, countries that hadn't made the short list would send delegations to Israel.

"We'd host them out of respect," Tursi said. "We wanted to take them seriously, not just to dismiss them. We figured it was OK to spend one or two days, or maybe even a week, to quantify an opportunity."

The one place where Better Place was moving steadily forward was in Denmark.

In January 2009, Better Place and DONG as the primary investor announced a round of 103 million Euros in financing (around $130 million at the time).

In conjunction with the new funding, Better Place had hired Jens Moberg as the head of its Europe, Middle East and Africa (EMEA) division, as well as chief executive officer of Better Place Denmark.

Moberg had an extensive and high-profile pedigree in Denmark with a reputation as a well-liked but savvy leader and negotiator. He had been employed at Microsoft in a variety of capacities since 1997, rising to corporate vice president of the software giant's enterprise business not just in Europe but worldwide. He had started his career 14 years earlier at IBM. He was well connected with the Danish government, serving on a number of advisory boards to the prime minister.

"In Jens Moberg, we've selected a world-class business executive to help us implement our model in Denmark, which will serve as a showcase for Europe and the rest of the world," gushed Agassi.

Moberg knew how to talk the Better Place talk.

"I firmly believe that the economics of a green industry such as sustainable mobility provide a compelling return for investors while creating jobs for industry and reducing our greenhouse gas emissions for the health of our people," he said.

A commitment to green was one area, at least, where everyone—at Better Place and at its partners—could agree.

ELECTRIC TAXIS

Other "land grab" discussions were happening outside of Europe.

In New York, Agassi envisioned creating a fleet of electric-powered taxis. In an email that Agassi sent to Joshua Steiner, former chief of staff for the U.S. Treasury Department under Bill Clinton and now running the private equity firm Quadrangle Capital Partners, Agassi laid out an audacious agenda.

"There are at least 100,000 cars in New York that do not leave the city; they are painted yellow, black or belong to the municipality," he wrote. "Every taxi or limo that will convert [to electric] will reduce 25 tons of CO2 emissions. City vehicles [will reduce] probably 15 tons and that is every year. So a conversion of 100K vehicles will reduce 2 million tons of CO2 emissions every year."

Agassi had come up with a financial model already.

"[It] requires no policy change—we are willing to let them drive a cab, pay us the cost of gas equivalency (daily calculated to roughly $70) and get a free cab with a 4-year contract. For a city vehicle, we will probably run the same model, only no free car."

Agassi had already met with some of then–Mayor Michael Bloomberg's staff, whom he said "were very supportive … and offered to let us start an experiment with an American-made car."

On the opposite side of the country, in the San Francisco Bay Area, serious discussions were also being held about creating an electric taxi "corridor" between San Francisco and San Jose along Highway 101.

The conversation started soon after Agassi became buddies with San Francisco Mayor Gavin Newsom, when both participated in the Young Global Leaders forum at Davos.

Newsom subsequently visited Israel in 2008 and was bullish on Better Place.

On the "CBS Sunday Morning" program, Newsom claimed in March 2009 that he and the mayors of San Jose and Oakland had collaborated on a plan to create "250,000 points of contact for electric charging," not an easy task given that there are "nine Bay Area counties that can't get along on any other issue."

It wasn't until October 2010, though, that the possibility of electric taxis in the Bay Area got real. The Bay Area's Metropolitan Transportation Commission (MTC) approved 17 grants, totaling $33 million, for its Climate Initiatives Program.

The largest single grant—$6.9 million—went to a consortium composed of the San Francisco Municipal Transportation Agency, the city of San Jose and Better Place "to demonstrate electric taxis in San Jose and San Francisco," according to an MTC press release.

According to the plan, 61 electric taxicabs and four battery switch stations would be deployed.

Two locations were announced—one at San Francisco's Embarcadero Center and another at San Francisco International Airport. San Jose Mayor Chuck Reed anticipated that the first battery switch station "could be installed in a year."

Despite the support from on high, the particulars proved to be Better Place's bugaboo.

The biggest hurdle for both the New York and San Francisco taxi plans, of course, was that Better Place didn't have an American car manufacturer on board, and Renault didn't sell in the United States.

"A bit of a chicken-and-egg problem, but we can get over that too," Agassi said.

Rumors began circulating.

CBS reported that the San Francisco taxi plan "could bring back Renault." Although the French car company "has been absent since the 1980s, [it] has recently made statements indicating a possible return with an American partner."

CBS quoted a spokesperson for the city of San Jose, who said the program's 61 cars would indeed be Renaults, "which implies they'll be the same swap-ready Renault Fluence Z.E.s that Better Place [will be] rolling out in Israel."

On the other hand, maybe this would create an opportunity for Better Place to push beyond Renault.

"There are discussions happening with other car manufacturers," Better Place director of communications Julie Mullins told CBS. "This presents them with a very high-visibility way to showcase their cars in the region that will likely buy the most electric vehicles in the United States early on." Taxis can serve "as the on-ramp for technology transfer to the mass market."

"We took it all very seriously," said Better Place general counsel David Kennedy. "We made it more than it was."

New York City in particular was "really the last place we should have approached as a startup," Kennedy continued. "There's so much regulation: the boroughs and the medallion owners. It's really a long run for a short jump."

Keeping every option open was expensive—in more ways than one.

"The real cost is your time. For a startup, opportunity cost is everything. If you're spending your time doing this, you're not doing something else," Kennedy said. "Even then, the out-of-pocket expense for developing a market like New York is in nine figures, once lobbyists and others are retained."

Whether it was taxis in New York or partnerships in Peru, Better Place had become expert at thinking big—and at spending money.

8

SHAI AGASSI, SUPERSTAR

S hai Agassi had 18 minutes.

That's the amount of time speakers on the TED stage have to make their case.

In the first decade of the new century, it seemed like the 18 minutes of a TED Talk could change the world. TED—originally an acronym for "technology, education, design"—started as a small group of digerati leaders in Silicon Valley. It grew into an annual conference with an admission price in the thousands. Videos of the talks themselves could go viral, leading to ideas catching fire on a broad scale. More important than the numbers, however, were the specific people a TED Talk could engage: influencers and leaders—people who could make a difference in the life and implementation of an ingenious idea.

By 2009, when Agassi took the stage, giving a TED Talk was an imprimatur of being an innovator who mattered. Only the most charismatic and persuasive entrepreneurs, philosophers, scientists, musicians, religious figures, philanthropists and business leaders were invited to present.

Agassi's talk, "A New Ecosystem for Electric Cars," was recorded and uploaded to the Internet in February 2009. Since then, it has been viewed more than a million times.

Agassi's success at TED was only one part of a wave of publicity and press that buoyed Better Place in its first years of operation.

In the TED video, Agassi hits the stage running. His black hair is freshly cut; his sideburns coming to a nice point. His black turtleneck directly emulates his hero Steve Jobs—but his charcoal gray suit jacket and matching slacks slightly up the formality. A tiny microphone abuts his left cheek; a piece of duct tape, not particularly well camouflaged, holds his earpiece in place.

"So how would you run a whole country without oil?" he asked the audience, with an initial timidity that would quickly be revealed as mere veneer for the polish to come. "That's the question that sort of hit me in the middle of a Davos afternoon," he continued. "It never left my brain. And I started playing with it more like a puzzle."

Agassi recounted the Better Place origin story—albeit without any mention of Andrey Zarur, who had chosen not to join the company. "The original thought I had: This must be ethanol. So I went out and researched ethanol ... about six months later I figured out it must be hydrogen."

Agassi explained that he quickly realized that only electric cars would make the solution "scale so this can be something that is used by ninety-nine percent of the population."

The car had to be convenient and affordable.

"Convenient is not something that you drive for an hour and charge for eight," he said, emphasizing that there's "no time for a science fair, no time for ... waiting for the magic battery to show up. [The question is] how do you do it within the economics that we have today?"

Agassi described charge spots and battery switch stations. 120 miles, the limitation of electric car batteries in 2009, "is good enough range for a lot of people," Agassi said. "But you never want to get stuck."

"If you had charge spots everywhere, and you had battery-swap stations everywhere ... it ends up that you'd do swapping less times than you stop at a gas station," he said.

Agassi then went off script.

"As a matter of fact, we added to the contract that if you stop to swap your battery more than 50 times a year, we start paying you money, because it's an inconvenience."

Mike Granoff, reviewing the TED Talk tape, was aghast.

"What was he talking about?" Granoff said incredulously. "We never had any model like this!"

It was the kind of visionary but not always entirely well-considered idea that would continue to blindside potential partners and even Agassi's own staff.

And yet people got up and cheered. Agassi had tapped into the tipping point.

Agassi presented another advantage: price. Electric miles were already cheaper than gas miles. And they were only going to become less expensive.

Electric miles, he said, follow Moore's Law. "They go from eight cents a mile in 2010 to four cents a mile in 2015 to two cents a mile by 2020."

MOORE'S LAW

Dr. Fred Schlachter, a researcher at the Lawrence Berkeley National Laboratory, stated it quite clearly. "There is no Moore's Law for batteries."

Moore's Law is based on an observation made in a 1965 paper by Gordon Moore, one of the co-founders of Intel, who noted that the number of transistors per square inch on an integrated circuit had doubled approximately every year since the integrated circuit was invented.

That "first articulation of a principle [became], after a little revision, elevated to a law," explained Seth Fletcher in Scientific American. "Every two years, the number of transistors on a computer chip will double."

Agassi was right that batteries would get better and cheaper—but Moore's Law would not prove to be as applicable for batteries as it was for silicon circuits and computer processing power.

Schlachter explained the problem, in an article in the National Academy of Sciences' journal.

"The reason there is a Moore's Law for computer processors is that electrons are small and they do not take up space on a chip," he wrote. "As lithography technology [used to make chips] improves, ever smaller features can be made on processors. Batteries are not like this. Ions, which transfer charge in batteries, are large and they take up space, as do anodes, cathodes and electrolytes. A D-cell battery stores more energy than an AA-cell [and is therefore larger] ... significant improvement in battery capacity can only be made by changing to a different chemistry."

Unfortunately, he continued, "scientists and battery experts, who have been optimistic in the recent past about improving lithium-ion batteries and about developing new battery chemistries—lithium/air and lithium/sulfur are the leading candidates—are [today] considerably less optimistic."

Christopher Mims echoed Schlachter's concerns in an article in the Australian magazine Business Spectator.

"Breakthroughs in energy storage technology aren't coming," he wrote. "Not in the foreseeable future, at least. That's because it takes years to convert 'breakthroughs' in the lab into something that works at scale, under all the conditions of real-life use. And the overwhelming majority of innovations don't survive the process."

Comedian and car enthusiast Jay Leno joked in 2010 that his 1906 Baker electric car had about the same battery range as the next-generation electric vehicles just hitting the market. Leno's line was more for yucks than science, but even Microsoft founder Bill Gates said that same year that "batteries have not improved hardly at all. There are deep physical limits [and] things that just don't move forward." The pace of innovation with chips "is rare," Gates concluded.

That doesn't mean electric cars can't make the most of the battery hand they've been dealt.

Lighter, more efficient designs, or more batteries packed under a car can help. It's the same principle with the latest mobile phones and tablets, where most of the guts of the device are taken up by the battery.

In addition, a 2012 McKinsey & Co. report suggested that slow, steady improvement driven by economies of scale as new battery factories come online—even if not at a Moore's Law level—may be enough. McKinsey predicted that the price for current technology lithium-ion batteries could fall by as much as two-thirds by 2020.

A GREEN CAR

Moore's Law was enticing, but green was gold as Agassi jumped into the meat of his TED presentation.

Better Place's car would be the most environmentally friendly electric vehicle ever.

"We do not use any electrons that come from coal," Agassi said with a flourish.

How Agassi could make such a sweeping statement is not clear. In Denmark, a good percentage of the country's electricity came from wind turbines, but in Israel, 60 percent of the country's electricity was generated from coal.

Yes, natural gas was coming, but Israel's Tamar offshore natural gas field had only been discovered one month earlier. Agassi could hardly have counted on it being online by the time Better Place began selling cars, let alone on natural gas supplying *all* the company's electricity.

Perhaps Agassi wasn't thinking of natural gas. Later in the talk, Agassi implied that Israel had given Better Place approval to develop a huge solar farm in the south of the country.

"People [in the government] said, 'Oh, that's a very large space you're asking for.' And we said, 'What if we had proven that in the same space we found oil for the country for the next hundred years?' And they said, 'We tried. There isn't any.' We said, 'No, no, but what if we prove it?' And they said, 'Well you can dig.' And we decided to dig … up, instead of digging down."

There were two problems with Agassi's statement.

First, no such approval had been given.

And second, the proclamation was not in sync with Israel's own stated energy goals, which set a target of generating just 10 percent of the country's electricity from renewable sources by 2020.

Was Agassi employing something like Steve Jobs' "reality distortion field" where, if he acted as if something were going to happen, it would (and very often did)?

Agassi frequently spoke of future events in the present tense. So "we do not use any electrons that come from coal" may not have been true immediately, or even in the next 20 years, but if solar or gas was even a remote possibility, it was only natural that he should speak of it as if it were already real.

Perhaps that was what was going on with his next over-the-top pronouncement: "Renault has put a billion and a half dollars into building nine different types of cars that fit this kind of model and that will come into the market in mass volume—mass volume being the first year, a hundred thousand cars."

Agassi knew full well that Renault had committed to just one model. And 100,000 cars—that was a prediction for five years down the road.

But Agassi was on a roll.

He explained how Denmark was creating a policy he dubbed the "IQ Test … they put a hundred and eighty percent tax on gasoline cars and zero tax on zero-emission cars. So if you want to buy a gasoline car in Denmark, it costs you about sixty thousand Euros. If you buy our car, it's about twenty thousand Euros. If you fail the IQ test, they ask you to leave the country."

The audience laughed and Agassi knew he had them.

President John F. Kennedy was remembered, Agassi said, because when he said we're going to send a man to the moon, "we didn't say we're going to send a man twenty percent to the moon, and that there will be about a twenty percent chance we'll recover him."

As his time was just about up, Agassi compared the imperative to go electric with nothing short of abolishing slavery.

Two hundred years ago, Agassi said, 25 percent of the United Kingdom's economic "energy" came from the slave trade—"just like 25 percent of emissions today come from cars. And there was an argument. Should we stop using slaves? What would it do to our economy?"

Some people said slavery should be ended gradually, others said its dissolution should be immediate, Agassi continued. But when the British government finally put an end to it, "the industrial revolution started within less than one year. And the U.K. had a hundred years of economic growth. We have to make the right moral decision. We have to make it immediately ... because if we don't, we will lose our economy, right after we've lost our morality."

MEDIA FRENZY

Agassi's TED Talk was a high point of the media frenzy about Better Place. But there was more to come.

In April 2009, Agassi was named to Time magazine's list of the 100 most influential people of the year.

A month later, Agassi also landed in the third-place spot in Fast Company magazine's "Most Creative People of 2009." He was preceded by Jonathan Ive, of Apple, and Melinda Gates, co-founder of the Bill & Melinda Gates Foundation.

Articles appeared about Better Place in The Washington Post, the Economist and VentureBeat.

Thomas Friedman called Agassi "the Jewish Henry Ford," adding that "he could sell camels to Saudi Arabia."

Agassi one-upped that, quipping that moving past oil is like getting "off heroin [and getting] addicted to milk."

New York Times reporter Clive Thompson called Agassi "a charismatic entrepreneur" and "amazingly persuasive," while describing Better Place's plans as "extraordinarily bold."

"Some people say I'm missing the fear gene," Agassi told Thompson, who mused that he "couldn't entirely tell if [Agassi] was joking."

Agassi wowed Thompson with his claim of expertise in, well, everything.

"I've learned every industry in the world," Agassi bragged. "One day, it would be Apple and Sony. The other day it would be [gasoline companies] BP and Chevron."

Thompson wasn't 100 percent sold.

"Agassi is an extremely charming guy; he has the born salesman's ability to read people and connect with them," Thompson wrote. "But he also has the obdurate quality I've seen in so many people who are drawn to computer programming and logical thinking. Once Agassi has convinced himself of the optimal solution to a problem, he develops a nearly pathological monomania about it."

THE COLBERT REPORT

Agassi rarely got flustered, but he wasn't sure how to react to interviewer Stephen Colbert's point-blank question:

"Let's cut to the chase here: Will this car get me laid?"

Colbert, who would go on to host "The Late Show," had at that time a highly watched late-night comedy show, "The Colbert Report." He did the show entirely in the character he had created, an insufferably (but hilariously) vain and smarmy U.S. conservative, modeled after some of the popular talking heads of the era. It was an extended inside joke that had caught on big, gaining high ratings; an appearance on the show was a major score.

So the question may have been out of line, but it wasn't out of character.

Agassi puffed out his lower lip and raised his finger as if to school Colbert, but his host dug in deeper.

"Because that's what young men care about with cars—will this get me action?" Colbert smirked.

Regaining his composure, Agassi tried to play along. "It will definitely get you the attention of the *right* chicks. It's the intellectual car ..."

"The intellectual car?" Colbert responded in play-acted amazement. "So they'll just *think* they're having sex, when in fact they're just having coffee?"

Agassi tried a different tack. A Better Place all-electric car would be "hotter than a Prius," Agassi said.

"What's the difference between this and a Prius?" Colbert asked.

"A Prius saves you about 20 percent of the gasoline and 20 percent of the emissions. This is 100 percent oil-free and 100 percent clean."

"But won't we just run out of batteries?"

"We have enough lithium, which is what makes these batteries, for about three billion cars, so I think we're safe for about two centuries."

"Can you clean lithium off a seagull? What if we have a lithium spill?" Colbert provoked Agassi, to peals of laughter from the studio audience.

Agassi fell into step: "First thing you have to be careful of is, when you see a seagull flying towards you, don't hit it."

"OK, if the model is a cell phone [with its lithium ion batteries], will I be able to download car horn sounds?"

Absolutely, Agassi responded. "We call them 'Drivetone' sounds."

"Seriously?" Colbert said.

"Yes. You can pick your own drive tone. Imagine you're driving behind someone on Fifth Avenue. And you go *ohhhh*—like a big ship."

"That was a ship? Sounds like an elephant giving birth to me," Colbert responded.

Agassi squirmed. Fortunately, his time was up.

"You know what," Colbert concluded. "If I can make it sound like whatever I want, if I can rev it, then I'm in!"

The crowd roared its approval.

9

"ALL YOU NEED IS A PLUG, RIGHT?"

As Shai Agassi was building his personal brand and promoting the Better Place message far and wide, there was one final attempt at a "land grab." This one targeted the biggest, most important territory of them all: the United States.

However, Better Place still had no U.S. car manufacturing partner.

No problem for an innovative entrepreneur. If he couldn't take Detroit, Agassi would capture the next best place: Washington D.C.

All he had to do was dazzle lawmakers with gumption and convince the people in power that Better Place could help the United States overcome one of its biggest financial and strategic problems: oil dependency.

Better Place aimed to convince legislators that the electrification of the United States was not only in the country's best interests but inevitable. And Better Place would lead the way.

Then, with Capitol Hill on Agassi's side, the recalcitrant carmakers would have no choice but to come crawling, the reasoning went.

The idea to take on Washington came from Mike Granoff, who through his years of political activism and fundraising was comfortable hobnobbing with congressmen, senators and lobbyists. With a winner like Agassi at his side, Granoff was sure new pro-electric laws and policies that would benefit not just Better Place but all of America could easily and quickly be enacted.

Their efforts didn't go exactly as expected.

Granoff and Agassi launched a nearly two-year attack on Washington, starting in March 2008. Agassi spoke to anyone in authority that Granoff was able to corral into listening.

There was House Democrat Steve Israel, of New York. Agassi made his pitch in a hotel near the U.S. Capitol.

At today's prices, the United States is spending $550 billion a year on importing crude oil, Agassi told Israel. The next president "will transfer two to three trillion dollars out of the economy."

"So what do we do?" asked Israel.

"We need tax hikes on gas-powered cars," Agassi replied immediately.

"That will never fly," Israel told Agassi. "And anyway, we don't make batteries in the U.S. So aren't we going to swap out foreign-oil dependence for foreign battery reliance?"

Then there was Senator Sam Brownback, a Kansas Republican, whom Agassi and Granoff met in the elevator after their meeting with Congressman Israel.

Agassi launched into his second literal elevator pitch. It didn't go quite as well as the previous one with Idan Ofer.

"How can I buy one?" Brownback asked, starting on a positive note.

"Well, we've got one problem," Agassi responded. "We need the infrastructure first."

"All you need is a plug, right?" Brownback shot back, although his intent was innocent. "You're like a long extension cord. Why would you need an infrastructure?"

Most of the meetings Agassi took in Washington went along these lines—representatives and senators listening politely, offering a hearty handshake, but clearly not getting it or willing to do anything to help.

As Daniel Roth wrote in Wired, "getting anything like the deal [Agassi] has in Israel [was] going to be impossible."

If Agassi harbored any sense of frustration, it wasn't on display when he appeared in July 2008 in front of the House of Representatives Select Committee on Energy Independence and Global Warming.

"For the price of two months' worth of oil, some $100 billion, we can put in place the infrastructure needed to power the nation's cars and end this oil dependence," he told the room full of representatives. "Of that $100 billion, moreover, some $80 billion will go into jobs that, by their nature, can only be performed in the U.S.—the construction of the infrastructure itself."

That wasn't all, though.

"For the price of one year's worth of oil, some $500 billion, we can go even farther—creating fully renewable electrical generation sufficient to power all of the nation's vehicles. In so doing … we will give a much broader stimulus to the renewables energy market."

Granoff meanwhile was running from office to office, phone call to phone call, trying to set up meetings. He met with Senators Evan Bayh (Indiana, Democrat) and Frank Lautenberg (New Jersey, Democrat) and Representative Eliot Engel, a New York Democrat whom Granoff described in an email to Better Place executives as "a good friend … and an immediate convert" to the cause.

At the Department of Energy, Granoff met with chief of staff Jeff Kupner and with David Strickland, staff director of the Senate Energy and Commerce Committee. Agassi took meetings with former U.S. Secretary of Transportation Norm Mineta and Senator Charles "Chuck" Schumer.

Perhaps the pinnacle of Agassi's Washington odyssey was the meeting held in the White House.

"We were in the West Wing, just like in the TV show, steps away from the Oval Office. We could see the door from where we were sitting," Granoff recalled.

Agassi and Granoff met with presidential advisor Pete Rouse for 45 minutes. Rouse appeared interested. He took notes but didn't say anything definitive. It was a chaotic time at the White House. Afghanistan was still a mess. Banks were failing.

"Dramatic things were happening every day in that period," recalled Granoff.

Nothing ever came of the meeting.

"It was never made a priority again," Granoff said.

Nevertheless, Granoff told his colleagues in an email, "The political climate in Washington is very much in our favor … there is a sense that new things are possible."

But were they? The Great Recession was about to upend the economy in ways no one could have anticipated. Banking on government in good times is already risky business. When crisis hits, the unknowns can multiply in wholly unpredictable ways.

THE PRESIDENTIAL TASK FORCE

After Barack Obama won the U.S. presidential election in November 2008, the first order of business for the incoming president was to straighten out a worsening economy, which was by now clearly in the midst of a major downturn. With credit nearly nonexistent, the already-hurting U.S. automotive industry was on the brink of collapse, with potentially millions of American jobs under threat.

In February 2009, the Presidential Task Force on the Auto Industry, an ad-hoc group of cabinet-level and other officials, convened to figure out what to do with General Motors and Chrysler, the two American automakers most at risk.

Should the government simply let them go bankrupt and start over? Should Washington actually buy the two companies?

Agassi and Granoff saw the Presidential Task Force as their last chance to capture the hearts of America's legislators. Why pump money into a dying engine and a moribund model when the future was clearly electric? Plus, the Task Force wasn't being run by yet another government appointee, but by businessman Steven Rattner, who had co-founded the private equity firm Quadrangle Capital Partners with Joshua Steiner, Better Place's contact in the Bloomberg administration for its New York taxi proposal.

Agassi and Granoff met with the Task Force four times, twice in June and twice in July 2009. The final meeting on July 31 was an intense all-day session.

Agassi was at his best.

"The relationship between the automotive companies and the oil makers is like an abusive marriage," Agassi told the Task Force members. "A marriage they've been in for a hundred years. Look at Exxon Mobil—it's the largest publicly traded company in the world. It's one of the most profitable companies anywhere. And the automotive companies—they're nothing. What do they get out of this relationship?"

Only Better Place could rescue Detroit, Agassi insisted. With all his charm and powers of persuasion engaged, cylinders firing at full throttle, he said without blinking, "Give us one battery-switchable car from GM, and we'll take care of the rest. We'll build the network from coast to coast."

The car Agassi had in mind was the Saturn.

Saturn was a relatively new GM brand, established in 1985 and originally marketed as "a different kind of car company." It had its own retailer network and an independent assembly plant in Spring Hill, Tennessee.

But the Saturn division had been losing money for years, and GM disclosed its decision to discontinue the car (along with GM's Hummer and Pontiac brands and its Saab subsidiary) during U.S. Congressional hearings in December 2008. Saturn production was scheduled to formally halt in October 2009.

In June, though, a deal looked likely to save Saturn: The Penske Automotive Group announced it would be buying the brand, but not the factories. Penske had a partner in mind, one that could have been highly advantageous for Better Place: Renault.

Renault was already committed to building an all-electric car for Better Place in Europe. It would not have been implausible for the company to bring some of its electric knowhow to the United States.

A Renault-made, Saturn-branded electric car could be Better Place's American savior, a way to finally crack the heretofore impenetrable promised land.

Agassi didn't know about Renault's possible involvement when he raised the idea internally, during an offsite meeting with the Better Place management team late in 2008.

A Better Place executive at the meeting remembers: Agassi's idea was that Better Place would "buy one of the factories GM was shutting down. We'd restart it and build our own cars. Shai said it would take two years."

The executive felt the discussions were a distraction.

"No one said anything. So I spoke up. 'This is not something we should discuss in any strategic timeline. We have no capability of running a car factory. We don't have the people or the expertise. It's a waste of time to even talk about it.'"

Nevertheless, the idea would be raised from time to time until it was formally put into play during the Task Force meeting.

"It was fun to float the idea," the executive admitted.

But it was not to be. Renault got cold feet, and Penske withdrew its offer to buy the Saturn brand in September 2009.

Agassi was also in the dark about the fate of the Presidential Task Force.

His tour de force in Washington took place just days before the Task Force was abruptly shut down. GM had declared bankruptcy (emerging a month later with the same name, a reduced product line and $51 billion in government bailout money), and Chrysler would soon be saved by the Italians, when it merged with Fiat later in 2009.

The Task Force's mission was deemed complete. The officials who had held all those meetings with Agassi and Granoff were caught off guard themselves. They didn't have time to tell Better Place yes ... or no.

It may have just been bad timing. But for Better Place, it was one more hard-luck example of the precariousness of putting too much stock in the good graces of government.

PUT A LITTLE PEP IN YOUR STEP

Better Place had one last governmental Hail Mary play to get into the U.S. market.

As Agassi was blitzing Washington throughout 2008, the United States was desperately trying to get ahead of the recession, which had set in big time.

The American Recovery and Reinvestment Act (commonly referred to as the Stimulus or the Recovery Act) was being finalized; it would be signed into law on February 17, 2009.

But in December 2008, a mini-scandal broke out when it was revealed that included in the draft of the Stimulus Act was a $200 million line item for reseeding the National Mall in Washington, D.C., which would be trampled on by the many well-wishers attending the presidential inauguration in January 2009.

The idea of spending so much money on a lawn didn't sit right with a public panicking from crashing home prices and spiking unemployment.

A week later, a new draft of the Stimulus Act came out. The $200 million for reseeding was gone. In its place was $400 million for vehicle electrification programs that would be allocated through the Department of Energy (DOE).

Granoff couldn't believe it. This was the chance they were waiting for. Most of what Agassi and Granoff had done to date in D.C. was stuck in neutral. But here was a fund specifically to promote electric vehicles!

Better Place proposed one last plan to pry away some of the DOE money for a Better Place–friendly project.

Dubbed the Pacific Electrification Program (PEP for short), it called for making the entire West Coast corridor along Interstate 5—from Seattle in the north to San Diego in the south—electric car friendly.

Battery-charging spots and full switch stations would be built at regular intervals, so that "if you lived in any of the cities on that corridor, you could get there solely with electric power," Granoff said.

The price: $100 million—only a quarter of the $400 million budget.

Better Place's head of global alliances Lawrence Seeff wrote an email to the entire Better Place staff laying out the details.

The money would cover the budget of Better Place's U.S. operation for three years, along with the deployment of 300 vehicles, 10,000 charge spots, 9 battery switch stations, 3 demo centers and a number of research and consumer studies.

"Our application comes with over 90 letters of support, among which are letters from the three relevant governors and from 8 members of Congress," Seeff wrote.

Granoff was confident this was the winning hand Better Place needed to establish itself in the United States.

"We never had a doubt that we'd get at least some of that money," Granoff said. "We were working with professional lobbyists who had a great track record."

But the money didn't come.

On August 5, 2009, less than a week after the final Presidential Task Force meeting, Better Place lost its bid for PEP.

The DOE's reasoning was a familiar one: Better Place had no U.S. car manufacturing partner, so how could it make good on its promises?

"In the proposal, we asked them to give us the money now and then we'd find the cars," Granoff said. "They basically said that wasn't good enough."

This became a pivotal moment for Better Place management.

"I was about to give a talk about the need for oil independence to an energy utility in New Jersey," Granoff recalled. "Just before the talk, I happened to check my email and received the news that the DOE had turned Better Place down. I broke into a cold sweat, but I continued with the talk anyway."

After he stepped off the podium, Granoff arranged an emergency conference call with Agassi and some senior staff members. Agassi was strangely calm.

"It's just a minor setback," he said. "We'll still win the war."

One of the call participants commented afterwards, "Who was that guy who just impersonated our CEO?"

But Agassi's cool demeanor was misleading. Something had shifted inside and it was soon to have radical implications for the company.

10

TWO SCOOPS OF ROCKY RENAULT

In January 2011, a spy scandal erupted at Better Place's French car manufacturing partner, Renault. It would soon engulf the entire country, dominating headlines for months.

The Chinese, it was claimed, had broken into the company with the aim of stealing Renault's intellectual property. Renault filed a criminal complaint with the Paris prosecutor accusing "unknown persons" of "organized industrial espionage, corruption, breach of trust, theft and concealment."

Renault CEO Carlos Ghosn put his reputation on the line and insisted that he had "factual proof" that the espionage had occurred.

"Of course we are sure. If we weren't sure, we wouldn't be where we are," Ghosn said. "We're not amateurs. We didn't just invent it all, you know."

Patrick Pelata, Renault's chief operating officer and a staunch supporter of the Better Place project within Renault, told reporters that "an organized international network" was behind the spying.

Beijing vociferously denied any links to the spying accusations, and French government officials sought to play down the Chinese connection. But the situation spiraled out of control.

Before long, allegations emerged that money had been deposited into three foreign bank accounts in Switzerland and Lichtenstein held by key Renault executives. The money was intended to compensate the executives for revealing information specifically about Renault's electric car plans.

The three alleged bribe-taking executives were identified as Michel Balthazard, director of advanced engineering at Renault; Balthazard's deputy Bertrand Rochette; and Matthieu Tenenbaum.

Tenenbaum had joined Renault at age 19 and had spent his entire career there, even getting a college degree through Renault's internal engineering course.

Tenenbaum was appointed deputy program director of the electric car program and was put in charge of the Better Place contract. The New York Times described it as "a plum job coordinating the engineering, marketing and design teams working on the project, and a sign that [Tenenbaum's] career was on a fast track."

But with accusations in the spy scandal swirling around Renault and the media, Tenenbaum and the other two men were promptly fired.

The French newspaper Le Monde reported that investigators at Renault discovered Tenenbaum had received 500,000 Euros in a Swiss bank account, and that the money originated from the China Aviation Industry Organization.

Better Place's Yoav Heichal, who worked closely with Tenenbaum, didn't believe it. He held that Tenenbaum was framed because "his image fit the description. He was like a playboy. He liked the good life; he used to travel a lot. He was not a corrupt guy, but he looked like he could be a corrupt guy."

"I want to be totally clean with French justice," Tenenbaum told The New York Times. "I want them to check my home, my phone, I want them to go fast and see I have nothing to do with this story."

Tenenbaum proved to be right. As investigators probed, the story began to unravel.

In February 2011, just a month later, France's domestic intelligence agency DCRI determined that the foreign bank accounts did not exist. Jean-Claude Marin, the Paris public prosecutor, informed the scandal-seeking public that Switzerland and Lichtenstein had confirmed there were in fact no bank accounts in the names of the three Renault executives.

Next, it was discovered that the source of the allegations against Balthazard, Rochette and Tenenbaum was a single anonymous informer whose identity was known only to one man, Renault's internal security official Dominique Gevrey, who was refusing to divulge the name of his source.

As the investigators continued to dig, they discovered that the anonymous caller had been paid 250,000 Euros by Renault and was demanding another 900,000 Euros for written proof of what he claimed. Patrick Pelata, in his role as the company's COO, had believed the rumors and authorized the initial transfer.

"We are in the presence of a possible intelligence fraud," prosecutor Marin announced.

Renault said it would press charges and was filing a civil suit.

Gevrey, who had previously worked as a French military intelligence agent, tried to flee the country. He was arrested at Charles de Gaulle Airport as he was attempting to board a flight to Guinea in West Africa.

Investigators turned their attention to examining the possibility that the "deep throat" who had revealed the scandal never existed, and that the money was actually embezzled by Gevrey and an unnamed private investigator.

Renault went into full spin mode, offering its "sincere apologies and regrets" to Balthazard, Rochette and Tenenbaum and promising that their careers and "honor" would be entirely restored.

Meanwhile, the government and public were demanding that heads roll—or at least be seriously set askew.

Carlos Ghosn was forced to take a pay cut, forgo his stock options for the year, and reimburse a performance bonus granted in 2010 worth 1.6 million Euros.

Pelata said that if the espionage saga proved to be a "manipulation," he would "consider the consequences … up to the highest level of the company, that is to say, up to myself."

Balthazard was offered his old job back, but declined.

"Working again in that atmosphere, with all those people who were so utterly convinced that I was guilty? I don't think so," he said.

Matthew Tenenbaum did go back to Renault—with two children, he explained, "I need to find work very soon … even though I had a good career at Renault, who would hire a person accused of such a thing?"

Tenenbaum didn't return to the electric vehicle team, though.

"I'd been gone already three or four months and it was difficult to come back," he said. "They had replaced me, and I didn't want to take the place of someone else. I wanted something new in the company."

Under pressure, Patrick Pelata stepped down as COO, taking on the amorphous position of "special advisor to the president."

Pelata had been "our key guy at Renault," remembered Yoav Heichal. "He was very into the future" and into the relationship with Better Place.

Now, his positive influence over Renault's electric car project was significantly diminished.

He resigned the following year.

Sidney Goodman commented on the turmoil at Renault and the loss of Tenenbaum and Pelata in an email to Mike Granoff and Dan Cohen.

"We don't know the implications yet, but suffice to say it isn't a positive move for us," he wrote. "That said, we have multiple fronts to work through with Renault ... so let's not panic nor have our internal teams start further rumors."

At the end of the day, the spy scandal was proven false and the affair ended for Renault with some public bruising and media anger. But for Better Place, the result would prove to be devastating.

Shai Agassi brushed off any concerns.

On a plane with Cohen when news of the scandal broke, Agassi told Cohen confidently, "This will blow over."

But it didn't. And the man who would take Pelata's place had an entirely different agenda when it came to both Better Place and Agassi.

CARLOS TAVARES

Carlos Tavares was a long-standing Better Place skeptic. While CEO Carlos Ghosn had given the initial go-ahead and Patrick Pelata had been enthusiastic about the partnership with Better Place, the Portuguese-born Tavares, who had already been at Renault for 30 years when the spy scandal broke, was in the opposing camp, in charge of the rival Nissan Leaf project.

So when Tavares was put in charge of Renault's "other" electric car, his loyalties were clearly with his first love, the Leaf.

Tavares also entered his new job replacing Pelata as COO at a difficult time for the company for reasons beyond the spy scandal. Renault was still smarting from the lingering effects of the global recession, with low sales, particularly in Europe.

"Tavares was a very straight person, who knows that two plus two is always four," Yoav Heichal recalled. "He could see the company was in crisis, he had to lay off workers, so his main priority was not R&D but how to sell more of what he already had. When you have something, you know how much it will cost you. If you develop something new—like the all-electric Fluence Z.E.—you don't know. That wasn't good for Better Place."

Tavares, Heichal added, was "a conservative guy who wanted to focus only on things that provided him immediate cash flow."

Tavares shut Agassi out.

"When Tavares came into the project, he had many urgent matters. Shai was not one of them," Heichal said. The two never met, "not even a single time."

But there was more to the chilly relations between Agassi and Tavares than just business.

In June 2008, Renault announced it had signed an agreement with the Portuguese utility Energias de Portugal SA to bring electric cars to the southern European nation. It was a logical next step beyond Israel in Europe; Tavares was Portuguese, after all, so this was his home turf and he knew many of the key leaders, including the Portuguese prime minister.

But although the cars would be designed to Better Place's specifications, Better Place itself wasn't included in the negotiations.

Agassi was furious.

Matthieu Tenenbaum explained that, when Renault and Better Place agreed to go steady, the idea was "we'll make you this awesome car and then Better Place and Renault will go everywhere together to make partnerships with utilities."

The deal with Energias de Portugal, however, only included the charge spots and grid management. The battery switch stations, the centerpiece to the Better Place offering, were not mentioned.

Perhaps Agassi shouldn't have been so quick to anger. Better Place had in fact been working in parallel to close a deal with a separate utility company in Portugal—this without Renault in the deal.

Still, the result of this family feud was swift.

Agassi was "really upset with Tavares for cutting him out of the deal," according to Tenenbaum.

He immediately retaliated.

"At the time, we were working together on the specifications for the Fluence Z.E., sharing progress all the time," Tenenbaum said.

"There will be no more exchanges," Agassi now insisted. "We're not giving Renault any more details because they'll just screw us again and give it to someone else."

Distrust built rapidly from there.

"We used to develop things together, but now Better Place said, 'We'll develop our own; we won't work with you,'" Tenenbaum explained.

It made sense up to a certain point, he said.

"Shai came up with this great idea of switching batteries, but there wasn't a lot of IP [intellectual property] that Better Place could actually protect," he explained. Creating boundaries was Agassi's response. "It was the way he saw that would create the most value for Better Place."

But Agassi "went a bit paranoid on the IP stuff," Tenenbaum said. "The way Shai decided where those boundaries should be was not the most efficient."

For Better Place, it meant developing its own solutions without concern for Renault.

"For OSCAR, this might have been OK," Tenenbaum continued. "We had experience at Renault developing navigation systems, but it's still software, so Better Place could do it. But for the battery switch stations, this is what we do in our plants every day. Every minute we're installing heavy engines into cars. It's something we know very well how to deal with."

The clash between software and hardware had reared its head again. It would play a major role in the unfolding drama between Better Place and Renault.

LIKE AN F-16 RELEASING A BOMB

Better Place had developed an innovative design for the battery-switch process based on the way an F-16 fighter jet releases a bomb.

"Check this out," Agassi bragged to The New York Times' Clive Thompson, dragging him over to an early prototype of a battery in a hollowed-out car intended for demonstration. "These latches use the same technology as those used to hold 500-pound bombs in place on bombers."

According to Better Place's design, hardware and software inside the car itself would unscrew the fasteners to release the battery. It was the system Better Place had demonstrated in Japan—it was fast, efficient and it worked.

But it was exactly this technology that Agassi was afraid Renault would steal.

"It was a fantastic design and Shai would go on and on about how great it was," Idan Ofer recalled. "But then he wouldn't give it to Renault, which led Renault to say, 'Fine, we're going to do our own,' and it resulted in this very complicated mechanism that caused great anxiety for everyone at Better Place."

The "great anxiety" Ofer was referring to was the alternative battery-switch mechanism Renault came up with, which moved the hardware and software for unscrewing the battery from the car to the robotic arm that was attached to the battery switch station.

For Renault, it was less about IP and mainly a matter of money. A single screw could push costs up too high.

The dilemma in a nutshell: If the software-controlled screws that released the batteries were built into the car, not the switch station robot as Better Place proposed, then Renault would have to absorb that cost—and pass it on to the consumer.

Each "smart screw" was estimated to cost up to $250. An extra $1,000 might not seem like a lot, but the Fluence Z.E. was already becoming an expensive car, and automotive sales margins are notoriously tight. It was Renault's job to put the Fluence Z.E. first and to save as much money as it could on manufacturing.

"Look at how a car manufacturer designs the door-locking mechanism," explained Yoav Heichal. "The door lock on the driver's side is different than the door lock on the passenger's side. Why? Statistics show that in most cases, you're alone in the car, so the driver's side door gets used six times as much. As a result, the door-locking mechanism on the driver's side costs twenty cents more than the other door locks. Multiply that by two million cars and it's real money for the carmaker."

Better Place pushed for its own design, where the battery essentially unscrewed itself on the car, because that meant all the switch station needed was a generic "palette"—a flat panel to "catch" the battery as it dropped out of the car.

But if the software moved to the robot, then the switch station was essentially hard-wired to the specific battery in the Renault Fluence Z.E.

The robotic arm and screwdriver in the station had to "match" the battery of the car coming in.

If Better Place later signed a deal with a different car manufacturer that used a different type of battery, the Fluence Z.E.-specific robot wouldn't know what to do. Renault's design meant the battery switch stations would work for only one type of car.

Renault's plan for the Fluence Z.E. also added complexity and time to the process, mostly in ensuring perfect alignment between the battery and the robotic screwdrivers.

The result: The one-minute switch that Better Place had shown off in Japan would, under Renault's concept, increase to a whopping three-and-a-half minutes.

Dan Cohen believed that Renault actually wanted to license Better Place's IP, not build its own.

"They just didn't want to be dependent on Better Place, especially if this would be as big as Shai said it would be and battery switch really took off," Cohen explained. "They wanted this to be a true co-development, but when Shai said no, they said if that's the case, we'll design it ourselves."

Matthieu Tenenbaum added that for Renault it didn't matter where the technology originated as long as they could use it freely.

"Renault didn't want to be stuck working only with Better Place," Tenenbaum said. "We had to have our own switching technology."

Agassi was ultimately forced to concede. What choice did he have? Renault was building the car itself, and there was nothing contractual that could be used to convince Renault to add an expensive system it didn't want.

During an all-hands meeting to mark Better Place's fourth anniversary in 2012, Agassi made a startling admission.

"I made a mistake," he told the 50 staff members assembled. "It was the biggest mistake I've made in my life. It cost us so much money, a year of burn, market delays, engineering incompatibilities."

What was the mistake?

Letting Renault "win the argument" about the switch stations, Agassi said calmly.

In Agassi's retelling of the story, Agassi and Yoav Heichal were in a meeting with Carlos Ghosn and Renault's chief engineer. Both sides laid out the benefits of their respective systems, then began bickering, each in their own language.

Agassi sensed the meeting was going in Renault's direction.

"I should have said to Renault, if we're going your way, we're not going anywhere, we're going to kill the deal right now," Agassi told his staff.

But how could he? Better Place had no closed deal with any other car vendor. It would have been a company-killing risk.

With the two sides at an impasse, it was Agassi who blinked first.

"We let them win," Agassi said. "And Renault killed us."

It wasn't a full admission of defeat, remarked Robby Bearman, who was in charge of grid integration at Better Place. Agassi "was admitting to losing an argument, not that he was making an error."

Matthieu Tenenbaum dismissed Agassi's story as pure fiction.

"Shai saying that he let Carlos Ghosn win, it never happened," Tenenbaum asserted. "Ghosn was never in those meetings. He was never directly involved in the negotiations. Shai always requested meetings with Ghosn, but he only rarely saw him. While Shai considered Ghosn his counterpart, Ghosn never thought of Shai similarly."

"I think Better Place loomed very small for Ghosn," Mike Granoff said. "He saw it as a small investment, something that he'd give a shot, and if it catches on, great, we'll lead the market; otherwise, it's just an 'experiment,' as he later put it."

An example: On the very day back in 2009 when Better Place and Renault announced their deal to put 100,000 electric cars on the roads of Israel and Denmark by 2016, Renault held a separate press conference with RWE, a German utility, on another project to supply 50 cars and install 100 charge spots.

Ghosn appeared on stage with the CEO of the German utility, but never again with Agassi.

As a result, "it was on the front pages of every German newspaper," Tenenbaum said, "the RWE deal—not Better Place."

It was worse with the other Carlos—COO Tavares. In a conversation with Mike Granoff, during a conference in Washington D.C. sponsored by Deutsche Bank in June 2009, Tavares admitted to Granoff that "he didn't think that switch wouldn't work, he just thought it was a bad investment—you can put lots of fast charge units there for the cost of one switch station," Granoff wrote in an email to Agassi.

Agassi responded to Granoff, also by email. "Now we know how he thinks. We need to continue embracing [Renault] until we have [another] option."

Perhaps the Renault-designed battery switch stations that Better Place now had to swallow wouldn't be so terrible. After all, the thinking might have gone, Renault was the only carmaker that had agreed to partner with Better Place. The company could deal with other battery types down the road, when it would be making so much money that adding an extra robotic palette and screwdriver kit to each switch station would constitute mere chump change.

Chump change is in the eye of the beholder, though.

According to Guy Tzur, who worked as research and development manager for the battery switch stations at Better Place, retrofitting a station with new robots for new types of cars might cost up to $1 million per station.

CULTURE CLASH

Yoav Heichal served as the main technical conduit between Better Place and Renault. He described his job as "an ambassador to connect Better Place's software mentality with the old school hardware of a car company."

That was often a challenge, given the wholly different worlds the two sides inhabited.

"Better Place was filled with these really smart guys, but they were all from the software industry, where you release a version, try it, and if it doesn't work, you restart," Renault's Matthieu Tenenbaum explained. The automotive industry operates far more conservatively. "We don't have the luxury of doing trial and error with a car."

Not when the physical safety of human beings is at stake.

"There's no real prototype, no physical mockup, until the last year or two" of a car's long development cycle, Tenenbaum continued. "But Better Place was telling us they wanted five hundred physical cars after six months, two thousand cars after a year and a half. Trying to deliver some kind of prototype to Better Place was new for us and very costly. All the parts are very expensive when they're being prototyped."

For an upstart like Better Place, getting accepted at the 120-year-old Renault, with its myriad of time-tested customs and ways of doing business, was sometimes akin to a fraternity house hazing.

"One time they left me waiting outside in the snow for two hours before they let me into the factory," Heichal recalled. "Another time I was told 'Don't come to France this week' when I was already on the bus from the airport in Paris to the factory. But at one point, the ice breaks and you become one of them. Then you can do the most foolish things and they'll forgive you. That's the French way of doing it."

It also helped that Heichal could speak French.

Heichal's partner in working with Renault was Sidney Goodman, whose main job—beyond trying to find a second auto manufacturer—was handling the alliance with Renault.

"Sidney was a good project manager," Heichal said. "It wasn't a problem that he didn't have an automotive industry background. He was someone who could listen. If you have someone who asks smart questions and tries his best to understand what's going on and to come at it all with a fresh pair of eyes, then it's really not an issue."

Others were more critical.

"We needed a former CEO of an automotive company in that role, not just Sidney," said Amit Yudan.

"I had nothing against him, but why did we have a software guy leading our car efforts? We needed someone from inside the industry who knows everyone by name," added Brian Goldstein, who headed Better Place's operations in Hawaii.

Goodman certainly had his hands full navigating the culture clash between the Israelis and the French. Much of what makes the Startup Nation work inside Israel—the *chutzpah*, the loose hierarchy and lack of conformity to accepted norms, the out-of-the-box quick thinking—Renault found off-putting.

The disagreements got so intense that at several junctures, Renault threatened to terminate its contract with Better Place.

"I remember at least four times when this happened," said Heichal.

The engineers at Renault also hated the concept of having a switchable battery.

"It's so un-auto-like, and there's no precedent in the industry. It was an entirely new concept and there was no guarantee that the model was going to work," charging system manager Emek Sadot said. "The only reason Renault committed is because of Shimon Peres."

Sidney Goodman tried to play peacemaker.

"We had a discussion with Sidney about Better Place being able to service all cars from Renault, as well as plug-in hybrids, in France and not being so dogmatic about battery switch," Tenenbaum said.

"All right, I understand," Goodman told Tenenbaum. "I understand that if we go into France and insist the cars must be switchable, it won't work, so we have to serve every car. It's obvious."

Even Better Place CTO Barak Hershkovitz came around, Tenenbaum added.

But not Agassi.

"Barak would come back to us and say, 'Shai vetoed it,'" Tenenbaum recalled. "I could see the frustrations of the engineers on both sides. I knew something was not going the right way."

THE FLUENCE Z.E.

Almost lost in the politics, paranoia, scandals and infighting was the fact that Better Place and Renault were actually building an all-electric car with a battery meant to be switched. It was something that had never been done before.

And they were doing it in record time.

Renault had set a timetable to create the Fluence Z.E. in just three years. In the automotive industry, creating a new car from concept to the time the first models roll off the production line generally takes a minimum of five years.

But the Fluence Z.E. wasn't entirely a new car. It was a slightly larger successor to Renault's popular Mégane—a boxy, uninspiring but solid family five-seater, meant to compete with similar vehicles like the Toyota Corolla or Mazda 3, top sellers in Israel.

Thinking about its design began before Better Place came on the scene—when the Fluence was intended to be gas-powered.

In fact, the aim was to release two models of the Fluence almost simultaneously—one with an internal combustion engine, and the all-electric Z.E. version.

The non-electric engine externals—things like window function, body exterior, steering column, safety features and trunk size—were already fast-tracked through development.

While this meant the Fluence Z.E. would be ready remarkably quickly for an entirely new model of car, the electric version would appear only slightly different in style from its gas-guzzling cousin.

The Financial Times described the Fluence Z.E. as "a classic three-box sedan, the shape children choose when drawing a car. The only sign that it is electric is its lack of an exhaust and front and rear lamps outlined in electric blue, a bit like the frames of designer glasses."

Indeed, other than the Better Place logo and the placement of two charging sockets on either side of the front end of the car, the Z.E. and the gasoline version looked identical.

This was a big mistake, said Mike Granoff.

Granoff was thinking of his pre-Better Place electric driving experience.

"I used to drive a Honda Civic hybrid," he said. "It was a good car, had even better gas mileage than a Prius, but they cancelled it. Why? Except for the H that stood for 'hybrid,' it looked exactly like a gasoline-powered Honda Civic. People wanted distinction. The Prius doesn't look like any other car. My thinking was that, for Better Place, if you're going to go with an existing platform, let's at least change the name. Call it something other than the Fluence."

Because the Fluence Z.E.'s body was identical to the gasoline-powered version, the battery had to go where the gas tank would have been. But the battery is much larger and, as a result, took up half the trunk. Compared to a Mazda or a Toyota, the Fluence Z.E. had a paltry amount of room for all the gear a family might need to transport, whether that would be groceries or luggage.

Yoav Heichal said that Better Place's team was well aware of the trade-offs the Fluence Z.E. presented.

"But looking from the point of view of Renault, we could understand why the car was built this way, why it had so many compromises," he explained. "Renault was launching something without knowing if it would turn a profit. It wasn't a perfect car, but it was cheap and easy to release from the perspective of a carmaker. When we started working with the Fluence Z.E., it had already passed the conceptual phase. They'd been working on it for two years."

The car Better Place really wanted from Renault was called the Zoe. It was everything the Fluence Z.E. was not—a smart, snappy vehicle with all the latest bells and whistles, a big trunk and a pancake battery under the car, all built from scratch, loosely based on Renault's existing Clio design.

The Zoe was seriously sexy, where the Fluence Z.E. was stodgy and staid.

But Renault wasn't offering Better Place the Zoe, at least not initially.

Why would they? asked Daniel Campbell, Better Place's head of telematics, web and mobile product management. "They already had an engagement from Better Place to sell 100,000 Fluence Z.E.s," he explained. "Renault was afraid that by introducing the perfect electric car they would cannibalize sales of the Fluence Z.E."

Still, Better Place's engineers were preparing for the day the Zoe would be ready. (It would launch two years after the Fluence Z.E., in 2013.)

The Zoe was designed to take a switchable battery, though it wouldn't have one at its debut.

"All it involved was changing four screws from static ones to dynamic screws, to allow the battery-switching mechanism," Campbell said.

Better Place did get some signs from time to time that a Better Place–compatible Zoe might be in the cards.

Jean-Christophe Pierson, who directed Middle Eastern affairs for Renault, told the Car Talk website that, "the new Zoe electric car … could be switch-friendly. Renault is waiting to see how Better Place does marketing … for the Fluence."

Better Place kept pressing Renault. It eventually came down to who should pay for "the last mile" to make the Zoe switchable.

The bill was $5 million, Heichal recalled, not an insurmountable amount in the larger scheme.

"Renault's position was that if we build this car with a switchable battery for you, no one else will use it, so you should pay for its development," Heichal said.

Agassi was adamantly opposed.

"You're going to be the ones selling and earning from this car, so you should pay for the development," was his stance.

It was a fight that would continue for the next two years.

In some ways, the Zoe represented a déjà vu moment for Better Place, harkening back to the company's thwarted relationship with General Motors.

By standing on principle ("we don't work with cars that have a tailpipe" for the Chevy Volt, "Renault should pay" for the Zoe), Agassi closed the door on two potential opportunities to broaden Better Place's product line and revenue stream. Both may have led nowhere (or worse). But the undeniable reality was that Better Place remained stuck with a single car, the technically advanced but visually vapid Fluence Z.E.

11

A STARTUP IN PINSTRIPES

Twitter was hardly a technical achievement when it first started. From 2007 to 2009, as the 140-character text messaging network giant grew faster than even its most optimistic founders and investors expected, its infrastructure couldn't cope.

During major events, people would want to tweet: the MacWorld conference in 2008, for example, or the death of Michael Jackson, in June 2009, where 100,000 tweets were posted. But the under-provisioned Twitter would slow to a crawl or even crash, leading to network outages and outrage among users, who would gripe and threaten to go to other competing services. Twitter's engineers worked frantically behind the scenes to build an entirely new backend that could handle the platform's unexpected popularity.

A whole mythology developed around the increasingly ubiquitous "Fail Whale," the image Twitter displayed when the site was "over capacity" and therefore inaccessible. An ironic "fan club," which made T-shirts and accessories with the iconic image of an optimistic beluga being transported heavenward by a flock of orange Twitter birds, cropped up on social media.

The site was eventually stabilized, and the Fail Whale was sidelined to a state of retired bliss. Twitter senior VP of engineering Christopher Fry told Wired that the whale image represented "a time when I don't think we lived up to what the world needed Twitter to be."

As early as 2006, founder and CEO Evan Williams admitted that, "like a lot of things, [Twitter] was built rapidly when we were small and had to be completely re-thought in order to support a much bigger user base ... we were (famously) having trouble keeping up with that demand in the core service."

Imagine if the same thing happened to Better Place—but with cars.

Drivers might run out of juice if OSCAR failed to accurately predict their state of charge and then couldn't direct them to the nearest switch station.

The electric grids of entire nations could fail if Better Place's smart charge management didn't properly handle the flow of a million cars plugging in at once.

If bills were sent late to customers, cash flow would crumble.

If customer service calls were routed incorrectly, drivers would grumble.

Agassi was determined that Better Place would not suffer the fate of a company like Twitter, and so he began building for the projected fabulous future.

This forward-thinking attitude resulted in Better Place's software systems striving for excellence on a truly grand scale. But it also betrayed one of the key rules for startups of all sizes: Keep expenses low at the start and stay nimble.

Shai Agassi's Better Place did not see itself as a lowly startup, though. Agassi had told Mike Granoff after the meeting with General Motors that Better Place would soon have the bigger market capitalization. Better Place compared itself not with companies just getting started but with blue chip stocks like IBM, Microsoft, Apple and Agassi's former employer, SAP.

It was a startup in pinstripes.

That thinking goes a long way toward explaining why Better Place established its data facility, which ran all of the company's billing and operations systems, in a drab industrial park in the outskirts of Madrid, Spain.

Operating Better Place's core computing systems in a secure location in Europe, where most of the company's planned business would eventually be, rather than setting up separate data centers in Israel, Denmark, Australia, France and elsewhere, made sense. Why reinvent the wheel time and again? And why court a Twitter-like disaster?

Indeed, anything that Better Place built—whether it was the data facility or the software—needed to be ready from the get-go to handle massive numbers of cars and their subscribers.

"We're building a network on Day One that can serve 100,000-plus cars," Agassi told the U.K.–based Financial Times.

The faulty lessons of thinking modestly had already been learned by less-fortunate companies.

AMDOCS

Nowhere was Shai Agassi's go-big attitude reflected more boldly than in Better Place's dealings with Amdocs, the Israeli enterprise software giant that describes itself as "the market leader in customer experience software solutions and services."

Agassi and Barak Hershkovitz contracted with Amdocs to create many of the key software systems Better Place would need to manage its network and keep its customers happy and paying.

Amdocs would build both the billing system and the customer relationship management (CRM) backend that handled everything from interaction with Better Place's Network Operations Center to helping the sales team follow up on leads and close deals.

The goal was to support not just the 100,000 cars Agassi had bragged about to the Financial Times, but a million subscribers around the world.

"We wanted Better Place to provide a mass solution, not just a niche," explained Eitan Hon, chief operating officer of Better Place's Israeli operations. "Shai believed that once we proved the technology and the business in Israel, it would scale very fast and, within two to three years, the billing system Amdocs was building would be the right one to handle that scale."

Amdocs had plenty of experience with billing systems for the cellular phone business. (It had started off creating digital versions of the yellow pages.) And they were local to boot—their Israeli headquarters was just a few minutes' drive from Better Place—yet with global clients Better Place could tap into as it grew.

Still, the scope of what Better Place required demanded a steep learning curve from Amdocs, one that Better Place had no choice but to finance.

Nor was it clear Amdocs was best suited for the job.

"Amdocs was great for billing and their revenues attest to that," explained Ariel Tikotsky, who had been with Agassi at TopTier and SAP in Silicon Valley, then followed his boss to Better Place, where he was in charge of knowledge management systems.

"There's not a huge difference between billing transactions of minutes, as with cell phones, and billing miles, as with electric cars," Tikotsky said. "But Amdocs knew almost nothing about building CRM systems, which is what we needed most of all. It's like coming to a tailor and asking him to build an aircraft carrier. The tailor says, I can do it, I have the best tailors around."

But it's not a tailor that you need.

The software Tikotsky's group required would categorize all the knowledge a Better Place customer service representative needed to know when solving a driver's problem. It depended on the work Amdocs was doing.

"Let's say I'm a driver, and I'm stuck with a flat tire," Tikotsky explained. "Better Place will call a towing company."

But which towing company would be best in that specific part of the country? What will the operation cost? How fast can they come? Can Better Place provide a temporary backup car if the fix entails more than a simple patch? Where is the closest backup car? Who has the keys?

The knowledge management system would guide Better Place's customer service representatives to the best answers. Everything had to be instantly accessible.

"We split any mechanical problem into many small scenarios," Tikotsky continued. "There was no question we couldn't answer. We thought about everything in advance."

However, Amdocs lacked the flexibility and speed needed by Tikotsky and his team. As a huge company, changes had to be approved up the chain of command, which took time—the opposite of a nimble startup.

"It cost us a lot of money and there were constant delays," Tikotsky said.

"Amdocs was like a big ship," said Motty Cohen, Better Place's head of innovation, echoing Tikotsky's nautical metaphor. "They simply cannot develop in an agile manner. For every change, you have to wait three to six months. Their development cycle was very different from ours. From the beginning, it was clear to me that this system is not suitable for us. We need agility from all the parties. When one party, like Amdocs, is holding you down, the entire process becomes very long."

Evan Thornley, watching from far-away Australia, also invoked a maritime metaphor.

"We were building a battleship for a dinghy race," he said. The software was "massive and gold-plated. It was totally unnecessary for the task at hand. We had the best software systems guys in the business, and the quality of their work was very high, but there was massive duplication, and people doing jobs that didn't need to be done or approaching tasks that in retrospect were completely irrational to the business reality."

No battleship survives its first contact with the enemy, Thornley emphasized. You have to study the marketplace carefully, "to be nimble and flexible in the early years, while still keeping an eye on scalability. But we were at the extreme end of the spectrum. Once you set that aircraft carrier in motion, it becomes impervious to reality when it hits the marketplace."

"With new technologies, building for scale in a single step is simply not possible," added Alan Finkel, Better Place Australia's chief technology officer. But "in his anxiety to reach scale in a short period, Agassi instructed the development team to use ... systems [like those] from Amdocs ... that were fundamentally unsuitable for a startup company."

Dan Cohen, Agassi's chief of staff, cautioned against looking back and second-guessing decisions.

"Yes, we built a platform that was way too big for the initial years," he said. "But it was because we didn't want to rebuild it later. It made sense at the time to not build it patchwork. It's not irrational to build a system for a company you expect to be huge. But it quickly got too complex."

Perhaps the most frustrating thing about the system Amdocs built was that it simply didn't work well.

"Everyone hated it," remembered Tal Bar, Better Place's lead salesman. "The idea and all the functions were great, but it had a lot of bugs; it would get stuck all the time."

IBM

Another huge company joined Better Place's list of third-party vendors: IBM won the tender to build and manage the Madrid data center.

Alan Finkel questioned the move to Madrid in the first place, at a time "when most other companies were shifting to cloud-based solutions," he pointed out.

Motty Cohen agreed.

"Today you can run everything on the cloud. You can lease servers from Amazon. You don't have to own the metal," he said. "To run a data center costs a lot of money. And you have to have more than one center in case of disaster and recovery. It was almost unmanageable. IBM had to have a dedicated department just to deal with the maintenance of the servers. You have to coordinate every time you publish a new version of the software. It was a nightmare, days of work of configuration management. For agile companies, you can publish a few dozen versions of software updates a day and it's automatic. For us, to publish a single version took up to a week."

IBM proved to be a huge headache, Tikotsky concurred.

"Our guys weren't allowed to touch the system in Madrid; only IBM could," Tikotsky said. "If we needed any kind of change, we had to open a ticket for an SLA—a service level agreement. The minute we handed the servers over to IBM, the systems started crashing. Delays set in. My knowledge management system went down for days, then data and documents were lost."

IBM was not as responsive as Tikotsky felt it should have been.

"For long periods of time, no one could tell us anything about what was going on," he recalled. "In one crucial period, there was only one person with responsibility for our servers at IBM, and he worked only two days a week. It got so bureaucratic. We were captives in their hands, totally at their mercy. It still amazes me to think about the huge amounts of money that were going their way and the miserable service we were getting."

BALLOONING STAFF

"We want to build a slim, mean machine," Moshe "Kaplan" Kaplinsky told Shelly Silverstein at their first interview. "We'll hire 30, maybe 60 people, and that will be the entire operation in Israel, the base of the company. I don't even think we need you to come on full time. Maybe just two days a week."

But the "startup in pinstripes" mentality pervaded Better Place's thinking about staffing, which quickly ballooned.

Silverstein was Kaplan's head of human resources, hired in early 2008 when Better Place had only seven people on staff. She would become responsible for much of the rapid hiring that would characterize the company in the early years.

"It developed like a geometric function. In the first year, every month I recruited ten, twenty, sometimes fifty people. Agile—that didn't happen," Silverstein joked.

Still, she loved her job in HR.

"It was like telling an artist to build the Sistine Chapel," she recalled. "We were going to create something huge, monumental. Everyone felt this narrative—that we were going to do something that had never been done before. We all felt so privileged. No one ever took a moment to ask if what we were doing was actually needed."

That was reflected in the opulence of the office itself—not so much in Silverstein's area, the Israeli OpCo, but in Agassi's TopCo floor, where he would park himself during his frequent visits to Israel.

"The luxury in the global office was amazing," Silverstein told Fast Company. "It was petty, but they had stuff we didn't have. We only had cookies from Israel; they had Nature Valley granola bars and Coke Zero."

One time, Silverstein said she saw one of the secretaries eating an apple. "I asked her 'Where did you get that from?' and she said 'I stole it from Global's kitchen. Go and do it yourself. I'll cover for you.'"

Silicon Valley startups have long been famous for their over-the-top perks and benefits. Among the more lavish: gourmet organic food at Dropbox, heated "endless pools" at Google, unlimited vacation at Automattic and Ask.com, $2,000 a year to travel for Airbnb staffers, a $4,000 baby bonus for new parents at Facebook, in-house yoga at Asana, and of course free massages and a fully stocked snack supply just about everywhere.

If Better Place wanted to reward at least some of its staffers with luxurious working conditions (if Nature Valley granola bars vs. chocolate chip cookies constitutes a real standard of indulgence), it was certainly in good company.

Debbie Kaye, Shai Agassi's personal assistant, dismissed Silverstein's concerns.

The differences in style, Kaye said, stemmed more from TopCo's California roots compared with Kaplan's Israeli OpCo "being run like the IDF, with a different culture. So we had Taster's Choice instead of Nescafé," she added. It wasn't a big deal.

In Paris, Better Place opened a *tres jolie* office on the Champs-Élysées, home to some of the city's most iconic brands and landmarks but also to some of its most expensive real estate.

"We committed over a million dollars to this space," said one of Better Place's finance guys who visited there. "We built an office with enough space for thirty people. It was all kitted out with desks and equipment. We envisioned we'd have an operation there, and we'd hire a prominent CEO and would need a place to put him, but there was only one guy who ever worked in it."

The rationale made a certain sense.

"Paris was going to be our European headquarters, and it was close to Renault," the finance team executive said.

Another staffer described the Paris office as a "chicken-and-egg" situation. "Why were we opening an office in Paris when we didn't have an operation in France?" he asked.

"You don't see the wasted money when you're in the middle of it," Shelly Silverstein lamented. "People were motivated by the vision: It was green, it was sustainable, and it was a little bit Zionist. It was a beautiful dream to dream; people got hooked. It was only later that you'd see the redundancy, the arrogance."

THE SERIES B

Given how much Better Place was spending, between third parties like Amdocs and fixed costs like staffing, it's not surprising that the initial investment of $200 million from 2007 was running out.

That wasn't unexpected, said Charles Stonehill, Better Place's chief financial officer.

"It was hard to imagine Better Place as a small company just growing incrementally," he explained. "Investors understood that electric vehicles were a big idea and that the Better Place version of electric cars was a big idea. The concept was always ambitious. No one pretended it wasn't. Either it would be extraordinarily successful or it would fail." There was no middle ground.

It was time to raise more money.

During the latter half of 2009, Better Place's finance team began making the rounds of some of the leading investment firms and banks in the world for a Series B fund raise.

They found a receptive ear at the Hong Kong and U.K.–based HSBC.

Dan Cohen made the introduction. He was close to John Thornton, who had joined HSBC a year earlier, in December 2008, after a 23-year career at Goldman Sachs, where Cohen had also worked. While the two were at Goldman, Cohen had heard Agassi speak on a panel at the Brookings Institution.

"Shai was unbelievably articulate," Cohen remembered. "You don't see so many Israelis speaking so eloquently in English, so passionately, convincingly and clearly. It was a fascinating talk on the future of electric vehicles and oil independence. I shared it with John."

Thornton gave Cohen the go-ahead to study Agassi and his Better Place proposition further.

"One thing led to another, and I met Shai. We began to build a good rapport," Cohen said.

That's when Thornton got the call from HSBC and decided to leave Goldman.

"John asked me if I wanted to join him, but at the same time, Shai had offered me a job at Better Place," Cohen said.

"Go for it," Thornton told Cohen. "If you're still as excited about Agassi once you're on the inside, I'll make sure the right people at HSBC take a look at it."

A year later, firmly in place as Agassi's chief of staff at Better Place, Cohen took Thornton up on his offer. Thornton introduced Cohen and the Better Place team to Kevin Adeson, head of global capital financing in HSBC's London office.

HSBC indicated it wanted in.

Agassi was at his best, bursting with bravado, in the Series B investor meetings.

"Shai had an extraordinary ability to bring people with him and convey his vision," said Macgregor Duncan, who was part of the Series B fundraising team. "I've worked with a number of exceptional people, but he's on a different plane altogether. His vision allied with his intense intellect. People would respond to something he said and say 'that's ridiculous,' and Shai would come right back and dismiss any concerns.

He'd marshal all the evidence on the spot, do the numbers in his head and completely outsmart the other side. I'd smile to myself and think, 'I've just witnessed a master salesman.'"

Even when Agassi was marginalizing an investor, he was winning.

"He'd say, you don't understand the company, the vision," Duncan recalled. "You don't understand how the market is about to tip, or how startups work."

During one pivotal meeting that Duncan attended, Alex Umansky from Morgan Stanley, which would come in with HSBC to co-lead the Series B, sat back in his chair and told Agassi, "I think I understand now what you're trying to do. You could become the next Google."

Agassi stared at Umansky for a few awkward seconds of silence.

"We will dwarf Google as a company," Agassi said with a straight face. "We will be the first trillion-dollar company in history."

Director of corporate development Jeff Johnson was in that meeting too.

"We all knew what the company was worth, and it wasn't that," Johnson said. "But Shai had raised two hundred million off a napkin with Idan Ofer; he'd built the partnership with Renault. It all seemed so easy. It set the context for what everything else was supposed to be like. I respected Shai. He so believed this was the right thing. That deep belief peppered every interaction with everyone around him."

"It takes a certain amount of *chutzpah* to say, forget Google, forget being a four-hundred-billion-dollar company, we're going to be a trillion-dollar company," Duncan said. "People were shocked by it. There was something exceedingly powerful in the way Shai used that sort of psychology, to make someone feel inadequate for saying we'll be the next Google. It would leave people with a sense of awe—that I just have to be part of it. This was Shai's true brilliance."

The Series B round closed on January 25, 2010. It was bigger than anyone initially imagined: $350 million with HSBC, Morgan Stanley Investment Management and Lazard Asset Management joining the Series A investors—Idan Ofer's Israel Corp., Alan Salzman's VantagePoint Capital Partners and Mike Granoff's Maniv Energy Capital.

HSBC contributed $125 million, which it described at the time as "one of the largest financial investments of its kind by HSBC."

Kevin Adeson joined Better Place's board of directors as part of the deal.

HSBC wanted to invest at $2.25 a share, which would have pegged the company's valuation at $850 million. Agassi wanted the share price higher, at $2.50 a share, so that Better Place would have a valuation of $1.25 billion, putting it in the rarefied category of startups that would later be dubbed "unicorns."

"Shai was insistent," Granoff recalled, "but HSBC said no way, this is ridiculous, we'll do $2.25 a share and not a penny more."

"Listen, we have to make it $2.50," Agassi told his counterparts at HSBC. He promised to meet a number of milestones. "If I don't accomplish these within six months, we'll issue you more shares to make the price just $2.25."

Among the milestones was setting up a full Better Place operation in France and raising another $500 million.

"We didn't even come close," Granoff said, "and yet when it was time to issue the shares to HSBC, Shai balked. HSBC had to push him and it eventually happened but only after enormous controversy."

The quibbling almost overshadowed the fact that the Better Place team had just pulled off one of the most dramatically successful rounds in startup history, even more so than the Series A "elevator pitch."

"We are confident that Better Place has the technical and commercial solutions to allow for the mass adoption of electric cars in the near term," HSBC's Adeson said in announcing the round. "We expect the Better Place model to be widely adopted across many countries and cities."

"Our technology and solutions, together with our strong partnership with Renault, provide us at least a two-year time advantage over all other alternative-energy vehicle approaches," Agassi asserted in a press release. "Today marks the end of an extensive process with the outcome being a decision by one of the world's largest, most conservative banks, HSBC, to take the validating step of investing in a private company intent on bringing innovation to the trillion-dollar automotive and energy industries."

The HSBC investment wasn't just about money, though.

HSBC originally stood for the "Hong Kong and Shanghai Banking Corporation." Through connections made by Adeson and Thornton, and through Ofer's own business in Asia, the door was now wide open to China.

12

PLUGGED IN AT THE GREAT WALL

China is the world's deadliest country in terms of outdoor air pollution, according to the World Health Organization. More than a million people died from dirty air in China in 2012, nearly double the number in runner-up India and seven times that of Russia, in third place.

China's pollution deaths are due primarily to a tiny particulate matter called PM2.5, which, at just 1/30th the size of a human hair, is small enough to find its way into and lodge in the human lung, causing a host of health problems ranging from coughing, chest tightness and shortness of breath, to asthma, heart attacks and premature death in people already suffering from heart or lung disease.

PM2.5 particles are generated by all manner of combustion activities, from motor vehicles and power plants to wood-burning and industrial practices. Many newcomers develop an ailment known as the "Beijing cough," a dry cough and itchy throat.

In 2008, just prior to the Olympic Games held in Beijing that year, several U.S. cyclists arrived at Beijing Capital International Airport wearing black masks to dramatize the problem. Their pictures were splashed across every Chinese media outlet.

China knows it has a problem.

In the immediate run-up to the Olympics, China banned some 300,000 trucks and 1.7 million private vehicles from entering Beijing. Ten months prior to start of the Games, many factories in the six provinces around Beijing were ordered to close down or partly halt production. The city's most polluting factories (including a large iron and steel plant) were moved entirely.

"The whole of northern China was making sacrifices for Beijing before and during the Games, but it [is] unrealistic, or simply not legitimate, for temporary measures to be sustained," Li Yan of Greenpeace East Asia told the South China Morning Post. "The drastic measures leading up to the Games" offer only a "temporary respite."

Indeed, with the Olympics far in the past, the Chinese capital is now seeing air quality deemed "safe" on less than 40 percent of days.

It's hit tourism to Beijing, too, which was down 14.3 percent in 2013 from the previous year. Expats are leaving as well, citing Beijing's filthy air as the No. 1 reason they're fleeing. The Chinese Academy of Sciences ranked Beijing the country's "least livable city" in 2016, with air pollution one of the main culprits.

Solving China's pollution pandemic has become a top priority for the Chinese government.

Li Junfeng, director general of the National Center for Climate Change Strategy and International Cooperation, described it as "like a smoker who needs to quit smoking at once, otherwise he will risk getting lung cancer."

It's no surprise, then, that when Better Place made its overtures to China at the end of 2009, it received perhaps its warmest welcome anywhere.

Idan Ofer made the initial introductions for Better Place in China.

Ofer had lived in Hong Kong during the 1980s, when he had helped expand his family's shipping business to the Far East. His goal now was to create a new car company—it would be called Qoros—as part of a joint manufacturing deal with the Chinese auto manufacturer Chery, one that would bring affordable Chinese-made cars to Europe and the United States.

When Ofer met Agassi in his Tel Aviv office in 2007, though, another thought had come to mind.

Like DONG in Denmark, Ofer wanted to diversify his operations (and separate his reputation) from the "dirty" business of coal, oil and Dead Sea mineral extraction. Electric cars were an ideal solution.

"That was the reason I went into Better Place with so much weight and invested so much of my own time," Ofer said. "Otherwise I would have invested just five million dollars."

Ofer recognized in Agassi's plans for Better Place a way "to marry my car-making business in China with Better Place's ability to build infrastructure," he said. "China has to go electric. They have a huge environmental problem. And they don't want to be fighting Middle East wars over oil. I actually thought that one day, there would be an edict to car manufacturers that you're going to have to go electric, or otherwise, you don't make cars here anymore."

China was so much on Ofer's mind that, had Agassi not been so gung-ho about Israel as a beta country, "we would have gone straight to China" and skipped the rest of the world. The Better Place story would have unfolded very differently, and the company might be the household name in China that Tesla is in the United States today.

Agassi put his chief of staff Dan Cohen in charge of the China opportunity.

"China was quickly becoming the biggest automotive market in the world," Cohen recalled. "There were emerging car companies, and we thought we could direct them in any way we liked. Many were government owned, which meant the government could take the ultimate decisions, making it potentially easier for Better Place. The electric utility companies were ready as well."

Mike Granoff added that China "could end up doing electric so big that it creates a global industry."

Indeed, China had just set a goal to get 5 million electric cars on the road by 2020.

Echoing Ofer, Granoff told the Green Prophet blog that the Chinese government had "made a clear policy, and I predict that before this decade is out, you won't be able to sell a gas car in China."

A year later, the Beijing government unveiled a subsidy program giving Chinese consumers purchasing 100 percent electric cars a discount worth nearly $9,000. Within a couple of years, that incentive would jump to as much as $19,000 per car.

CHINA STATE GRID

Better Place began its Asian sojourn in 2009 in Shanghai, where a third party made a connection for Idan Ofer and Dan Cohen to the region's electric utility, State Grid Shanghai.

"Idan and I pitched the Better Place concept," Cohen said, complete with battery switch stations and battery-switchable vehicles. "The head of State Grid Shanghai liked it. He wanted to start a pilot project."

That would have been some pilot project: The city of Shanghai has one-and-a-half times the entire population of Israel. A demonstration in Shanghai could have been bigger than a full-blown rollout in Israel.

A week later, Cohen got a call.

"We spoke to our headquarters and they felt this is such a big project, it should be managed from our headquarters in Beijing," Shanghai told Cohen. "Can you fly to Beijing to meet there?"

"At first I thought, this is bad news," Cohen said. "It's the Chinese bureaucracy kicking in. This will slow everything down. But the truth was the exact opposite."

Better Place had hit the radar of Liu Zhenya, the chairman of China State Grid, which oversaw operations in Shanghai and, as the country's largest utility, covered some 88 percent of the country.

"He said he wanted to make it his own project," Cohen recalled. "He wanted to own it. I said, 'This is fantastic.' We were just a speck on the wall for a company like China State Grid. Now the door was open for us."

Dan Cohen wasn't interested in relocating full time to China, nor was it necessarily in the best interests of the company for him to do so. He tapped Quin Garcia to be Better Place's on-the-ground guy to open up the Chinese market.

Better Place had given Garcia the opportunity to work in parts of the world he'd never dreamed of when he was studying at Stanford and had first met Shai Agassi.

Better Place had flown him to Israel, where Garcia had built the first electric car prototype. He did the same for Better Place's battery-switch demonstration in Japan. China was a logical next destination for a young engineer with high-tech wanderlust on a mission to change the world.

Garcia flew to Beijing in November 2009, set up a small office, hired a few local staff members and began negotiations in earnest with China State Grid as well as several Chinese automakers.

While Better Place remained tight-lipped about the identity of these automakers, Forbes reported that the state-owned Beijing Automotive collaborated with Better Place "to build prototypes of a battery-switchable car based on Saab models the Chinese company had acquired from GM's former Swedish subsidiary."

The prototype cars never got beyond the garages at Beijing Automotive, though. No tricked-out electric Saabs were ever seen on the streets of China's capital.

But negotiations with China State Grid—which serviced most of the north and central regions of the country and was slated to be Better Place's infrastructure partner—were progressing well.

That is, until Shai Agassi stepped in and put an abrupt kibosh on the budding deal.

It was a surprising development for Cohen and Garcia given that, despite the occasional public pronouncement from their Better Place boss, the two were never able to get Agassi's full attention.

Agassi rarely visited China. It wasn't just that his never-ending schedule and responsibilities on multiple fronts were keeping him away; in China he felt out of his comfort zone.

Agassi's gift of gab, the power of his confident persuasion, was all but irrelevant when working with a translator.

"The back-and-forth goes slower, and you're never sure if you're being translated correctly or not," explained Dan Cohen. "Shai's charisma was literally lost in translation."

Kiyotaka Fujii had a similar observation from Agassi's engagement with Japan.

"Shai's a very effective communicator and negotiator in English, but if it's not in English, he loses interest," he said.

Garcia recalled a meeting in China that exemplified what Agassi was up against.

"We were in a beautiful conference room with one of China's top automakers," Garcia said. There was a long table made out of exquisite mahogany; it emanated a deep, almost red glow. Everyone was smoking.

"At the head of the table were two seats at an angle where the most senior people sit. There was a big potted plant between them. Behind were two more seats where the translators sat," Cohen, who attended the meeting as well, remembered. "The executives sat down first, and only then the rank and file. It was very formal."

Formality is the antithesis of how business is done in the Startup Nation, of course.

"Israelis are loud and aggressive in meetings while the Chinese are much more subtle," Garcia pointed out. "So negotiating between these two cultures can be challenging. I became the man in the middle, trying to form a consensus."

Garcia bounced back and forth between the two sides, working with a translator, while here and there using the bits of Chinese he'd picked up during his brief stay in the People's Republic.

"I was trying to show I was on their side, too," he said, referring to the Chinese automaker.

In such an environment, it's little wonder that Agassi felt like an Israeli without his hummus.

There were also deeper issues at play.

Already on guard about protecting Better Place's intellectual property with Renault, Agassi was doubly afraid with China.

"He'd heard all kinds of war stories about China," Cohen said, "about the Chinese eating you alive and stealing your IP. He was extremely reluctant to go there. I'd say he was truly afraid."

It was more than fear.

"He did everything he could to put spokes in that wheel," Cohen said. "Every time we were about to sign an agreement, he'd drive us crazy. He'd turn it around. It was not necessarily on purpose, but he was so suspicious of their motives, it became impossible to create something."

"Shai resisted China from Day One," added Ofer. "Oh, he went through the motions because I was the chairman and largest shareholder and I wanted to do business in China. But he never followed my guidance on China. I set up a meeting once with the mayor of Beijing. The mayor said, 'Just come to the meeting and we'll do this business.' But Shai didn't want to come. And then he actually destroyed our relationship with China State Grid."

Agassi had good reason to be suspicious about China State Grid's intentions, it turned out.

Better Place had a standard clause in the contracts it wrote to work with infrastructure partners that gave Better Place first right of refusal if the partner went into a new territory.

Dan Cohen explained the rationale.

"We had a couple of clauses that simply said if we set up this joint venture, you cannot go and create a similar entity independently," he explained. "It was reasonable. We didn't want to give them all the technology and the next day become irrelevant. We thought it was pretty straightforward."

China State Grid didn't agree.

In December 2007, prior to Better Place's entrance onto the scene, China State Grid had joined a multi-country consortium that was awarded a 25-year, $4 billion license to run the power grid in the Philippines.

In its negotiations with Better Place, China State Grid insisted that it be given the rights to operate the charging infrastructure in the Philippines, including possible battery-swap stations. Even though the Philippines wasn't on any Better Place road map, Better Place wasn't willing to cede that control. Plus, it would set an ominous precedent.

Cohen agreed with Agassi in the Philippines case.

"Even though we were just this small technology company with no real clout, trying to do business with the gigantic China State Grid, it was a red line for us," Cohen said. "We could have bypassed it, but we didn't."

The blame for the deal blowing up didn't all fall on Better Place's side, Cohen insisted. China State Grid was dragging its feet too.

"They were already being perceived as being too much of a monopoly in the energy sector," he said. "They were concerned that if they put their foot in the electric vehicle field, it could be seen as trying to take over a whole new area, the transportation sector. They were trying to stay under the radar."

At the same time, "it was still early days for electric vehicles in general, and State Grid was being careful not to overcommit itself to things that may not happen," Cohen added.

QOROS

While negotiations were wobbling—and then falling apart—with China State Grid, and attempts at putting a deal together with Beijing Automotive never materialized in a drivable prototype, in April 2010, Better Place signed a Memorandum of Agreement with Chery Automotive to develop switchable-battery cars.

It was an unsurprising move to insiders familiar with Idan Ofer's partnership with Chery to create the new Qoros brand, but it certainly got the attention of the media.

A picture of an electric car plugged into one of Better Place's already iconic blue-and-gray charge spots under a large banner reading "Chery" at the 2010 Beijing Auto Show appeared along with a gushing article in Wired magazine.

"The two companies say the partnership offers the potential to lead what could become the world's biggest electric vehicle market," Wired's Chuck Squatriglia wrote. Although China's "global share of the electric vehicle segment is [only] 2.7 percent, HSBC research expects it to surpass Japan by 2016 and the United States by 2019."

"With only two percent of China's population owning cars and eighty percent of sales in 2009 to first-time car buyers, China has the opportunity to create and lead an entirely new category around clean transportation," Dan Cohen added. "With the scale of Chery's design and manufacturing capability and an industrial policy that favors electric cars over [internal combustion engines], we believe China represents an unprecedented opportunity for Better Place."

Chery was China's largest private (that is, not state-owned) automotive maker and its top automotive exporter in 2009. It built about 500,000 cars, most of them sedans, the year before. An electric-powered Chery or Qoros would go even farther.

"China never developed a globally competitive automobile industry," Mike Granoff told Green Prophet. "However, the zero-emission car— the electric car—is really more of a big consumer electronic device— something China has excelled at producing for export. And the other major component for electric cars—the batteries—is another industry in which China is in a global leadership position. So their plan is to leapfrog American, European and Japanese legacy carmakers by becoming the leaders in all-electric cars—first for their domestic market, and then for export."

Every day, 3,000 new cars hit the roads of the city of Beijing alone, Granoff continued. "Just as they are doing cars much faster than the United States ever did, China is realizing the detrimental impact of oil dependence on economy, environment and security much faster as well— and they are responding."

China was key for Better Place and for the world, Granoff added. "China is what's going to make this revolution happen faster than anyone thinks. I believe they will tip the world market toward electric cars before 2015."

Idan Ofer wasted no time in gathering his team for the Qoros, which Jim Motavalli described on the Car Talk website as "China's Lexus."

"We want to create a brand with Western levels of quality but at a lower price than comparable European cars," Ofer told Motavalli.

Ofer hired former Volkswagen head honcho Volker Steinwascher as Qoros's vice chairman and recruited engineers from both VW and BMW. Although most of Qoros's cars would be gasoline-powered, at least a few would be electric models.

Ofer instructed his Qoros managers to cooperate fully with Better Place's engineers on building a battery-switchable electric vehicle. While the technical teams worked together diligently, Shai Agassi was continuing to cause headaches for his counterparts in China.

The most significant was a disagreement over price.

Qoros worked up a detailed specification for what it would take to make an all-electric Qoros: 11,000 Euros.

Agassi pushed back.

"You should be building this car for 8,000 Euros," he said.

"Come to China and see for yourself," Ofer replied. "You can check every component. We're willing to do what no other company in the world would do—we'll give you full carte blanche to look around. If you can do it better, go ahead."

Agassi couldn't do it for cheaper, but that wasn't necessarily the point.

"Shai was complaining about how bad our people are at Qoros, how dysfunctional and incompetent they are. He was undermining the viability of Qoros as a company," Ofer said. "That's when I realized: He's going to destroy my company."

For Ofer, that would have been doubly disastrous.

"Qoros was always a hedge for me against Better Place," he admitted. Better Place might be gone someday, "but I'll still be in the car business."

Ofer limited Agassi's access to Qoros.

"I told Shai that from this day onward, you are no longer allowed to speak to one another," he said. "This relationship is over."

Qoros began selling its first model in 2013 and has released several other gasoline-powered cars since then, including an SUV and a hatchback, but never a battery-switchable electric car.

"It was all designed," Ofer said. "It was a truly beautiful car."

CHINA SOUTHERN POWER GRID

With China State Grid off the table and Qoros closing the kimono, so to speak, Cohen and Garcia turned their attention south—to China Southern Power Grid, the smaller sister to the mammoth State Grid utility.

China Southern Power covered only 12 percent of the country, but that still accounted for 250 million subscribers. It was the eighth-largest utility in the world at the time, according to the Fortune Global 500.

"The conversation was much friendlier," Dan Cohen recalled. "They had no R&D arm and no aspirations to go abroad, so they had no problems with our non-compete clause."

In April 2011, after almost a year and a half of fruitless negotiations with China State in Beijing, Better Place went for the smaller prize: It signed its first solid contract in the People's Republic with China Southern Power, which "pledged to help the company develop an electric car infrastructure supply chain and to encourage regional Chinese automakers to make battery-switchable cars."

The Guangzhou municipal government, where China Southern Power had its headquarters, said it would push automakers like the Guangzhou Automobile Industry Group to go electric.

"Electric cars present a great opportunity for China and are critical to achieve a low carbon economy," Wu Yimin, executive vice mayor of Guangzhou, said. "We will support this rapidly growing industry by encouraging production of electric cars in the region and promoting adoption in fleets," including taxis, buses and other public sector vehicles. "The cooperation between China Southern Grid and Better Place is a strategic step, and both companies will have our full support."

Shai Agassi chimed in as well—this time positively.

"China Southern Grid is an important partner in a huge market that is moving quickly toward the mass-market development of electric cars and is embracing battery switch as the primary means of range extension," he said in a press release. "Our collaboration with China Southern and the support of the Guangzhou government open the door to new opportunities for switchable-battery electric cars made by Chinese manufacturers for the domestic and export markets."

The deal also called for the creation of a 1,900-square-meter Demonstration Center in Guangzhou with a working switch station. The operation occupied the downstairs of what would now be Better Place's official Chinese headquarters. Quin Garcia transferred his operations there following the fallout in Beijing.

The Guangzhou center opened to the public in December 2011.

Carlo Tursi, Better Place's director of corporate development, had been assigned to oversee the launch. Politicians and investors had been invited as well as local government officials.

Tursi recalled that two nights before the doors were to open, an unexpected discovery almost stopped the unveiling from happening.

"We found a mouse living in the space between the battery and the car," he said. "It was winter and Guangzhou is very cold. I guess it was a bit warmer in there. So he went to sleep. One of the Chinese security guys saw the mouse and got so excited, he spent the night installing mouse traps all around the battery-switching lanes. We didn't want to have a demo in front of the local Communist Party officials and have a mouse walk out from under the car!"

The mouse could have caused more than embarrassment if it had chewed on some of the wires connecting the battery to the car.

The story ended anti-climactically.

"We never caught him," Tursi said. "I think he just ran away."

The team had bigger problems, though. Just a few hours before the launch, the batteries wouldn't charge.

"We had some strange voltage readings on the battery," Tursi said. "Maybe something happened when they shipped the battery from Israel. It had been sent by sea and was on a ship for a long time. We didn't want to have a big failure—you know, the car finishes the swap, drives out of the lane and then it just stops. So we did some last minute ER. There was a faulty battery cell. Dan Cohen and I stayed all night to give moral support to the engineers."

By 4 a.m., the battery cells were finally charging and, later that morning, the demo went off without a hitch.

Idan Ofer, who had flown in for the Guangzhou launch, waxed effusive about the significance of finally having a public face in China.

"Most Chinese are new buyers who don't have a history of car ownership," Ofer said, "so they don't know what it is like to drive such a car. In the West, most people are not first-time buyers. They have a long history of using gasoline-powered cars. If you tell Chinese buyers what an electric car is and how convenient it is to charge the battery, they will prefer the green car."

China Daily reported China Southern Power had agreed to build 14 charging stations in Guangdong, Guangxi and Guizhou provinces as "a step to support the country's national energy-conversation and low-emission strategy."

As hundreds of people visited the Demonstration Center in Guangzhou (which would continue running for two years with its small Chinese-speaking staff), there was little doubt in Ofer, Cohen and Garcia's minds that it wouldn't be long before battery-switchable cars would be seen plugged in near the two most iconic walls in the world: the Western Wall in Jerusalem and the Great Wall of China.

13

U-TURN

Shai Agassi and his family spent the summer of 2009 in Israel, as they had done most summers since moving to California, visiting family. At the end of the summer, Agassi made an announcement that shocked his staff: He would be taking a "sabbatical" from Palo Alto for the year to stay in Israel.

A few months later, he made it permanent—he wasn't going back to Palo Alto at all. He asked his senior staff to move with him: to make Israel the new global headquarters for Better Place, in practice if not according to the company's articles of incorporation (by which the company was registered in Delaware, a common tax-saving practice in the United States).

Agassi assembled his staff in Palo Alto to share the news. There wasn't enough room in the conference room for all 60 Palo Alto staff, so they met in an open area amidst the cubicles.

Agassi stood in the middle and explained that he had decided to move to Israel. It wouldn't be so terrible, he told them, as he was so frequently on the road that they rarely got significant in-person face time with him.

"You can expect to see me at least twenty-five percent of my time, as well as via tele-presence between Palo Alto and Israel on a regular basis," he said. "We're at a critical point in the development cycle of our solution and it's essential that I'm closer to the R&D team. From the start, we have always stated that executing in Israel and Denmark has been our key strategic plan, and we are a hundred percent committed to our success there. We've got a lot of work to do … regardless of where I am in the world, I need you to stay focused."

Then, without any warning whatsoever, Agassi proceeded to denigrate his team.

One of the staffers who was there recalled that "he degraded into a kind of calm but very nasty rant on the global operation. It was one of the oddest meetings I've ever been in."

"You guys don't deliver value to the rest of the operation," the executive recalled Agassi yelling at his team. "I don't know where you guys came from, but I was never on your side. No one cares about you, and neither do I."

Afterward, the executive remembered thinking, "OK, if you don't think we're important, then shut it down. But why did he have to attack us so personally?"

Agassi and his assistant Debbie Kaye, along with a few key staffers, including Sidney Goodman, director of communications Julie Mullins and chief of staff Dan Cohen, decided to join him in Israel. Those who remained quietly began planning their departures.

It wasn't that they necessarily disagreed with Agassi's decision to relocate.

Indeed, it made objective sense that the company should be consolidated in Israel. But the company they joined had been meant to be a Silicon Valley startup, with all the cachet and connections that implied.

"At first Shai tried to maintain a routine of coming to Palo Alto regularly," recalled Cohen. "But there was no reason to go there. Even though that's where the main financial markets for Better Place were, and where the company's founders were, the weight was clearly shifting to Israel."

It was hard for the staff.

"We thought we'd lose that Silicon Valley edge, with Better Place as a disruptor, an innovator, a thought leader," Cohen continued. "We were afraid Better Place would become more tactical, operational and local. It definitely impacted morale and the ability to maintain good people."

Lawrence Seeff, David Kennedy, Charles Stonehill and Aliza Peleg would all be gone within the year.

BEHIND THE MOVE

What was behind Agassi's decision to move himself and corporate headquarters to Israel? Was it purely a business decision? Or was there something else going on?

The official reason: The main action in Better Place at that point was happening in Israel, and Palo Alto was 10 time zones away. But an equally plausible explanation was that Agassi was still smarting from the failure to secure funding from the Pacific Electrification Program (PEP) and from the general lack of tangible results achieved in Washington, D.C.

If the United States didn't want Better Place, Agassi may have thought, then Better Place didn't want the United States.

"He was bitter about the whole American situation," Dan Cohen corroborated. "That no one was listening, no one was delivering and he couldn't get funding, while Tesla did."

In 2009, rival electric carmaker Tesla Motors had hit hard times. Although later it would be seen as a high-profile purveyor of all things sexy when it comes to electric cars, batteries, solar energy and even spaceships (from its sister company SpaceX), in 2009, Tesla was so broke that its founder Elon Musk was pouring his personal fortune (largely from his online banking startup, which became PayPal) into the company.

In October 2009, Musk claimed to be out of cash and living off loans from friends.

And then, the U.S. Department of Energy—the same agency that shut out Better Place for the PEP project—offered Tesla a loan for $465 million in June 2009. (The loan was approved and went through in January 2010.) Tesla's profile subsequently rose, and the company was able to pay back the loan by May 2013, with Musk bragging that Tesla was "the only American car company to have fully repaid the government."

Better Place, meanwhile, was flush with cash, but the rivalry with Musk and the contrast to Better Place's American experiences weighed on Agassi.

One more reason for the move to Israel wouldn't become clear for another few months.

In the fall of 2009, Agassi hired Tami Chotoveli as his personal coach. Before long, she was taking an informal role in the company as a business advisor.

Chotoveli ran a family-owned luxury watch company and was a well-known Israeli Internet personality, maintaining a highly active social media presence.

Nir Gilad, Idan Ofer's business partner and CEO of Ofer's Israel Corporation, recalled the first time he heard about Chotoveli.

"The company had become huge, with hundreds of employees, and we needed a nice org chart," Gilad said.

Agassi was at first reluctant, but after a vacation in Thailand, he showed up with the very document Gilad wanted. Everyone in the company was listed.

"He told us he had consulted with an organizational behavior expert to create it," Gilad said.

Mike Granoff met Chotoveli with Agassi a few months later as the three of them returned to Israel from a meeting in London.

As they shared a taxi home, Agassi referred to Chotoveli not as his advisor but as his girlfriend.

Granoff was surprised.

"I didn't know she existed before that moment," he said.

"She's the first person I've met who's smarter than me," Agassi would later tell Granoff.

Chotoveli soon began showing up at social events. At one party, thrown at Idan Ofer's home in the exclusive village of Arsuf, just north of Tel Aviv and overlooking the Mediterranean, Chotoveli arrived with a "fancy Louis Vuitton bag that cost seven or eight thousand dollars," Ofer recalled. "So I asked her what kind of bag it was. She said 'Oh, I don't know, I just got it from a customer.'"

She had to have known, Ofer felt. "From that moment on, I didn't trust her."

Chotoveli started appearing in more than just social settings. As Agassi's unofficial business advisor, she was at his side in meetings with prospective investors.

Ofer and Gilad noticed that Agassi began to change; he lost some of his self-assuredness and bluster.

"She would write notes to him in meetings," Ofer said. And Agassi began using notes during his presentations.

"This is a guy who never read from paper," Gilad pointed out. "He could get into a room without knowing anything about the crowd and give you a speech that you'd think took hours of preparation."

Chotoveli was eroding Agassi's confidence, Gilad thought. "He was afraid of saying something that she didn't agree with. Shai was not the same Shai after Tami."

Ofer felt he had to put his foot down.

"I forbade Shai from taking her to any more meetings," Ofer said. "And she wasn't allowed to come into the Better Place offices. I learned afterward that he did take to her a couple more meetings, one in Germany and one in Los Angeles, against my wishes. I instructed him not to, but he did anyway."

Not everyone was upset that Chotoveli was part of Agassi's life.

Better Place finance team member Macgregor Duncan recalled being in a car together with Agassi and Chotoveli on the way to an investor meeting in Los Angeles.

"It was just the three of us for two days," Duncan said. "When Shai and I had done these road trips before together, it was often awkward. We'd have nothing to say. But Tami was always very warm to me. We talked about her kids and her passions, ordinary topics that Shai never approached."

It's not clear when Agassi's wife, Nili, learned about Chotoveli—or when Agassi and Chotoveli's relationship became romantic—but Agassi's marriage was already in trouble.

Earlier in 2009, when Granoff told Agassi he needed him for another meeting in Washington D.C., Agassi responded that he wasn't sure if he could make it.

"I need to figure some things out," he told Granoff. "I'm on some thin ice at home."

Agassi's father was not happy with his son's behavior.

Nir Gilad called Reuven Agassi to ask what was going on.

"I cannot even approach Shai with these rumors," the elder Agassi admitted to Gilad.

It wasn't long before Chotoveli's Facebook and Twitter feeds filled up with pictures of her and Agassi: tender poses with over-the-top language and lots of hearts and smileys, which Agassi previously would have found much too public.

And he began opening up personally.

Ofer described Agassi before Chotoveli as "a very tight guy, stingy. For the last five years, he's worn the same pair of shoes." Now he was posting about love.

In the end, the question demanded an answer: Was Agassi's return to Israel entirely in the company's best interest? Or did he come to be closer to Chotoveli?

"We have no tangible facts to back up this theory, that Tami was part of the excuse he gave of coming back to Israel," Ofer said. "Maybe it was just that he needed to be closer to the R&D, like he said. I somehow suspect there was a hidden reason."

STOCK OPTIONS

Better Place staff found no shortage of topics to grumble about in 2009. A key complaint: the way Agassi set up the company's stock options.

Employees in startups routinely receive the right to buy company stock at preferential rates. These "options," which are above and beyond their already generous compensation, "vest" over a period of time, usually four years, in equal amounts month to month.

This motivates employees to stick with the company. If you leave early, you don't get the option to buy as much stock. If a company goes public or is bought by another public company, stock options are how high-tech millionaires are made.

Agassi was so convinced of Better Place's success that he created a highly irregular stock option program that vested not over four but over ten years. It also tied stock ownership to company performance.

The number of options an employee received was based on a complicated matrix of profitability, how many cars would be sold and how many subscribers Better Place signed up. Indeed, the final tranche of options wouldn't vest until Better Place had a million people driving its electric cars.

But what if Better Place didn't meet its own ambitious goals? Why should employees who had nothing to do with the bigger picture of sales and marketing or the politics of the company suffer by not receiving the type of package they could elsewhere?

"Four years is already more than you can predict in business, so we don't generally talk about options for that amount of time," explained Dimitri Dadiomov, who had been with Better Place since nearly the beginning.

"The stock option program was a motivational disaster," a Better Place executive added. "If you're in Silicon Valley and you're coming out of Stanford, and all your friends are getting stock options that are x amount higher and that vest over four years, and yours are tied to this weird performance criteria, that causes issues."

There was never a revolt, the executive said. "But the option program kept us from attracting top executives.

"The Israelis didn't quite get it; it wasn't in their culture as much, although they knew the stock option program wasn't good," the executive continued. "SAP didn't do options at all, they just paid a very high salary. But those of us who came from other startups in Silicon Valley knew it was a raw deal. People didn't talk about it, but it was very disappointing. Shai assumed that people would take it and say OK, that they wouldn't figure it out because he was so much smarter than everyone. But the team in Palo Alto said, this can't be serious, this sucks. It was clear from all this that Shai didn't give a hoot."

Agassi did give a hoot, but it was from an entirely different kind of owl.

"Shai thought that four-year stock option programs were bad plans that incentivized wrong behavior," the executive continued. "He was certain he was right and that everyone else at thousands of companies must be wrong. It showed a lack of respect and commitment to the staff and what they were worth."

Mike Granoff put it this way: "Shai would say that Better Place is going to be the biggest company in the world. We're going to be worth a trillion dollars. So even if your stock options are only 25 percent of what you might get at another company, they're going to be worth more than anywhere else you could go. If you want to go somewhere else, that's fine. But this is the best you're going to get."

TOKYO TAXIS

In the midst of all the contention about stock options and the role of Tami Chotoveli, Japan stood out as a bright spot for the company.

Just under a year after the successful demonstration of battery switch in Yokohama, Better Place was back with an even more ambitious prototype—this time in the very heart of Tokyo.

The goal: to determine whether there was a business case for electrifying the city's fleet of 60,000 taxis.

Although the taxi concept had been floated in the United States, it got much farther in Japan: an actual working prototype serving actual delighted customers.

Tokyo's ubiquitous taxis are operated by the world's politest cabbies who, in their white gloves and pressed shirts, come across more as mass-market chauffeurs than the quirky iconoclasts played by Andy Kaufman and other TV and movie taxi drivers. The taxis represent only 2 percent of all the cars in the city, but they are responsible for 20 percent of vehicle CO_2 emissions.

No wonder: At any given time, half the taxis in the fleet are circulating the city's streets looking for customers.

"A single internal-combustion taxi produces twenty-nine tons of CO_2 a year," explained Ryuji Kaneda, director of sales and operations for Nihon Kotsu, the taxi service that would partner with Better Place in the Tokyo taxi project.

Better Place could not have found a more visible showcase for its technology.

"Tokyo's taxis define the face of the city, just like the black cabs in London and New York's yellow taxis," Kiyotaka Fujii, CEO of Better Place Japan, explained.

Electric taxis had a number of key selling points.

Because taxis, which can drive up to 20 times more miles than private cars, are such a major source of city pollution, "the government and the politicians loved the idea of going electric. It was an easy sell," continued Fujii.

Another selling point: There were only two types of taxis in Tokyo—a model made by Nissan and another by Toyota.

"If taxis went electric, you could more easily standardize the batteries," Fujii said. "You wouldn't have to have such a huge inventory of different types" and the battery switch stations would be easier to operate.

Finally, the only way to electrify a taxi fleet would be through switchable batteries.

"Taxis in Tokyo run two hundred to three hundred miles a day. They don't have time to stop for a fast charge that takes thirty minutes to an hour," Fujii said. But they could handle a five-minute battery switch. Taxis were a perfect match of functionality and need.

Fujii used his personal connections to secure a former parking lot in the Toranomon district, not far from Tokyo's fashionable Roppongi neighborhood, as the location for Better Place to build a switch station.

A visitor's center for curious passersby was built as well. The main pickup station for passengers was nearby at the Roppongi Hills business and shopping plaza at the base of a 54-floor office tower.

"This is the equivalent to Rockefeller Center in Manhattan," Fujii noted with satisfaction.

There was always a long line of taxis and passengers ready to ride.

The taxi trial began on April 26, 2010, and lasted for three months. Three taxis were put into service with real taxi drivers. A fourth taxi was stationed for display at the visitor's center, which at its peak gave tours to some 1,500 people a week.

The base model for the taxis was a modified Nissan Dualis, the Japanese equivalent of the Rogue sold in the United States. The small electric fleet was licensed to Tokyo's largest taxi company, and most of the financing came from the Japanese Ministry of Economy, Trade and Industry. The batteries were provided by American battery maker A123 Systems. The investment from Better Place was primarily person hours and travel to and from Israel and Palo Alto.

The taxis were meant to mainly serve the city itself; they could range as far as Haneda Airport, Tokyo's domestic flight hub, but not the farther out, and larger, Narita Airport. Customers who needed longer rides were referred to another cab. The idea was that the taxis would duck into the switch station between passengers.

Some riders were so intrigued, though, they asked if they could tag along during a switch. The drivers were happy to indulge ... and they kept the meter running.

The feedback, according to Quin Garcia, who helped convert the Nissan Rogues to electric, was *sugoi*.

"It means 'cool,'" Garcia said. "We would hear that a lot. From people that got into the cab. The drivers would tell us."

Yasuhiro Kobayashi was one of those drivers.

The 23-year-old worked for Better Place partner Nihon Kotsu. In a video interview with Edmunds AutoObserver, Kobayashi commented that, "Compared to the other taxis I've driven, it's a very good ride, and easy to drive. There's not much lurching around, and customer reaction is quite good. [It's] making my job easier."

Did the drivers find switching batteries annoying? Not really.

"Yes, you have to do it frequently, but it goes by very fast, so I've found it hasn't really affected my business," Kobayashi said about the three, sometimes four trips he had to make into the Toranomon district each day to switch out his power pack. "It's less troubling than filling up with gasoline."

Kobayashi added that because the car is so silent, "you must be very careful coming up on pedestrians from behind. But there are benefits to being silent too, so you have to strike a balance."

Although the trial ran only for three months, Better Place had already scoped out what would be necessary to convert all of Tokyo's taxis to battery-switchable electric: 200 stations, each serving approximately 200 cabs, for 40,000 in total, about two-thirds of Tokyo's total fleet.

During the trial, only one cabbie pushed his luck and ran out of juice before he could get back to the switch station. Other than that, the program concluded without any major hitches. There were no breakdowns or lengthy out-of-service periods in the thousands of runs the taxis made; operating costs were far cheaper than for internal combustion models; and the battery exchange station functioned smoothly.

Better Place released a video promoting the project. In it, Shai Agassi commented: "If you have a passenger going to Tokyo every day ... I guarantee that they're going to ask the driver, does this thing really work? And when they say not only does it work, it works better, it's quieter and I actually like it better than my older taxi, you get the ultimate demonstration."

VISITOR CENTER

North of Tel Aviv sits Pi Glilot, a ramshackle outdoor shopping center that had once been a sprawling gas- and oil-storage depot. Huge empty drums punctuate the landscape, which has in recent years become dotted with automotive dealerships. A large water-storage drum looms over the northern entrance.

For Shai Agassi, that drum was emblematic less of its fossil fuel past than of how it could showcase the vibrant electric future Better Place envisioned.

Five million dollars later, the drum had been transformed into a combination Visitor Center and pre-sales showroom. Its round contours perfectly fit the design for the semicircular theater that would be constructed inside to show off what Better Place was cooking up in Israel and around the world.

Like its counterpart in China, the Pi Glilot Visitor Center, which opened on February 8, 2010, was Better Place's public face in the Holy Land. It quickly caught on as a must-see stop on the agendas of everyday Israelis seeking a family outing slightly more unusual than a brisk hike followed by a beachside barbecue.

Because a typical startup generally consists of nothing more visually exciting than a sea of cubicles and the occasional artisanal beer tap in a communal kitchen, the Visitor Center became a place to show off Startup Nation. Tour groups from abroad flocked to Pi Glilot, as did Israeli high-school classes, their teachers looking to inspire the next generation. Mike Granoff brought dozens of visiting politicians in steady succession as part of his ongoing courting of Washington D.C.

It was also a popular spot for Birthright groups—a free program offering college students and young adults a 10-day "Jewish identity" trip to Israel. They made the Pi Glilot pilgrimage, even though virtually none of these young Birthright participants either lived (or planned to live) in Israel or had, as poor college students, the kind of cash needed to buy a car of any type, let alone a pricey electric one, in their home countries.

The Visitor Center included three main components: a dramatic movie that laid out the Better Place value proposition, a peek at a live battery-switch housed outside in the parking lot inside a sweltering makeshift tent, and a test drive on a short kilometer-long track around the Visitor Center.

Enthusiastic drivers would triple or quadruple up in the cars to grab their chance at a minute or two of piloting one of the few all-electric cars Better Place had running (at first the Mégane, later the Fluence Z.E.).

If it was a pleasant day, and the air conditioning or heating was turned off, the absolute, stunning silence of an all-electric car when it was parked but turned on was exhilarating. Accelerating brought on a high-pitched whir that sounded like an airplane on the runway preparing for takeoff.

Not everyone liked those sounds—neither the whir nor the quiet.

Amos Shapira, CEO of Cellcom, one of Israel's big three mobile telephone providers, was paralyzed by the silence. His Better Place guide, prepared for every eventuality, popped in a CD with the sounds of a Harley-Davidson's engine revving up.

"Now I can drive," Shapira told his guide with relief.

Shai Agassi had big plans for the Visitor Center.

"We will allow every citizen of Israel to experience driving the electric car," he said.

Over the next three years, more than 80,000 people were exposed to Better Place through the Pi Glilot Visitor Center, a stunning achievement in marketing.

But would it translate into sales?

The 25-minute Better Place movie, available in Hebrew or English, was an over-the-top, inspiring and masterful work of environmental salesmanship. Visitors would often leave in tears at the very thought of what this plucky Israeli startup with a dream of making the world a better, cleaner, safer place had already achieved.

Visitors would enter from the rear of the theater and grab one of the 30 chairs made from refurbished car seats.

John Reed from the Financial Times sat in a seat that came from a 1995 Mazda Lantis. He described the film in 2010.

It "begins with images of carefree people relaxing on a beach, getting married, and buying their first car, before moving into a montage of more worrying images: burning oil wells in a desert, a stranded polar bear, houses underwater after Hurricane Katrina."

Agassi's image appeared.

"We've all become slaves to the price of oil," Agassi intoned. "The economic effect of cars can't be measured just as the cost of gasoline or the cost of the cars."

Rather, you have to look at the bigger picture—"the cost of deaths, the cost of sickness, the cost of climate change."

As Hollywood-style music swells, Agassi concluded with a dramatic flourish. "This is a new era of transportation. We're ready, the car is ready, the system is ready. The question is: Are you ready to switch?"

Better Place spared no expense in creating a full Disneyland-style experience. Agassi's image wasn't just on the screen; he was holographically projected—a full-size representation of the company's CEO and chief evangelist.

As the movie ended, the screen slid to the side to expose a model of a Renault electric car sliced open so that visitors could see its guts. Visitors exited the screening room into a second rounded chamber called the

"Vision Room." It was filled with wiry stands; an electronic garden of willowy stems, each with its own tablet computer perched like a flower on top where enthusiastic electric converts could enter their details for future sales.

Surrounding the room was another screen, this one displaying a map of Israel with the locations of future battery switch stations. Visitors' names would magically appear in the middle of the map.

The Visitor Center became a juggernaut for publicity, especially when an A-list Hollywood celebrity came to visit.

Leonardo DiCaprio brought his then-girlfriend, Israeli supermodel and Sports Illustrated cover girl Bar Refaeli. Pictures posted to the Better Place website showed Agassi accompanying a beaming Refaeli as she returned to the Visitor Center after her electric whirl. (Refaeli came back several times, bringing her family and some of her famous friends.)

Ashton Kutcher came too, escorted by his then-partner Demi Moore, who tweeted after her visit that she hoped the United States would get involved in Better Place, which she called "a system that could change the world, our dependency on oil and the quality of our planet."

When a star came calling, "we had to clear the entire building," recalled Lilach Gon Carfas, who managed the interface between the Visitor Center and Better Place's corporate headquarters, which had moved from Kyriat Atidim to a high-tech industrial park in the Tel Aviv suburb of Rosh HaAyin.

"Only three or four people were allowed to stay. Shai was one of them," Gon Carfas said. "Paparazzi would try to bribe the guard, but they didn't get in."

Agassi was less forthcoming to the delegations of senators, governors and members of Congress shepherded to Pi Glilot by Mike Granoff. Former Massachusetts governor Mitt Romney drove an electric car, as did New Jersey Governor Chris Christie, who spent an hour and a half at the center.

Agassi initially didn't think it was worth his time to meet Christie. A series of increasingly frantic emails and phone calls to Agassi's assistant, Debbie Kaye, eventually wore down Agassi's resolve.

Agassi showed up for a 20-minute meet and greet during which he cornered Christie and bluntly asked for $200 million to set up Better Place operations in Christie's home state.

"That's doable," Christie replied genially, although nothing ever came of it.

The theatrics and celebrities worked: Agassi boasted in a 2011 interview with technology journalist Om Malik, that Better Place inventory was sold out for two years.

However, unlike competing electric car company Tesla, which asked its early customers to secure their spot with a deposit of $5,000 or more, Better Place reservations were not binding; no one was committed to following through on their intentions.

Would they?

IN-FIGHTING

With the Visitor Center generating rave reviews locally and abroad, the successes of Tokyo splashed all over the media, his key executive team now relocated to Israel with him, and a new woman by his side, Agassi should have been at the top of his game.

But he wasn't. He became increasingly moody and lost focus, former Better Place staffers recalled.

Meetings with Agassi became increasingly abrasive.

"He would sometimes humiliate people," a staff member recalled. At an all-hands meeting, "the marketing guys had come to give a presentation and he just mocked them, in front of everyone. It was unfair."

Charles Stonehill noticed the changes too. "Shai was finding it harder and harder to accept contradictory views. He was more convinced of his own vision of the electric car future and was less willing to hear other perspectives."

Now that he was full time in Israel, Agassi and Israeli OpCo head Moshe "Kaplan" Kaplinsky butted heads with increasing frequency.

"They shook hands and would smile around one another, but ultimately they were two alpha males, and you can't have two roosters in the same compound," said Shelly Silverstein, who worked for Kaplan.

Kaplan's attitude didn't help.

"If you were painted with Kaplan's colors, you couldn't be faithful to anyone else in the company, and definitely not to TopCo," Silverstein recalled. "I thought that everyone wanted the company to succeed, but there were all these gladiators going around behind the scenes, fighting for their turf from competing entities. Sometimes, Better Place seemed more political than the Knesset [Israel's parliament]."

"The *esprit de corps* that was present in the first years of the company was quickly going away," said Granoff. In the beginning, "everybody was just so excited to be there, to be a part of this project and they were so convinced that with Shai's leadership, with all the money we had, and with the relationships we had developed with Renault, there was no doubt in anyone's mind we were going to be succeed. But now, Better Place had become a den of camps, with fighting and politics and pettiness and walls. It was just mind-boggling."

Yoav Heichal, who calls himself a "good friend" of Agassi's, said part of the problem was that, even though Agassi had moved to Israel, he simply wasn't as present as before.

"He was going through a difficult personal period, with his divorce, and he was not really involved with the company for a long period of time," Heichal recalled. "And when he was involved, it was to have a drink with [French President Nicolas] Sarkozy," who Agassi was courting to start up a Francophone Better Place, "not to sit with the guys and hash out details as he would before."

LONDON

Things came to a head in June 2010, when the Better Place board of directors held a meeting in London. The night before the meeting, the Executive Committee had dinner without Agassi.

Idan Ofer was at that meal.

"We wanted to have a discussion about Shai without Shai being there. It was perfectly normal for a board to have that kind of conversation," Ofer explained.

In the meeting, the board hoped to cover overall strategy as well as whether Better Place had the right executives in place. As the company had grown larger, Agassi's choice of so many friends and family for senior positions was now a matter of concern.

"I have made some of the best friends I ever had in the company,"

Mike Granoff said. "And yet, that does not mean that I have boundless confidence that each of these people are the right people to be in the key positions as we get deep into the execution phase. For that, my instinct would indicate that we need a fair amount of people who have super-deep experience and talent and have succeeded at other, somewhat analogous, hugely ambitious tasks in the past. And I just don't see enough of them around."

But Agassi found out about the dinner and became convinced the real purpose of the meeting was to try to get rid of him.

"In the middle of dinner, I got this long email from Shai bitching about the fact we're having this meeting without him," Ofer said.

"How dare you do this thing!" Agassi wrote Ofer.

The next day, the board meeting was held in Series B lead investor HSBC's corporate offices. Agassi was uncharacteristically on edge, remembered Dan Cohen, who also attended.

"He felt like people were stabbing him in the back," Cohen said.

Agassi started up again about not being invited to the dinner the previous night. The conversation quickly reached a boiling point.

"Listen, Shai, I can have a conversation with anyone I want to," Ofer challenged Agassi. "I'm the largest shareholder here; you're not going to tell me who I can talk to. I won't take this shit from you. Either you go or I go. You decide."

Agassi responded quickly and unequivocally. He stood up, flung open the doors and stormed out of the room.

"This is over. I'm finished with him," Ofer fumed.

Granoff was sweating bullets.

"We can't fire someone after he's just raised three hundred and fifty million dollars," he thought to himself. "This will be utterly devastating."

Ofer stayed firm.

"The cemetery is full of people who couldn't be replaced," Ofer quipped.

But Agassi himself hadn't gone far. He remained sitting outside the meeting room.

Cohen believed Agassi had realized that "he'd overplayed his hand."

Granoff wondered whether what he was witnessing was just a game, Agassi's poker skills in action. Was it a bluff? A test to see if the board had the courage to find another CEO?

Despite the high-stakes tension, the drama was resolved remarkably fast. Half an hour after Agassi had walked out, he was reinstated—not that he'd ever formally quit.

The board had made nice, but the repercussions were long-lasting.

"That day defined all of Shai's relationships going forward," Cohen explained. "If it happened once, it could happen again. Shai began thinking how to manage the board differently, tougher."

Ofer later said he regretted bringing Agassi back. "We bowed to peer pressure and didn't make the right decision." His interactions with Agassi were never the same.

"Everything changed after this," Granoff recalled. "Shai took even the smallest effort by the board to assert some authority as a *casus belli*. And the first criterion in his management team was not operational capacity but personal loyalty. As a consequence, there was never [again] any serious deliberation of issues—whether it was the structure of the organization, terms of partnership agreements, the pricing, or anything else. Shai was always difficult, but before this meeting, at least he was manageable."

ON THE FARM

Halfway around the world, Better Place Australia took notice of what had happened in London.

Shortly after the tumultuous board meeting, Macgregor Duncan, Better Place's Australian-born, New York-based vice president of global corporate development, joined a staff retreat at Evan Thornley's huge colonial-era private farm, an hour-and-a-half's drive outside of Melbourne.

It was 11 at night and Duncan and Thornley were sharing a bottle of wine.

Duncan had spoken with Alan Salzman after the board meeting.

"I was telling Evan about some of my reservations about what was going on at TopCo," Duncan recalled, "and I mentioned to him what happened in London."

"Shai has tremendous talents," Duncan said to Thornley, "but he has blind spots that are deeply problematic for the company. There has to be a formula that can accommodate Shai as an inspiring figurehead and strategist but that allows someone else to run the company day-to-day. You are the obvious guy. You're a fantastic manager of people, a wonderful CEO, you instill intense loyalty among your colleagues. The only plausible solution is for Shai to take on the role of visionary founder or even chairman and for you, Evan, to come on as global CEO."

Duncan and Thornley picked up the conversation again in the morning.

"We talked for another two to three hours," Duncan recalled.

Thornley was uncomfortable with the direction the discussion was going.

"He was happy running his Better Place business in Australia," Duncan explained. "As a result, he was nervous about getting on Shai's wrong side. He didn't want Shai to think he was disloyal. If you were disloyal to Shai, you'd get shut out. He was afraid he'd be isolated or fired, and he really wanted to grow the Australia business."

Thornley remembered the conversation with stronger finality and with less of the Machiavellian tenor.

"I'm flattered by your confidence in my ability," he told Duncan, "but you've got to stop right there. If you're looking for a candidate to replace Shai, I'm not your guy. I'm not moving to Israel. I live in Australia, I just got divorced, so I've got a lot of things going on with my kids. I share your concerns, but if you're trying to hook up some grand plan, well, that's not going to work."

And with that, the matter was dropped—for the time being, at least.

AGASSI RESPONDS

Following the tumultuous board meeting that nearly led to his dismissal, Agassi penned a detailed email to the members of the Better Place board, in which he broadly defended his own actions while simultaneously berating the board—at first gently and then with increasing vigor.

"Instead of asking the CEO to provide … information in a transparent and coordinated fashion," Agassi wrote, "some board members started back-room discussions directly with management. Some of these conversations led to direct instructions conflicting with the CEO as to alternate courses of action, leaving team members confused as to chain of command."

Agassi was at times contrite.

"This is not about whether the board can meet without the CEO. By all means the board can and should do so periodically," he wrote. "I regret the chain of events of last week and needless to say Better Place does come first for me. I cannot do it alone. I need a strong and involved board, one that supports me, advises me and together makes the best decisions for Better Place. I am open to constructive criticism ... but we should end up acting in unison."

At other times, he demanded transparency and respect.

"Transparency ... is a fundamental value underpinning this company," he wrote. "If the board demands transparency it has to do so with transparency at all times ... Respect was lacking not only to the role the CEO plays ... but more importantly to the value system upon which we founded our interactions to date ... I never compromise on trust and transparency."

He apologized only once outright in the letter.

"It is well understood that the CEO's actions following said gathering represented lack of credit towards the Chairman of the Board's ability to conduct the board appropriately, and for that I apologize," he wrote.

"I hope this resonates," he concluded his letter. "If needed, I am happy if the Chairman convenes a special board session to regain our footing and begin reestablishing the trust and transparency we all need to succeed."

14

BAIT AND SWITCH

How many miles could the Fluence Z.E. get on a single charge? Renault promised 115 miles (185 kilometers)—and it even included an official sticker inside the car attesting to that.

But as Better Place engineers began testing the first Fluence Z.E.s to arrive in Israel, they discovered something astonishing. The car's true range was no more than 85 miles, or just under 140 kilometers.

That was 25 percent less than what Better Place expected.

And that was under good conditions.

If there were too many hills, or if it was a particularly cold or hot day—when the car's climate-control system would put a greater burden on the battery—the Fluence Z.E. would be lucky to get as far as 60 miles before needing to stop at a battery switch station or plug in.

That was nearly a 50 percent drop from what Renault had promised.

Renault hadn't meant to deceive Better Place. It based its estimate on an accepted standard among European car manufacturers.

The New European Driving Cycle, or NEDC, was developed in the 1970s. It specifies that a car being tested must be run at a certain temperature (20 to 30 degrees Celsius) and be driven on a flat road in the absence of wind.

The car doesn't even have to be driven outdoors for the test. Sometimes manufacturers test on a "roller bench," and aim an electric fan at the car to simulate aerodynamic drag. All "ancillary loads"—that means air conditioning, fans, lights, heated rear windows and any extras—must be turned off to conduct the test.

In Renault's product literature, the Fluence Z.E. was described as having a "homologated range of 185 km over an NEDC combined cycle. In real usage, range varies between 80 km [50 miles] and 200 km [125 miles] depending on driving conditions."

Electric cars have ways to squeeze out a few more miles and extend the range.

"Regenerative braking" technology is one: The second you lift your foot off the accelerator pedal, mini-generators kick in to slow the wheels. It feels like the car is facing down a strong wind, rather than slowly gliding to a stop as in a non-electric car. The drag recovers energy, which the system immediately transfers to the battery.

Imagine you have just driven up a fairly steep and long incline, and you're worrying about the Fluence Z.E.'s rapidly depleting battery. You've reached the summit and now you've got an equally steep descent.

If you resist your instinct to brake, the car does it for you, all the while creating its own electricity. By the time you get to the bottom of the hill, you might discover your battery percentage has made back all the charge it lost on the way up—and then some.

Savvy drivers of cars with regenerative braking could turn motoring into a kind of car-sized puzzle: How much charge could you get back if you braked only when absolutely necessary, or if you took turns occasionally too fast in the quest for more power?

It could be exhilarating but at the same time exhausting: Brake too much and you might not have enough charge to get home. Obsessively watching the percentage meter go up and down makes driving far more stressful than in a conventional car. It's like constantly having to keep your eyes on the gas gauge—as well as on the road.

The reality of the Fluence Z.E.'s reduced range had a ripple effect on everything Better Place was building, from marketing to construction of the battery switch stations. One changed number tripped the switch on the entire Better Place business plan.

And it was only the first in a series of assumptions that would be upended in the months to come.

In a new business, change is inevitable; it's how you react that counts. How Better Place responded would define the company's success or failure.

Dan Cohen explained the impact of the range revelation: The whole system in Israel was based on the car being able to go at least 100 miles between charges, he said. "If not, you won't be able to drive from Tel Aviv to Haifa and back without a switch in between."

It was the same for Jerusalem to Tel Aviv, a 90-mile round-trip commute. Switch would go from an infrequent occurrence to an everyday activity for Better Place's longer-distance commuters.

It wasn't just the inconvenience.

"When you have just five percent left on your battery, you feel a little bit afraid," Eitan Hon explained. "I like a little bit of risk, so if I get home with zero percent, I know the car, so it's OK. But normal people don't like this feeling. You need to start with at least a hundred miles of range to know the battery will support you."

Better Place's sophisticated in-car operating system was not built for such risky behavior, either. The version of OSCAR that shipped with the first Fluence Z.E.s "was never designed to squeeze out the last five kilometers before getting home," said Daniel Campbell, who headed up the telematics division at Better Place. "It was not meant to be that accurate," but when it was discovered that the car's range was lower than expected, "it became critical."

Also hit: the battery switch station locations. These had been planned according to the assumption of the originally promised 115-mile range.

"You couldn't drive from Yotvata to Mitzpe Ramon [in Israel's southern Arava and Negev deserts, respectively] in the winter when the car gets just 50 miles to the charge because it was all uphill and you have to use the heat," Campbell said. "So you'd have to go on a parallel route where there was a battery switch station," adding close to an hour to the trip.

Better Place customers would be compelled to concoct elaborate work-arounds.

"We would drive to the hotels near Masada, plug in to an electrical outlet in the parking lot and charge up for a couple of hours while getting a cup of coffee," one Better Place owner would later describe the 170-mile journey from her home at Kibbutz Kalia along the Dead Sea to Eilat. "That gave us enough power to get to the next switch station."

Hon, however, defended Renault. Despite the NEDC sticker in the car, he said, Renault had never promised Better Place the full 115-mile range.

"They always said just that 'we'll try to get there,'" he recalled.

Matthieu Tenenbaum of Renault backed that up.

"If you look at our press release from 2008, we were talking about only a hundred kilometers [or 62 miles] of range, and that was in every condition," he said.

Patrick Pelata, Tenenbaum's boss at Renault, admitted as much, telling the French newspaper Le Monde that the Fluence Z.E. "would offer a range of about a hundred kilometers in 'Israeli' conditions—that is, in urban areas and with the heavy use of air conditioning."

Renault CEO Carlos Ghosn had said the same at the January 2008 Better Place launch in Jerusalem, although he added that the car could get up to 160 kilometers "under normal driving conditions."

One hundred kilometers was OK, Pelata added: Israel "is a small country ... where ninety percent of the population drives less than seventy kilometers a day."

"We knew that in tests the car could reach a hundred and eighty kilometers, but because of all the auxiliaries, you'd never drive like this," Tenenbaum admitted.

"It was Shai who was saying it had to be two hundred kilometers and was going crazy, although internally, he told everyone 'Don't worry, there will be switch stations everywhere, and OSCAR will tell drivers when to switch,' so it seems he didn't care so much about this. On the actual performance of the car, the range we delivered was better than expected."

HADERA

The ideal locations for the battery switch stations in Israel—and the ones Better Place wanted—would have been alongside the hundreds of gas stations off the country's major highways. Better Place could piggyback off their visibility, turning each station into "a billboard for the business," as Hugh McDermott dubbed them.

But that's not what happened.

The battery switch station in Hadera was a telling example.

Located deep inside a grimy industrial zone, far off the main road, it was hard to find, with little lighting, and in a neighborhood so dicey that Better Place's Ariel Tikotsky admitted he wouldn't feel comfortable having his wife pull in for a switch alone after dark.

The majority of Israel's population lives in the crowded Tel Aviv metropolitan area—a drive not more than an hour from the northernmost tip of the *merkaz* (the center) to its south.

The rest live in relatively far-flung outposts: the cities of Haifa in the north, Jerusalem to the east, and Beersheba at the tip of Israel's southern Negev desert.

The city of Hadera is about halfway between Tel Aviv and Haifa. With the Fluence Z.E.'s real-world range, there was no way for commuters to avoid stopping at the sketchy switch station on the way home.

Worse, the station wasn't even close to the main commuter highway.

Most drivers traveling from Tel Aviv to Haifa take Highway 2, a speedy route along a modern, well-kept limited-access highway.

The Hadera station was off the old Highway 4. For the typical commuter, getting there meant an extra 20 minutes, navigating an obstacle course of traffic lights, strip malls, speed bumps and roundabouts.

The options for commuters from Tel Aviv to Jerusalem weren't much better. One switch station was on the grounds of a cement factory. Another was on the outskirts of Jerusalem, adjacent to the city's recycling center and creepily close to Jerusalem's main cemetery (giving new meaning to the expression "gone to a better place").

Only two of the 40 stations that would eventually be built in Israel were located along any of the country's key highways—and there were no stations at all inside the main city centers.

In Denmark, however, it was another story. The 18 stations being built to serve the greater Copenhagen area were nearly all along well-traveled and easy-to-reach highways and intersections. And Australia had plans to build its switch stations next to gas stations, shopping malls and markets.

Why was Israel's switch-station situation such a mess?

The problem was regulation. Most of Israel's gas stations were built illegally, explained Yoav Heichal, and owners didn't want to call attention to that by applying for a new permit to add a Better Place facility.

"Tama 18" is the Israeli regulation for gas stations, and it grants a station only 200 square meters of "built area" beyond the pumps. Because gasoline is so heavily taxed in Israel, the real profit is earned by the convenience stores selling sandwiches and popsicles. Station owners use every square inch—and often some extra illegal space—to add money-makers such as restaurants and carwashes. Risk going back to the zoning board and getting dinged, just to add a Better Place station? No thanks.

How had Better Place overlooked the infuriating, albeit entirely to-be-expected intransigence of the gas station owners it hoped to partner with? Was this another example of the disconnect between software and hardware expertise?

Better Place considered lobbying the government to make changes to the Tama 18 rules to benefit both gas station owners and Better Place. "It's been done a few times before, but it would take about five years," Heichal said.

Better Place needed to start selling cars in two.

Better Place hired a consultant who brainstormed switch station locations.

Could they be considered residential facilities? the consultant asked.

No.

Tourism or recreation?

No.

The only place where Better Place could find a match that wouldn't require diving into Israel's famously tangled bureaucracy was to locate the stations within industrial zones. After all, the switch station had a machine in it—the robot. Cars go in and out. The whole facility could be classified as a hanger or a machine workshop.

"It was the wrong concept, but it was the only way we could deliver on time," Heichal said.

That pressure to deliver, fast, was always present.

The idea was to get metal in the ground as quickly as possible, to demonstrate that Better Place could do it. A second batch of stations could always be built later in the "right" locations, Heichal said.

What should have happened, said Guy Pross, who had by now left his job at the Australia-Israel Chamber of Commerce to join Better Place as director of governmental relations in Australia, was a conversation with the top echelons of government.

"We needed the prime minister himself to say, 'This is a national project,'" Pross said, and that Better Place must have its switch stations in the right locations.

For example, Highway 6—Israel's first toll road—seemingly had plenty of room to add stops along the way for a switch station or two.

But Highway 6 was run by a private operator that, without outside intervention, didn't see the value.

Eitan Hon said that getting access to Highway 6 could have taken 10 years, even with a wink and a nudge from the top.

"So we built the stations off an exit," he said. "We said we can live with a bigger detour."

Hon felt that the company did the best it could under the circumstances.

"The fact that the battery switch stations got built at all is something amazing," he said. Like the creation of the battery-swappable Fluence Z.E. by Renault, it had never been done before.

The situation in Australia was very different.

Although no stations had been built yet, planning was meticulous—the opposite of the often fly-by-the-seat-of-your-pants style of the Israeli team.

Geoff Zippel was head of deployment for Better Place Australia. Before that, he had worked at Mobil and Exxon/Mobil in Australia overseeing 11,800 gas stations across Asia.

That might not seem relevant to a company like Better Place—whose mission was to put oil companies out of business—but Zippel brought his 20 years of experience building and finding locations for service stations to bear when negotiating with Australia property holders for Better Place.

"When we went into an oil company in Australia, the first thing we did is say, we're actually not your competition," Zippel explained. "Once a customer drives a new car off the lot, the energy supplier has been chosen. It's either oil or electricity. There's nothing you can do about that."

But an oil company can still make money from electric car drivers.

As in Israel, "a significant amount of a gas station's profit comes from what customers buy at the convenience store—the soft drinks, packets of cigarettes and newspapers," Zippel continued. "So we told them, we'll preferentially direct a vehicle requiring a battery switch station to your site, not to the gas station down the road. The electric car driver will be on your site for five minutes, or 15 minutes if there are cars waiting in front. If you can't convince that driver to get out of the car and buy something from your shop, that's your problem. But I can deliver electric cars to your store."

Zippel made the same "what's in it for you" pitch to supermarket chains.

"We'd attract electric vehicle customers to their site on the idea that they'd do a switch, then run in and buy something. Plus, it gave them environmental sustainability credentials. And they'd get a commercial return for it, since we'd be paying rent."

Zippel had one more incentive for the oil companies: an integrated fuel credit card that could manage both electric kilometers and gas kilometers.

"Petrol cards are a big deal in the oil industry in Australia," Zippel said. A family with two cars—one gas-powered and one electric—could now use a single credit card for all their fill-ups. "The oil industry loves when motorists have one of these cards in their pocket because it brings them back to that company's gas network."

The pitch worked.

"We had 200 switch station locations confirmed in Australia—120 in the five major capital cities and 80 as part of the highways connecting them. Seventy-five percent of them were co-located with gas stations or supermarkets."

That's not to say that Better Place Australia had signed any formal memoranda of understanding.

"We had agreements based on the knowledge that the sites we'd chosen would be available to us when we were ready," Zippel said.

Meanwhile, Better Place was missing its construction deadlines in Israel—and the press took notice.

Agassi acknowledged this, in a sit-down with The Jerusalem Post and other Israeli publications.

"We didn't know anything four years ago," he admitted. "This is something regulatory that has never happened in any other place in the world, and we are all learning. Better Place is learning, and the state is also learning how to manage the process."

Anybody who has ever done a home renovation can understand what it is like to go through the process once, Agassi emphasized: "Imagine what it is like to do this simultaneously in dozens of locations on three separate continents."

INCONVENIENCE

Better Place had sold investors and excited electric car enthusiasts on the "guarantee" of a five-minute battery swap.

It will take "less time than it takes to fill your gasoline tank," Shai Agassi told The New York Times' Clive Thompson in 2009.

But as it became more difficult to secure locations, and Better Place scaled back its switch stations in Israel from 120 to just 40, the swap time increased. It wasn't the robots and screwdrivers that were the problem this time—it was because so many stations were so far off the beaten path.

For the occasional battery switcher, for whom the stations were mainly meant as a psychological safety net, that might have been bearable. But for daily commuters between Israel's big three cities? The extra time might make the difference between deciding to go electric or sticking with a tried-and-true gasoline-powered car.

Even the most convenient switch station—on the Jerusalem–Tel Aviv route, off Highway 1—added an extra 15 minutes to a trip, plus time for the switch itself.

Besides, smart commuters had long been taking the alternate road—Highway 443—instead of Highway 1, with its heavy traffic, sharp turns and inevitable accidents. But there was no switch station anywhere near Highway 443. Electric car drivers would have to change their commuting habits, increasing travel time sometimes by up to 50 percent.

On top of this, they might face a wait at the switch station. Unlike a gas station, with its multiple pumps, each switch station only had one lane. If there were two cars ahead of you, tack on another 10 minutes of waiting time. If there were three or more cars, there was a distinct chance that the switch station wouldn't have time to recharge the spent batteries it had just swapped, leading to even further delays.

In determining where to build, Better Place had gone to great lengths to ensure that customers could drive "anywhere" in the country and find one of the 40 stations—even if there was no one there to use it on a regular basis.

That led to some odd locations—such as the switch station on the edge of the Ramon Crater, Israel's version of the Grand Canyon, in the tiny, isolated town of Mitzpe Ramon.

Rebecca Shliselberg, Better Place's Global Network Planner, pointed out how the station had an excellent location—right off the street. "But who cares?" Shliselberg complained. "No one is driving to Mitzpe Ramon."

Shliselberg also criticized the station in Katzrin, in the Golan Heights, as "wasted money."

"It would have been cheaper to let you rent a gasoline-powered car for a once in-a-blue-moon vacation until the demand increased enough for full national coverage," she added.

It wasn't an unheard-of idea.

For instance, Nissan—Renault's sister company—gave U.K. owners of its Leaf all-electric vehicle a voucher to rent "a petrol or diesel car, free of charge, for up to 14 days during the first three years of ownership. All you pay is the insurance."

CURSED FROM THE GRAVE

At times, it seemed the battery switch station project was cursed from beyond the grave.

To build anything in Israel, you need to keep the Israel Antiquities Authority on call. If you run into anything that looks vaguely ancient, the IAA will conduct a survey of the area to determine what treasures from Israel's rich past may lie beneath the earth.

On the one hand, this policy causes bureaucratic impediments to promoting business.

On the other, this attention to the past is part of what preserves Israel's heritage. And that heritage can go a long way back.

For instance, in the mid-1990s, the construction route of Highway 6 would have meant bulldozing Tel Hadid—an ordinary-looking mound of dirt that held within it artifacts from the early Iron Age, in the days of the biblical Joshua. Plenty of pottery, as well as a more recent mosaic floor (from the 6th century of the common era) depicting a boat sailing on the Nile River in Egypt, were retrieved in the Hadid area.

In 2000, a compromise resulted in the highway's planners building a half-kilometer-long tunnel under the site so that archaeologists (and nature lovers) could still have access to the remarkable discoveries of Tel Hadid.

The conflict between digging and archaeology in Israel is not just academic; it can escalate quickly if ancient graves are found.

Atra Kadisha, an ultra-Orthodox organization dedicated to the preservation of Jewish burial sites (the name means "holy site" in the Talmudic language of Aramaic), is at the forefront of the battle to prevent desecration of Jewish bones buried for thousands of years.

Jewish law prohibits removal of the dead from a grave—or even opening a grave for no reason. Atra Kadisha members are sure to be present when a suspected burial site is found during construction work. If the construction crews or politicians don't accede to their demands, protests bordering on riots can erupt.

When burial remains were found at the proposed location of a new hospital emergency room, for instance, protesters came out, climbing the fences around the excavation, blocking roads and burning tires. Leaflets were distributed calling for "the land of Israel to go to war."

Better Place didn't run into any graves or ancient bones while building its battery switch stations, but ensuring that it wouldn't—and avoiding publicly embarrassing protests by the Atra Kadisha—cost money and took time to do the extensive and proper ground surveys required before digging.

And Better Place needed to dig—and deep—for its battery switch stations.

Agassi insisted that the stations look and feel like carwashes and that drivers could just sit in their cars on a mostly flat track while the batteries were being changed.

Better Place could have done less digging and forced the cars to be raised up in the air—as in a garage—but this would either have required drivers to exit the car before the switch started, or exposed them to the risk of falling. Agassi was all about user experience; he knew that if the switch stations were perceived as dangerous, customers would resist.

"Digging is not just the process of bringing a machine," explained Guy Tzur, Better Place's switch station research and development manager. "It's getting the permits to dig and paying for them—that's what's complicated and expensive."

In addition to archaeological ruins and graves, the diggers had to keep away from modern electrical and plumbing infrastructure.

"Unfortunately, in some parts of the world, including Israel, the mapping of underground cables and pipes is not complete," said Tzur.

Some locations weren't even fit for building—but Better Place wouldn't know that until the location had been chosen and the survey completed.

Better Place's battery switch stations eventually reached a depth of 13 feet—that was the space required to house the battery storage and cooling system underground and avoid a sizable and unsightly building.

Despite the depth, the switch-station also required a very large footprint. The battery warehouse had to sit alongside the switching area itself; it couldn't be positioned directly beneath.

That kind of space was a tall order in Australia, explained Geoff Zippel.

"Gas stations don't want a big and imposing structure on their forecourt," he said. "They want you to clearly see the pumps and the convenience store when you're driving down the highway."

POWER UP

Building the switch stations was just the start. Once they were open, how much would it cost to keep them going?

"The rent for a regular battery switch station in the center of the country was $2,500 a month," explained Efi Shahak, who headed up the Association for the Advancement of Electric Transport in Israel, a nonprofit organization of Better Place drivers. "But that was almost twice the real value for the property."

Shahak wanted to know why.

"I talked to an employee who told me that people assumed that Better Place was rich. They were a big company, they were 'champions in signing checks,' so the land owners said to themselves, 'I can ask for more,'" he discovered.

Rent was only half of the monthly cost to run a switch station. A big chunk of the rest went to the electricity that powered the intense air conditioning Better Place needed.

Anyone who owns an iPhone or a laptop computer knows that the battery degrades over time as it's recharged over and over. The batteries in an electric car use the same lithium ion chemistry. The more rapidly the battery is charged, the quicker it loses its capacity.

But if the battery is fast charged under extremely cold conditions, it stays usable much longer.

The cost of 24/7 air conditioning, spare parts, taxes and maintenance added another $2,000 a month per station.

All told, it could cost up to $5,000 per station for rent and operation. Multiplied by 40 stations in Israel, that was $200,000 per month that had to be accounted for. To that, add in the cost of building the stations: $500,000 on Better Place's spreadsheets, but with a real-world cost, as Mike Lindheim had pointed out, that was closer to $3 million per station.

In the end, though, Better Place barely paid for the stations. Seventy percent of the money was fronted to Better Place as a four-year loan by Baran, the construction company hired to build the stations in Israel. The first 20 were included in the loan agreement.

But Baran was getting antsy.

As the final stations were being finished, Baran reported in a public earnings statement that Better Place owed it nearly $15 million.

Baran wasn't an entirely innocent bystander.

"They looked at us as a milking cow," explained Yoav Heichal. Like the switch-station landowners, Baran perceived Better Place as a company with unlimited financing and investors who would always pony up more.

"They didn't ask for cash up front, but they padded the bills by huge amounts," Heichal said.

Heichal was shocked by some of what he saw.

"I used to come to make fixes on the stations and I saw different contractors smoking cigarettes for the whole day," he said. "At the end of the day, Better Place would get an invoice for ten people for ten hours doing nothing. But at Better Place, no one cared. The goal was to launch as soon as possible."

Baran, as a contractor, would often outsource its own outsourced work.

"A guy would come, drill a hole to hang a sign and bill us for five hundred dollars," Heichal continued. "There were contractors of contractors of contractors, and each station had a different set, so no knowledge was being built up and transferred between the stations. I'd estimate the contractors were charging Better Place three to four times more than the amount required for hardware and services."

BATTERY FINANCING

Better Place's business model to build an electric car for the masses at a reasonable price point depended on separating ownership of the battery—the most expensive "extra" for electric cars—from the car itself.

Better Place's big idea was that *it* would own the battery and drivers would pay for that battery through their monthly subscription package.

It was a bold move, but it presented a big challenge: Better Place had to pay—up front—for the tens of thousands of batteries it was expecting to sell as part of the Fluence Z.E.

At up to $15,000 a battery, that represented a cash-flow conundrum of electrifying proportions.

When a customer bought a Fluence Z.E., the money went nearly entirely to Renault. That put all the pressure on the battery-subscription packages.

Better Place planned to charge upwards of $300 a month for a subscription package. That came out to an average of $4,000 a year, to cover the battery, electricity costs, installation of a home charge spot, and all of Better Place's internal costs.

The solution was to get a third party to finance the batteries—to loan Better Place the money to buy them.

Better Place assumed the battery loans would be paid back in four years. Because no one knew how long the relatively new battery technology would last, this seemed like a reasonable approach. But it didn't add up: The $4,000 annual subscription amounted to only $16,000 over four years—enough to cover a battery, but none of the extras.

And what if the battery didn't last that long?

Better Place had assured drivers they would always have a battery with a reasonable capacity. When a battery's ability to be charged degraded too much, it would be retired (perhaps to be used in a storage facility, as was proposed in Denmark). When second-generation batteries with larger capacity and greater range became available, drivers would receive them seamlessly at their next switch.

That meant more batteries to buy.

In real-world use, drivers would discover their batteries would degrade to an unacceptable level in as little as two to three years.

But Better Place had never planned to pay full price for the batteries. They were to be financed, like a mortgage.

Better Place imagined pooling these battery loans into vehicle-specific versions of the home mortgage industry's infamous collateralized debt obligations (CDOs)—the same type of instruments that helped bring about the Great Recession.

The pooled assets could then be sold to investors, who would receive a stream of income based not on monthly mortgage payments but on the recurring subscription fees paid by Fluence Z.E. drivers. And, as with CDOs in the mortgage industry, the more car owners involved, the more the risk could be spread.

But by 2010, when the company needed to come up with the money to buy the first batteries, mortgage bundling had become one of the great tragedies in Wall Street history.

Better Place turned first to its own investors, but they refused.

"No one wanted to take the risk," explained Mike Granoff, referring to his contacts at HSBC and Morgan Stanley. "They didn't want to put their jobs on the line."

Even if CDOs hadn't played such a role in tanking the housing market, they would have made investors nervous, because bundling for batteries had no track record. No Better Place electric cars were yet on the roads or in the hands of consumers.

Most troubling of all, there wasn't enough money in it.

"Financing the batteries would only generate a seven to eight percent return," explained Ben Keneally, Better Place Australia's head of marketing. "That would be OK for a debt investor who was expecting a safe, modest rate of return. But equity investors, like venture capitalists, are looking for a return of twenty to forty percent for their money."

VantagePoint CEO Alan Salzman was more outspoken when Agassi proposed that VantagePoint kick in to help finance the batteries.

"These are bullshit numbers by someone who has no understanding in finance," he bellowed over dinner one night in late 2010.

Better Place had better luck with General Electric.

In September 2010, Better Place announced with great fanfare that it was partnering with GE in a deal that would "finance a total of 10,000 batteries for electric vehicle drivers through various pilot projects."

GE also committed to making sure its own WattStation home charging spot would be compatible with Better Place's service network.

The director of GE's Ecoimagination investment arm, David Searles, praised Better Place for having a "solid, strong vision about how the electric vehicle will evolve." He added that GE found Better Place's battery swap plan "compelling" and that he was "pleasantly surprised" by the performance of the all-electric Renault Fluence Z.E.

Behind the scenes, though, GE's financing offer was "not any better than what we could have gotten from the bank," lamented Amit Nisenbaum, Better Place's head of strategic alliances.

Agassi wasn't happy.

"He'd say, 'This is just small change; they should be investing in multiples of this,'" one of the Better Place staff members involved recalled. "The GE guys got turned off. In the end, they invested twenty million dollars basically to get Better Place off its back."

That $20 million wound up as a general investment in Better Place; GE would not be taking on the battery financing.

Better Place was finally forced to turn to Renault, which made a deal—but for only 50 percent of the total.

Better Place still had to come up with $7,500 for every car it sold.

NO CFO

Shortly after the Better Place board meeting in London in June 2010, Charles Stonehill, the company's chief financial officer, told the board he wanted to leave.

He agreed to stay on during the Series B fundraising and while a search for another CFO was launched, but scaled back his day-to-day activities in the company. He formally resigned in early 2011.

"I left because of some private disagreements with Shai," Stonehill said diplomatically. "It was not so much the performance of the company but other areas we disagreed on."

Like what kind of company Better Place should be.

"Could we vary the business model to be more inclusive of other electric vehicles" and not just those with switchable batteries? Stonehill asked. "Could we work with other cars on their charging structure? Should we strike partnerships with companies like General Motors that had showed interest in cooperating? I was extremely concerned that the company was not open to a different set of ideas."

Stonehill's absence created a vacuum at a precarious time, when the cost of the batteries and of building and operating the switch stations was contributing to a worsening financial position for Better Place.

The individual OpCos and Barak Hershkovitz's Better Place Labs had their own financial teams and internal CFOs, but without Stonehill, there was no corporate-wide point of financial oversight, no single officer at the top who could gather all the data on income and expenses and present it to the board in a concise report. What was the company's headcount, for example? What was the "burn rate"—the amount of money a company needs to spend to keep going?

Delays compounded the company's woes.

Production and delivery of the first Fluence Z.E. cars was late, and the switch stations weren't faring any better.

"We were originally supposed to go to market in 2010," remembered Hugh McDermott, who spent most of his time on the road in Europe, pitching potential utility partners on how a Better Place system could operate as a virtual power plant.

"When you're venture-capital backed and have no revenue, every month you push out that launch date means another month of burn. Do the math. A year of delay equals several hundred million dollars."

Yet with no CFO, the company's situation hovered mostly under the radar, while spending continued unchecked.

"Every time I came to visit Israel, it seemed like another floor had been built at the company's corporate headquarters," McDermott said. "I couldn't figure out what we were doing. We were spending like drunken sailors."

"The size of the staff was ridiculous and entirely unnecessary," added Macgregor Duncan. "We probably needed one-third that number. You'd go to Israel at that time and you just didn't know what everyone did."

Hiring a new CFO proved to be difficult. Indeed, the job would remain empty for nearly a year and a half after Stonehill left.

The decision to relocate the company headquarters from Palo Alto to Israel had dramatically shrunk the pool of available executives. Instead of being able to draw from the best of the best worldwide, future executives were limited to those who either lived in Israel or were willing to relocate.

David Shlachter, who worked in global marketing in the Palo Alto office, remembered that "every time an American quit, he or she was replaced by an Israeli."

"The management became more provincial at that time," chief counsel David Kennedy commented. "I hate to say that, because I have such high regard for Israeli business culture. And you can't find a group of harder-charging, gritty, practical entrepreneurs than in Israel. But for some reason, we weren't able to use that pool."

Although the search for a CFO was supposed to be handled by a committee, it was in reality micromanaged by Agassi.

"Don't worry," Agassi would say as the process dragged on. "We've got three candidates. I like this guy. I'm interviewing this other guy. I've got it."

But nothing happened for 18 months.

"Shai didn't want to have a CFO who would ask too many questions, or one who would be recording what we were discussing," said Idan Ofer. "I can show you reams of paper and discussions we had rewriting what the role of the CFO was vis-á-vis the board. We tried to find a way of appeasing Shai but we didn't succeed."

Mike Granoff suggested Agassi was not stalling per se, but perhaps had set his sights too high.

"We have to get someone who was formerly the CFO of General Motors or Microsoft," Agassi told Granoff.

"Basically, the 'ungettables,'" Granoff lamented. "The executive recruitment firm we paid to conduct the search said they never had an account as impossible as this."

Australia's Geoff Zippel felt that the board, not Agassi, was ultimately responsible for the CFO debacle.

"The entire governance by the board was exceedingly poor," he said. "You can draw your own conclusions, but when a company is allowed to operate without a CFO for 18 months, when Shai is the only person who knows the position of the business—*are the battery switch stations working, are car sales on time and on plan, are we overspending and in what areas?*— it's the board who should be managing the executive team, not the other way around. It's the role of the board to make sure that the business was running on track."

———

Despite the climbing costs, there was no sense of panic. Rather, an attitude that "we can always raise more money" prevailed, Granoff admitted. Employees believed that Idan Ofer would never turn the spigot off, "that he was in too deep and couldn't let it go."

Dan Cohen said an IPO was already being discussed although, given that the company didn't have a single paying customer yet, it would have been highly unorthodox.

"It was like, we've already done the impossible; we've been so successful at raising money—from Idan, from HSBC—that it's easy," Yoav Heichal recalled. "We can just raise more and more."

THE SERIES C

Enough information was available to the board, even without a CFO, to make it clear that by mid-2011, a key financial planning assumption had been upended. The Series B money—$350 million—wasn't going to last until cars started selling and revenue was coming in. Better Place had burned through it in a year and a half.

There was no choice. It was time for a third round—a Series C.

According to the terms of the Series B, at least half the money for any new round needed to come from new investors.

But investors had questions—plenty of them. Wasn't the company supposed to be operational now? Why had it used up its previous round so quickly? Could they rely on management to stick to its business targets?

Better Place's finance team snapped into action. Previous Better Place investor Morgan Stanley took the lead from the banking end. Mike Granoff donned his fundraising hat again.

Shai Agassi wanted another huge round like the $350 million Series B. When the initial road show was met with surprising investor resistance, he settled at $200 million. But he insisted on a stunning valuation of $2.25 billion—nearly double that of the Series B.

It was too high, Granoff warned Agassi.

"If we set that price, no sophisticated investors will want to get in," Granoff said.

But Agassi stood firm.

"In Shai's mind, that was what we needed to get to launch," Granoff said. "Everyone will see that we've been right all along about disrupting the market."

Agassi's pitch resonated with the company's existing investors, who agreed to come back for a third round, committing $130 million. That was too much, though—it was already more than half the amount to be raised.

"We needed a fig leaf," Granoff realized: a new, unrelated investor who would provide some cover from accusations that Better Place was breaching the terms set for the Series C.

Investment banker Alex Umansky had already been at Morgan Stanley some 20 years when Better Place came calling for its previous round. He had been instrumental in convincing his investment-banker bosses to join the Series B.

As the Series C search began, Umansky had jumped to Baron Capital. If he could get Baron on board, Better Place would have a "new" investor. It might not meet the 50 percent requirement, but it could assuage concerns.

Ron Baron, Umansky's boss, agreed to put in $20 million—"as a personal favor to Umansky," Granoff said. But he questioned the numbers.

"The way you're spending, you don't need $200 million, you need $400 million," Baron told Agassi. "I'll only come in if you can raise a total of $250 million."

"No problem," Agassi replied. "Give me until the end of the year and I'll get you the other fifty million."

"And what if you don't?" Baron asked. "I want you to put in some of your own money. Five million at least."

Up to this point, Agassi had never invested a dime of his considerable personal wealth. This didn't sit well with some of Better Place's investors, who had watched as rival electric car CEO Elon Musk pushed himself to the verge of personal bankruptcy by investing $35 million of his own savings into Tesla.

Sammy Ofer, Idan Ofer's father, would drive his son crazy about it.

"My father kept complaining, why isn't he putting any money of his own into this?" the younger Ofer recalled. "I tried to make excuses—he gave up this fantastic career at SAP, he put in his intellectual property, his time, before 2007."

While Agassi agreed to Baron's end-of-the-year demand, he never did invest—not even when the round closed at $200 million, rather than the $250 million Baron wanted.

Baron's "fig leaf" investment solidified the new valuation. That would turn out to cause new problems for raising money.

"The valuation was excessive. It led to us getting the wrong investors," explained Macgregor Duncan.

In particular, only large investment banks and institutional money managers could justify that price. Regular venture capitalists—the type Mike Granoff had called "sophisticated investors" who normally would get involved in a startup company like Better Place—found it too expensive.

"I had many conversations with Shai, saying 'Why are you pressing for such a large valuation?' You're crowding out other participants by asking for such a price," Duncan said. "A valuation of $800 million would have been more attractive. At $2.25 billion, no venture capitalist will look at us."

"The price today is irrelevant because we'll be so big in the end," Agassi replied, with his stock answer.

"Shai thought that the massively inflated valuation was part of the story," Duncan continued. "It created the impression of this juggernaut, a company created on a PowerPoint presentation worth $2.25 billion. People were seduced by Shai's charm. They put aside rationality."

The difficulties in raising the Series C were compounded by Agassi's presentations, which became increasingly erratic.

Duncan accompanied Agassi on several of his fundraising meetings. He remembered one particularly memorable pitch early on to Morgan Stanley.

"We were having a due diligence discussion about the financial model," Duncan recalled, "and Shai stated that Better Place would have a million subscribers around the world, including Israel and Europe, by 2014."

"Sorry, can you repeat that?" the Morgan Stanley guys said.

Agassi did. They drilled deeper.

"OK, so your financial models are predicting you'll have 2,000 customers in 2012 and 10,000 in 2013," they continued. "Are you telling us you will have 988,000 more customers in 2014?"

Agassi looked the Morgan Stanley guys straight in the eye. "Yes," he said, without missing a beat.

"The whole thing had veered into the absurd," Duncan recalled. "It wasn't clear to me any more where the line was between selling the vision and a realistic assessment of what was taking place."

Perhaps that's because of who Agassi's fictional hero was: Ender Wiggin, the lead character of Orson Scott Card's best-selling science fiction series.

Duncan and Agassi were driving to an investor meeting when Agassi mentioned Wiggin.

"Shai was in this kind of ruminative mood and he's unexpectedly sharing with me about his childhood," Duncan recalled. "He told me that his favorite book was 'Ender's Game,' which is about this kid who was basically raised to become a superhero to defend Earth against alien invaders. You don't have to be a Freud or a Jung to see that Shai saw in this book a parallel with his own life. That, like Ender, I think he genuinely saw himself as having a mission to save the world. It was his moral responsibility."

The Series C closed on Friday, November 11, 2011. "Not bad for a startup that has yet to launch its networks of electric car charging posts and battery swapping stations," Forbes' Todd Woody wrote.

The day after the Series C was wired and entered Better Place's bank account, the entire finance team resigned.

"None of us wanted to be involved in a company we believed was going south," Duncan explained. "I was the most senior finance person in the organization and I didn't have a voice with Shai."

Duncan says the team didn't quit until the end of the Series C partly out of loyalty to the company but also because they were offered significant cash bonuses to stay.

"If I had left three months earlier, the Series C may not have been signed," Duncan said. "I had the relationships with the investors. What would they say if the most senior finance person in the organization leaves just prior to the round?"

Duncan also harbored a secret hope.

"I thought there was a possibility that after Charles Stonehill left, I could develop a different kind of relationship with Shai and speak some sense to him," he said. "I hoped I could help steer the company to a more sustainable business model. But I quickly realized the futility of that ambition."

Duncan says deep down, Agassi must have known that the difficulties in raising the Series C meant Better Place was headed for trouble.

"He had to keep going through the motions, like a politician running for office who sees he's 30 points behind in the poll and will get decimated, who sees that all his senior advisors have bailed, but still has to go out every day and say 'I'm going to win.' Maybe the other candidate will get involved in some scandal and have to drop out. For Shai, that might have been a war in Iran. Oil prices would spike to $250 a barrel and we'd be back in business. That was the mentality of the organization."

In some ways, Better Place always felt like a political campaign, Duncan added: "that we were working on a mission bigger than ourselves, trying to convince the skeptics—and that Shai was still going to be able to pull a rabbit out of a hat."

15

HOW TO LOSE MONEY
WITHOUT REALLY TRYING

To say the public and press in Israel were shocked would underestimate the feeling of deep betrayal that set in when the price of the Renault Fluence Z.E. was announced.

At $35,000, it was no less expensive than a competing Toyota Corolla or Mazda 3 in Israel.

Hadn't Shai Agassi said that Better Place's electric offering would be inexpensive, affordable, even free? What happened to that massive tax discount the Israeli government had granted to Better Place for its all-electric vehicles?

The price announcement came at a news conference May 15, 2011, at the tony David InterContinental hotel, fronting Tel Aviv's glittering boardwalk, with the gentle waves of the Mediterranean Sea providing a soothing soundtrack.

Inside, though, the mood was anything but calm.

Murmuring turned into ill will: Better Place had gotten greedy. They didn't really care about the environment. They just wanted to make money on the backs of the suckers who had led the cheer for so long.

The basic five-door sedan was given a sticker price of $35,623. (The price in Denmark was roughly equivalent.) The "premium" model, which included such luxuries as leather seats, an improved sound system and height adjustable seats, was $2,000 more. Both versions included the full OSCAR navigation and energy management system, and could be charged—at home, at public charge spots, in a battery switch station—in the same way.

Zohar Bali, Better Place's vice president of sales, was at the press conference.

"The media just killed us," he said. "It was a huge disappointment to them. 'This is not what Shai promised us,' they said."

Lilach Gon Carfas was in the Visitor Center and heard the same grumbling.

"People thought they'd get the car for free," she remembered. "Or at least for half price."

At Better Place, the staff was equally stunned. It wasn't the price they'd wanted either. It had come from Renault.

The actual price of the Fluence Z.E. from Renault to Better Place was just over $31,000, including the 8 percent (highly reduced) purchase tax from the Israeli government and 16 percent VAT (value added tax, Israel's equivalent of national sales tax).

That left Better Place with only the thinnest profit margin. It made barely a blip on the bottom line and left no wiggle room for negotiations, depriving buyers of the time-honored "joy" of haggling for a better deal.

How did Renault come up with that price? A car manufacturer applies two main factors when calculating the cost of a new car.

One is simply spreading the development costs across the number of cars expected to be sold.

Agassi had told Renault CEO Carlos Ghosn that Better Place would buy 100,000 Fluence Z.E.s—enormous for Better Place, but for a car manufacturer used to selling in the millions, quite small. Renault plugged that number into its spreadsheets, and Agassi's "free" car concept took a quick spin down the off ramp.

Carmakers also price cars by gut. Bali was involved in the pricing discussions at Better Place, applying experience he'd gained working for other car companies in Israel.

"A carmaker doesn't have a specific set price list," Bali explained. "When they want to come into a market like Israel, the first thing they do is a comparative analysis with similar vehicles."

Better Place considered the Fluence Z.E. comparable to family sedans like the Toyota Corolla or the Mazda 3. But Renault "wanted to compare it with other electric cars, or plug-in premium vehicles like the Toyota Prius," Bali said.

That bumped the price up significantly. In fact, the only reason the

Fluence Z.E.'s final retail price was on par with other family sedans was because of the tax break Better Place had received.

Renault may have had another consideration: It didn't want to cannibalize sales of the gasoline-powered version of the Fluence that it had released into the market only a year earlier. If the Z.E. price was too low, Renault might have worried, who would buy its "other" Fluence?

As a result, "the price from Renault to Better Place for the Fluence Z.E. was fifty to sixty percent more than the wholesale price of gasoline-powered cars of a similar class sold to importers in Israel," Eitan Hon explained.

Renault's Matthieu Tenenbaum disagreed. Renault's price for the Fluence Z.E. was where it always was, he said.

"If you look at our first discussions, you'll see that the target price of the car we gave, which was used by Shai in Better Place's business plan, was maybe five or ten percent off from where it ended up," he pointed out. "There was never a scenario where the Fluence Z.E. would be cheaper than an internal combustion engine vehicle. We were very transparent; we showed them the cost of every component. Why would Better Place expect it to be lower?"

In the end, Better Place simply may have been outmatched—a pipsqueak upstart compared with an international powerhouse like Renault, which made decisions according to its own internal logic and not out of any overt malice. Agassi may have believed Better Place could compete with and even best Renault, like the biblical David slew Goliath—but his slingshot was filled mostly with bluster.

"It was an argument we didn't win," Dan Cohen conceded, referring to Better Place's objections to Renault's pricing. It resulted in "a price that didn't help us penetrate the market."

CARASSO

Renault's Israeli distributor, Carasso, was nervous.

"In the entire time it's operated in Israel, Renault has never sold ten thousand cars in a single year, and certainly not one model," explained Zohar Bali. "But Shai was telling the market that we would deliver fourteen thousand cars in our first year, and one hundred thousand in six years, in Israel alone."

No other car brand had ever launched with these kinds of numbers, Bali said. "In Israel, Mazda sells ten thousand to twelve thousand Mazda 3s a year. It's one of the best-selling cars in the country, and it took them twenty years to get there."

The facts outside Israel didn't support the numbers, either.

"We couldn't point to an example from another market and say, they did ten percent market share in their first year, so we can do fifteen percent," Bali said.

Indeed, Jean-Christophe Pierson, the head of Renault in the Middle East, told the French newspaper Les Echos that a market share of 3 percent over the coming two to three years "would be a good score for the Fluence Z.E."

But Bali backed up his boss. "I thought, maybe this is so new, maybe Shai knew better. I couldn't believe it, but there's a first for everything, and maybe Shai knew what he was doing. He'd raised all that money. So I said I'll support it, even though my instinct was saying 'no way.'"

Bali eventually became a believer. "After a few months driving the car, I came to the conclusion that we had the right solution for this stage. It was an amazing car."

Carasso didn't share Bali's enthusiasm.

"They didn't want to commit to the numbers in our business plan," Bali said.

Carasso was also afraid that Better Place would be so successful that Renault would grant Better Place the entire Renault franchise in Israel.

"We told Carasso, 'We don't want to be a distributor,' but they didn't believe us," Bali said. "Their top manager said, 'When you understand how much money you can earn from this business, you'll never give it up.'"

As a result, Carasso refused to sell the Fluence Z.E. at first.

This thrust Better Place into yet another unanticipated situation: It had to become a car importer as well as a technology and infrastructure provider.

Better Place set up a new entity, Better Place Motors, as the official importer for the Renault Fluence Z.E. in Israel, with Bali as its general manager.

It was not an easy fit.

"We weren't built to be a car distributor," Bali complained. "We couldn't afford to have our own stock of cars, and we didn't have a leasing program like Carasso."

And then there was financing: Better Place would have to absorb the full price of buying the Fluence Z.E. from Renault up front and get paid back from the buyer over the course of a four- to five-year loan.

"It was a huge headache," Bali said. "We had to use our balance sheet for this legitimate consumer need."

It was also unsustainable—a financial drain that would have bankrupted the company before it sold its first car.

Eventually, Better Place was able to cut a deal with the smallish Bank Igud to take on the financing risk. Bank Igud was given a prominent office in the Visitor Center directly opposite the salespersons' cubicles, which raised some eyebrows from customers who wanted to compare prices.

A $10,000 CAR?

In a four-part series on LinkedIn's "Pulse," Shai Agassi described how traditional American carmakers in Detroit could tackle the "disruptive threat" posed by electric car companies by going electric themselves.

Without referring specifically to Better Place, Agassi argued that a sub-$10,000 car would succeed "not because it is an electric vehicle, but because it is a great car at an unparalleled price point. Much like the $499 iPad succeeded not because it was a keyboard-less tablet, but because it was an amazing computer at an unbelievable price point."

It was all about slipping in under a psychological ceiling.

If Agassi had his druthers, the Fluence Z.E. would be selling at $9,999, not $35,000.

If that wasn't possible, then NIS 99,000 instead of NIS 120,000, the shekel price for the basic Fluence Z.E.

Tal Bar, who became the company's top salesperson, thought the total price should be even lower—no more than NIS 80,000.

Where did these notions of a lower price originate?

"What Shai had in mind was that once we got a second car company, we could renegotiate with Renault," a Better Place executive told Fast Company. That second car deal would force Renault CEO Carlos Ghosn to come back to the table begging for new terms, the executive added.

"Because Shai's an optimist … he didn't think the price was an issue; it was an interim number."

Perhaps Better Place could have subsidized the Fluence Z.E. to bring the sale price down.

Better Place head of marketing strategy and planning Yishai Horn thought a higher monthly subscription fee would do it.

"That's HP's business model. The printers are cheap and the ink is expensive," he said.

Price perception was a key success factor "that we apparently missed," Horn added. "The pain of adoption should have been balanced with a super-attractive car price. We'd only need to do it for a year. After that, we'd be selling 15,000 cars a year," momentum would be unstoppable and the price could go back up.

The subscription packages, however, were about to become a major headache of their own.

THE SUBSCRIPTION PACKAGE

Better Place created a guerrilla-marketing program called the "Champions," into which it enlisted its most highly engaged supporters and early adopters to become brand ambassadors.

Their job was to give feedback to Better Place on the driving experience and to get the word out to the general Israeli public. The Champions had grumbled about the price of the car, but their real beef was with the monthly subscription packages revealed at the David InterContinental press conference.

There were two tiers: The first package allowed for up to 20,000 kilometers (12,000 miles) a year of driving. The second covered up to 30,000 kilometers of driving a year (18,000 miles). Both included all the electricity and battery switching a subscriber required. The packages were priced between $300 and $500 a month.

Agassi was upbeat. In an interview after the announcement, he boasted that the deals were so good, buyers "are actually showing up for financial reasons and less for altruistic reasons. When you get a car that is actually cheaper than a gasoline equivalent, you open up a much broader market than just the niche early adopters."

The Champions, meanwhile, were livid.

The packages were too expensive; they didn't show a big enough savings over gasoline-powered cars, the Champions said. Not everyone was as committed as they were.

Two months after the prices had been revealed and the media rolled up its collective sleeves to lunge at Better Place, Zohar Bali convened a meeting at the Visitor Center for a group of 15 Champions, to hear their complaints and suggestions.

It lasted four hours.

Bali was supposed to "support the Better Place offering, to convince the Champions," he explained. "I didn't have any other idea at the time. The Champions' commitment to the Better Place project was unbelievable. They were very smart and very opinionated. There was a physics professor among them and some very clever electrical engineers. They came with graphics to make their points."

Their main message: The packages were not just overpriced; they were too complicated.

"They wanted something much simpler, like pay-as-you-drive," Bali said.

Better Place sales manager Tal Bar agreed.

The original package pricing "was not a good business offering," Bar said. "20,000 kilometers a year was too high. You're paying for something you don't use."

The meeting was combative, Bali remembered. "We struggled for the full four hours."

By the end, Bali had been convinced.

"Even though I backed the original offering, I understood now that Better Place had made a mistake," he said. "So I told them, from today on, I'll be your representative at Better Place. I can't assure you all of your ideas will be accepted, but I'll present your ideas exactly as you've said them."

Bali confronted Better Place vice president of marketing Dafna Agassi, Shai Agassi's sister.

"I can't keep going with this offering. You should listen to what they're saying to us," Bali told her.

"No way—this is crazy," Dafna Agassi replied. "Shai is adamantly opposed to anything resembling pay-as-you-drive. You know that!"

Bali went on the sly to one of Better Place's sales managers, Odelia Cohen, who worked up a new idea, with some of Better Place's sales representatives.

The revised proposal lowered the number of kilometers in the starting package to just 12,000 a year, more clearly linked the price to the number of kilometers driven, and introduced a rollover policy—missing from the initial offering—where unused kilometers could be used for up to three years. The starting price: just $160 a month.

"It was very simple: Pay only for what you drive. Just what the Champions had asked for," Bali explained.

To sweeten the deal, Cohen came up with a new option where drivers could "lock in" a lower per-kilometer price if they agreed to prepay for the first four years.

Bali knew he could sell it to the Champions. Dafna Agassi eventually agreed.

They called a meeting with Shai Agassi.

Dafna was afraid of her brother's reaction, so Bali made the presentation with her.

Agassi shocked them with his response.

"You're right, that's the way to deliver it," he said, before adding, "I was always against the original proposal."

Bali was baffled. "How is it that he said this was the pricing he had wanted from the beginning and we had all been so afraid?"

Tal Bar also breathed a sigh of relief.

"From that point on, the packages became a lot easier to sell," he said. "Before that, it was almost impossible."

After the new pricing was announced, Bali received a phone call from Idan Ofer.

"Thank you," Ofer told Bali. "Now I understand it and can sell it myself."

The initial pricing for a Better Place subscription package in Denmark was also high—and it stayed that way. (There was not a similar Champions group in the country to generate the requisite outrage.)

But there was a silver lining.

Michael Kanellos, writing for the website Green Tech Media, analyzed the total cost of owning a Fluence Z.E. in Denmark. The car itself cost 27,496 Euros, and a five-year subscription plan would add 23,490 Euros, for a total of 50,986 Euros. An equivalent gasoline-powered car, including Denmark's 180 percent tax on vehicles with an internal combustion engine, Kanellos wrote, would cost around 40,230 Euros—10,000 Euro less—but that didn't include gas, whereas "the Better Place option includes all the electrons you need."

"The Fluence Z.E. in Denmark with all these factors looks like a good deal," he concluded.

"Good deal" were not the words Israelis associated with Better Place. Even with lower monthly rates, "when you said the name 'Better Place,' people said, oh, this is a car only for rich people," Tal Bar explained.

The negativity was coming too soon in the game. Bar switched jobs from Visitor Center guide to "switcher"—Better Place lingo for car salesperson—in 2011. But the cars weren't ready to sell—and wouldn't be for almost another year.

And when they were, the lower prices for the subscription packages would come back to bite Better Place—big time.

16

"WHO TRUSTS SHAI?"

The Series C had raised $200 million. But there was still $50 million missing that Shai Agassi had promised investor Ron Baron would be raised. More important, Better Place's business plan needed those funds to get through 2012.

An "investor's day" was convened March 26 at Better Place headquarters in Israel to put people at ease. Every investor, big or small, was invited to receive a complete briefing on where the company stood, financially and technologically, and where it was headed.

Andrey Zarur was one of the key organizers of the day.

Zarur, who had come up with the idea for Better Place with Agassi back in Davos, but who had then stepped out when he received another job offer, was back.

Zarur had stayed close with Agassi; now, Mike Granoff wanted to get him more involved as "someone external to the organization who could help identify gaps and screen the appropriate talent."

Agassi started the meeting by showing a chart on which colorful bubbles represented a supposed $50 million to be raised by Granoff and Zarur and another 50 million Euros that Agassi said was coming from the European Union Bank.

The two "50 million" bubbles surrounded a central figure: an operating budget of $250 million. The impression was that the money was already in the bank.

"So you see, we have two-hundred and fifty million coming in; there's nothing to worry about," Granoff recalled Agassi saying. "But we were, like, what if that doesn't happen? Shai presented all these vague ideas—it made it difficult to know what the real numbers were."

But there was no time for questions. Investors were whisked off to a show-and-tell field trip at the Rosh HaAyin headquarters.

"We went through all the ancillary products that the team was cooking up—like solutions for older homes with electricity management issues or where it was hard to install a charge spot, what to do with the second life of the battery," Granoff said. "Shai wanted to show that he was developing all these business pop-ups. It was comforting. Like we were on top of all these things. It seemed like we were creating value."

"Everyone left in high spirits," Zarur recalled.

The next day, Better Place convened a meeting of its top management in Rosh HaAyin. Despite Zarur's not having a formal day-to-day role in the company, Agassi invited him to join.

Agassi and Zarur opened the computer and called up the numbers they'd shown to the board the previous night.

"I immediately sensed a high level of discord," Zarur said.

On the screen were the projections for how many cars the business plan said needed to be sold in Israel—in 2012 and the years to come.

Moshe Kaplinsky was the first to fire back.

"No way," he barked, going full army chief. "I'm not signing up for those. Forget it."

"Tough luck," Agassi shot back. "I just showed those numbers to the board, so … "

"Hold on a minute," Zarur interrupted. He turned to Agassi and said in a hushed voice, "I assumed that you'd met with our people first. Are you saying that it was the other way around—that the numbers presented to the board hadn't been approved by management?"

But it was too late. The meeting devolved into finger pointing, Zarur remembered.

"People were yelling 'you haven't done this,' or 'I can't move that until R&D gives an answer.' The body language in the room was horrendous," Zarur said. "Kaplan and Shai were looking at the ground, not making eye contact. Shai is telling Kaplan he has to deliver on these numbers, and Kaplan is looking viscerally uncomfortable."

Then Agassi said something that shocked Zarur.

"Trust is the most important thing in a company. But trust is gained, trust is earned. And there are only two people in this room that I can trust."

The room turned deafeningly silent for what seemed like an eternity.

"There were only ten people in this room, and everyone knew I was one of the people Shai trusted. So who was the other?" Zarur wondered to himself.

Zarur broke the quiet. "Who feels Shai doesn't trust them?"

Five hands shot up.

"Who feels they can trust Shai?" Zarur continued.

Only two hands went up.

"OK, guys, this is a problem," Zarur said. "Do you realize how dangerous this is? This is not about science or financial projections. This is a management team that doesn't have cohesion. But this is a good thing. Now that it's out in the open, you all can start working on communication and alignment. You don't need me in the room now; you need to start sorting things out as a management team."

Zarur got up to leave. As he headed to the door, "Shai was beaming laser shots out of his face at me," Zarur recalled. "It led to a massive fallout."

Several managers approached Zarur afterward to thank him for getting everything out into the open.

Agassi, on the other hand, sent a furious email to Zarur.

"What you did in that meeting was out of bounds, it was bullshit. How could you do that to me?" Agassi yelled at Zarur from behind the safe boundaries of Microsoft Outlook. "You betrayed my trust! You stabbed me in the back!"

"What are you talking about?" Zarur responded. "Do you not understand that these people don't trust you and don't feel that you trust them? Don't you see how dysfunctional that is?"

"That meeting was very negative to the CEO," Agassi wrote.

"Why? What was so bad?" Zarur replied.

"Because you're giving them an excuse to not do their job," Agassi said. "Now there's a 'board member' on their side. And they're going to use that to hide, to not do what they need to do."

Zarur thought about what Agassi had just written for a moment.

"Were they really not doing their jobs? Was Shai in any way correct?" he wondered. "But even if he was, that was still not a good thing. It was a symptom of a much bigger problem. That these people were not doing their jobs, and there was no plan to replace them or help them or anything else."

Mike Granoff had been uneasy about the trust and communication problems in the company for a few years. After Agassi's meltdown at the contentious 2010 London board meeting, Granoff had written Agassi a detailed email:

"Like everybody, you have strengths and weaknesses," Granoff said. "The complication, I think, is that one of your weaknesses is that you can be reactionary to critiques, thereby deterring people from offering them in good faith, and as a result, problems can continue to fester. It is not often that I have enough confidence in my own insight to second-guess yours. But on those rare occasions, I have certainly hesitated to discuss it with you, and I am sure there are others for whom the same can be said."

Zarur and Agassi's relationship never really recovered.

"It was gradual," Zarur said. "It wasn't that one day there was a change of attitude. It took many months to unravel."

The change took place mostly on Agassi's side.

"I never had Shai on a pedestal like the rest of the company," Zarur continued. "I knew him from the beginning. I knew he was capable of brilliance but also of some stupid stuff. I met him first as a friend, not as a boss or a co-founder. I knew his kids, went out with him and his wife. I'd seen how he could exaggerate and employ hyperbole in investor meetings. It was my job to bring things back to reality. To temper expectations. That worked for many years. But when he told me he had no plan to get back on track, that made me very nervous."

At the same time, Zarur felt strangely liberated. Freed of the need to defend Agassi or the company's policy, he became Better Place's walking prophet of doom, holding meetings and exchanging emails with the other board members.

"I would say, 'Guys, I don't like this plan, it's overly aggressive, it doesn't have a lot of room for failure, if anything goes wrong we'll be in trouble,'" he recalled. "Fortunately, we had just closed the Series C round, so we still had enough money in case a course correction was necessary."

But how much did Better Place actually have in the bank? It became an obsession for Zarur. Not knowing, he said, "scared the shit out of me. Did Shai know? I don't think anyone really knew."

The lack of a CFO was the biggest problem, Zarur felt. "We had all this information being put forth by a fragmented finance group, with no head to pull it all together and show the board what we're spending. We needed a world-class CFO who could do a better job of handicapping all these different opportunities we were going after."

As Zarur gathered more data and spoke with more people in the company, he came to a stunning conclusion: Better Place's burn rate—the amount of money it was spending every day on salaries, offices, travel, equipment, suppliers, utilities and importing cars—had reached a staggering $1 million a day.

At that rate, and assuming the company didn't make a last-minute pivot from its increasingly unsustainable business plan, the $200 million Series C would run out by October.

"By May, I was now screaming, yelling at the top of my lungs to anyone who would listen that we need to cut down expenses," Zarur said. "If I were to say to the public the magic words—'we have six months of cash'—everyone would panic. The auditors would say 'You're not a going concern.' And then it would be, holy shit, what are we going to do?"

Michael Edelcheck, GE's representative looking after its investment in Better Place, had come to the same conclusion.

On a visit to Israel, he confronted Agassi: "By my calculations, you'll run out of money by October." But Agassi reassured him.

"We're done building the switch stations, that's the biggest burn," Agassi replied. "Now we'll cut back on the deployment team, we'll reduce headcount. And remember, we have the fifty million Euros from the EU Bank and the money Mike and Andrey are bringing in."

Edelcheck calmed down. Agassi had bought a bit more time.

MAMILLA

The turmoil inside the company hadn't leaked out beyond the gleaming facade of Better Place's Visitor Center, now converted into a full-fledged sales facility.

The Vision Room had been dismantled and the tablet computers and their stands were retired. A small sea of tasteful cubicles with bright colors was erected in their place, housing a sales team of half a dozen.

The press, still antagonistic, was mainly angry about the price of the car and the packages—it wasn't privy to the situation inside the company. In

May 2012, when the first Fluence Z.E.s for sale arrived in Israel, it was an opportunity to do some damage control.

Better Place's PR team organized a three-day press "event."

A dozen automotive and technology journalists from Israel and around the world met on the morning of May 9 at Pi Glilot. After a morning briefing on the technology and business model behind Better Place, Julie Mullins, the company's head of PR, divided the journalists into twos and threes. Each group was given a Fluence Z.E.

The OSCAR unit in each car had been pre-programmed with a driving route to Jerusalem. Each was a slightly different "adventure," so that the journalists could swap stories upon arrival. Every itinerary included a stop at a switching station, for the full Better Place experience.

Jerusalem is 70 kilometers from Tel Aviv, but a world away spiritually, architecturally and, in particular for the Fluence Z.E., topographically.

While Tel Aviv is mostly flat, with a good share of wide straight boulevards and sleek expressways, just getting to Jerusalem involves a series of steep ascents and perilous turns, punctuated by sudden drops. There wouldn't be much opportunity to try out the Fluence Z.E.'s cruise control, still an unusual accessory for Israeli cars in 2012.

Once in Jerusalem, the roads—while modern enough and paved—often follow narrow old donkey and horse paths, twisting maddeningly and changing names without reason.

It was the perfect opportunity for OSCAR to show off its GPS and power management chops and for drivers to play the regenerative braking "game" to gain back power on declines.

A press conference was scheduled for early evening, after everyone had arrived in Jerusalem, checked in, showered and met for dinner at the city's swanky Mamilla Hotel, with its rooftop restaurant directly overlooking the Old City.

Before and after the meal, the journalists had the opportunity to meet and mingle with Better Place's executive team. Agassi was there, of course, along with Barak Hershkovitz, Moshe Kaplinsky, Sidney Goodman and Dan Cohen. They were peppered with questions throughout the evening.

Some were mundane. "Will there be enough time to buy potato chips while the car's battery is switched?"

Others reflected the worried-parent trope. "Will my neighbor's child get electrified if he tries to plug his bike into a charge spot?"

One journalist, seemingly serious, asked, "Will OSCAR reveal your latest route to your mistress when your wife gets behind the wheel?"

The press event worked.

The resulting articles were flattering, gushing at times. They reversed—at least for the moment—some of the damage caused by the price announcements.

The New York Times' Jim Motavalli rode to Jerusalem with Hershkovitz, "the ophthalmologist who doubles as Better Place's chief technical officer," as Motavalli wrote. "I never got an eye exam, but I did learn quite a bit about the interface in the Fluence," which he described as "a delight to drive."

"I thought it handled well," he continued. "It's a well-appointed and finished five-passenger sedan," not as nice as the standalone Leaf or Chevy Volt, but "comfortable and nicely built … that should prove attractive on the world market."

The price of the Fluence Z.E. was high, Motavalli pointed out, but "in line with similarly equipped gas cars in Israel, which fulfills Agassi's mission of not forcing consumers to pay more to go electric."

Better Place had "if not an assured future, at least a bright vision of what the future could be," he added.

Simon Rozendaal, from the Dutch publishing house Elsevier, wasn't so sure.

"I do not know if this system holds a future," he wrote, "but it sounds somewhat nice. Many sensible people think so too: That's why Shai Agassi, who founded Better Place, has been given $750 million."

Rolf Bos from the Netherlands' Volkskrant drank liberally from the Better Place Kool-Aid. He reported Agassi boasting during the press event that by 2016, Better Place expected that half of all cars sold in Israel will be electric.

"Is that too optimistic?" Agassi wondered. "We are a country of early adopters. We cannot afford to be dependent on oil."

Bos also revealed a previously undisclosed (and never implemented) trade-in plan whereby Better Place "will swap a petrol car for an electric," a Better Place representative told the reporter.

Bos had only one complaint: When you go for a battery switch, there's no station attendant "to clean the windshield."

Nikki Gordon Bloomfield from Green Car Reports liked that OSCAR could differentiate between individual drivers, thereby providing "accurate range predictions based on each person's individual driving style and history." (The car greeted each driver by name.)

Danish journalist Mette Winkler, from the Copenhagen newspaper Borsen, compared OSCAR favorably to KITT, the artificial intelligence in David Hasselhoff's 1982 Pontiac Trans Am from the American TV series "Knight Rider."

"Just noiseless," he added.

Indeed, Winkler added, "it is impossible to say if the car is 'on' at all. It's all silent. No motor buzz, just a green 'go' indicates the car is ready."

Julie Mullins summed up the press event with an anecdote about a particular reporter, "a well-respected car journalist who had been really hard on us. After a day with the car, going through a switch and talking to Shai, she was so moved, I saw actual tears welling up. All her writing had been negative up to that point. She had been very skeptical about coming to Israel, but afterward, she was so moved by what we were trying to accomplish that she asked, 'How can I help you?' She told me, 'What you're doing is really important. And it's not just about a car.' I remember thinking, if only we could bottle this and get everyone into the same experience."

CHARGE SPOT INSTALLATION

The journalists were happy. And by the end of May, 113 cars had been sold.

Agassi boasted in a tweet that this "was five cars every day ... 113 people who decided to lead the change."

But getting the car into a customer's garage led to a distressing discovery.

Better Place's spreadsheets were built around the expectation that to install a home charge spot would require a single technician working for a few hours.

Here's what actually was involved.

Before a sale could even be initiated, a Better Place representative had to come out to the potential customer's house to ascertain that the buyer had a place for the charge spot, and that Better Place could manage all the appropriate wiring and electrical connection.

Customers needed a dedicated parking spot, which excluded most renters and people with on-street parking. Better Place fought but ultimately lost a regulatory battle to receive permission to install charge spots on the street; the Israel Electric Corporation claimed that as its domain.

Even if the IEC had agreed to install charge spots on the street, regulations to earmark parking spots for electric cars, similar to parking reserved for people with disabilities, would be needed to make it work. That process would have had to go all the way up to the Knesset for approval.

Better Place did manage to install a few charge spots in public parking lots. But no laws prevented non-electric cars from taking the spaces.

If a customer had a designated space, the Better Place representative would bring all the appropriate paperwork so that the homeowner could get approval from any relevant bodies. For Israelis who owned their own freestanding home, this was easy. But the vast majority of Israelis live in condominium complexes.

And as with condominiums everywhere, Israelis have to go through the homeowners' association, or the *va'ad habayit,* to receive signed approval to make changes of any kind to the exterior of the building or in shared spaces that would affect the other residents.

Many *va'ad habayit* members were concerned about who would pay for the electricity.

The Israel Electric Corporation allowed only its own people to open an individual's power box to connect the Better Place charge spot. It could take several months to get a technician.

So Better Place created a workaround. They would connect the charge spot to the overall apartment complex first (the *va'ad habayit's* domain) rather than an individual's power box. When the IEC was ready, they could come and switch the cables.

In those months, however, the bill would come to the *va'ad habayit,* and the car owner would have to write a reimbursement check.

That led to worried questions.

"What if the Better Place driver refuses to pay us back?" *va'ad habayit* members asked.

"Will the other apartment owners complain about paying for someone else's electricity?"

"Who's responsible if there's a malfunction? Or a fire?"

"What if Better Place goes out of business? Will we be stuck with the bill?"

Better Place came up with legal solutions for everything—documents assuring the *va'ad habayit* that the homeowner committed to pay his or her bill, and caps on the amount of time the cumbersome arrangement would last.

Faxes and emails streamed back and forth between Better Place, the *va'ad habayit* and the potential car owner, all before the Fluence Z.E. was even purchased. Some cases required in-person meetings. Technicians and Better Place representatives returned again and again to convince reluctant *va'ad habayit* members that driving electric was the future, and that having an environmentally friendly Better Place charge spot in their building would reflect well on the community.

Frustrated, some drivers bailed after the initial meeting. But in most cases, Better Place prevailed.

"We convinced the *va'ad habayit* that we'd provide what they needed. If they had concerns, we'd answer them, one by one, patiently," Zohar Bali said.

Once the papers had been signed, Better Place usually sent not one but two technicians in a truck loaded with equipment to complete the installation. The process inevitably took more time than expected.

A few hours became a few days and a few visits.

All this was over budget, as was any kind of technical support: Once a charge spot was up and running, what would happen if a problem required a technician to come back? Better Place's spreadsheets had never accounted for this.

Indeed, Better Place had promised free installation of the home charge spot as part of the purchase price of the car in Israel. (Better Place Denmark took a different approach and tacked on a one-time fee of $1,868 to the subscription package for installation.)

Home charge spot installation is generally not free in other countries. In North America, an off-the-shelf charge spot such as a GE WattStation or a Bosch Power Max will you set you back $600 to $800. The average installation cost is $1,350, according to the U.S. Department of Energy.

In that respect, the Israeli costs were in line with their international counterparts. Eitan Hon estimated that the total cost to Better Place for installation, including the cost of the charge spot itself, was $2,000 to $3,000.

INFLECTION POINT

The result of the real-world cost implications of "free" installation in Israel, exacerbated by the need to pay for 50 percent of the expensive electric batteries up front, was that Better Place was losing money on every car it sold.

Better Place had only one source of ongoing revenue: the subscription packages. Other options—such as becoming the infrastructure provider for non-switchable battery, plug-in electric cars like the Chevy Volt—had been vetoed years earlier as not fitting into the company's laser-focus business vision. Any profits from acting as a virtual power plant for utility partners was far off in the future—and in any case, that plan was slated only for Denmark, not for the main "beta" country of Israel.

But that single source of revenue dropped by half when the Champions rebelled. Calculated over a four-year period, subscription revenue barely covered Better Place's share of the battery, let alone the company's considerable overhead. Now add in up to $3,000 for a free charge spot and the full cost of installation.

The inescapable conclusion: *The more cars Better Place sold, the more money it would lose.*

The small profit margin Better Place made on each car—a few thousand dollars—wasn't enough to close the gap.

The Champions weren't wrong—at the higher prices, no one would have bought the car. But the lower prices created an untenable Catch-22.

Maybe in a few years, if battery prices dropped; if installation could be streamlined; if cheaper charge spots could be designed or even bought from a third party; if Better Place could cut headcount and stop giving out granola bars; if revenue from operating virtual power plants for utilities would kick in—there might be hope.

Better Place critics have charged that this was the inflection point, the moment of realization that the model that Agassi and his team had doggedly been pursuing since Davos did not and could never work.

The most dramatic response would have been to shut down operations. Short of that, the company's management might seriously have considered pivoting to a different approach.

What might that have looked like?

A more open attitude toward fast charge as an alternative to switch.

A more limited test instead of a full-blown rollout—perhaps just in a few-mile corridor between Herzliya and Ra'anana, two wealthy suburbs north of Tel Aviv.

A turn to China and departure from Israel, where the numbers weren't adding up.

Better Place instead insisted the company just needed enough time—a long enough runway—and costs would surely come down.

Better financing than Renault's paltry 50 percent deal for the batteries could be secured.

Battery prices could drop.

General Motors or some other manufacturer might agree to make a switchable-battery car.

Renault would see the light and reduce the price tag for the Fluence Z.E., restoring some of the lost profit margin Better Place had been counting on, while driving up sales, until Better Place became the unstoppable juggernaut it was meant to be.

"It is true that we needed a little bit longer than we thought at the beginning," Agassi conceded to Matthias Lambrecht of Financial Times Deutschland. "But it is absolutely fine to be delayed in a project of such dimension. It really doesn't matter if we start our business six months earlier or later."

Still, if change of any sort—big or small—was going to happen, this was probably the last time it would have been practical: prior to the launch of a full-blown sales and marketing campaign, before a significant number of real customers began buying the company's cars, and while much of the Series C round's $200 million was presumably still in the bank.

JANTELOVEN

Better Place needed to put on a happy public face. The arrival of the Fluence Z.E. in Denmark presented the opportunity.

"We invited all our customers who'd already received their Fluence Z.E., as well as Better Place employees, to come down to the harbor, where we organized a big brunch with eggs, bacon, beans, fruit and lots of fish," said Susanne Tolstrup, Better Place Denmark's director of communications. "There were blue Better Place balloons everywhere and about 50 Fluences. Our CEO gave a speech, and then we set out in a parade of Fluences through the streets of Copenhagen."

The parade stretched from one end of the city to the other. It drove past the parliament, through the part of town that dates from the 16th century, then ended up in a suburb, where several cars pulled into one of Denmark's switch stations to give the visiting journalists a demonstration.

One of the Fluence Z.E.s was driven by the private chauffeur of the Danish royal family. It pulled out of the parade line when the car passed the Amalienborg Palace and parked there.

"It was a very proud moment," Tolstrup recalled. "That day, we felt like we were going to conquer the world."

First, though, they'd have to conquer Danish public opinion, which was not kind to Better Place.

Tolstrup says that so-called *Janteloven*—or "the Law of Jante"—was partly to blame.

"*Janteloven* is an integral part of Danish culture," she explained.

It began as a list of 10 rules, created in 1933 by Danish author Aksel Sandemose to govern how Scandinavians should think about one another, and to instill a sense of collective modesty.

Among the rules:

"You're not to think you are anything special."

"You're not to think you are as good as us."

"You're not to think you are smarter than us."

"You're not to convince yourself that you are better than us."

"You're not to think you know more than us."

And the ultimate keep-you-in-your-place commandment: "You're not to think that you can teach us anything good."

By every definition of *Janteloven,* Better Place failed the test.

"When Better Place was first established, its ambitions were outrageously high," Tolstrup explained. "Better Place positioned itself like it wanted to conquer the whole world in one attempt.

"The Danes didn't like that too much. Many people said, 'That idea is pretty crazy, you can't do it.' To believe in your vision so strongly and be so confident of your idea is not very Danish. Obviously, there were some people cheering for Better Place to become a success, but many were expecting us to fail."

Better Place investor HSBC's Anthony Bernbaum said there was no other choice.

"Better Place is a small company in an ocean of big car manufacturers and oil companies, and therefore has had to make some noise to be recognized," he told the Danish publication Borsen.

DONG—Denmark Oil and Natural Gas—also got caught up in the *Janteloven* tendency towards suspicion of overachievement.

"People here were surprised that a state-owned energy company would invest in a project with a risk profile like Better Place had," Tolstrup said. "DONG's share in Better Place Denmark was only 18.3 percent, but DONG got a lot of criticism for its decision to invest in the first place. People thought it was an extremely risky way to spend taxpayer money."

On March 12, 2012, Anders Eldrup was ousted as CEO of DONG. The official reason was that Eldrup had hired four individuals with huge bonuses and extraordinary severance deals to build up DONG's green portfolio. DONG's board of directors called Eldrup's behavior "a breach of his duties as CEO" and removed him without warning.

Tolstrup thinks that DONG's involvement with Better Place might also have played a role.

"The media blamed Eldrup for using Better Place as a sort of 'greenwashing' project," she said. "It wasn't that DONG was hiding something, but that it was pointing attention away from its fossil-fuel energy projects which were, at the time, the company's main business."

Johnny Hansen thinks that's overreaching.

Hansen replaced Jens Moberg as CEO of Better Place Denmark in March 2011, after Moberg had had a heart attack six months earlier. Hansen had been the CEO of transportation giant Arriva Scandinavia, which he had transformed into the largest private transportation company in the region, with 7,000 employees and revenues of $600 million.

"DONG was doing all sorts of investments," Hansen said. "Better Place was very small. I wouldn't say that Better Place didn't factor into what happened at all, but that would be exaggerating our role."

Whatever the official reason, a $25 million round of local financing for Better Place Denmark being discussed at the time never happened.

"If the CEO hadn't been kicked out, we probably would have gotten that money," Hansen said.

Just as with the Renault spy scandal, bad luck had struck Better Place again.

17

"NOT FOR EVERYONE"

"**S**he's not for everyone. Only for people who won't accept things as they are."

"She's not everyone's kind of thing. Just for those who are fed up with unstable gas prices."

"Not everyone's going to love her. Only the ones who no longer want to poison the air that we breathe."

"She's definitely not going to be love at first sight, except for those who want great performance without the fuss."

"She's not for everyone. Only for those who believe they have a right to make the world a better place."

Better Place's first commercial dropped on Israeli television and the Internet in July 2012 and was met with a collective head scratching.

If it's not for me, then who is it for exactly? viewers wondered. And *are they talking about a car or a woman?*

The response to Better Place's carefully crafted marketing production was exacerbated by the commercial's faux-subversive style: fast cuts, swirling smog, pensive teenagers looking longingly out of windows, all set to the kind of imminent-apocalypse musical score that plays in action films during the penultimate moment before the hero regains his purpose and returns to slay the bad guys.

The hero in this case was a racy male model in a tight black T-shirt with a voice so inelegantly dubbed into English as to make early 1980s MTV videos look like the paragon of lip-sync perfection.

In the ad's 30 seconds, a car—presumably a Fluence Z.E., although it's never shown—drives through a generic European city. (It was filmed in Prague.) A pretty woman sipping coffee at an outdoor cafe rises robotically to follow the car, a man pumping gas drops the nozzle and lurches in the car's direction, while drivers stuck in a traffic-clogged highway tunnel impulsively abandon their vehicles to Zombie-walk toward the Fluence, which speeds away.

The commercial reflected Better Place's attitude that the company need do little more than sit back and watch consumers flock to its showroom doors.

It was exactly how Agassi had defined the issue back in 2008.

During his interview with Daniel Roth of Wired, Agassi told his team in Palo Alto during a three-day strategy meeting that the problem is "We still think we're selling to them. We're not. It's not us to them. It's them to us. You see, people want this to happen; we just happen to be in the way of their getting what they want. We can't give them the car fast enough … This is going to be a community. We just need to get out of their way."

Agassi concluded his speech succinctly. "They're going to be zealots."

Better Place's commercial did not exactly inspire Israelis to run out and buy a Fluence Z.E.

The stigma that had started with the high price of the car and subscription package was the first blow. But there was a bigger problem, one that no commercial could remedy: Ordinary Israelis simply don't buy "C" class cars like the Renault Fluence.

They get them free from their employers. They even get free gas.

The vast majority—some 70 percent—of five-seat family sedans on Israel's roads are company cars, provided to employees as corporate perks and leased from one of the big Israeli fleet operators—Hertz, Avis, Shlomo Sixt and Eldan.

Some are used for commuting to work. Others become the family car, ferrying the kids to classes and soccer matches and transporting the average Israeli family of five to its annual summer camping trip at the Sea of Galilee.

And when these drivers gas up, they don't even need to swipe a credit card. A system known as a "Dalkan" (a play on words with "delek"—the Hebrew word for "fuel" and also the name of one of Israel's leading service station chains) makes pumping gas an almost magical experience. Sensors recognize when the nozzle has been inserted into the tank and automatically turn on the pump. You can throw away the receipt—it's all on the house.

But if you were getting your gas for free, a potent part of Better Place's main sales pitch—that driving electric would save you money—went out the window. That left the environmental argument, but unless you were a "greenie," as Zohar Bali put it, why would you choose a car that forced you to change your driving behaviors, cope with range anxiety, and stop every 120 kilometers or so to switch batteries?

The market didn't see the Fluence Z.E. as a budget-conscious leap into an electric future. It saw it as inconvenient. It certainly wouldn't go to the top of the list of cars to choose from when one's current three-year lease ran out.

USAGE TAX

As good as the company car deal is in Israel, it's not entirely free. Employees who receive a car from their job have to pay a "usage tax." It's deducted straight from the employee's paycheck, along with income tax, social security and national health insurance, and is calculated as a percentage of the retail price of the car.

The $35,000 Fluence Z.E. was no exception—its usage tax was the same as any comparably-priced gasoline-powered "C" class car.

It could have been even higher: The government wanted to tax the $15,000 battery, too. Determined petitioning from Ziva Patir helped nip that extra charge from the bill.

"Everyone was against us," Patir recalled. "All the other importers said, if that's the case, I can say that the tires are not part of the car and I don't want to pay taxes on the tires. But we were able to persuade the authorities that the battery is more like fuel and shouldn't be included. It was really unprecedented."

Patir kept pressing for an even lower usage tax—as an incentive for drivers to try out a new technology.

"We asked the government to make an exception for the Fluence Z.E., to say that even though a fleet operator would buy the car for NIS 100,000, it should be treated for the purposes of usage tax as if it costs only NIS 60,000," Patir explained.

The tax authorities were not impressed.

"'We want more efficient small cars on the road,'" Patir recalled the response. "'We don't want to help with a big car like the Fluence Z.E.'"

Globes reporter Dubi Ben-Gedalyahu had a more cynical take.

"The government didn't want to lose the income it made from taxing gasoline," he said. "They get about five billion shekels [$1.3 billion] a year from that."

Patir had one final argument.

Usage tax is considered to be on employees' "enjoyment" of their vehicles. Because the all-electric Fluence Z.E. was less convenient, requiring frequent stops at battery switch stations, drivers would enjoy it less—and therefore the car should be taxed less.

Shai Agassi quickly nixed that idea.

"If you use that argument," he told Patir, "we'll never sell the car to individual buyers."

In the end, the only discounts available to Better Place drivers receiving corporate cars came from the companies themselves; several big Israeli firms, including IBM and Amdocs, kicked back a few hundred shekels to drivers as an incentive.

IBM and Amdocs were Better Place clients and may have wanted to stay in the company's good graces, but that impulse didn't extend to Israel Chemicals. Idan Ofer remembers trying in vain to persuade his company to bring a few Fluence Z.E.s into its large fleet of company cars.

"Israel Chemicals employees travel long distances," a source close to the company told Globes. "The electric car isn't suitable."

A different kind of tax issue was hitting the "C" class car market in Denmark, making the Fluence Z.E. unexpectedly unattractive.

In 2008, the average car in Denmark sold for about $30,000. By the time the Fluence Z.E. hit the market, four years later, the average price was down to $17,000.

Had car manufacturing become miraculously cheaper? No. Turned off by Denmark's crushing 180 percent tax on gasoline-powered cars, Danes were going for tiny, two-door "A" class cars instead.

The Fluence Z.E. was out of fashion before it even came to market.

RESIDUAL VALUE

Shai Agassi and Better Place's management knew that most "C" class cars were provided as company benefits. But they were convinced the Fluence Z.E. could overcome employee resistance and become a fleet favorite. As one Better Place executive explained, "Shai believed 'If you build it, they will come.'"

The leasing companies weren't buying it; the numbers didn't make sense.

Leasing companies make money by providing brand-new cars to corporations for three to five years, then reselling those cars to consumers.

Better Place boasted early on that "it would sign its 'main agreements' for the purchase of electric cars with dozens of fleets that together owned over 70,000 cars," Dubi Ben-Gedalyahu reminded readers in Globes. "The assumption was that the 'fleets would wait in line to receive their cars.'"

But the leasing companies were worried. Their business model is heavily based on the "residual value" of the car—that is, how well does a car hold its value when it comes time to sell it to the public?

The electric Fluence Z.E. had no sales history, so its residual value was impossible to predict.

"The leasing companies would say to us, 'It sounds great, but let's wait a year to see if it works. We're not early adopters,'" Zohar Bali recalled. "They preferred to go with a safe purchase, like a Toyota Corolla, that they knew they could easily sell after three years."

The Fluence Z.E. suffered from yet another strike: It was a Renault.

"Renault doesn't have a very good image in Israel," Ben-Gedalyahu says, bluntly. The Fluence Z.E. "wasn't terrible—the quality and specifications were decent and the car had a big screen. But since Renault doesn't have the best brand reputation here, it leads to a lower resale value and a faster depreciation. Better Place knew all this, they knew it was a compromise, but they didn't have any other choice."

The Fluence Z.E. was also more expensive for a leasing company to buy than a comparable gasoline-powered car.

Fleet operators like Hertz and Avis generally expect to receive a 15 to 25 percent discount off the retail price of the car. But because Better Place's profit margin was so small, "our discount always came in 10 percent less than everyone else," Bali said. "If I'm Avis and I have to purchase 1,000 cars, and Toyota is offering me a 20 percent discount for Corollas but

Better Place is only offering a 15 percent discount," well, you can do the math.

And so did the leasing companies.

LONDON REDUX

"The objective is to keep Shai as CEO," Andrey Zarur told the Better Place board of directors in a special session in Idan Ofer's London apartment.

The agenda: to discuss the board's growing concerns with disappointing sales and unrestrained spending.

"But we have to create a support organization around Shai to allow him to do the things he knows how to do, like build a product and sell," Zarur continued. "We need to allow Better Place to function as a real company."

The board had returned to London, nearly two years to the day from Agassi's near resignation. And like that previous meeting, the June 2012 special session was being held without Shai Agassi.

"I had just given them my *shpiel*," Zarur said, "about how I believe, based on what I know so far, not on any materials we may see from Shai later today, that by October we'll have just 30 days left of cash. And how we have no plan if we reach this point."

Zarur wasn't proposing that Agassi be deposed. Instead, he was calling for an executive-level restructure: Hire a proper chief operating officer to run the company day-to-day, and—his longtime request—bring in a CFO, "so that I can pick up the phone and ask, what are our accounts receivable, our payables, our burn rate—basically so I can know when we're running out of money," Zarur explained.

"A powerful CFO might have to make some pretty harsh decisions as to what needed to be cut. Those might even be projects near and dear to Shai's heart."

Agassi hadn't moved on the CFO hire and Zarur was exasperated. The CFO, he proposed, would have a dual reporting structure—to Agassi as CEO and directly to the board.

Zarur outlined his plan to the group: In two hours, when it met formally with Agassi, the board should set up a nominating and recruiting committee to fill the COO and CFO positions. Zarur also proposed a mechanism to keep costs (and Agassi) in check: All expenses over $10,000 would have to be approved by the board. Agassi would need the board's OK to make any new hires.

Finally, Zarur wanted to form an audit committee that could get to the bottom of whether his analysis was correct: Was the company on the verge of bankruptcy?

Everyone agreed—except Agassi.

"Shai did not take it well," Zarur remembered.

"You're taking my company away from me!" he said. "Why don't you just fire me?"

"It was very clear that he was going to fight this tooth and nail," Zarur said. "In hindsight, I should have known that this wouldn't have flown with Shai, that he would take this as a huge slap in the face. I was naive in thinking that this had even a chance of happening."

Agassi tried to assure the board that money was not going to be a problem. He was still working on that 50 million Euro loan from the European Union Bank, which he predicted had "a ninety percent probability of happening."

"No, Shai," Zarur countered. "It has maybe a three percent probability. We are not in agreement. You have a very different perception than I do of what's going on."

Agassi claimed that the $50 million that was missing from the Series C "was in progress. We have people working on it."

It turned out that Agassi had started quietly meeting with investors without informing the board.

Zarur thought this was crazy; he'd already tried.

"New investors don't want to put money into a company if it hasn't met the milestones set in the previous round," Zarur explained. "And we were way behind schedule. In the Series C we said we'd have cars on the road by January, but they didn't start selling until May. We said we'd have the switch stations all up and running, but they weren't.

"This is what's known as the 'don't throw good money after bad' rule. Every large group of investors we talked to told us that. At this point, the entire world had seen our plan. It was clear we wouldn't be able to raise any more money until we'd met our deliverables."

Agassi scored one major point: a week to review the resolutions before they were voted on.

Agassi left the room, allowing the board to discuss for a few more minutes what had happened.

"We came to a decision that, although Shai may kick and scream and threaten, these things are necessary and must be implemented," Zarur said.

Zarur assured the board that he still believed Agassi was the best CEO for the company. "I was conflicted by the loyalty that I had to my friend, and my legal responsibility to the shareholders. The economic upside for me from Better Place was very small, and I didn't want to lose my best friend over all this shit."

Indeed, once a CFO and COO were hired, Zarur planned to leave the board "and try to salvage whatever relationship I could with Shai. I told the board this."

GOING WOBBLY

In the following weeks, though, little changed.

No committees were formed to find and hire a CFO and COO, there were no cuts to staff and spending, Agassi still had carte blanche to write checks as he saw fit and the burn rate continued to soar. Zarur's only success: An audit committee was formed to follow up on the company's cash position.

"Shai was very smart about it," Mike Granoff explained. "After everyone went their separate ways, he flew back to Israel and went over to Idan's house. He spent a day or two there persuading Idan how no CEO could accept such limitations, how no CEO could be managed like this, and that this is the death knell of the company if it goes through. I remember talking to Idan before that and saying 'Don't go wobbly,' but he went wobbly, and the resolution was never adopted."

Board member Alan Salzman quit in frustration, in July 2012. He had been moving this way since Agassi's relocation, complaining at the time that "I didn't invest in an Israeli company; I invested in an American one."

It was a big blow to the prestige and stability of the company.

Even Granoff was on the verge of getting out.

"I didn't quit, but I wish I had," he said. "It would have shaken people up."

A month after the board meeting, Agassi summoned Granoff into his office in Rosh HaAyin. The meeting lasted more than an hour. Agassi was pacing.

"Where's the fifty million dollars you promised me?" Agassi demanded. He pointed to a picture of a battery switch station on the wall. "You see that? I put that in the ground. Five years from dream to implementation. No one in the world could have done that."

Andrey Zarur, who was already on shaky ground with Agassi, had it even worse. He became *persona non grata*.

"Horrible things were being said about me, in social media, in meetings," he recalled.

Tami Chotoveli lobbed a flurry of oblique messages on Facebook and Twitter. They didn't name names, but the intended destination was hard to mistake.

"I have zero tolerance for back stabbers!!!"

"Sometimes, the person you'd take a bullet for ends up being the one behind the gun."

"Nobody likes a liar. In the long-run, the truth reveals itself. Either you own up to your own actions or your actions will ultimately own you."

Agassi wasn't silent either.

One tweet: "Those who disappoint, cheat themselves … I am easily fooled, ONCE!"

And another: "Friends are either True or not friends."

In perhaps the most spiteful and painful public declaration of their business and personal "divorce," Zarur's founding role as Agassi's partner in coming up with the idea for Better Place back in Davos was erased from the company's website and materials.

Chotoveli balanced her angry tweets with lovey-dovey status updates and photos of the happy couple. Agassi was now living with Chotoveli, who stood by her man even as the world was crumbling around them both.

"Being loved by the right person allows you to move forward because you know someone always has your back," Chotoveli declared on Twitter.

"When you find your ONE … you become someone different, someone better."

Andrey Zarur was definitely not feeling the love.

"What did Andrey do?" Granoff asked. "He had the best interests of the company at heart. He told Shai more than once, 'I'm here to help you. You're going to get yourself fired if you don't do this.' But Shai heard this only as 'This guy is turning against me too.' Paranoia is a self-fulfilling prophecy."

ROAD TRIP

During the heady days surrounding the signing of the Oslo Peace Accords, in 1993, and the subsequent peace treaty with Jordan, in 1994, many Israelis dreamed of making a truly international road trip, driving from Tel Aviv to Damascus for a plate of hummus and beans—a farfetched fantasy considering the state of the Middle East today.

But a lengthy road trip within Israel is definitely doable.

While the country is only 9.3 miles wide at its most narrow point, it is nearly 300 miles from northern Metula, along the Lebanese border, to Eilat, situated at the intersection of Jordan and Egypt, in the south.

Shai Agassi may have been trying to clear his head as he set out August 19, 2012 on exactly that trip, in his midnight-blue Fluence Z.E. But the result was a triumph of publicity that captivated the media once more and, at least temporarily, changed the conversation inside Better Place.

Agassi made his country-spanning journey entirely by switching batteries at stations along the way, demonstrating that the Better Place network worked. Drivers could feel comfortable that nowhere in Israel was out of range.

Agassi took to Twitter to document his trip.

At 7:51 a.m., he tweeted that he would be "driving around the whole of Israel today," with his brother, Tal, and father, Reuven, in tow.

Agassi wore a black T-shirt and a pair of faded jeans. His father wore blue shorts and a pink button-down shirt.

The first battery switch was in Haifa, at 8:15 a.m. An hour and a half later, Agassi tweeted a picture of his car "at the border with Lebanon ... one day we will be able to drive to the other side and shake hands."

By noon, Agassi had reached Mount Hermon in the Golan Heights, where he snapped a photo of himself with his arms spread wide in a victory salute in front of his Fluence Z.E.

There were no more pictures for the next seven hours until Agassi surfaced again, posed with Tal and Reuven, in front of the Eilat Airport.

"7:30 p.m. south most point in Israel Eilat ... In less time than it takes to charge a single battery ... Israel covered," he tweeted.

Agassi would have been forgiven for taking a break after an exhausting day behind the wheel and checking into one of the Red Sea resort's luxurious 5-star spa hotels. But a few hours later, Agassi was tweeting again—this time a picture of his dashboard, showing 1,000 kilometers covered so far that day, with the caption "Possible only (with battery switch) #Betterplace."

By 12:42 a.m., Agassi was home. "1,150 km ... round-trip around Israel ... Same distance as California South-North ... #onlyInIsrael."

The whole trip took 16 hours and involved 11 battery switches.

Agassi called his road trip "an amazing epiphany [to realize] what it means to have a country that runs completely on electricity."

In an email to Better Place staff the next day, Agassi commented that "we drove fast (sometimes really fast ...), with full air-conditioning blowing...snacks, diet Cokes, USB sticks with our favorite music, and a certain awe at how this system of ours actually works."

Agassi thanked the Better Place team "for converting this dream into reality ... you have built an amazing machine ... it is bigger than any robot, charge spot or any piece of software we put in it ... this distributed machine has a soul ... and yesterday it smiled upon us."

Brian Thomas, a Fluence Z.E. owner and frequent blogger about all things Better Place, was blown away.

"No other electric car in the world with any other fast charging technology could do that," he gushed. "Not one. Not even the most expensive in the world."

Thomas was right: Only a network of battery switch stations could propel a single car that many miles without needing to plug in. It was a shimmering reminder, blasted across the web for posterity, that no matter what came next, Agassi could go to sleep that night buoyed by the satisfaction that he had realized his vision—and that this knowledge, this success, could never be taken away.

It was to be a short-lived victory.

COPENHAGEN

The Better Place board of directors met again in Copenhagen on August 30, 2012. Andrey Zarur resumed his role as the messenger bearing bad news. Nothing had changed, he warned. The company would still be broke by October.

"I was more convinced than ever that the company would be out of cash then," he said.

But this time, Zarur's crowing about the upcoming electric carpocalypse was met with resistance by the other board members.

"You're wrong about this, Andrey," one board member told him. "Shai will secure more capital; we're making progress."

"Thank you for having raised the alarm so enthusiastically in the past," said another. "But you don't need to worry about it anymore."

Zarur was baffled. Had the social media slams against him taken their toll?

"My reputation had been dragged through the mud; I knew that," Zarur said. "By now, it was clear that all the credibility I had with the board was shot. Apparently, I was the Boy Who Cried Wolf."

The Copenhagen board meeting lasted 12 hours. Agassi was grilled; his plans were ripped apart; but Agassi prevailed. He emphatically assured the board that the 50 million Euro loan from the European Union Bank would be arriving any day. He declared that the cash crisis Zarur had been warning about either never was, or was about to pass quietly.

At the very end of the meeting, Agassi threw out one backhanded request.

"There could be a gap between when we need the money and when we get the loan," he said. "Are you guys prepared to step up and do a quick bridge if needed?"

Mike Granoff remembered the response. "No one said 'yes' loudly, but no one said 'no' loudly either. So Shai took it as a 'yes.'"

ON THE GOOD SHIP "BETTER PLACE"

After the board meeting, Idan Ofer decamped to his private yacht, where he would remain for the better part of the next month. So deeply invested, emotionally as well as financially, in Agassi and his electric car company was Ofer that he had named his yacht the *Better Place*.

The media attention it garnered also made a public relations splash.

The 50-meter yacht had first made waves at the Monaco Yacht Show earlier that year for its luxury and environmentally friendly features. Built by the Monegasque yacht maker Wally, at a cost of $10 million, the vessel *Better Place* was notable for its extensive use of carbon fibers, making it one of the first yachts in the world to receive a "Green Star" award for sustainable excellence from the RINA standards company. On board was a 300-square-meter cabin with a salon and kitchen, an 86-square-meter deckhouse, a 60-square-meter main suite, a huge Jacuzzi and no fewer than 20 sunning lounges.

For those who could only gaze at the yacht's opulence from afar, the most notable design feature was the sails: One had the blue Better Place logo writ large; the other featured the words "Better Place," visible from miles away.

Ofer sailed the *Better Place* to nearby Greece. He considered all that had transpired over the past several months, and then over the past several years. On his nightstand was a printout of an article that had appeared in the Harvard Business Review.

Within a few weeks, it would change everything for Ofer, Agassi and Better Place.

The report, written by Michael Maccoby for the Review's January 2000 issue, was called "Narcissistic Leaders: The Incredible Pros, the Inevitable Cons."

Maccoby, a well-known psychoanalyst and organizational consultant, won a Harvard Business Review McKinsey Award for the taut seven-page paper, which the reviewers called an outstanding work "likely to have a major influence on the actions of business managers worldwide."

As Ofer began to read, he felt his world shake. It was a chilling revelation.

"I saw all the prerequisites, all the data points," he said. "Every single one matched Shai Agassi's character."

Until now, Agassi could have been described as focused, driven, single-minded, unbending.

Never had anyone dared to diagnose him.

Maccoby began his analysis by noting that the CEO superstars at that time—he mentioned Bill Gates, Andy Grove, Steve Jobs, Jeff Bezos and Jack Welch—embraced the limelight in ways unheard of in the past, hiring publicists, writing books and appearing on television talk shows.

Seen through a Freudian lens, Maccoby said, these larger-than-life business leaders exhibit clear narcissistic behaviors.

"Throughout history, narcissists have always emerged to inspire people and to shape the future," Maccoby wrote. "When military, religious and political arenas dominated society, it was figures such as Napoleon Bonaparte, Mahatma Gandhi or Franklin Delano Roosevelt who determined the social agenda. But from time to time, when business became the engine of social change, it too generated its share of narcissistic leaders. That was true at the beginning of the [last] century, when men like Andrew Carnegie, John D. Rockefeller, Thomas Edison and Henry Ford exploited new technologies and restructured American industry. And I think it is true again today."

The Mayo Clinic defines narcissistic personality disorder as one "in which people have an inflated sense of their own importance, a deep need for admiration and a lack of empathy for others. But behind this mask of ultra-confidence lies a fragile self-esteem that's vulnerable to the slightest criticism."

Narcissism is not entirely negative. Indeed, the personality disorder can be productive—even necessary.

Jack Welch and George Soros, Maccoby wrote, "are gifted and creative strategists who see the big picture and find meaning in the risky proposition of changing the world and leaving behind a legacy."

The most productive narcissists are "not only risk takers willing to get the job done, but also charmers who can convert the masses with their rhetoric," Maccoby wrote.

Productive narcissists "come closest to our collective image of great leaders," Maccoby continued. "They have compelling, even gripping visions for companies, and they have an ability to attract followers ... they are by nature people who see the big picture. They are not analyzers who can break up questions into manageable problems; they aren't number crunchers either ... to paraphrase George Bernard Shaw, some people see things as they are and ask why; narcissists see things that never were and ask why not."

Narcissists are masters of language, and their skillful oration is part of what makes them so charismatic. A narcissistic leader believes that "inspiring speeches can change people [and] indeed, anyone who has seen narcissists perform can attest to their personal magnetism and the ability to stir enthusiasm among audiences," Maccoby wrote.

Ofer thought back to the first time he'd met Agassi in his office in the Millennium Tower. He recalled Agassi's electrifying appearance on the TED stage, his command in front of investors, employees, board members.

But charisma can be a double-edged sword, Maccoby warned. "It fosters both closeness and isolation."

As the narcissistic leader becomes more self-assured, he or she also becomes more spontaneous.

"He feels free of constraints. Ideas flow. He thinks he's invincible. This energy and confidence further inspires his followers," Maccoby wrote. But it also leads the narcissistic leader to listen less "to words of caution and advice. After all, he has been right before, when others had their doubts."

The darker side is always there, Maccoby wrote. Narcissists, Freud pointed out, "are emotionally isolated and highly distrustful. Perceived threats can trigger rage. Achievements can feed feelings of grandiosity."

The more successful the narcissist becomes, the more pronounced his or her faults become. They shun emotions and keep others at length. They are sensitive to criticism or perceived slights.

Narcissism ultimately turns unproductive, "when, lacking self-knowledge and restraining anchors, narcissists become unrealistic dreamers. They nurture grand schemes and harbor the illusion that only circumstances or enemies block their success," Maccoby wrote.

Ofer put the paper down for a moment. Was Agassi an "unproductive narcissist?"

Despite their high self-regard, narcissists can be extremely thin-skinned.

"They bruise easily," Maccoby wrote. "They cannot tolerate dissent [and] can be extremely abrasive with employees who doubt them—or with subordinates who are tough enough to fight back."

Ofer thought of the clash with Andrey Zarur—who had had the tenacity to stand his ground.

Narcissistic leaders may say they want teamwork, but in practice "they want a group of yes-men," Maccoby added. "That's why, even though narcissists undoubtedly have 'star quality,' they are often unlikable." Narcissistic leaders want to win at all costs, which can lead the unproductive narcissistic leader to see everything as a threat.

Perhaps the biggest problem Maccoby pointed out was that narcissistic leaders don't want to change. "As long as they are successful, they don't think they have to."

When the narcissistic leader is productive and kept in check, "these will be the best times," Maccoby concluded. But when narcissistic leaders self-destruct, "their organizations can be led terribly astray."

Dan Cohen had also read the Harvard Business Review article. He'd received it from Evan Thornley in Australia.

Cohen, as chief of staff, had been as close as anyone ever really got to Agassi, at least professionally. But he had fallen out with his boss and quit Better Place a few months earlier.

"There was no one event that sparked and finished it," Cohen explained. "It was a slippery slope. Things were happening in Shai's personal life, which impacted the business and the professional environment between the two of us."

Out of Agassi's direct orbit, Cohen was able to take a more critical look. When he read the Harvard Business Review article, he said, "I felt like it was describing Shai."

Agassi had become so synonymous with Better Place that Cohen had once told the board, "If you have any illusions that Better Place can succeed without Shai, you'd better think again."

Now Cohen was thinking again.

"Could someone else take Shai's role? That wasn't easy to say," Cohen said. "But the company was definitely going nowhere with him."

On the calm waters of the Mediterranean, Ofer had time to think again, too.

Ofer had backed Agassi when no one else would. He had looked past the warning signs.

And yet, as his yacht returned to Israeli waters, he still wasn't sure what to do.

AMSTERDAM

While Ofer was at sea, Better Place kept up a public image of progress and positivity.

On September 3, 2012, Better Place opened a new battery switch station, at Schiphol airport, five-and-a-half miles outside of Amsterdam.

The station was intended to serve a fleet of 10 taxis that would run into town and back. Three local taxi providers signed on: Connexxion, BIOS and TCA. Each would get two cars, with two spare vehicles shared between them. The switch station was given a great location—on the airport grounds adjacent to the main terminal.

The Schiphol-Amsterdam corridor is a particularly demanding route—more than 700,000 taxi trips originate from Schiphol each year. A second station in Amsterdam city was announced, along with plans for 28 more across the Netherlands in the coming years.

Agassi flew out to help cut the ribbon on the shiny new station with the Dutch Minister of Economic Affairs Maxime Verhagen; Olivier Onidi, directorate general for mobility and transport at the European Commission; and Jean-Paul Renaux, managing director of Renault Netherlands.

Better Place even announced the hiring of a CEO for Better Place Netherlands, Paul Harms, who came to the company from European car-leasing leader Athlon.

From Amsterdam, Agassi continued on to New York to meet Mike Granoff. The search for the missing $50 million was afoot, and Granoff was back in his familiar role as matchmaker to Manhattan.

But something wasn't right, Granoff noticed. Agassi was off his game; he seemed deflated.

Granoff remembered stopping for a quick lunch at Frank's Express Pizza.

"Tell me about the next meeting," Agassi said to Granoff. "Why are we meeting with them, anyway?"

A previous meeting with the same investors hadn't gone well, Agassi pointed out.

"If you can't move them, Mike, how do you think I can do it?" Agassi said.

Granoff was flabbergasted. Where was Agassi's usual bravado, his never-give-up attitude?

"This wasn't the Shai Agassi I knew," Granoff said.

It was true that the investors they'd met with so far were reluctant to commit. But it was more than that.

"Shai was defeated. He probably knew better than anyone else the reality that was about to hit him in the face," Granoff said.

WHO WILL LIVE AND WHO WILL DIE?

The reality came a week later in a double blow that left Idan Ofer with no doubt about what he had to do.

Israel and the Jewish world had just celebrated Rosh Hashanah, the Jewish New Year.

Rosh Hashanah, according to Jewish tradition, is when God decides who will live and who will die in the coming year.

In the *Unetanneh Tokef* prayer said during synagogue services, the possible means of one's demise are delineated in painstaking detail and sung by worshipers in a passionate petition to heaven.

Who will die at his predestined time and who before his time?

Who by water and who by fire?

Who by sword and who by beast?

Who will rest and who will wander?

Who will live in harmony and who will be harried?

Who will enjoy tranquility and who will suffer?

Who will be impoverished and who will be enriched?

Who will be degraded and who will be exalted?

Ten days after Rosh Hashanah comes Yom Kippur—the Day of Atonement.

If on Rosh Hashanah, tradition says that one's fate is written down, on Yom Kippur, God seals the books. The in-between days are a last chance for making things right—both with God and with those on the earthly plain.

It was during those auspicious days that Idan Ofer and the other members of the Better Place board received two emails.

The first was from Agassi.

Agassi asked the board members to step up with the bridge loan that he had mentioned at the end of the Copenhagen board meeting. He needed this "safety net" to make payroll and pay suppliers.

The second message was the long-awaited report from the audit committee. It confirmed what Zarur had been saying all these months: Better Place would be out of cash in a matter of weeks.

No wonder Agassi was asking for more money.

Finally facing the electric abyss, Ofer was aware that he had the power to play God at this point. What he did next would determine the fate of more than 1,000 people worldwide, chief among them Shai Agassi.

"Who will rest and who will wander, who will enjoy tranquility and who will suffer, who will be impoverished and who will be enriched?"

Ofer made his decision.

18

THE END OF THE ROAD

The Jewish calendar packs its biggest holidays into an intense four-week period in the early fall. After the severity of Rosh Hashanah and Yom Kippur comes a week of lightness: the holiday of Sukkot, which commemorates the Israelites' journey from Egypt back to the Promised Land by commanding observant Jews to build temporary huts called "sukkot" outside of their homes.

Traditional Jews will spend the next seven days eating, sleeping and passing the time playing cards in these flimsy structures, built on porches, balconies, in backyards or in parking lots outside their apartment and condo buildings.

A holiday that prompts Israelis to literally dwell amongst their vehicles would seem an ideal time to stage a car show presenting the latest and greatest models. Which is exactly what the Automania car fair set out to do that Sukkot at the Tel Aviv Exhibition Grounds.

Many Israelis are given the entire Sukkot holiday as vacation from work, so the Automania show was guaranteed high attendance. Every major car importer in Israel was there, including Better Place.

Automania came at a pivotal point for Better Place: To date, only 457 cars had been delivered in Israel, many of those to Better Place employees and suppliers; in Denmark, the number was less than 200.

Agassi wasn't concerned. When challenged in an interview with the Israeli business publication TheMarker, Agassi spun the low numbers as being entirely according to plan.

"We said that before we'd deployed the entire network, we cannot sell more than 500 cars. We've reached 500 cars now, the network is open, so now we can deliver cars to fleets and companies," he explained. "Oil prices are rising and the prices of batteries are down. There's no stopping this model. It is only a matter of time."

A week before the show opened, Better Place came up with an idea that would prove more enticing for consumers.

Better Place persuaded Albar, one of the country's leading fleet operators, to offer a leasing option to consumers, not just to businesses. For NIS 9,900 (around $2,500) down and NIS 1,990 ($500) a month for 36 months, an individual could lease a Fluence Z.E. The deal included a subscription package covering 1,000 kilometers and unlimited battery swaps.

The offering was an instant success.

When the Automania show opened on the first day of the holiday, the Better Place booth was packed, as was Albar's pavilion.

Forty-eight consumers signed lease deals with Albar during the show.

Idan Ofer called up Zohar Bali.

"You made me so happy today. I'm so proud of you," Ofer said.

But it wasn't enough. Ofer's commitment to making Better Place the best it could be was about to take a very different turn.

ARSUF

A few hours before the Sukkot holiday was due to start, Ofer summoned Shai Agassi to a private meeting at his home in Arsuf. Agassi came prepared with the latest spreadsheets to prove Better Place could turn the corner, even as the audit committee reported the company was teetering on insolvency.

He brought a flower for Ofer's wife, Batya.

"It was like a peace offering," Ofer recalled. "He knew this was going to be a problematic meeting, but I don't think he knew to what extent."

As Agassi began pulling papers out of his bag, "he started to explain how the budget he conjured up was actually doable, how it was working," Ofer said. "But I'd made up my mind. I said to him, 'I don't want to bother with this. I don't want to hear any more from you.'"

The two sat facing each other—the final showdown between the billionaire and the man who wanted to save the world.

Agassi tried to speak but Ofer shot him down again. He wasn't interested in hearing any more excuses.

"The board has lost confidence in you," Ofer said simply.

He didn't raise his voice, but he didn't waver either. Not this time.

"I don't want you to work for me anymore. I don't want you as CEO of the company. It's time to make a change."

Agassi was flustered, but for only a moment.

"You will fail without me," he said to Ofer.

"That's OK," Ofer responded. "I will take the consequences."

Ofer stood up. The meeting had lasted all of 15 minutes, including a few brief opening pleasantries. On September 30, 2012, Shai Agassi, who had nearly single-handedly created Better Place from scratch, whose name was as synonymous with his company as Steve Jobs's was with Apple, whose vision stayed true even when the business was crumbling around him, had been fired.

Agassi didn't give up—at least not immediately. He called on the other members of the board in a desperate attempt to convince them to reverse the chairman's decision.

Ofer headed him off at the pass.

"I had told the board already," Ofer recalled. "I said, 'I don't care. I've fired him.'"

In the end, Agassi was rebuffed by all sides. The power had finally shut down around him, leaving him stranded—like an electric vehicle languishing helplessly on the side of the road, or like Moses, forbidden by God to enter the promised land after toiling 40 years in the desert, tantalizingly close but ultimately just out of range.

The news dropped on the second day of the Automania car show in Tel Aviv. The timing could not have been worse for Tal Bar and the other sales staff, who had been riding a much-needed crest of optimism from the Albar deal.

From that moment, sales stopped short. Anyone who paused at the Better Place booth only wanted to exchange gossip, to extract some insider clues as to what had happened and what was coming next.

Buyers who had purchased vehicles in the previous days called Better Place, frantically demanding to cancel their orders.

"It felt like a big hammer came from above and slapped us all on the head," recalled Bar. "Everything came to a standstill."

Inside Better Place, it was pandemonium.

"Everyone was in disbelief that this can happen," Bar continued. "No one saw it coming."

Debbie Kaye was one of the first people Agassi called to break the news. Ofer called Agassi's personal assistant shortly afterward.

"Why haven't you cleaned out Shai's office yet?" Ofer demanded.

"The employees don't know yet," Kaye sputtered. "You want them to see me packing him up?"

With Agassi's glass office in the center of the TopCo floor, there would be no hiding the significance.

"Yes, let them see," Ofer said.

"Fine, but I'm not at the office," Kaye deflected the demand.

"Why not?" Ofer wanted to know.

"I was fired, too," Kaye said.

"No you weren't. You have nothing to do with this. You will continue in your role as assistant to the new CEO."

"I want to be fired," Kaye said, emphatically. She was.

Agassi's brother, Tal, didn't wait to be laid off—he quit in solidarity with his brother. Agassi's sister, Dafna, left a month later, in November, while CTO Barak Hershkovitz stuck around for another couple of months.

Outside Agassi's house, loyalists had created a graffiti wall, painting the concrete separating Agassi's ground floor garden from the sidewalk with words of love and gratitude scribbled in colored paint.

"Shai, we love you" and "Thanks for 5 amazing years" took center stage. Dozens of supporters and staff members signed their names. A picture of the graffiti wall was posted all over social media.

Also posting was Tami Chotoveli, unable to hide her feelings. In the days following Agassi's ouster, she unleashed her anger on Idan Ofer, first in a harsh tweet that read, "Whoever makes a deal with the devil pays the price."

She followed that up with a longer post on Facebook, in Hebrew:

Everyone knows who Shai Agassi is. Everyone ... I don't need to send messages through Twitter and Facebook ... Shai Agassi is Better Place and Better Place is Shai Agassi. This will always be the truth.

Agassi, meanwhile, was not taking the news well.

"It's very difficult to get fired from any role," Kaye recalled, "but to have it be so public, and then on top of that, he'd lost his company and his dream, the goal he'd focused on for so long. To be out of the picture all of a sudden was pretty shocking. I don't know if he saw it coming. I would find it hard to believe he knew it would happen the way it happened."

Idan Ofer issued a short, carefully worded statement that suggested the public not read into Agassi's departure anything more than normal business.

"Under Shai's leadership, we've successfully achieved our goals in the first chapter of Better Place, and we owe Shai our gratitude for turning his powerful vision into a reality. It is almost five years to the day since Shai launched Better Place and a natural point in the company's evolution to realign for its second chapter and for the challenges and opportunities ahead."

Better Place corporate was careful to say publicly that Agassi's ouster was a "joint decision."

Ofer's first public comments on Agassi's dismissal were made not to the Israeli press but to a Chinese newspaper—not surprising given that Ofer still saw China as his future, especially now with Better Place imploding locally.

Speaking to the China Southern Weekly, he tried to put a positive spin on Agassi's departure.

"Shai Agassi is a smart man, and I like him and his idea," Ofer said. "But building and operating a company are different things, which require different skills. It is ordinary for a founder to leave management in Israel, and Shai Agassi still owns 10 percent of Better Place."

Ofer did admit that there was bad blood between him and Agassi.

"I'm honest and always hope that others will be as honest as I am. But I've always discovered that other people are different from me, and I am sometimes bitterly disappointed."

But he insisted he would stick with a post-Agassi Better Place. "I also never give up, and almost never buy or sell companies. I prefer to constantly expand."

Ofer thanked Agassi in his official statement.

Shai Agassi's leadership and innovative vision have "successfully positioned the company's goals in the first chapter of its life … the board of directors has prepared in advance for this change and now, after five years of construction," has experienced management in place "that will lead to the realization of these challenges."

The board, of course, had no such succession plans. Ofer had taken his decision in Arsuf alone. When Forbes' Todd Woody interviewed Ofer just three weeks prior, Ofer gave no indication of what was to come.

"As far as I'm concerned, Better Place has proven what it set out to do successfully," Ofer told Woody. "There isn't a single issue that was put into the business plan that we haven't done."

EVAN THORNLEY STEPS UP

Evan Thornley got the call at midnight the day before Ofer planned to fire Agassi.

"We want you to be the CEO of all of Better Place," Ofer told him on the phone.

Thornley was on a plane at 10 that same morning. He barely had time to pack a suitcase before he began the 22-hour journey.

"I didn't know how I was going to work it out with my family," he said. "But right now, we had to do triage and try to keep the company alive."

Ofer expressed full confidence in his new CEO.

"In his four years as CEO of Better Place in Australia, Evan has built an impressive track record, particularly around establishing a strong set of industry partners there," Ofer said in his statement announcing Agassi's departure. "Evan brings the right combination of entrepreneurship and coalition and team-building to take Better Place to the next level."

Thornley returned the compliment.

"Four years ago, Shai asked me to join the Better Place mission and bring it to Australia," he said. "It has been my pleasure to lead that effort along with my colleague CEOs in Israel, Denmark and now the Netherlands. Today, it is an honor for me to step up and lead this fantastic global team on a day-to-day basis … we start the second chapter with a tremendous strength of global investors and management team."

Privately, though, Thornley was not so sure.

"Was I the right guy?" Thornley wonders. "Others can judge if I had the right skills. But one thing I know for certain, I had the right motivation. I knew the job would be a nightmare—for me personally and for my family. The only reason for me to be in Israel was that we had to complete our mission. But I was ready to do it."

THE MEDIA RESPONDS

The media wasted no time springing to action, analyzing what went wrong and assigning blame. Some publications expressed understanding.

Forbes: "It is not uncommon for a startup to replace a visionary founder with a corporate veteran when it comes time to move beyond the startup phase. Though as a former top executive at software giant SAP, Agassi was not exactly a typical startup guy."

The Wall Street Journal: "It's part of the business school literature: a transition from an entrepreneurial manager to a business manager. The vision is established, and now they need a hard-nosed manager to manage the thing, to make the business ties, and do the selling."

Fortune: "The press is calling the resignation of Shai Agassi, CEO of electric car company Better Place, a surprise, but it isn't really. Truth is, the company hit the same wall that the vast majority of startups do. Visionary entrepreneurs don't necessarily have the skills to build a big corporation, especially in an industry as complex as autos."

But Agassi "did what entrepreneurs are supposed to do," Fortune continued. He turned "an idea into a company ... the next step is the hard blocking and tackling needed to make the company scale globally, something entrepreneurs aren't particular good at because it's less about vision than hard, routine, back-breaking work."

Agassi deserved credit "for taking a radical notion and getting to the proof of concept stage." That said, "the challenges it faces are daunting. Better Place has said it lost nearly $131 million in the first half of this year and expects losses to continue." The company is now "in a race to generate revenue before its cash runs out."

Or put another way, as TheMarker reported, Better Place had blown through an estimated "$477 million since the beginning of 2010, including $64 million in the second quarter of 2012" alone.

The Israeli business newspaper Globes was less circumspect. Its analysis of Agassi's firing was peppered with unnamed sources eager to point fingers.

Idan Ofer "could absorb a lot," one source said: "The wasteful financial practices of Shai, his self-aggrandizement, not to mention his messianism and arrogance, but when the bottom line is not providing results, that's when the trouble starts." Ofer would not "be the sucker who lost money while the global CEO travels the world and repeats the same messages."

Agassi's "dealings were extravagant and arrogant," said another. "He didn't recognize that there was a problem. He spent all his time fiddling with how big his vision was. Vision is great, but when you are impervious to criticism, the road to failure is just a matter of time. He was given a rope, but instead of pulling it and taking things forward, he put the noose around his neck."

Agassi had "a thousand tons of charisma" but was "not a man of details" and "wasn't bothered by things relating to finances."

It was an unavoidable collision course. "The burn rate was incomparable. Sales penetration was slower than expected and the deployment of switch stations more expensive. All this put a great amount of pressure on the shareholders and investors to cut spending."

"There's a lot of black humor running around the corridors of Better Place," Hadas Megan and Shlomit Lan wrote in Globes. They cited an example of a book about the company that Agassi had produced and distributed to his staff just prior to Rosh Hashanah, a few weeks earlier. It was called "Chapter 1."

The 120-page full-color book was stuffed with pictures and stories describing Better Place's remarkable past and its inevitable future. Sections of the original blueprint were included. There was a letter of encouragement from Bill Clinton, sketches tracing the evolution of the switch stations, charge spots and cable design, smiling photos of celebrities and investors. The names of all 1,000 Better Place employees were printed in the front and back inside covers.

Now, Globes pointed out, staff were joking ruefully that another "1" should be added to the book's title.

Not "Chapter 1" but "Chapter 11."

Agassi's supporters, meanwhile, called his firing a "putsch"—a German word used to describe a sudden revolt or attempt to overthrow a government.

"When all over the world the brand is associated with you, and you are considered a success story, you assume that they will let you get on with the job," wrote one.

"This whole thing reminds me of how Apple ousted Steve Jobs and came to regret it bitterly," a senior Better Place staffer told TheMarker.

Agassi issued a single brief statement to the press.

"Five years ago, I followed the vision of weaning the world from oil and last month, I circled the state of Israel in an electric car, from Dan [in the Golan Heights] to Eilat. Very few people get to turn a vision of this complexity into reality in just five years. I'm proud of the team of people who developed the vision and I'm confident of their ability to take the company to the next level."

Fluence Z.E. owner Brian Thomas tried to see the bright side to the chaos that was unfolding around the company.

Even if Agassi's dismissal meant Better Place "were to fail completely, someone would pick up the local assets at a discount price and continue to run the service. Too much has been spent for it to be written off completely," Thomas wrote.

"Knowing what I know today I'd still buy my car. I'd take that chance," he concluded.

GOODBYE

Shai Agassi sent an email to the entire Better Place staff to say goodbye. No matter how personally defeated Agassi may have felt, he still wanted his dream to succeed.

Better Team,

This month, five years ago, we announced in New York the formation of Better Place. At the time, we were viewed as an audacious plan that was mocked by most people in the industry. Today we are no longer a plan, but a reality—one that drives millions of miles on the roads of two countries.

To a certain degree, each and every one of you experienced the same road that I had been through, these last five years. Each of you can personally state that there is no greater happiness than seeing our dream take form and become reality in front of our eyes. A dream that started as a set of schematics drawn and erased with marker on windows and walls. A dream realized in mass-produced cars driving on the road powered by electricity, served with a national grid of charge spots and battery switch stations. This physical network will realize the dream of taking countries and the world off their dependency on oil.

The next chapter in this historic book written at Better Place I leave for you, dear people full of drive, to write on your own.

I will continue this journey as a board member and a large shareholder in Better Place, but no longer as CEO. I am proud of all that we have accomplished together over these years, the incredible change that we drove, the proof that no one can dispute—an electric car with a switchable battery is the future. And the future was invented here, by all of us.

Evan [Thornley] and Kaplan [Moshe Kaplinsky] have been a significant part of this road over the last four years. They were entrusted as managers of this company by our board. I wish them and my fellow board members the best of luck as we face the tremendous challenges ahead of us.

Regardless of the fact that I am no longer your CEO, my heart will always stay with you in Better Place out of full belief in our shared vision. I have full belief in the tremendous people that realized that vision along this magical road that we have shared. I am forever indebted to all of you, and will never forget you, regardless of where you will end up or where I am. I love you in a special way that only comes from this kind of shared experience. An experience that created a brotherly bond amongst all of us.

One thing you can all be sure of, I will think of you every morning as I enter my electric car, start it and smile as I see OSCAR come up to greet me.

Thank you all,

With great love,

Shai

19

SAVING PRIVATE BETTER PLACE

Evan Thornley was at an immediate disadvantage: With still no CFO at the top, the number of people on the payroll was more a matter of debate than fact. And that affected Thornley's ability to determine whether there was enough cash to get through the end of the week and what he was going to do about it.

After a shower and a power nap following his long flight to Israel, Thornley set up a makeshift office in the lobby of the West Hotel, about a mile from the Visitor Center, where he conducted back-to-back interviews with key Better Place staff, a kind of corporate speed-dating.

Thornley needed to get a very quick read on what everyone did in the company, but he didn't want to get too close to the main office in Rosh HaAyin—he didn't know how he'd be perceived. Usurper? Savior? Traitor?

He certainly didn't relish what was to come next—radically cutting staff, projects and locations. It would only exacerbate how Better Place staff, except maybe those in Australia, saw him: an executioner parachuted in from several continents away by an uncaring chairman who had stolen the company's dream from its visionary.

Thornley spent the next two days in interviews. Staffers were instructed to treat Thornley like a potential investor for whom they were doing a "roadshow," presenting their numbers and plans and "selling" him on their function within the company.

Meanwhile, at the Rosh HaAyin office, the OpCo and TopCo teams had descended into a turf war, with OpCo staff scouting out the TopCo floor and eying its fancy equipment. The assumption had been that Kaplan, as head of the Israel OpCo, would get Agassi's CEO slot. Now that he hadn't, his people were miffed. Instead, Kaplan was promoted to deputy chief operating officer of the global side, in addition to his role as CEO of Better Place Israel.

"Evidently, it wasn't enough," wrote Haaretz's Daniel Schmill.

Kaplan abruptly quit on November 14, 2012, just a month and a few days after Agassi was fired.

CRACKING THE CODE

As Idan Ofer surveyed the disaster his beloved company had become, he made a critical and commando decision, one that bypassed most business standards: He pledged an additional $100 million for Better Place. Of that, $67 million was transferred immediately. Mike Granoff raised another $100,000 from the investors he represented.

Protocol would have demanded a comprehensive plan be put in place to ensure the money would be spent appropriately and that the company had pivoted toward profitability. But there was no time. Without Ofer's emergency bailout, there would have been nothing left to work with. Bankruptcy proceedings would have already started.

Ofer was also working to calm another development: Shai Agassi was leaving the board, despite the pledge made to Better Place employees in his goodbye letter.

Ofer offered Agassi a newly created position, deputy chairman, but Agassi declined.

"The decision is said to be personal and has not been explained," Ynet reported.

Nevertheless, the public bought the new narrative: that Ofer believed in Better Place and had put his money where his mouth was; that Agassi's dismissal was in fact a sound and well-planned move; that sales would pick up and the dream could be salvaged.

And sales did pick up.

The consumer leasing option announced during the Automania show proved remarkably resilient. Although December's numbers were atrocious—just five cars sold—and half the orders for the 48 cars sold through Albar at Automania were canceled shortly afterward, by the beginning of 2013, Zohar Bali and his team had bounced back and were moving dozens of cars per month, mainly through the lease option.

January saw an unprecedented 102 cars sold.

Bali, at this late date and with Agassi no longer in the picture, had finally cracked the leasing code.

In addition to the consumer partnership with Albar, Better Place started its own direct leasing program with an unprecedented carrot—a money-back guarantee stating that if Better Place went out of business, the driver could return the car with no penalty and no further monthly payments owed.

"It was like a gold rush," Bali said. "People were saying, 'Save me two!'"

For the leasing companies, who had complained that they didn't know what the residual value of an electric car would be three years down the road, Bali came up with a new formula.

"We fixed the price in advance as the resale price of a Toyota Corolla," he explained. "That made it almost one hundred percent risk free."

For such a scheme to work, the leasing companies needed a financial guarantee. But the banks were unwilling to go out on a limb for an unproven technology, especially one from a company that appeared to be faltering.

"So we came up with the idea to use our balance sheet to finance the car for the leasing companies," Bali said.

Better Place would essentially offer up its own assets as collateral. It was a short-term fix, Bali admitted, but it was effective. "It was the missing link," he said.

Bali even got Carasso, Renault's initially reluctant Israel distributor, to begin selling the Fluence Z.E., by lowering the sales commitment from 14,000 for the first year to just 2,000 for a two-year period going into 2014.

"We kept adjusting the number down until we got to one that was realistic," Bali said.

Carasso was never enthusiastic, though.

"Their strategy was to fake an orgasm—to let everyone know they are willing to do it, but then not to do much of anything. They didn't go all the way," Bali said.

PAINFUL CUTS

Slowly, the media came to see Evan Thornley as a calmer, more professional version of Shai Agassi. Cars continued to sell, and the remaining switch stations were steadily opened, one or two at a time until, by January 2013, Agassi's dream was fulfilled *ex post facto,* and all 40 stations were operational.

Inside Better Place, however, Thornley never had a real honeymoon. He was shocked by what he discovered.

"Better Place had three silos—the Israeli OpCo, the global head office and the tech group," Thornley said, and each was "at war with each other. They really didn't like each other. Everyone seemed to think that this was OK and acceptable, that at a time of absolute crisis, parts of the organization wouldn't talk or work with other parts of the organization."

This communication breakdown only contributed to the financial woes of the company.

"I would ask people in the Israeli OpCo's finance department for information," Thornley recalled. "I was trying to assemble how much money we really had in the bank, and they'd say, sorry, we can't give you that information. You're global, and we're the Israeli OpCo. I had to assemble the number manually in this very hostile non-sharing environment."

It took Thornley seven weeks to determine the actual headcount of the company.

"I had thought there were about 700 staff," he said. "When we finally got a stable estimate, including contractors who might as well have been employees, it was 1,165 people."

This included "massive duplication" in the company but also "people doing jobs that didn't need to be done, or approaching tasks that in retrospect were completely irrelevant to the business. The software guys, for example, were incredible; the quality of their work was very high. But we had fewer than one thousand customers and they were building this massive, complex and gold-plated system to cope with ten million."

Agassi had considered that good planning for the future.

"It was well thought out and thorough," Thornley said. "But we needed to be nimble and flexible while at the same time keeping an eye toward scalability. We were at the extreme end of the spectrum."

Thornley made a number of changes quickly. He merged the three silos so there was just one finance and HR team for the entire company. And the company finally hired a CFO: Alan Gelman, who came to Better Place from Bezeq, Israel's leading telephone provider. Gelman was actually hired by Agassi just before Ofer sacked him, but the CFO didn't start until Thornley had taken over.

Thornley's most painful task in fixing Better Place was layoffs. They were announced the last week of October. Up to 200 people would be fired.

The initial group came mostly from R&D. Thornley spun that to the press as natural, now that the company had completed the development of most of its infrastructure.

Thornley and his team would eventually lay off 500 people—half the staff.

"It was a continuous process, an awful thing for the organization," Thornley said.

But what choice did he have?

Perhaps the most surprising staff decision Thornley made was keeping on Sidney Goodman.

"Sid was stunned when we kept him on. But he was doing a really good job managing the Renault account," Thornley said. "He built good relationships there and earned their respect. He had to work at all levels of the organization, learn who the decision makers were, deal with a bunch of practical engineering problems. It was an absolutely massive job to secure that partnership. It was hard not being an automotive guy, but his knowledge grew a lot over time."

Goodman had been hampered by Agassi, Thornley felt.

"His main problem was that he had to carry Shai's bag; he had to take Shai's brilliant but sometimes crazy strategies into Renault and make them work," Thornley said. "He was the meat in the sandwich between how Shai wanted to do business, and the cardigan-wearers at Renault wanting to do business as usual."

SALVAGING RENAULT

Immediately after Shai Agassi was laid off, Renault sent a delegation to Israel. The Renault people returned to Paris "deeply concerned about what they saw and heard," recalled Evan Thornley.

A damage-control team of Thornley and Ben Keneally, head of

marketing in Australia who had come to Israel to help with the transition, flew to Renault's headquarters.

"We started with the usual five minutes of diplomatic posturing," Thornley said of their late December meeting with the Renault representative now in charge of the Better Place relationship.

But as the door to the conference room closed, the Renault executive's expression turned dark.

"Enough of the bullshit," he told his Better Place counterparts.

"He then launched into a two-hour monologue about how screwed up things were in Israel," Thornley remembered. "Only at the end did he pause for breath."

The crux was that the Renault executive was under pressure to make a call before the end of the year: Would Renault's investment in switchable-battery Fluences be written down as a loss on the company's balance sheet?

If Renault declared the project a loss, it would stop producing the Fluence Z.E. And with Renault as the only car manufacturer, that would spell the end of Better Place.

"What do you have to say for yourselves?" the Renault executive demanded.

"I agree with you," Thornley replied. "And I'll give you two more things you didn't even think of. Now, here's what we can do it about it. And here's where we'll need your help."

Thornley laid out "why the business was not a bust, but was behind schedule, and how that was not going to be the case forever."

Keneally jumped in and went through the data Better Place had been able to crunch in the months since the Fluence Z.E. had been on the roads.

"We showed him how many miles people were driving each day, that people were in fact driving long distances, that they were swapping on average about once a week, and that this was the only real way, other than the Chevy Volt, that someone could get all the financial benefits of electric without their range being limited," Keneally recalled.

"Yes, you're right," the Renault executive finally admitted. "No one is buying those limited-range city cars."

"Look, we're not disguising the fact that we messed up," Thornley said, coming clean. "But if you give us a bit more time, we think this is quite an exciting—and different—story. You haven't wasted your money."

The group reconvened over dinner where the Renault executive revealed what was at stake.

"We came into the meeting fully planning to shut this whole thing down today, but you had good answers," the Renault executive said. "In the past, all we got was denial. OK, let's solve this together. Let's see what you can do with a few more months."

CENTER OF GRAVITY

"The Israeli business is hemorrhaging money, and it is going to keep hemorrhaging no matter what we do, even if we sell more cars," Thornley told the Better Place board of directors in December 2012.

Thornley had internalized the harrowing truth that the company's costs in Israel were always going to outstrip the revenue it could earn from customer subscriptions, and that its current business model, where it was losing money on every car delivered, was unsustainable.

Thornley had put together a 160-page PowerPoint presentation with every aspect of the company laid out in painstaking detail—from the bleak financials to future plans. Among the data points: The company had sold only 330 cars to non-employees in Israel. In Denmark, the number was half that.

"There isn't a snowball's chance in hell we can get to positive cash flow in Israel," he emphasized.

Thornley instead proposed shifting the company's "center of gravity" to Western Europe, with the Netherlands—which had now been running the switchable-battery taxi trial between Schiphol airport and Amsterdam for several months—as its main market.

Australia would play an important role too.

Starting in 2011, Better Place Australia had been quietly working on a side project to make a General Motors car battery-switchable.

A Better Place–led consortium, called EV Engineering, had pulled in big-name companies such as Bosch, Continental, Futuris and GE. The Australian government got behind it as well, kicking in $3.5 million. The project refitted seven Holden Commodores—GM's top-selling car in Australia—with an electric motor and battery where the gas engine and tank used to be.

"It was a large, rear-wheel drive, V6-engine muscle car," Thornley said.

"We set out to show GM they could make a battery-switchable version of the vehicle that would be a huge hit in the corporate fleet market."

Thornley knew that Detroit "would never let GM in Australia do that kind of experimentation. So we said, let's build a prototype, a hundred miles from GM's office, totally off the balance sheets, and come back with a finished car.

"They were without a doubt some of the finest prototype electric vehicles anyone has had the privilege of driving," Thornley said.

Beyond the Holden experiment, "the Australian market represented a proof of concept and a set of business plans, technologies and analytics that could help Better Place grow to other suitable markets," explained Better Place Australia's head of deployment Geoff Zippel. "If we could make Melbourne work, the same model would work for any typical U.S. city."

The board meeting presentation also shed light on the expensive agreements the company had with third-party vendors like Amdocs, which had built Better Place's million-subscriber billing system.

As part of Thornley's reorganization, he wanted out of that contract.

Amdocs, however, claimed that, no matter how much Better Place had paid the company, Amdocs had also "provided Better Place with a system worth $50 to $60 million dollars, free of charge as an investment in the company" and had written into its contract an 80 million Euro termination fee.

Thornley countered in his presentation that the Amdocs investment in Better Place was "only" about $12 million, and that he hoped to negotiate with Amdocs "to explain that the current situation was neither anticipated nor contracted."

All arguments were eclipsed, however, by the stunning bottom line presented to the board: In order to continue, Better Place needed to raise an additional $300 million by March 2013.

The only way to do that would be with big countries and big numbers.

"We need to prove the concept with a growth story," Thornley explained to the board. And that meant doubling down on Australia and shifting focus to Europe, particularly the Netherlands.

"If you look at any numbers in the company and don't include Australia or Western Europe, no one will ever invest money," Thornley said. "It wasn't viable to shut down Israel entirely, which is what you'd normally do in business at a time like this, but we said we'd figure out how to deal with that over time."

Thornley won full backing from the board.

Relieved yet confident that a plan was finally in place, Thornley took a vacation with his girlfriend, who had flown in from Australia.

"I hadn't seen her in three months," he said. "I'd been working these hundred-hour weeks. So I said, 'Let's go to Athens for a couple of days.'"

But something was brewing in Israel.

As soon as he landed in Greece, Thornley recalled, "I started getting phone calls from Idan, ringing all kinds of alarm bells."

In just three days, the board had rescinded its approval of Thornley's plan and now wanted to put its energies exclusively on Israel and Denmark.

"When I returned, there was a lot of politics going on. Intrigue was at full tilt," Thornley said.

Thornley was no stranger to politics—he had been in the Australian government, after all—but he was out of his league in Israel. It was not unlike how Agassi had felt in China.

"I didn't speak the language; I wasn't connected with any of the players. I couldn't even begin to understand what was going on," Thornley said. "But what was clear was that Idan's demeanor had changed. He wanted to roll up his sleeves and get involved personally in trying to turn things around in Israel, to show how passionate he was for the mission."

Under the increasing pressure, Ofer had become overly focused on small issues, Thornley felt.

Ofer had learned, for example, that when Better Place technicians went out on a service call or to install a new charge spot, they used gasoline-powered cars. Ofer demanded they drive the Fluence Z.E.

It wasn't possible, Thornley tried to explain. The technicians were actually sub-contractors and used their own trucks.

"No, they have to use the Fluence," Ofer barked. "What I say goes!"

Ofer then turned his attention to one of the battery switch stations in the Negev desert that was not connected yet to the Israeli electric grid and was being run off diesel-powered generators.

"A bunch of locals kept stealing the diesel, and it was driving Idan crazy," Thornley recalled.

These were not the sorts of issues that should be given priority, Thornley felt.

"We had to deal with things costing us $300,000 a day. We shouldn't be wasting energy on the theft of diesel cans costing us $300 a day."

"Idan, I don't want to belittle your concerns," Thornley told Ofer. "I'm a big believer in the messages these kinds of symbols are sending, but we're in the middle of a massive crisis. We have to set priorities here. We need a chain of command."

"I feel like I'm not being listened to here," Ofer complained to Thornley. "It's my money, and my company."

Ofer and Thornley argued back and forth for several days.

"I know what it's like being a leader who's being undermined," Thornley said. "I've been in that situation before. I think we ended up on a pretty clear collision course."

The disagreement was cut short when, after a particularly brutal interchange with Ofer calling in by videoconference from his home, Thornley suffered what he thought was a heart attack.

"It turned out to be not life-threatening, but it was quite scary," Thornley recalled. "My doctor said, 'You are off the reservation for three days.'"

Thornley holed up in his hotel room and laid low while Mike Granoff and Dan Cohen ran interference. With Agassi gone, Cohen, who had resigned earlier that year, was back at Better Place, after a brief stint with Ofer's private venture firm, Quantum Pacific, in London.

"Dan and I went to Evan's room to talk to him," Granoff remembered. "He acted like he was sick. But Dan said, 'How is it he can talk to us but not to Idan? He's just pretending to be too sick to work.'"

"To be fair, I wasn't very forthcoming about it," Thornley admitted. "Where I come from, health is a private matter. If your doctor says you're out of action, you are. It's no one else's business. I didn't want to have a lengthy discussion about my medical prognosis with people who were trying to stick knives in my back."

It was clear to Granoff and Cohen that Ofer was about to fire Better Place's second CEO.

Granoff was despondent.

"We won't be able to survive another CEO shift so soon. We'll be a laughingstock," Granoff worried.

But Ofer was in full-on panic mode.

Even with Ofer's new money, "we still only had six months left of cash, so Idan had a point," Granoff said.

Thornley's departure was announced on January 16, 2013. A Better Place spokesperson said in a statement that Thornley was leaving the company in good spirits.

"Evan Thornley felt that he had reached the end of his road in the company and asked to retire."

THE THIRD CEO

Stepping into Thornley's shoes was Dan Cohen.

Cohen was perhaps the only executive who knew Better Place intimately—and whom Ofer trusted at this point. In his role as chief of staff, Cohen had been supportive of Better Place's China operation, which was still critical to Ofer's hopes for the company.

Cohen's appointment generated a not-inconsiderable number of raised eyebrows. He was seen as a political appointee, a yes-man to Ofer rather than an independent thinker.

Debbie Kaye, Agassi's former assistant, now watching from the sidelines, was aghast.

"It was a clear conflict of interest," she said, still loyal to her old boss. "And with all due respect, Dan was just as responsible as Shai for any failures—maybe more so—because he was the one on the ground doing it!"

Cohen continued the cutting Thornley had begun.

More staff departed, including the attendants who had worked in the battery switch stations. Now, if you had a problem when pulling into a station, you called one of Better Place's operators in the Rosh HaAyin control center (although it had been downsized too).

Thornley's dismissal meant bad news for Better Place Australia. Cohen decided to shut it down entirely. Thornley's final job at Better Place was to lay off his own management team and close the office he had only recently proposed as one of the company's saving graces.

Cohen also moved quickly to shutter the U.S. office, including canceling still-simmering plans to launch a switchable-battery taxi project in the San Francisco Bay Area.

All these moves led journalist Daniel Roth to tweet that the headline of his Wired article from 2008, "The Future of the Electric Car," should be amended to end: "But Probably Not."

"NO LONGER PART OF OUR BUSINESS MODEL"

Just when it looked like things couldn't get much worse for Better Place, Renault CEO Carlos Ghosn gave an interview to the Danish website EnergiWatch.

"When you look at the overall trends, we must conclude that replaceable batteries are no longer the main track for electric vehicles," Ghosn said in the article, published the first week of May 2013. "The main track is flat batteries in cars with charging. We believe that people want flexibility in the technology, and we can see that the demand is for rechargeable standard batteries."

As a result, the Fluence Z.E. would be the last battery-switchable car made by Renault. After it fulfilled its commitment to supply the 100,000 cars Better Place had ordered, production would stop. Cohen had hoped he could salvage the European market with a switchable-battery version of the Zoe. But that was now officially off the table.

"Swappable batteries are no longer the central part of [our] business model for electric cars," Ghosn added definitively.

It was a death sentence for Better Place, and Dan Cohen knew it.

Cohen called Carlos Tavares at Renault.

"We're in a very serious situation here," Cohen said to Tavares. "Before we make some tough decisions, I wanted to give you one last opportunity to say you're in."

Maybe Ghosn's comments didn't reflect official Renault policy, Cohen suggested to Tavares. "I'm sure he didn't really mean it."

Cohen implored Tavares to ask Ghosn to issue a "corrective statement," Cohen said. "But he just said, 'I'll relay your concerns.' He sounded almost happy."

THE END

With Renault now pulling out, Cohen and his team had to take a hard look at what remained of Better Place.

Despite all the cutting and savings (there were just 100 people left in the company at this point), the future looked bleak.

Not only had Better Place not raised the $300 million Evan Thornley had said it needed back in December, but the latest calculations indicated the company would need an additional $500 million in investment to reach profitability under its new, more focused model. Another $70 million was needed immediately to keep the lights on.

But there was a snag.

According to the rules of the previous round, Idan Ofer was unable to invest any more from his Israel Corporation unless all the other investors who had participated in the Series C did so too. And even if they wanted to, just as with the Series C, to go forward required the addition of new investors.

Given Better Place's disarray, that seemed unlikely.

How about looking toward the more risk-tolerant venture capitalist community? The company's $2.25 billion valuation was too high for them. As Macgregor Duncan had told Agassi when Better Place was raising the Series C round, only the big banks like HSBC could consider that kind of price, and their conservative nature was not a match for a company in trouble.

A company sale or IPO? Out of the question.

Cohen's only hope was China.

"They liked what Idan was doing in China," Cohen said. "We had a relationship with China Southern Power and we were ready to reopen the doors with China State Grid. The story of the three CEOs didn't hit their radar at all."

But an investment from China would take at least six months, Cohen reckoned. And there was no time or money for that. Even though the company still had some of Ofer's money in the bank, it was clear there was nowhere left to go.

And so, on May 26, 2013, 5 years, 6 months and 25 days after launching to the public at the Essex House in New York, the board of directors of Better Place voted to formally file for bankruptcy.

"Unfortunately, after a year's commercial operation, it was clear to us that, despite many satisfied customers, the wider public take-up would not be sufficient and that the support from the car producers was not forthcoming," Cohen said in a statement.

"This is a very sad day for all of us," the board of directors added. "We stand by the original vision as formulated by Shai Agassi of creating a green alternative that would lessen our dependence on highly polluting transportation technologies. Unfortunately, the path to realizing that vision was difficult, complex, and littered with obstacles, not all of which we were able to overcome."

Mike Granoff wrote a letter to his investors summing up his experience over the previous half decade.

The Better Place idea, he explained, "always envisioned and required great scale."

Referencing the business philosophy made famous in the 1991 best-selling book by Geoffrey A. Moore, Granoff added, "Crossing the chasm to that scale—to adding many thousands of cars to the network very early on—required perfect execution. And we failed to execute perfectly."

There were some fits and starts in the months to come; attempts to keep the dream alive. Two groups briefly bought the company. Both lost it.

First came solar-energy entrepreneur Yosef Abramowitz, co-founder of the Arava Power Company, who went by the nickname "Captain Sunshine." Abramowitz teamed up with the Association for the Advancement of Electric Transport in Israel, hoping to turn Better Place into a national infrastructure project. But when government bureaucracy kept some 350 Fluence Z.E.s he intended to sell locked in the Ashdod port, his investors backed out.

Then came a group called Success Parking, led by parking lot magnate Tsahi Merkur. It planned to rebrand the company as "DRiiVZ" and keep only a dozen of the original 40 battery switch stations open. Success Parking lost the bid for Better Place when Merkur was caught trying to pass a $500,000 check drawn on a fictitious foreign account.

Within a few months, all the switch stations were padlocked, the control center was turned off, and drivers were left on their own.

One painful and highly visible reminder reported by Better Place drivers: The clock on the dashboard of the Fluence Z.E. was stuck in perpetual Standard Time; it could only be updated to Daylight Savings Time though the control center, which was now shut down.

Carasso promised to honor its agreement with Renault to service the cars for five years, but if the battery died or malfunctioned, there were no ready replacements in the region.

Renault closed its Turkish production line for the Fluence Z.E. shortly after Better Place's bankruptcy and moved it to South Korea. There, the car would have a moderately successful run as a fixed-battery electric vehicle known as the Renault Samsung SM3 Z.E.

A version of the all-electric Fluence Z.E. also appeared at the 2016 Beijing Auto Show under the name "Fengnuo"—a Chinese approximation of "Fluence."

Back in Israel, fewer than a thousand Fluence Z.E.s were sold or leased, with another 400 in Denmark. The electric vehicles languishing in the Ashdod port would eventually be so damaged by the sea air that Renault claimed they would need to be destroyed entirely. It was an ending not unlike that of the General Motors EV1, which entirely vanished from the United States in 2002.

Renault quietly "bought back" the few cars tooling around Copenhagen, offering customers a gasoline-powered Fluence or—in perhaps the most painful irony of all—a non-switchable-battery powered Zoe. In Israel, however, most remained on the roads in the years to come. Drivers kept up their enthusiasm about their purchase despite the limited range and lack of the Better Place company to support them.

Drivers could power up at home, making the car workable for short distances. A local Israeli distributor, Freedom eBikes, which assembled and marketed electric bicycles in Israel, adapted its charging cable for two-wheelers to work with the Fluence Z.E., providing added wall-pluggable portability.

Drivers banded together on social media for support and adopted several mobile apps that allowed them to locate and share home-charging spots if a driver got stuck.

"We're a band of brothers, a very cohesive community, and we need to help each other," explained a Better Place car owner to Ynet reporter Nir Ben-Zaken. "Anyone who bought the car becomes part of the family."

"Electric car owners are a special population," added Shlomo Kedar, who used an app called Pony Express to share his charge spot. "If you ask for help, you'll immediately get ten suggestions, including a cup of coffee or lunch."

"Start-up Nation" author Saul Singer said he hoped Better Place's bankruptcy wouldn't scare off future Israeli initiatives to make the world a better place.

Israel is "a big solution factory," he explained. "We love to tackle big problems, particularly if they seem impossible to solve. I would hope that we get even better at thinking big, and that our failures will not rein in the audacity of our best entrepreneurs."

For now, Better Place's legacy lives on beyond Israel.

The company's involvement with European standards groups like the TEN-T consortium for electrifying the continent's roadways, the EZ-Batt project to create a standard electric battery to be used in all electric vehicles, and Green eMotion, which was aimed at setting a framework for pan-European interoperability and cell phone-like "roaming" for electric cars, helped create facts on the ground and policies that will impact future electrification projects.

"When we started, there was no awareness that electric vehicles were a viable option, that they could go longer distances than city cars or golf carts," said Amit Yudan, whose job included working on public policy programs for Better Place in Europe.

And although Yudan was never able to sign on another European utility, "Better Place created huge attention with heads of state, politicians and regulators to develop the infrastructure and provide the consumer services," he said.

Better Place's notion of an electric taxi service in the Netherlands didn't disappear entirely either. In 2014, it was reincarnated as Taxi Electric, a service connecting Schiphol airport with the city of Amsterdam, using a fleet of 137 Tesla Model S electric cars. In 2016, Madrid's La Ciudad del Taxi announced plans to put 110 all-electric Nissan Leafs on the streets of Spain's capital city.

Nor is battery switching entirely dead; it's just been scaled back.

In Taiwan, a startup called Gogoro has built a network of switchable-battery motor scooters. You pull up to a Gogoro roadside stand the size of a small vending machine and swap the 20-pound battery yourself. The company is expanding to other countries in Asia.

But large-scale battery swap seems to have gone out of favor.

A company called Greenway in Slovakia proposed developing switchable battery delivery vans in 2012 and even built a couple of simple prototype switch stations, but the idea didn't catch on.

In another ironic twist, a month after Better Place went belly-up, rival Tesla announced that its high-end Model S would have a switchable-battery option. Tesla founder Elon Musk demonstrated a 90-second battery swap on stage to wild applause (Better Place was never mentioned) and built a switching station between Los Angeles and San Francisco.

But drivers gave the idea a decidedly lukewarm response.

"We've invited all the Model S owners in the area to try it out, and of the first round of 200 invitations, only four or five people were interested," Musk told shareholders and investors in 2015. "Clearly it's not very popular."

"Being willing to take risks is essential," emphasized "Start-up Nation" author Singer. The collapse of Better Place is actually "a good example of how Israelis have a tolerance for failures. We don't just hide them. We get up, brush ourselves off and do the next thing."

Mike Granoff, who in many ways jumpstarted the Better Place story by introducing Shai Agassi to Idan Ofer, echoed that assessment in the letter he sent to his investors explaining Better Place's decision to liquidate.

"Israel was home to the world's first full-service network for electric cars allowing uninterrupted travel across the whole country, and history will ultimately tell the significance of that milestone. While that might be little comfort to heartbroken customers, to investors, or to the hundreds of employees who need to find other work, all of us should hold our heads high in the knowledge that we played an important role in this burgeoning revolution. As [famous short seller] Jim Chanos has said, 'In investing you can be really right, but temporarily quite wrong.'"

Granoff concluded on an honest but optimistic note.

Speaking for all of the pioneers who had put their faith into Better Place, he wrote, "I am sorry we were not able to bring the company to the glorious success that it deserved, but I have no regrets for having tried."

AFTERWORD

In the wake of Better Place's bankruptcy, the desire to play the blame game is understandable. After all, investors lost nearly a billion dollars, and more than a thousand drivers could no longer switch batteries.

How did a startup that seemed to have everything going for it end up so totaled?

The crash of Better Place was not the result of any single factor. Rather, it was in many ways a perfect storm of unexpected changes that upended the company's business plan and assumptions, combined with some flat-out bad luck and an unbending commitment to a singular vision. That commitment, in retrospect, might be deemed short-sighted, but at the time was business as usual for a company that sincerely wanted to change the world.

Indeed, startups can thrive only in an environment that acknowledges and embraces risk and uncertainty. Enterprising companies—and the investors who back them—get into bed together fully aware that the majority of startups will fail, but a few will grow big enough to make the whole system worthwhile.

Still, the Better Place story holds lessons—for business and perhaps for wider application as well.

Here are seven such lessons.

1. HOW YOU MANAGE CHANGE MAKES ALL THE DIFFERENCE

That change is inevitable has long since become a business and pop culture cliché. Some might say recognition of this started with Spencer Johnson's "Who Moved My Cheese?" But it's how a company and its management respond to changing circumstances that determines whether a business succeeds or stalls.

Changes hit Better Place on multiple fronts, sometimes all at once.

The public expected a free or at least inexpensive car, but Renault assigned a high price to the Fluence Z.E., leaving Better Place only the thinnest profit margin.

Driving range for the Fluence Z.E. was 25 percent less than Better Place had anticipated when planning its network, resulting in some poorly located switch stations and increased "range anxiety" for drivers.

The battery switch stations cost six times what Better Place's spreadsheets had accounted for. And because the stations worked only with the Fluence Z.E., it would have cost another $1 million to retrofit each station for additional battery types down the road.

The charge spots cost more than 10 times the original estimate, once installation costs, including repeat visits by technicians and the involvement of Better Place's lawyers, were factored in.

Customers balked at the monthly subscription package. Result: too little revenue to cover expenses.

There was only one type of car, and it wasn't a hit. Better Place had planned to sign multiple car manufacturers but couldn't get any traction. Customers didn't like the Fluence Z.E.—it was too big, too boxy; it had a tiny trunk and it looked too much like the gasoline-powered version of the Fluence. The biggest obstacle: It was a Renault, which the target market deemed a second-rate family sedan, compared with Mazda or Toyota.

Company cars were off the table. Better Place had planned on getting to these markets through the big leasing companies, but because no one knew what the Fluence Z.E.'s residual value would be in three years, or how well the battery would hold up, Hertz and Avis balked.

There was no incentive for electric. The majority of "C" class cars in Israel are provided as corporate perks and come with free gas. What's the consumer benefit in such a market? Better Place believed individuals would still buy them. They didn't.

Israel's Renault distributor said "no," forcing Better Place to set up its own sales subsidiary at considerable time and expense.

Branding was hidden. Co-location with existing gas stations along major highways would have been perfect for Better Place's switch stations, allowing fast access and high visibility. But illegal building blocked that path. Instead, the switch stations were set up in grimy industrial zones and next to cemeteries.

Better Place was religious about battery switch. But the public (and every other electric car manufacturer) came to prefer the less complicated and less expensive fast charge model.

Bad relationships took a toll. Better Place had imagined a healthy working relationship with its only car-manufacturing partner. Instead, the two companies barely talked. Suspicion and paranoia ruled the day, and the poor luck of a spy scandal removed Better Place's few advocates at Renault.

The Great Recession—enough said. Better Place had planned to finance its expensive batteries through mortgage-like CDOs. The housing crisis killed that notion.

One country in Europe wasn't enough. Better Place wanted to be everywhere on the continent. It cut deals only in Denmark and the Netherlands.

Washington, D.C., was gridlocked. Shai Agassi's charm and vision wasn't enough to get U.S. government attention and overcome obstacles to funding—leaving Better Place with no presence in its largest potential market.

Investment dried up. Better Place was sure Idan Ofer would never shut off the funding spigot, but the billionaire eventually had no choice.

The bottom line: No matter how smart you and your team are, or how well planned your business, unexpected change is the only certitude.

Managing change often demands a radical rethink. But Shai Agassi and his team stayed the course, digging in deeper while doubling down on dogma, even as they watched their every assumption fall away or get turned on its head.

At what point do you realize the original business plan no longer works? By the time new management was ready to make the hard decisions, it was too late.

2. STARTUPS MUST REMAIN NIMBLE

Better Place grew so fast that, even before it had had a single product ready for sale, it could no longer be described as agile. And agility is the key element that gives up-and-comers a competitive advantage over the entrenched players they hope to disrupt. Better Place's sky-high burn rate, runaway staffing and expansive worldwide operations cost it the easy ability to recalibrate.

It was done with the best of intentions.

Hiring Amdocs to build software that could support a million drivers from the get-go meant Better Place would not fall into the "Twitter trap" of not being prepared for customer growth—a logical and even laudable goal.

But the dilemma could have been approached in a way that preserved agility: Build what was needed today—and maybe a little more—without overspending on massive scaling capabilities. Wait until it's clear what shape the product will take. Don't count on the form defined in early projections.

"Future-proofing is fine," Better Place Australia CEO Evan Thornley said. "But not when you have hundreds of software engineers involved in that future-proofing. Startups require the ability to change fast. We were bloated."

3. REMAIN OPEN TO NEW SOLUTIONS

Staying nimble also requires not committing too strongly to ideas and ideals, or getting stuck on any particular solution—because the rules change.

Shai Agassi made it clear when he met with General Motors in 2008 that Better Place was not interested in becoming the infrastructure provider for the Chevrolet Volt. He eschewed "anything with a tailpipe."

That kind of commitment had its advantages. It certainly differentiated Better Place. And the company could afford that stance at first, with the 100 percent–electric Fluence on board.

But when it became clear that no other car manufacturers were willing to sign on, the commitment became a liability. Better Place might have benefited from some tinkering, some opening up to other opportunities.

Similarly, Better Place had sold investors on the benefits of turning all of Israel into a "beta" country, and had invested considerable resources into its Israeli infrastructure. But when it became clear that the company was set to lose money on every car it sold in the Holy Land, did it make sense to continue?

Companies in both software and hardware have successfully pivoted. Indeed, doing so is the hallmark of some of the all-time greatest business success stories.

Mobile phone maker Nokia started by making rubber boots.

IBM is no longer in the personal computer business at all.

Western Union rose to fame with telegrams; today it's the world's largest money transfer service.

Nintendo originally made playing cards.

Twitter started as Odeo, a podcasting company that was made irrelevant when Apple released iTunes.

What alternative pathways to success might Better Place have considered?

4. KNOW WHEN TO FOCUS

The corollary to not getting stuck is to resist the desire to explore any and every opportunity that comes your way.

Especially in the early days, when nothing is set in stone, it is tempting to answer every call, take every meeting and fly to any country that expresses an interest in your product.

Better Place's Series A round investment was large enough to enable the company to explore potential partnerships from Beijing to Bahrain, Chile to China. Operations were launched in five continents at once. Resources were poured into taxi trials in New York, San Francisco, Japan and the Netherlands.

Was all that too much for a single startup, however well-funded, to handle? Would a narrower demo centered on a single geography, or a proof of concept, have been more prudent?

Better Place had an aversion to focus when the opportunities seemed boundless. When do you need to keep your options open and when is it time to settle down and go steady?

Being discriminating about opportunities can help a startup succeed. Multiple partnerships and contacts may look good in a press release, but they are rarely sustainable.

5. THE BUSINESS YOU THINK YOU'RE IN MAY NOT BE THE ONE YOU'RE REALLY IN

Better Place was at its core a hardware company: It built switch stations, charge spots and a smart grid with physical cables and connectors, and it sold two-ton electric cars that required all those components. But the company's top management all came from software.

That mismatch would grate when it came to placing metal in the ground, where a mistake couldn't be fixed by pushing out a software update and where iterating a better interface design wouldn't reduce the costs of physically installing hardware in the field. Most of all, there's no easy way to cut corners when human lives are at stake and you need to keep your drivers safe while they're hurtling down a highway at 70 miles an hour.

Know your industry and hire appropriately.

6. BE WARY OF "PROTEXIA"

Many executives hire friends, past work colleagues and sometimes even family. It's often an excellent starting point and can be invaluable while getting going. But as the business grows, the initial team is invariably replaced by professionals with more solution-specific experience.

Replacing an executive you trust, someone with whom you've shared battle experience either in a previous job or in the military itself, with an unknown from a search firm can be intimidating. It can even be a mistake. (Look how well Apple's John Sculley worked out for Steve Jobs.)

But was that reason enough for Better Place to stick with its initial team? Were they all the absolute best for a company with such great ambitions?

Did personal issues cloud management's judgment at times?

Was there another role for Shai Agassi that would have allowed him to remain the visionary without getting trapped in the day-to-day details? It turns out you do have to sweat the small stuff.

7. INDIVIDUAL VISION AND CHARISMA CAN TAKE YOU ONLY SO FAR

Shai Agassi's confidence in his ability to sell anyone on anything was not unlike Steve Jobs' famous "reality distortion field"—which more often than not resulted in Apple staff building revolutionary products even they didn't think were possible.

Both Jobs and Agassi pushed their teams to create remarkable software and hardware. But there is a limit; at some point, the magician can't produce the next rabbit and cold business calculations take over.

Hyperbole eventually will wear thin, and whether it's in the boardroom or on the TED stage, it can come back to hurt a company. When you promise a free car, or one that runs entirely on renewable energy, and don't—or can't—deliver, your customers may not forgive you.

Grandstanding for a better deal may mean no deal at all, or bridges burned rather than built.

Dismissing employee concerns as irrelevant to a trillion-dollar company doesn't engender loyalty.

The dangers of running a one-man show have been communicated since the days people first started telling stories around the fire. The message is clear: Seek out and listen to your advisors, especially the least powerful among them, or pay a price.

Early in his career, Shai Agassi played competitive poker. But as the game goes on, you're dealt new cards. If you keep playing based on the same cards you had at the beginning, eventually someone will call your bluff.

Audacious vision and ambitious goals are critical to inventing innovative products and solutions, but they cannot operate in a vacuum. They must be balanced by smart hires, prudent spending and ever-agile development and business planning.

Get it right and you might be the next big thing. Overplay your hand and, as with Better Place, even a billion dollars won't keep the power on.

ACKNOWLEDGMENTS

In 2012, I bought a Renault Fluence Z.E. 100 percent electric car from Better Place. Like the other Better Place drivers interviewed for *TOTALED*, I loved the car—it was fast, quiet, powerful and green. After the company went bankrupt, I wanted to know more about what happened. This book is the result of that search.

TOTALED would never have come together without the support of the nearly 80 former Better Place executives, journalists, investors and car owners who agreed to be interviewed. I was continually amazed at how generous they were with their time in answering my questions—by phone, in person and via Skype.

I had hoped to interview Shai Agassi for the book. Although he declined to participate, I appreciate the time he spent explaining his concerns—and ultimately his objections—to me.

Even though everyone I spoke to gave so much to this book, a few stand out. In particular, Mike Granoff, Zohar Bali, Dan Cohen, Andrey Zarur and Evan Thornley spent many hours over multiple sessions and follow-up emails to help me tell the story accurately. Mike was instrumental in introducing me to key Better Place staff. I also met my first (and only) Israeli prime minister while interviewing Idan Ofer, as we ate Passover cookies in his Tel Aviv penthouse.

After I conducted the interviews, I got stuck. Esther Goldenberg helped me get past my writer's block. Esther is the best book coach imaginable. This book came together through our weekly sessions of encouragement, smart suggestions and timely feedback. If you are looking for a stellar coach for your next book, Esther should be your first call.

Also instrumental in crafting the narrative was my editor Sara Wildberger, who not only pared down a significant amount of my overly pearly prose but also suggested new directions and framing that ultimately made *TOTALED* a more compelling tale. Business book editors don't come much better.

Abigail Leichman was the first editor to read *TOTALED*, and she made sure that the language was clean and my facts were straight.

My agents, Deborah Harris and Michael Palgon, helped me craft a killer proposal which guided the overall structure of the book.

To Mishy Harman, Yochai Maital, Zev Levi and everyone on the Israel Story team—thank you for believing that *TOTALED* could be turned into compelling radio.

To my children—Amir, Merav and Aviv—who put up with their father squirreling away extra hours to write with the upstairs office door closed, thank you for giving me the space to immerse myself in the world of *TOTALED*. I hope I maintained some semblance of family balance!

Last—and certainly not least—I want to acknowledge my wife Jody who never wavered in her faith that I had this book in me and could write it. Her willingness to listen to my every up and down, her unflagging enthusiasm and mindful support as the book rounded the final corner were my ultimate inspiration.

In the dedication to *TOTALED*, I wrote about "Jody, who loved her Fluence Z.E." That was in the past tense. Just as the book was coming out, Renault made an offer we couldn't refuse to buy back our electric car. Like the General Motors EV1, our Fluence Z.E.—and those of all the other Better Place owners who took Renault up on their overture—will probably be crushed and destroyed, leaving only several dozen shuttered battery switch stations to remind occasional passersby of the Better Place story in Israel.

I hope that this book will in part keep the best of the Better Place legacy alive.

ENDNOTES

Much of the research for *TOTALED* was based on personal interviews conducted by the author with nearly 80 former Better Place executives, journalists, Fluence Z.E. drivers, investors and industry insiders. These interviews were instrumental in reconstructing dialogue where one of the participants in a discussion or meeting did not provide his or her own quotes. These are indicated in the notes to follow.

While the majority of the people interviewed for *TOTALED* spoke on the record, a few asked that they remain anonymous. These are indicated in the notes as well.

TOTALED uses U.S. figures in most cases; as a result, if an interviewee referred to kilometers, shekels or Euros, it has generally been converted into miles and dollars in the quote itself.

Introduction

1   *"For a moment, suspend your disbelief":* Author's interviews with Mike Granoff from December 2013 until July 2014.

1   *Today, he was saying it to one of the wealthiest men in Israel:* Details of the meeting between Agassi and Ofer from the author's interviews with Idan Ofer, April 17, 2014 and Mike Granoff. The overview of the Better Place solution presented here will be expanded on in the rest of the book.

1   *At the time worth nearly $4 billion:* Michal Yoshai, "Stef Wertheimer Richest Israeli on Forbes' Middle East Ranking," *Globes*, October 1, 2007. Idan and Sammy Ofer were worth $3.9 billion together according to *Forbes*.

3   *Ofer's Israel Corporation held stakes in a dozen companies:* Israel Corp. website.

3   *Ofer's luxurious suite on the 25th floor of the Millennium Tower:* Author's interview with Mike Granoff.

4   *Wired magazine called it the fifth-largest startup in history:* Daniel Roth, "Driven: Shai Agassi's Audacious Plan to Put Electric Cars on the Road," *Wired*, August 18, 2008.

4   *perhaps the most spectacularly failed technology startup of the 21st century:* Max Chafkin, "A Broken Place: The Spectacular Failure of the Startup that Was Going to Change the World," *Fast Company*, April 7, 2014.

Chapter 1 - The Early Days

5 *Agassi had sold another company, TopTier:* Doron Avigad, "TopTier Acquisition Unprecedented for SAP," *Globes*, January 4, 2011.

5 *Reuven Agassi immigrated to Israel from the southern Iraqi city of Basra:* Senor and Singer, *Start-up Nation: The Story of Israel's Economic Miracle.*

5 *"In Baghdad, the government even carried out public hangings":* ibid.

5 *the Agassis joined a flood of 150,000 Iraqi refugees:* ibid.

5 *Reuven Agassi eventually was drafted into the Israel Defense Forces:* Shai Agassi, "Israel Technology Generations," *The Long Tailpipe—Shai Agassi's Blog*, June 29, 2007.

5 *that's where he met Paula:* ibid.

5 *the army had a program where the state would pay for education:* ibid.

5 *Shai Agassi was born on April 19, 1968:* "Shai Agassi—Israeli Entrepreneur," *Encyclopedia Britannica.*

5 *When Reuven retired from the military:* ibid.

6 *"I got exposed to American culture and to my first Apple II computer":* ibid.

6 *in exchange for 10 percent of his "lifetime profits" from writing software:* Clive Thompson, "Batteries Not Included," *The New York Times*, April 16, 2009.

6 *Agassi graduated from the Lincoln International School in Buenos Aires:* Yatedo website.

6 *he was hit by a truck:* Eleanor Fox, "Electric Shock," *Mako Magazine*, May 30, 2013.

6 *while trying to cross an expressway on foot:* Author's interview with Mike Granoff.

6 *"He lay for months in the hospital":* Fox, "Electric Shock."

6 *he was taken instead into the Intelligence Corps:* "Agassi, Shai Ben Reuven," Wertheimer. info website.

6 *more companies listed on the NASDAQ:* Start-up Nation Central website.

7 *"How is it that Israel— a country of":* Senor and Singer, *Start-up Nation: The Story of Israel's Economic Miracle.*

7 *Just about every major tech company:* ibid.

7 *Intel entrusted its Israeli team to develop the 8088 chip:* David Shamah, "Let a Billion Chips Bloom: Intel Israel Celebrates 40 Years," *The Times of Israel*, January 26, 2014.

7 *convinced Reuven Agassi "to do the unthinkable":* Shai Agassi, "Israel Technology Generations," *The Long Tailpipe—Shai Agassi's Blog.*

7 *the two started Quicksoft:* Dan Yachin, "Still a Prodigy," *Globes*, June 10, 2013.

7 *In 1995, Quicksoft landed a deal with Apple:* ibid.

7 *"Someone at Apple decided":* Shai Agassi, "My Best Career Mistake," *LinkedIn*, April 22, 2013.

7 *It created a sense of urgency:* ibid.

8 *"We huddled and concluded that the lesson from this failure":* ibid.

8 *Quicksoft had signed on five new long-term clients:* ibid.

8 *By Friday, all five companies were gone:* ibid.

8 *We have only two more weeks of cash in the bank:* ibid.

8 *Could the Quicksoft technology become a kind of Yahoo for business:* ibid?

8   *It was an answer "for visionary corporate CIOs":* ibid.

8   *14 angel investors, which injected $800,000 into the company:* ibid.

8   *Quicksoft's corporate portal division was renamed TopTier:* Guy Grimland, "Taking High Tech to New Heights," *Haaretz,* October 23, 2008.

8   *In 1998, Agassi sold 56 percent of TopTier:* Avigad, "TopTier Acquisition Unprecedented for SAP."

8   *By 2000, the company was generating $20 million in revenue a year:* "SAP to Pay $400 million for TopTier," *IT World,* March 30, 2001.

9   *With 13,000 employees:* "SAP—a 44-Year History of Success," SAP website.

9   *An analyst report by AMR Research:* Avigad, "TopTier Acquisition Unprecedented for SAP."

9   *he held 8.8 percent of TopTier, worth about $35 million:* Tzvika Paz, "TopTier President, CEO Shai Agassi to Head New SAP subsidiary," *Globes,* May 4, 2001.

9   *Agassi was put in charge of the entire portals business:* ibid.

9   *Hasso Plattner relinquished his role guiding technology development:* Alorie Gilbert, "SAP Chief Gives Up Development Duties," *CNET,* February 4, 2003.

9   *"There was a huge sense of pride and excitement":* Author's interview with former TopTier executive.

9   *"Plattner built a corporate culture in his own image":* Steve Hamm, "Meet the New Hasso Plattner," *BusinessWeek* (which became *Bloomberg Businessweek* in 2010), July 9, 2001.

9   *insular and slow to change its ways:* ibid.

9   *Plattner launched mySAP.com,* ibid.

10   *"Agassi suggested nearly a dozen heretical ideas":* Roth, "Driven: Shai Agassi's Audacious Plan to Put Electric Cars on the Road."

10   *Plattner had anointed him as imminent successor:* Dawn Kawamoto, "SAP Tech Honcho Shai Agassi Resigns," *CNET,* March 29, 2007.

10   *Instead, Agassi found himself competing with SAP's head of marketing:* ibid.

10   *"It changed him forever":* Author's interview with Andrey Zarur, August 1, 2014.

10   *he had already made up his mind several months earlier:* Josette Akresh-Gonzales, "Energy CEO Shai Agassi on Recognizing a 'Sliding-Doors' Moment," *Harvard Business Review,* May 2009.

10   *"The moment could have passed me by quite easily":* ibid.

11   *"I've never seen someone as skilled as Shai at selling abstract concepts":* Vauhini Vara, "Software Executive Shifts Gears to Electric Cars," *The Wall Street Journal,* October 29, 2007.

11   *he took home only $125:* Ranking Hero website.

11   *35th annual World Series of Poker's* "No-Limit Hold'em": Global Poker Index website.

11   *he placed well ahead of several celebrity players:* J. Bonsai, "Bluffing? SAP Exec Hopes So," *Investor's Business Daily,* October 31, 2005.

11   *he won $3,964:* Global Poker Index website.

11   *"Shai is very private":* J. Bonsai, "Bluffing? SAP Exec Hopes So."

11 *"I'd say that my poker game is uneducated"*: ibid

12 *"The way he talked about it, it was just so easy"*: Author's interview with Macgregor Duncan, May 28, 2014.

12 *"In business you can't bluff too much or you'll get caught"*: Bonsai, "Bluffing? SAP Exec Hopes So."

12 *"Poker helps develop that level of awareness"*: ibid.

Chapter 2

13 *Forum of Young Global Leaders:* World Economic Forum website.

13 *Among the attendees:* ibid.

13 *achieved their success young - under the age of 40:* Forum of Young Global Leaders brochure, PDF.

13 *started by German-born Klaus Schwab:* "WEF and Davos: A Brief History," *The Telegraph,* January 18, 2016.

13 *"how do you make the world a better place by 2020":* Francesco Anesi and Carolina De Simone, "Global Shapers of the World Unite!" *Global Shapers Community,* a World Economic Forum website, November 7, 2012.

13 *"It was intended as a conversation starter":* Akresh-Gonzales, "Energy CEO Shai Agassi on Recognizing a 'Sliding-Doors' Moment."

14 *"There were no assignments; everything was self-selection":* Author's interview with Andrey Zarur, which also includes Zarur's description of Klaus Schwab, of how Zarur and Agassi met, what Agassi originally thought about the science and how his views changed, and Zarur's impressions of Agassi's "unparalleled intelligence."

15 *by a complete and total cessation of vehicular traffic:* Author's experience living in Israel.

15 *levels of nitrogen oxide drop by 83 percent to 98 percent in the Tel Aviv area over Yom Kippur:* David Shamah, "Study Shows Yom Kippur's Empty Roads Make for Cleaner Air," *The Times of Israel,* September 13, 2013.

16 *"A change in vehicle fleet to low-emission vehicles":* ibid.

16 *"Reducing oil consumption was also a national security issue":* Author's interview with Andrey Zarur.

16 *"Electric cars were just one of ten different things we looked at":* ibid.

16 *"I created a fairly sophisticated Excel model":* ibid.

16 *they briefly considered hydrogen:* ibid.

16 *"We also looked at things that would make you laugh":* ibid.

16 *At one point, they wondered if they could build highways with the power to charge cars:* Author's interview with Mike Granoff.

16 *"the most cost-effective technology was electric":* Author's interview with Andrey Zarur.

17 *The internal combustion engine had to be retired:* Roth, "Driven: Shai Agassi's Audacious Plan to Put Electric Cars on the Road."

17 *A short history of electric cars* based mainly on research from: David Kirsch, *The Electric Car and the Burden of History*, Rutgers University Press, July 1, 2000; and Ken W. Purdy and Christopher G. Foster, "History of the Automobile," *The Encyclopedia Britannica.*

19 *Members of two student groups at Stanford University:* Author's interview with Dimitri Dadiomov, March 30, 2014.

19 *About 40 people attended:* ibid.

19 *"I'm imagining this software executive in a suit":* ibid.

19 *Agassi and Zarur needed help to flesh out the details:* ibid.

19 *the university Agassi admits he applied to—and was rejected from:* Shai Agassi, "Stanford Presentation," *The Long Tailpipe—Shai Agassi's Blog.* April 27, 2007.

19 *Of the students who attended Agassi's lecture:* ibid.

19 *Agassi spent many hours with the group:* ibid.

19 *The result was an 18-page document:* Shai Agassi and Andrey Zarur, *Transforming Global Transportation: Fuel Independence at Country Level as a Business Opportunity. A Modern Day Moon-Shot*, December 2007, sixth draft.

19 *"an ambitious, exploratory and ground-breaking project":* "Moon Shot Thinking," GDTM.org website.

20 *"the bravery of Churchill, the vision of JFK, the determination of Reagan":* Agassi and Zarur, *Transforming Global Transportation.* The details and calculations in the following section are taken from this paper.

22 *"Shai never intended to say that he was JFK, putting a man on the moon":* Author's interview with Andrey Zarur.

23 *The paper "was only meant as an exercise":* ibid.

23 *"Almost word for word":* ibid.

23 *Yergin posited that the world had enough oil to last for decades:* Daniel Yergin, "It's Not the End of the Oil Age," *The Washington Post*, July 31, 2005.

23 *dire predictions about the imminent approach of "peak oil":* Dave Cohen, "Getting to Know Daniel Yergin," *The Oil Drum*, August 18, 2006.

23 *saw no reason to panic:* Daniel Yergin, "Ensuring Energy Security," *Foreign Affairs*, March/April 2006.

23 *"There will be a large unprecedented buildup of oil supply in the next few years":* Yergin, "It's Not the End of the Oil Age."

23 *Yergin delivered this prognosis in front of a crowd of international leaders:* The Saban Forum 2006 - A U.S.-Israel Dialogue Proceedings, PDF, *Brookings.*

23 *billionaire Israeli Haim Saban:* "232 Haim Saban—Forbes 400," *Forbes*, February 2, 2017.

24 *he was quietly nervous:* Roth, "Driven: Shai Agassi's Audacious Plan to Put Electric Cars on the Road."

24 *Among the participants seated near him:* ibid.

24 *he started off with an uncharacteristic stammer:* ibid.

24 *"As he talked, he read the body language of the audience":* ibid.

24 *"Do you have this written down anywhere":* Author's interview with Mike Granoff.

24　*Agassi briefly stepped down from the dais:* ibid.

24　*"You are my witnesses":* ibid.

24　*"You're solving the right problem at the wrong time":* Shai Agassi and Mike Granoff, *Chapter One: The Start of the Story,* Better Place internal publication, September 2012.

25　*"The average Joe doesn't go to a dealership":* ibid.

25　*"And how exactly should I do that?":* ibid.

25　*"You're the smart guy. You figure it out":* ibid.

25　*Agassi was lying in bed when his phone rang:* Roth, "Driven: Shai Agassi's Audacious Plan to Put Electric Cars on the Road."

25　*"Nice speech. Now what?":* ibid.

25　*"What do you mean?":* ibid.

25　*"You spoke so beautifully. You have to make this a reality":* ibid.

25　*"Can you really do it?":* Shai Agassi, "President's Conference," *The Long Tailpipe—Shai Agassi's Blog,* June 3, 2008.

25　*"merely solving a puzzle":* Agassi, "President's Conference."

25　*"I wasn't thinking about it as a company, but more as an arm of government":* Shai Agassi and Mike Granoff, *Chapter One: The Start of the Story.*

25　*"agencies don't do things. Entrepreneurs do":* ibid.

26　*"What can I do to help?":* Agassi, "President's Conference."

26　*He started his 60-year career in politics: President Shimon Peres (1923-2016):* Knesset website.

26　*"Oil is the greatest problem of all time":* Steve Hamm, "A Better Place for Cars," *BusinessWeek, January 21, 2008.*

26　*"Why should we hang on oil when we can hang on the sun?":* Roth, "Driven: Shai Agassi's Audacious Plan to Put Electric Cars on the Road."

26　*"When you are small, you can be really daring":* ibid.

26　*"You cannot say: I'm going to negotiate pollution for 10 or 20 years":* ibid.

26　*Shai Agassi flew to Israel at the end of December:* Senor and Singer, *Start-up Nation: The Story of Israel's Economic Miracle.*

26　*"Each morning we would meet at [Peres's] office and I would debrief him":* ibid.

27　*He set two conditions:* ibid.

27　*"You don't know anything about cars":* Author's interview with Mike Granoff.

27　*"The Israeli government is not a venture capitalist":* ibid.

27　*"We only intended to raise five or ten million dollars in seed capital":* Author's interview with Andrey Zarur.

27　*Olmert promised he would put pressure:* Roth, "Driven: Shai Agassi's Audacious Plan to Put Electric Cars on the Road."

27　*Under Olmert's proposed tax scheme* ibid.

27　*The tax would rise sharply afterward:* ibid.

27　*the revenue losses could add up to $700 million over five years:* ibid.

27　*The potential hit to tax revenues:* ibid.

28   *He also sent letters to the CEOs of the five biggest automakers:* Senor and Singer, *Start-up Nation: The Story of Israel's Economic Miracle.*

28   *Peres and Agassi flew together to Davos:* ibid.

28   *Of the two who showed up, Toyota was the first to arrive:* Author's interview with Mike Granoff.

28   *he spent most of the meeting trying to talk Peres out of pushing it any further:* Senor and Singer, *Start-up Nation: The Story of Israel's Economic Miracle.*

28   *"How about we give you guys a big discount on bringing our hybrids to Israel?":* Author's interview with Mike Granoff.

28   *"I had completely embarrassed this international statesman":* Senor and Singer, *Start-up Nation: The Story of Israel's Economic Miracle.*

28   *"They're really nervous about what you have to say":* Author's interview with Mike Granoff.

28   *there was even a manga comic book:* James Macintosh, "Carlos Ghosn: Superstar Car Executive," *Financial Times,* November 19, 2004.

28   *"the hardest-working man in the brutally competitive global car business":* Joann Muller, "The Impatient Mr. Ghosn," *Forbes,* May 5, 2006.

28   *Japanese media nicknamed him "Seven-Eleven":* Macintosh, "Carlos Ghosn: Superstar Car Executive."

29   *"I read Shai's paper and he is absolutely right":* Senor and Singer, *Start-up Nation: The Story of Israel's Economic Miracle.*

29   *"So what do you think of hybrids?":* ibid.

29   *"A hybrid is like a mermaid":* ibid.

29   *Agassi went so far as to propose that Renault actually manufacture its electric cars in Israel:* ibid.

29   *Why not make it 100,000?:* ibid.

29   *Ghosn's enthusiasm was part of a long term play to differentiate Renault:* Roth, "Driven: Shai Agassi's Audacious Plan to Put Electric Cars on the Road."

29   *Toyota had its Prius hybrid, GM had been pursuing hydrogen fuel cells:* ibid.

29   *A tiny electric Nissan that maybe Renault could sell to government facilities:* ibid.

30   *"Ghosn doesn't get up in the morning unless there's money in it":* Chris Paine, *The Revenge of the Electric Car,* documentary, 2011.

30   *"We're the only ones on the offensive":* ibid.

30   *"My great advantage is that I'm ignorant":* Roth, "Driven: Shai Agassi's Audacious Plan to Put Electric Cars on the Road."

Chapter 3 - Building a Better Place

31   *Mike Granoff was sitting in the lounge of the David Citadel Hotel:* Author's interview with Mike Granoff.

31   *"Israel would be a great test bed for electric cars":* ibid.

31   *to explore opportunities in new energy technology:* ibid.

31 *a Washington D.C.-based group that works to address "the economic and national security threats posed by America's dependence on oil"*: Securing America's Future Energy website.

31 *raise some of the initial capital for Israel Cleantech Ventures:* Author's interview with Mike Granoff.

31 *"to fund a company with ambitions to scale electric cars":* ibid.

31 *"Before this, I had never associated Israel with anything to do with cars":* ibid.

32 *"Within an hour, I got a message asking if I could come for breakfast":* ibid.

32 *"It was all very exciting to me, but I also knew Shimon Peres":* ibid.

32 *"People used to say he's had a hundred great ideas for Israel":* ibid.

32 *"You're not going to do this yourself":* ibid.

32 *"Shai Agassi," Peres replied:* ibid

32 *Granoff had never heard of Agassi:* ibid.

32 *"Here's this guy, he's number two at one of the world's largest software companies":* ibid.

32 *"to pursue interests in alternative energy and climate change":* Phred Dvorak and Vauhini Vara, "SAP AG Loses Key Executive as Agassi Quits," *The Wall Street Journal,* March 29, 2007.

32 *"OK, I'll take his contact information now":* Author's interview with Mike Granoff.

33 *shipping magnate Sammy:* Ben Hartman, "Hundreds Bid Farewell to Billionaire Sammy Ofer in TA," *The Jerusalem Post,* June 5, 2011.

33 *Within several years, Idan Ofer would rocket to the top spot as Israel's wealthiest man:* Alistair Dawber, "Israel's Wealthiest Man Idan Ofer Set to Move to London Amid Tax Row," *The Independent,* April 9, 2013.

33 *Ofer projected the confidence of a wrestler:* Roth, "Driven: Shai Agassi's Audacious Plan to Put Electric Cars on the Road."

33 *Ofer actually played rugby and squash in high school:* Author's interview with Idan Ofer.

33 *"Climate change is real":* Thompson, "Batteries Not Included."

33 *"Even if this ends up destroying - for lack of a better word - my refinery business":* Roth, "Driven: Shai Agassi's Audacious Plan to Put Electric Cars on the Road."

33 *"Suspend your disbelief":* Author's interview with Mike Granoff.

33 *In the midst of the presentations, Agassi flew to California to meet with VantagePoint Capital Partners:* Author's interview with Mike Granoff.

33 *"Our approach to clean tech is to invest in accelerating the inevitable":* Camille Ricketts, "Vantage Point's Alan Salzman on Tesla and How VCs Should Think Green," *VentureBeat,* June 30, 2010.

34 *"If you think of Tesla as the iPhone, we're the AT&T":* John Markoff, "Reimagining the Automobile Industry by Selling Electricity," *The New York Times,* October 29, 2007.

34 *"Every car in the world is going to become electric":* Yoni Cohen, "An Interview with VantagePoint CEO Alan Salzman," *Forbes,* January 23, 2012.

34 *"I think it's one of those seminal companies that is going to change how the world functions":* David Pogue, "Jump-Starting the Electric Car Dream," *CBS Sunday Morning,* March 16, 2009.

34 *"Electric vehicles are software-driven vehicles"*: Thompson, "Batteries Not Included."

34 *Agassi was "a visionary, technologist and businessman"*: Alan Salzman, "2009 Time 100," *Time*, April 30, 2009.

34 *"If you're going elephant-hunting"*: Vara, "Software Executive Shifts Gears to Electric Cars."

34 *As the buzz built, Granoff brought investors through his own Maniv operation:* Author's interview with Mike Granoff.

34 *The Israeli venture capital firm Pitango was interested too:* ibid.

35 *at $200 million, it was one of the largest Series A rounds in history:* Chafkin, "A Broken Place: The Spectacular Failure of the Startup that Was Going to Change the World."

35 *"I was told we needed to build a prototype electric car in six weeks"*: Author's interview with Quin Garcia, April 13, 2014.

35 *a self-avowed "car guy"*: ibid.

35 *He had met Shai Agassi six months earlier:* ibid.

35 *Agassi's talk, entitled "The Physics of Startups"*: Entrepreneurial Thought Leaders series, Stanford University, April 25, 2007.

35 *He approached Agassi after the lecture:* Author's interview with Quin Garcia.

35 *Garcia set up operations at an auto body shop called 4x4 Projects:* Author's interview with Quin Garcia.

35 *4x4 was located in a mustard-yellow warehouse:* Roth, "Driven: Shai Agassi's Audacious Plan to Put Electric Cars on the Road."

36 *"we basically ripped out the engine"*: Author's interview with Quin Garcia, which also includes Garcia's description of the ill-fated test drive with Idan Ofer.

37 *Better Place launched to the world in a press conference:* Katie Fehrenbacher, "Shai Agassi Launches Electric Car Startup, Raising $200M," *GigaOm*, October 29, 2007.

37 *"I wasn't sure why we were launching so early"*: Author's interview with Mike Granoff.

37 *Joe Paluska, head of the technology practice:* ibid.

37 *Granoff punched the buttons to swipe through the slides:* ibid.

37 *"literally overnight"*: Shai Agassi, "Launch Day," *The Long Tailpipe—Shai Agassi's Blog*, November 1, 2007.

37 *"Our global economy urgently needs an environmentally clean and sustainable approach"*: Shai Agassi Launches Alternative Transportation Venture," press release, *BusinessWeek*, October 29, 2007.

37 *"The tailpipe problem has always been the most challenging wedge"*: ibid.

37 *"The car companies won't build cars for this until they see a commitment on infrastructure"*: Vara, "Software Executive Shifts Gears to Electric Cars."

38 *"lot of momentum"*: ibid.

38 *"By removing the battery cost from the vehicle price"*: ibid.

38 *provided, of course, Tesla vehicles could be charged with Better Place's infrastructure:* Fehrenbacher, "Shai Agassi Launches Electric Car Startup, Raising $200M."

38 *"it would be very compelling"*: ibid.

38 *"It's definitely a technology that we're very interested in":* Vara, "Software Executive Shifts Gears to Electric Cars."

38 *Better Place launched its Israeli operations on January 21, 2008:* Lilach Weissman and Dubi Ben-Gedalyahu, "Renault CEO: Israel Ideal Test Ground for Electric Car," *Globes,* January 22, 2008.

38 *A banner proclaiming in Hebrew "Making peace between transport and the environment":* "Project Better Place & Renault-Nissan to Electrify Israel," *The Auto Channel,* video, January 22, 2008.

38 *Renault CEO Carlos Ghosn spoke first:* Carlos Ghosn speech from *Auto Channel* video, "Project Better Place & Renault-Nissan to Electrify Israel." Ehud Olmert and Shai Agassi speeches from original drafts written by Mike Granoff.

40 *"It means that I'm a magician":* Doron Avigad and Noa Paraq, "Agassi: Morgan Stanley Doesn't Invest Without a Business Plan," *Globes,* January 22, 2008.

40 *one of 94 publications and websites that covered the Israeli launch:* "Media Coverage Report," Better Place internal memo, January 23, 2008.

40 *be a few thousand electric cars on Israeli roads within a year and 100,000 by the end of 2010:* Steven Erlanger, "Israel Is Set to Promote the Use of Electric Cars," *The New York Times,* January 21, 2008.

40 *"You'll be able to get a nice, high-end [electric] car at a price roughly half that of the gasoline model today":* ibid.

40 *"the total costs of owning one of these cars will be as much as 50 percent less":* Steve Hamm, "A Better Place for Electric Cars," *BusinessWeek,* January 21, 2008.

41 *"If the world is to end its oil addiction":* Akresh-Gonzales, "Energy CEO Shai Agassi on Recognizing a 'Sliding-Doors' Moment."

41 *"I am willing to lose my 'wunderkind' status":* Shai Agassi, "General Press Observation," *The Long Tailpipe—Shai Agassi's Blog,* November 11, 2007.

Chapter 4 - Hiring the Team

42 *"The challenge isn't the batteries and it isn't the cars":* Chuck Squatriglia, "Better Place Unveils an Electric Car Battery Swap Station," *Wired,* May 13, 2009.

42 *Originally from South Africa:* Author's interview with Mike Granoff.

42 *a business development background entirely in the software industry:* "Q&A with Sidney Goodman of Better Place," *Charged Electric Vehicles,* January 5, 2012.

43 *"Tal was a very intelligent guy":* Author's interview with Geoff Zippel, April 16, 2014.

43 *"It's great to say 'I can do anything'":* Author's interview with a former Better Place executive.

43 *Tal was an earnest employee:* Author's interview with a different former Better Place executive.

43 *Shai Agassi also hired his sister, Dafna:* Roth, "Driven: Shai Agassi's Audacious Plan to Put Electric Cars on the Road."

43 *he had originally trained to be an ophthalmologist:* ibid.

43 *"Here I also save lives"*: Inbal Orpaz, "Car of the Future: Electric and Full Applications," *Computerworld*, March 20, 2012.

43 *"He told me to do a calculation comparing the number of patients affected by lung disease"*: ibid.

43 *"catastrophic damage to health"*: ibid.

43 *"My supreme goal is to get off oil, not just to make Better Place profitable"*: Matthew Kalman, "Baby You Can Drive My Car," *The Jerusalem Report*, February 24, 2012.

44 *"Barak knew how to design a product"*: Author's interview with Ariel Tikotsky, April 17, 2014.

44 *one of Hershkovitz's most important qualities was that he "didn't yell"*: Author's interview with Emek Sadot, June 15, 2014.

44 *"not what you know but who you know"*: "Protexia, Who Do You Really Know?" Aliyahpedia section of Nefesh B'Nefesh website.

44 *"Israel is like one big family"*: "Hebrew Slang and Common Israeli Expressions," eHebrew website.

44 *The founding team of Check Point*: Neal Ungerleider, "How Check Point Became the Fortune 500's Cybersecurity Favorite," *Fast Company*, June 4, 2013.

44 *"Israel is geographically smaller and there's a lot less transitory behavior"*: Author's interview with Bob Rosenschein, April 16, 2014.

45 *"an important source of talent"*: ibid.

45 *Moshe Kaplinsky was brought on board to head up the Israeli operating company*: "Project Better Place Israel Appoints CEO," *Green Car Congress*, March 13, 2008.

45 *His name was on a short list to become IDF chief of staff*: Hanan Greenberg, "Candidates for Replacing Halutz: Kaplinsky, Ashkenazy," *Ynet*, January 17, 2007.

46 *"I came to this project mainly because of a deep understanding of Israel's dependence on oil"*: John Reed, "Electric Cars are All the Rage in Israel," *Financial Times*, September 17, 2010.

46 *"I came because of Shai's enthusiasm"*: Shlomit Lan, "The Future has Been Delayed," *Globes*, May 13, 2009.

46 *"extreme scenarios"*: Reed, "Electric Cars are All the Rage in Israel."

46 *the brigade's graduates have gone on to some of the highest positions in the military*: "Finally, Golani Brigade is on Top of the Heap," *The Jerusalem Post*, January 18, 2007.

46 *"Well, no one's perfect"*: Author's interview with Shelly Silverstein, May 19, 2014.

46 *Golani soldiers are considered "the salt of the earth"*: ibid.

46 *"Like we used to make on the bonfire during boot camp"*: ibid.

46 *"There was a gap of cultures in the company"*: Author's interview with Dan Cohen, February 26, 2014.

46 *Kaplan didn't simply "give orders, and say 'Do it and leave me alone'"*: Author's interview with Eitan Hon, April 2, 2014.

47 *"The one thing Shai always told me was that he didn't want a general"*: Author's interview with Mike Granoff.

47   *Former IDF chief of staff Dan Halutz, for example, was hired directly out of the army:*
      Golan Hazani, "Dan Halutz Named CEO of Kamor Motors," *Ynet*, October 10,
      2007.

47   *"Certain units have become technology boot camps":* Dwyer Gunn, "How Did Israel
      Become 'Start-up Nation?'" *Freakonomics*, December 4, 2014.

48   *"IDF service in 8200 is without a doubt an important training ground for future
      entrepreneurs":* Moran Bar and Reut Shechter, "Beyond Israeli Army Unit 8200 -
      That's Not What Startup Nation is All About," *Geektime*, May 31, 2015.

48   *"There are job offers on the Internet and want ads that specifically say meant for 8200
      alumni":* Gil Kerbs, "The Unit," *Forbes*, February 8, 2007.

48   *8200 alumni went a step further and set up a five-month intensive high-tech accelerator:*
      David Shamah, "8200 Start-up Boot Camp Turns Entrepreneurs into Tech Warriors,"
      The Times of Israel, March 31, 2014.

48   *Israel's compulsory service "produces a maturity not seen in Israelis' foreign peers":* Gunn,
      "How Did Israel Become 'Start-up Nation?'"

48   *Zarur, meanwhile, had received a job offer:* Author's interview with Andrey Zarur.

49   *"They want me to make a ten-year investment to them":* ibid.

49   *"I'm getting all these signals from Hasso Plattner":* ibid.

49   *"Let's turn our vision into a real business plan":* ibid.

49   *"We've got a problem, my friend":* ibid.

49   *"We got into a big fight":* ibid.

49   *"Look, I'm totally bummed too":* ibid.

Chapter 5 - Nuts, Bolts and Robots

50   *Tal Agassi was standing in front of three gray-and-blue foam mock-ups:* Roth, "Driven:
      Shai Agassi's Audacious Plan to Put Electric Cars on the Road."

50   *in Better Place's spanking new offices in Kiryat Atidim:* ibid.

50   *Fresh chilled watermelon was served:* ibid.

50   *"The first looks like a giant Pez dispenser":* ibid.

50   *Better Place's business plan called for charge spots to be installed in 500,000 parking spots:*
      Barbara Kiviat and Tim McGirk, "Israel Looks to Electric Cars," *Time*, January 20,
      1998.

51   *NewDealDesign in San Francisco:* Alissa Walker, "Branding Better Place: Building an
      Electric Vehicle Movement," *Fast Company*, September 28, 2009.

51   *Israeli industrial design firm called Nekuda:* Jonathan Shapira, "Project Better Place
      Appoints Israel CEO, Declares Israel as Primary R&D Center," *Cleantech Investing in
      Israel*, March 12, 2008.

51   *vandalized by thieves:* Kalman, "Baby You Can Drive My Car."

51   *open automatically with the swipe of a member's smart card:* Author's experience driving
      a Renault Fluence Z.E.

51   *created a non-verbal feedback loop:* "Welcome to the End of Oil," NewDealDesign
      website.

51 *He wore a tight-fitting button-down shirt that day:* Roth, "Driven: Shai Agassi's Audacious Plan to Put Electric Cars on the Road." Description of the design meeting including discussion and quotes has been adapted from this article.

53 *"Originally we thought they would cost fifty to a hundred dollars each":* Author's interview with Emek Sadot, which also includes Sadot's comments on how Better Place tried to reduce the cost of the charge spots, why third party products like the WattStation couldn't be used, and how the company briefly toyed with becoming a "charge spot plant."

54 *"Shai's got two big traits":* Roth, "Driven: Shai Agassi's Audacious Plan to Put Electric Cars on the Road."

54 *Tal wanted Better Place to develop its own cable:* Author's interview with Ziva Patir, June 24, 2014.

54 *"like going to Coca-Cola and telling them every bottle should come with my straw":* Author's interview with Emek Sadot.

54 *"Better Place wanted to impose its own proprietary standard on the industry":* Author's interview with Ziva Patir.

55 *At 57, she was the oldest employee at Better Place:* ibid.

55 *climbed the ladder to the CEO position, the first woman to do so:* ibid.

55 *Patir also held the chair:* "SII's Ziva Patir Elected VP of ISO and Chair of Technical Management Board," press release, *The Standards Institute of Israel,* October 8, 2013.

55 *Patir retired from the SII in November 2007 and met Shai Agassi a few days later:* Author's interview with Ziva Patir, which also includes Patir's description of her interview with Agassi, discussion of standards, the Swiss electric car driver and Agassi's Apple mantra.

56 *"Ever been to a carwash":* "Moment of Transportation" conference, NDN, video, March 12, 2008.

56 *As the car approaches, the station identifies it:* Author's experience driving a Renault Fluence Z.E., which also includes description of the various steps in swapping a battery, from the hydraulic clamps to the jukebox of batteries stored in the bowels of the station.

57 *gives the underside of the car a quick wash:* Kalman, "Baby You Can Drive My Car."

58 *"We're not dealing with electrons moving in and out":* "Moment of Transportation" conference.

58 *The first switch station to be prototyped took one minute and 13 seconds to swap a battery:* Domenick Money, "Better Place Battery Swapper Demonstrated," *AutoBlog,* May 13, 2009.

58 *"If we can't do this in less time than it takes to fill your gasoline tank":* Thompson, "Batteries Not Included."

58 *"social contract":* Moment of Transportation" conference.

58 *"Technologists will tell you":* ibid.

58 *"So we're actually giving you a better contract":* ibid.

58 *No one goes out to the movies or dinner for less than an hour:* ibid.

58 *Better Place won a government competition sponsored by the Japanese Ministry of the Environment:* Money, "Better Place Battery Swapper Demonstrated."

59 *set a goal of having electric-powered cars account for 50 percent of the cars sold in Japan by 2020:* ibid.

59 *the Leaf, which would, seven years later, become the best-selling 100 percent electric vehicle in the world:* John Voelcker, "Nissan Leaf Sets New Annual Record for U.S. Electric Car Sales," *Green Car Reports,* January 5, 2015.

59 *Subaru had a car called the Stella and Mitsubishi was pushing the i-MiEV:* Josie Garthwaite, "Mitsubishi, Subaru Gear Up for Electric Car Rollouts, Starting in Japan," *GigaOm,* June 5, 2009.

59 *dispatched to the Land of the Rising Sun:* Author's interview with Quin Garcia.

59 *The vehicle chosen for the trial was a Nissan Qashqai:* ibid.

59 *"It's much easier from an engineering perspective":* ibid.

59 *"We were tasked with building both the car and the station in Japan":* Author's interview with Yoav Heichal, May 20, 2014.

59 *"Everything we wanted them to do, they did":* ibid.

60 *he admitted the company's tireless focus on switch "never made sense" to him:* Author's interview with Danny Weinstock, July 21, 2014.

60 *"When you come from low-tech like me":* ibid.

60 *They're setting up "the world's biggest puncture repair shop":* Shlomit Lan and Hadas Magen, "Can Better Place Get Better?" *Globes,* October 11, 2012.

60 *"It's a solution that belongs in the nineteenth century":* ibid.

60 *"The chemistry is still changing":* Clive Thompson, "Batteries Not Included."

60 *they'd use batteries from a relatively small number of manufacturers:* Squatriglia, "Better Place Unveils an Electric Car Battery Swap Station."

61 *"an electric vehicle battery pack needs to be weather-tight to keep water out":* Jay Yarow, "The Cost of a Better Place Swapping Station: $500,000," *Business Insider,* April 21, 2009.

61 *"then they will blame Ford, not necessarily Better Place":* ibid.

61 *a trailer with a compact generator:* White Paper, "Electric Vehicles for Israel," Stanford Graduate School of Business, March 22, 2007.

61 *Danny Weinstock was a big fan of fast charge:* Author's interview with Danny Weinstock.

61 *"Shai always considered himself an average person":* ibid.

61 *"Fast charging is just electricity; there are no moving parts":* ibid.

61 *it's done so infrequently it's a non-issue:* Author's interview with Emek Sadot.

61 *"really energized people with thinking outside the box":* interview on C-SPAN, transcript sent via email by Mike Granoff to Sidney Goodman and Dan Cohen, January 26, 2010.

62 *With a background in electrical design and engineering:* Author's interview with Mike Lindheim, July 3, 2014.

62 *Lindheim put together a detailed spreadsheet:* ibid.

62 *The price: $3 million per station covering everything:* ibid.

62 *The robot alone was $900,000* ibid.

62 *Agassi had a different cost in mind: $500,000 per station:* Yarow, "The Cost of a Better Place Swapping Station: $500,000."

62 *"It didn't come from anywhere":* Author's interview with Mike Lindheim.

62 *"I have the original spreadsheet":* Author's interview with Andrey Zarur.

63 *"We have to cut it down to $1.5 million at the most":* Author's interview with Mike Lindheim.

63 *"The numbers don't lie":* ibid.

63 *but it would require significant redesign and sourcing:* ibid.

63 *"Tal and Shai didn't understand the intricacies of a construction project":* ibid.

63 *"In every company meeting when Shai would speak":* ibid.

64 *Sitting in the dashboard's pride of place:* Kalman, "Baby You Can Drive My Car" and the author's experience driving a Renault Fluence Z.E.

64 *"If I want to drive from here to Jerusalem":* Kalman, "Baby You Can Drive My Car."

64 *OSCAR learns each driver's habits:* ibid.

64 *"We will know how you drive, how your specific battery behaves":* ibid.

65 *Apple CEO Tim Cook had to write a letter of apology to customers:* Jordan Crook, "Tim Cook Apologizes for Apple Maps, Points to Competitive Alternatives," *TechCrunch,* September 28, 2012.

65 *Waze's secret sauce is that it generates real-time traffic maps based on data from drivers:* Brian Blum, "Waze Steers You Clear of Traffic," *Israel21c,* December 19, 2011.

65 *Users can also proactively report accidents:* ibid.

65 *Waze had just raised an initial seed round of $12 million:* Tzahi Hoffman, "Mobile GPS Co Waze Raises $25 m," *Globes,* December 8, 2010.

65 *"We like what you're doing":* Author's interview with Motty Cohen, which also includes recounting the dialogue and negotiations between Waze and Better Place.

66 *50 million drivers were now using Waze:* Rip Empson, "WTF is Waze and Why did Google Just Pay a Billion+ For It?" *TechCrunch,* June 11, 2013.

66 *One fan even reported Waze accurately predicting traffic on the eponymous Monkey Forest Road:* Author's personal story traveling in Bali.

66 *the search engine giant acquired Waze for a stunning $1.1 billion:* David Shamah, "How 'Disruption' Won Waze its $1 Billion Exit," *The Times of Israel,* February 9, 2014.

66 *Hershkovitz turned to another mapping company:* iGo: Author's interview with Daniel Campbell, June 9, 2014.

66 *iGo was founded and run by two Israelis:* Author's interview with Motty Cohen.

66 *"Because Waze relied on remote maps":* Author's interview with Daniel Campbell, which also includes Campbell's description of how drivers don't update their in-car maps, how car specifications are frozen years in advance and the total budget to build OSCAR.

67 *In 2008, around 18 percent of Denmark's total energy came from the wind:* Roth, "Driven: Shai Agassi's Audacious Plan to Put Electric Cars on the Road."

68 *so much so that Denmark has to export much of its night-time energy:* Dave Andrews, "Danish Wind Power and Electricity Export in 2007," *Claverton Energy and Research Group,* December 6, 2008.

68   *Denmark actually had to pay Germany to take its excess electricity:* Author's interview with Johnny Hansen, March 21, 2014.

68   *"Since DONG Energy was formed, in 2006":* "Dong Energy Profile," UN-Business Action Hub website, December 4, 2015.

68   *DONG and local investors put around $25 million into Better Place:* Eva Obelitz Rode, "DONG Chief Slams Checkout for Electric Cars," *JydskeVestkysten,* January 18, 2013, and author's interview with Susanne Tolstrup, February 23, 2014.

68   *"a small [nation] with a well-connected road system and a lot of green idealism":* "Germany Launches Electric Car Initiative," *UPI,* May 4, 2010.

68   *nearby Iceland was its recommendation:* Author's interview with Dimitri Dadiomov.

69   *Although gasoline-powered vehicles faced a crippling 180 percent tax levy:* Steve Hanley, "Electric Car Sales Plummet After Change in Tax Policy," *Gas2,* September 12, 2016.

69   *Shai Agassi spoke at the closing event of the Copenhagen Climate Council:* Shai Agassi, "Denmark Launch," *The Long Tailpipe—Shai Agassi's Blog,* March 30, 2008.

69   *"How do you run all cars in Denmark without gasoline":* ibid.

69   *"Let's say that we'll have ten thousand or one hundred thousand cars":* Author's interview with Hugh McDermott, February 26, 2014.

70   *turn down the throttle on a gas-fired power plant:* ibid.

70   *"If you reduce it by ten percent for an hour, no consumer is going to notice":* ibid.

70   *"it looks just like a real power plant going up and down":* ibid.

70   *The smart grid:* background provided by author's interview with Hugh McDermott and Robby Bearman; and Barak Hershkovitz interview by Inbal Orpaz in "Car of the Future: Electric and Full Applications."

71   *"Better Place came up with the idea of smart charging":* Author's interview with Emek Sadot.

71   *Better Place had even grander plans:* Author's interview with Robby Bearman, July 2, 2014.

71   *Better Place could discharge the batteries in its customers' cars temporarily:* ibid.

71   *those batteries could be "retired" and moved to a warehouse:* ibid.

71   *It's a model that Tesla has adopted today with its Powerwall:* Sebastian Blanco, "Tesla Expands EV Battery Tech to Homes, Businesses," *AutoBlog,* April 30, 2015.

72   *"Utilities do ten- to twenty-year forecasts of energy usage":* Author's interview with Hugh McDermott.

72   *"Their whole business is built on probabilities":* ibid.

72   *"There's always a tension between minimizing costs and maximizing service":* Author's interview with Emek Sadot.

Chapter 6 - Tailpipes Not Invited

73   *GM was looking at liabilities of close to $200 billion:* Jay Alix, "How General Motors was Really Saved: The Untold True Story of the Most Important Bankruptcy in U.S. History," *Forbes,* November 18, 2013.

73   *heavy union and health care obligations:* "The Collapse of General Motors into Bankruptcy is Only the Latest Chapter in a Long Story of Mismanagement and Decline," *The Economist,* June 4, 2009.

73   *as gas topped $4 a gallon in the United States:* ibid.

73   *A plan to generate $3 billion through a sale of bonds or shares:* ibid.

73   *when Shai Agassi and a small team of Better Place executives arrived:* Author's interview with Mike Granoff.

74   *The Volt had made its debut in Detroit:* Kristi Piziks, "Green at the 2007 Detroit Auto Show," *TreeHugger,* January 8, 2007.

74   *the Volt runs strictly on electricity until the battery is depleted:* Sam Abuelsamid, "Detroit Auto Show: It's Here. GM's Plug-in Hybrid is the Chevy Volt Concept, *AutoBlog,* January 7, 2007.

74   *a distance greater than the typical commute for 80 percent of U.S. workers:* Alex Davies, "More Range in Chevy's Volt Means You Hardly Ever Need Gas," *Wired,* August 4, 2015.

74   *His goal for the meeting with GM:* Author's interview with Mike Granoff.

74   *when Mike Granoff saw a Newsweek article featuring Bob Lutz:* ibid.

74   *"the electrification of the automobile is inevitable":* Keith Naughton, "Bob Lutz: The Man Who Revived the Electric Car," *Newsweek,* December 22, 2007.

75   *The Swiss-born Lutz:* Blake Z. Rong, "Stories with Bob Lutz," *AutoWeek,* November 25, 2013.

75   *before coming to stateside GM's cross-town competitors Ford and Chrysler:* Executive Profile of Bob Lutz, *Bloomberg.*

75   *His babies included such gas guzzlers:* Naughton, "Bob Lutz: The Man Who Revived the Electric Car."

75   *he had called climate change "a total crock of shit":* Glenn Hunter, "GM's Lutz on Hybrids, Global Warming and Cars as Art, *D Magazine,* January 30, 2008.

75   *"I'm a skeptic, not a denier":* ibid.

75   *"We saw Toyota getting highly beneficial rub-off from their Prius success":* Naughton, "Bob Lutz: The Man Who Revived the Electric Car."

75   *They didn't believe a car could be run on lithium ion batteries:* ibid.

75   *In 1996, GM introduced the first modern electric car:* details on the EV1 compiled from Chris Paine's 2006 documentary, *Who Killed the Electric Car?,* Jessica Donaldson's description of the EV1 on the Conceptcarz.com website, and from the EV1.org website.

76   *"That tore it for me":* Naughton, "Bob Lutz: The Man Who Revived the Electric Car."

77   *"This is like JFK's call for the moon shot":* ibid.

77   *"I read that and I thought, oh my God, this is it":* Author's interview with Mike Granoff.

77   *"I had a friend, Richard Demb, in New Jersey":* ibid. The company Granoff was referring to is Gourmet Popcorn Creations.

77   *The headquarters of General Motors in downtown Detroit sprawls across 14 acres:* Renaissance Center, "The Encyclopedia of Detroit," *Detroit Historical Society.*

77   *Opened in 1977 and purchased by GM in 1996:* Colin Marshall, "The Renaissance Center: Henry Ford II's Grand Design to Revive Detroit," *The Guardian,* May 22, 2015.

77   *At 73 stories:* "Tallest Buildings in Detroit," WorldAtlas website.

77   *Tower 300 on the 30th floor, in conference room A21:* email from Mike Granoff to Better Place executives participating in meeting, April 22, 2008.

77   *At Agassi's side were two of his top lieutenants:* Author's interview with Mike Granoff.

78   *Administrative assistant Sandy McElroy:* email from Mike Granoff to Better Place executives participating in meeting.

78   *representing a healthy sprinkling of relevant GM departments:* ibid.

78   *In his place was Larry Burns:* ibid.

78   *a down-in-the-trenches guy who understood the technology intimately:* Susan Hassler, "Larry Burns on Electric Vehicles and the Future of Personal Transportation," *IEEE Spectrum,* August 16, 2013.

78   *He laid out what Better Place was building:* Author's interview with Mike Granoff.

78   *Agassi extolled the virtues of battery swap:* ibid.

78   *The GM team nodded in agreement:* ibid.

78   *"It took the Toyota Prius 15 years to get to just 1.5 percent market share in the U.S.":* Chafkin, "A Broken Place: The Spectacular Failure of the Startup that Was Going to Change the World."

78   *"The GM people were not convinced that battery switch was the future":* Author's interview with Mike Granoff.

79   *"We could never really figure out how to make that work with our switching mechanism":* ibid.

79   *"All you need to do is take the engine out, redesign the carriage and put in a flat battery":* ibid.

79   *the latter would barely say a word the entire meeting:* ibid.

79   *Would Better Place be interested in becoming the global infrastructure partner for the fixed battery Volt?:* ibid.

79   *He told Agassi by phone afterward, "We've got to do this?":* ibid.

79   *"Mike, you don't understand. That car, the Volt, it has a tailpipe. It's a stupid car":* ibid.

80   *"It's true that it would have been a low-margin business":* Author's interview with Dimitri Dadiomov, March 30, 2014.

80   *"We don't work with cars that have a tailpipe" would become a mantra for Agassi:* Author's interview with Mike Granoff.

80   *And the numbers: as low as $30 a barrel:* Peter Taberner: "2016 Oil Price Forecasts: Why is Everyone Getting it Wrong?" *OilPrice.com,* October 16, 2016.

80   *which these days is generated nearly entirely by sources other than oil:* Wendy Lyons Sunshine, "What are Sources of Electricity that Charge Your Life?" *The Balance,* June 21, 2016.

81   *Agassi had predicted that the price of oil would spike to more than $100 a barrel:* Shai Agassi, "Oil at $100 a Barrel - the Halfway Point," *The Long Tailpipe—Shai Agassi's Blog,* January 4, 2008.

81   *It hit $98 in November of that year:* "Crude Oil Price History," FedPrimeRate website.

81   *peaked the following July, just two months after the meeting at GM:* Rebeka Kebede, "Oil Hits Record Above $147," *Reuters*, July 11, 2008.

81   *"What I find exciting about Better Place":* Thomas Friedman, "While Detroit Slept," *The New York Times*, December 9, 2008.

81   *"The gas bill on an annual basis for the average car in Europe":* Author's interview with Mike Granoff.

81   *with the cost of gasoline in Europe approaching $8 a gallon at the time:* ibid.

81   *"driving an electric vehicle is like getting your gasoline at 75 cents per gallon":* Ron Adner, *The Wide Lens: What Successful Innovators See That Others Miss*, Portfolio/Penguin, 2012.

81   *Agassi's magic number was $500 per month:* Author's interview with Mike Granoff.

81   *"So, let me give this to you straight":* ibid.

82   *"I'll be offering $20,000 cars in a market where you're selling $60,000 cars":* Roth, "Driven: Shai Agassi's Audacious Plan to Put Electric Cars on the Road."

82   *"So, if it's free, why don't you just swap the car instead of the battery?":* Chafkin, "A Broken Place: The Spectacular Failure of the Startup that Was Going to Change the World."

82   *"That's a stupid question":* ibid.

82   *The entire leasing and financing business:* Author's interview with Mike Granoff.

82   *"You won't be able to sell those cars at all":* ibid.

82   *"He was saying 'disruption, disruption, disruption":* ibid.

82   *"This was all the validation that Shai needed":* ibid.

82   *"The next meeting we have … we'll have the bigger market capitalization":* ibid.

83   *Afterward, though, Granoff was uncomfortable:* ibid.

83   *"Everything was said without regard to the fact that this was General Motors":* ibid.

83   *Nor was the free car idea supposed to be brought up:* ibid.

83   *"It was a complete absurdity":* Chafkin, "A Broken Place: The Spectacular Failure of the Startup that Was Going to Change the World."

83   *He sent a letter to the organizers:* Author's interview with Mike Granoff.

83   *"It was comforting to find":* email from Mike Granoff, May 7, 2008.

84   *"Based on our analysis, we have decided to remain focused on our E-Flex EREV":* letter from Beth Lowery of General Motors sent to Shai Agassi, Mike Granoff and Sidney Goodman, July 17, 2008. For background on E-Flex technology see: "GM Introduces E-Flex Electric Vehicle System; Chevrolet Volt the First Application," *Green Car Congress*, January 30, 2017.

Chapter 7 - Electric Land Grab

85   *It was 6 a.m., and he was woken up by "a firestorm of email and text":* Marc Moncrief and Paul Austin: "Thornley: Why I Shunned Cabinet Seat," *The Sydney Morning Herald*, January 21, 2009.

85 *An Australian cabinet minister had been charged in a rape:* ibid. The cabinet minister was Theo Theophanous.

85 *"I want you to take up his role":* Author's interview with Evan Thornley.

85 *"People wait twenty years to get offered such a position":* ibid.

85 *Thornley was in discussions with Better Place to become CEO of its Australian division:* Moncrief and Austin: "Thornley: Why I Shunned Cabinet Seat."

85 *"It would have been completely politically and ethically untenable"* Author's interview with Evan Thornley.

86 *"If you're serious, we need to talk":* ibid.

86 *"Why don't you route your trip from France back to Melbourne the long way, through San Francisco?":* ibid.

86 *where the state's Renewable Energy Development Venture would kick in a grant of $500,000:* Author's interview with Brian Goldstein, director, Better Place Hawaii, May 11, 2014, and "Better Place, Sheraton Waikiki and Hawaiian Electric Partner on EV Charge Network in Hawaii," press release, *BusinessWire*, September 30, 2010.

87 *His revised itinerary included a three-hour layover in San Francisco:* Author's interview with Evan Thornley, which also includes the details of the discussion between Thornley and Agassi and Thornley's calls to the premier.

87 *One member of parliament told him that his behavior was a "f—ing disgrace":* Marc and Austin: "Thornley: Why I Shunned Cabinet Seat."

87 *"There were TV cameras parked outside my house":* Author's interview with Evan Thornley.

87 *"Rumors flew that I was going to be a high paid lobbyist for some French company":* ibid.

88 *In 1995, Thornley co-founded LookSmart:* Garry Barker and Sue Cant, "Microsoft Dumps LookSmart," *The Age*, October 8, 2003.

88 *LookSmart signed a deal in 1998 with Microsoft:* "LookSmart International Signs Deal with Microsoft," *Telecompaper.com*, February 15, 2009.

88 *relocated to San Francisco:* "LookSmart—the Australian Connection," Salient Marketing website.

88 *The stock debuted at $12 a share:* Andy Wang, "Stock Watch: LookSmart Looks Smarter," *TechNewsWorld*, August 30, 1999.

88 *climbed to more than $70 per share:* J.R. Parish, *You Don't Have to Learn the Hard Way: Making it in the Real World: A Guide for Graduates*, BenBella Books, 2009.

88 *LookSmart ran into trouble:* Matt Hines, "LookSmart's Microsoft Deal Looks Rocky," *ZDNet*, August 18, 2003.

88 *Microsoft accounted for 64 percent of LookSmart's revenue:* ibid.

88 *LookSmart is still in business and receives some 6 billion search queries monthly:* LookSmart media kit, PDF. 2016.

88 *Several years earlier he had visited Israel:* Author's interview with Guy Pross, February 26, 2014.

88 *"Any Israeli ministers who would travel to Australia":* ibid.

88 *Pross headed up the search for a local CEO:* ibid.

88 *Thornley was chatting with David Carlick:* Author's interview with Evan Thornley.

88 *"I'd be glad to help, give them a few tips"*: ibid.

88 *"Two of the four guys on our list used to work for you"*: ibid.

88 *"No, no, I'm trying to change the world through politics now"*: ibid.

89 *"non–bar mitzvah, bar mitzvah trip"*: ibid.

89 *"Why don't you meet with Shai Agassi while you're over here?"*: ibid.

89 *Australia was a "stand in" for the United States:* ibid.

89 *Moreover, Australian car owners were used to driving long distances:* ibid.

89 *"The best way to prove that was to target a country with plenty of high kilometer drives"*: Derek Fung, "How Better Place Plans to Revive the Electric Car," *CNET*, February 25, 2009.

89 *"Australia spends around twenty to twenty-five billion a year on petrol"*: ibid.

90 *"we can electrify the Hume Highway"*: ibid.

90 *"It's not a trivial amount, but it's not mind boggling"*: ibid.

90 *"They were saying, 'What—you're leaving a cabinet position for this?'"*: Author's interview with Evan Thornley.

90 *"My story moved to page 11"*: ibid.

90 *Terry was a 20-year veteran and senior executive for General Motors' Australian operation:* Author's interview with Alison Terry, April 22, 2014.

91 *"GM made a strategic call to develop the Volt with range-extension capability"*: ibid.

91 *The way Agassi conducted the discussions"*: ibid.

91 *Better Place Australia raised $25 million:* "Better Place Australia Raises $25 million in First Round Financing," *Electric Vehicle News,* November 30, 2009.

91 *"That amount, from Australian investors, at a $230 million pre-money valuation"*: Author's interview with Antony Cohen, April 17, 2014.

91 *"I didn't want to go to war with the automotive industry about switch"*: Author's interview with Evan Thornley.

91 *Thornley and Agassi argued about this plenty of times:* ibid.

92 *"Even Shai said that switching was only ever meant to be a backup"*: ibid.

92 *the very first battery switch station opened to the public in Yokohama*: Squatriglia, "Better Place Unveils an Electric Car Battery Swap Station."

92 *Some 5,000 people visited in the first months of its operation:* internal Better Place email from Kiyotaka Fujii, June 11, 2009.

92 *A white Nissan Qashqai with the words Better Place written across its rear left*: description of car and switching in Yokohama from "Better Place Electric Car Switching Station," YouTube video, May 13, 2009.

92 *"creating a truly-zero emission solution"*: "Better Place Unveils First Automated Battery Switch for Japan," press release, *AutoBlog*, May 13, 2009.

92 *The Danish and Israeli ambassadors to Japan were there:* Squatriglia, "Better Place Unveils an Electric Car Battery Swap Station."

92 *"Today marks a major milestone"*: "Better Place Unveils First Automated Battery Switch for Japan."

93 *"a great achievement"*: Dubi Ben-Gedalyahu, "Better Place Presents Automatic Battery Changer," *Globes*, May 13, 2009.

93 *it was somewhat surprising that Fujii was … not a confirmed believer:* Author's interview with Kiyotaka Fujii, which also includes Fujii's subsequent comments on fast charge vs. battery switch.

94 *"Fixed-battery cars are a dumb idea":* ibid.

94 *"What we learned is that just because Renault has a deal with us":* Author's interview with Yoav Heichal.

94 *Fujii had another theory about what was going on:* Author's interview with Kiyotaka Fujii.

94 *"Shai was convinced that there will be many car manufacturers lined up":* ibid.

95 *Over a period of two years, Yudan worked tirelessly to convince Verbund:* Author's interview with Amit Yudan, June 30, 2014.

95 *More than 80 percent of the electricity Verbund generated in 2008:* "Verbund is a Pioneer in Renewable Energies," press release, Verbund website, August 8, 2008.

95 *"It took a lot of time to develop confidence with them":* Author's interview with Amit Yudan.

95 *Verbund wanted a more or less even split:* Author's interview with Dan Cohen.

95 *was more akin to an intense but reasonable negotiation:* Author's interview with Amit Yudan.

95 *"It was the right decision from our end":* Author's interview with Dan Cohen.

95 *"will come to Austria as soon as the government wants us to":* Shai Agassi, tweet, February 18, 2012.

96 *"We can't do this":* Author's interview with Amit Yudan.

96 *account for 14 percent of the country's gross domestic product:* "Just How Important are Cars to the Germans?" *The Local*, September 24, 2015.

96 *Cars are Germany's top export, and Germany is the fourth-largest producer of cars in the world:* ibid.

96 *"It's OK, we can make this a private meeting":* Author's interview with Amit Yudan, which also includes the rest of Yudan's discussion with the German minister.

96 *Agassi was creating enemies elsewhere in Germany:* Author's interview with Ziva Patir.

96 *his positioning of Better Place as an "equal partner":* Chafkin, "A Broken Place: the Spectacular Failure of the Startup that Was Going to Change the World."

96 *It was held with "all the big shots of the German car industry":* Author's interview with Ziva Patir.

97 *"You will see that you don't understand what I'm talking about":* ibid.

97 *"They never forgave him for that":* ibid.

97 *Idan Ofer set up a meeting at the Frankfurt Auto Show:* Author's interview with Idan Ofer.

97 *It wasn't easy to get, but "they took it seriously because of me":* ibid.

97 *"I wouldn't invest $750 million in Better Place":* Author's interview with Ziva Patir.

97 *"If we hadn't been such assholes":* Chafkin, "A Broken Place: The Spectacular Failure of the Startup that Was Going to Change the World."

97 *"What is the reason you were not successful in Germany?"*: "Goodbye Gas Station, Hello Battery Charger!" *DW*, September 16, 2009.

97 *"The question is only—when"*: Matthias Lambrecht, "Charge Inhibition," *Financial Times Deutschland*, May 15, 2012.

97 *"Shai correctly wanted to create a situation where the automakers would move quickly to electric"*: Chafkin, "A Broken Place: The Spectacular Failure of the Startup that Was Going to Change the World."

97 *Better Place was spun "as being a very neat, easy solution"*: Author's interview with Lawrence Seeff, May 7, 2014.

98 *"We had a guy who wanted to be our man in Chile"*: Author's interview with Carol Tursi, May 28, 2014.

98 *Seeff remembered that there would be conversations with the Chile contact "once or twice a month"*: Author's interview with Lawrence Seeff.

98 *There were inquiries from Southeast Asia, Eastern Europe, "even some in Africa"*: Author's interview with Carol Tursi.

98 *a "random" meeting with the head of industrial research at a company in Taiwan*: Author's interview with Dimitri Dadiomov.

98 *"It was an island, after all"*: ibid.

98 *"It took us months for someone to say no to the Bhutanese"*: Author's interview with a former Better Place executive.

98 *"I like the Bahrainis"*: email from Jeff Keswin, Lyrical Partners LP to Shai Agassi and Mike Granoff, November 23, 2008.

98 *"Beijing, Singapore, Hong Kong and Tokyo all in four days"*: internal status update to Better Place management from Josh Steinmann, February 1, 2008.

98 *"in the last six weeks, I've been in thirty countries"*: "Moment of Transportation" conference.

99 *"there is a limit to how many we can do at any point in time"*: "Goodbye Gas Station, Hello Battery Charger!"

99 *"We'd host them out of respect"*: Author's interview with Carol Tursi.

99 *Better Place and DONG announced a round of 103 million Euros in financing*: Ucilia Wang, "Better Place Grabs €103M, Names new Danish CEO, *Green Tech Media*, January 27, 2009.

99 *Better Place had hired Jens Moberg*: ibid.

99 *He had been employed at Microsoft in a variety of capacities*: Jens Moberg CV. JensMoberg.dk website.

99 *"In Jens Moberg, we've selected a world-class business executive"*: Jonathan Shapira, "Better Place Raises €103 Million, Names New Danish CEO," *Cleantech Investing in Israel*, January 27, 2009.

99 *"I firmly believe that the economics of a green industry"*: Better Place, Dong Energy Close €103M Deal for Danish Electric Car Network," *FINalternatives*, January 28, 2009.

100 *"There are at least 100,000 cars in New York that do not leave the city"*: email from Shai Agassi to Joshua Steiner, January 2, 2008.

100 *"[It] requires no policy change":* ibid.

100 *Agassi had already met with some of then–Mayor Michael Bloomberg's staff:* ibid.

100 *Newsom subsequently visited Israel in 2008:* "San Francisco Mayor in Talks with Project Better Place," *AutoBlog,* May 14, 2008.

100 *a plan to create "250,000 points of contact for electric charging":* Pogue, "Jump-Starting the Electric Car Dream."

101 *the Bay Area's Metropolitan Transportation Commission (MTC) approved 17 grants:* Sean Hollister, "Better Place's Electric Taxis Coming to SF Bay Area, Thanks to $7 Million Grant," *Engadget,* October 31, 2010.

101 *The largest single grant—$6.9 million:* ibid.

101 *According to the plan 61 electric taxi cabs and four battery switch stations would be deployed:* ibid.

101 *Two locations were announced:* Author's interview with Mike Granoff.

101 *San Jose Mayor Chuck Reed anticipated that the first battery switch station "could be installed in a year":* Jim Motavalli, "Better Place Rolls Out Bay Area Battery-Swapping EV Taxi Fleet," *CBS MoneyWatch,* November 1, 2010.

101 *"A bit of a chicken-and egg-problem, but we can get over that too":* email from Shai Agassi to Joshua Steiner, January 2, 2008.

101 *has been absent since the 1980s:* Motavalli, "Better Place Rolls Out Bay Area Battery-Swapping EV Taxi Fleet."

101 *"which implies they'll be the same swap-ready Renault Fluence Z.E.s":* ibid.

101 *"There are discussions happening with other car manufacturers":* ibid.

102 *"We took it all very seriously":* Author's interview with David Kennedy, June 30, 2014.

102 *New York City in particular was "really the last place we should have approached as a startup":* ibid.

102 *"The real cost is your time":* ibid.

Chapter 8 - Shai Agassi Superstar

103 *a TED Talk could change the world:* Nathan Heller, "Listen and Learn," *The New Yorker,* July 9, 2012.

103 *"A new ecosystem for electric cars":* quotes and description of Shai Agassi's appearance in this section come from Agassi's TED Talk, February 2009.

104 *"What was he talking about?":* Author's interview with Mike Granoff.

105 *"There is no Moore's Law for batteries":* Fred Schlachter, "No Moore's Law for Batteries," *Proceedings of the National Academy of Sciences in the United States of America,* April 2, 2013.

105 *Moore's Law is based on an observation made in a 1965 paper by Gordon Moore:* Annie Sneed, "Moore's Law Keeps Going, Defying Expectations," *Scientific American,* May 19, 2015.

105 *"first articulation of a principle":* Seth Fletcher, "Computing After Moore's Law," *Scientific American,* May 1, 2015.

105 *"The reason there is a Moore's Law for computer processors"*: Schlachter, "No Moore's Law for Batteries."

105 *"Breakthroughs in energy storage technology aren't coming"*: Christopher Mims, "Tech World Vexed by Slow Progress on Batteries," *The Wall Street Journal,* October 5, 2014.

106 *Comedian and car enthusiast Jay Leno joked in 2010:* Katie Fehrenbacher, "Dear Friedman: There is No Moore's Law for Batteries," *GigaOm,* September 27, 2010.

106 *"batteries have not improved hardly at all"*: ibid.

106 *slow, steady improvement driven by economies of scale:* Brad Plumer, "Expensive Batteries are Holding Back Electric Cars. Can That Change?" *The Washington Post,* April 2, 2013.

106 *"We do not use any electrons that come from coal"*: Shai Agassi, TED Talk.

106 *60 percent of the country's electricity was generated from coal:* National Coal Supply Corporation website.

106 *Israel's Tamar offshore natural gas field had only been discovered one month earlier:* "Tamar - Building Energy Independence," Delek Drilling website.

107 *"People [in the government] said, 'Oh, that's a very large space you're asking for'"*: Shai Agassi, TED Talk.

107 *a target of generating just 10 percent of the country's electricity from renewable sources by 2020:* Rona Fried, "Israel Gets Its First Big Solar Project: 5th Largest in the World," *SustainableBusiness.com,* October 21, 2013.

107 *Steve Jobs' "reality distortion field"*: Harrison Weber, "The Curious Case of Steve Jobs' Reality Distortion Field," *VentureBeat,* March 24, 2015.

107 *Agassi frequently spoke of future events in the present tense:* Author's interview with Mike Granoff.

107 *"Renault has put a billion and a half dollars into building nine different types of cars"*: Shai Agassi, TED Talk.

108 *Agassi was named to Time magazine's list of the 100 most influential people of the year:* Alan Salzman, "The 2009 Time 100."

108 *the third-place spot in Fast Company magazine's "Most Creative People of 2009"*: "Most Creative People of 2009," *FastCompany,* May 8, 2009.

108 *"the Jewish Henry Ford"*: Thomas Friedman, "Texas to Tel Aviv," *The New York Times,* July 27, 2008.

108 *getting "off heroin [and getting] addicted to milk"*: ibid.

108 *"a charismatic entrepreneur"*: Clive Thompson, "Batteries Not Included."

108 *"Some people say I'm missing the fear gene"*: ibid.

109 *"I've learned every industry in the world"*: ibid.

109 *"Agassi is an extremely charming guy"*: ibid.

109 *"Let's cut to the chase here: Will this car get me laid?"*: quotes and description come from Agassi's appearance on The Colbert Report, September 22, 2009.

110 *"We call them 'Drivetone' sounds"*: Agassi's only other on-air mention of Drivetones was on the CBC (Canada) program "The Hour." Described in "What's Your Drivetone?" *The Intersection of People and Process,* February 4, 2009.

Chapter 9 - "All You Need is a Plug, Right?"

111 *The idea to take on Washington came from Mike Granoff:* Author's interview with Mike Granoff.

111 *Granoff and Agassi launched a nearly two-year attack on Washington:* ibid.

111 *There was House Democrat Steve Israel, of New York:* ibid.

111 *At today's prices, the United States is spending $550 billion a year on importing crude oil:* "Moment of Transportation" conference.

112 *"So what do we do?":* Roth, "Driven: Shai Agassi's Audacious Plan to Put Electric Cars on the Road."

112 *"We need tax hikes on gas-powered cars":* ibid

112 *"That will never fly":* ibid.

112 *"How can I buy one?":* ibid.

112 *"Well, we've got one problem":* ibid.

112 *"All you need is a plug, right?":* ibid.

112 *Most of the meetings Agassi took in Washington went along these lines:* ibid.

112 *"getting anything like the deal [Agassi] has in Israel [was] going to be impossible":* ibid.

112 *"For the price of two months' worth of oil":* Domenick Yoney, "Shai Agassi Pitches $100 Billion Plan," *AutoBlog*, July 1, 2008.

112 *"For the price of one year's worth of oil":* ibid.

113 *He met with Senators Evan Bayh ... Frank Lautenberg ... Representative Eliot Engel:* internal status update to Better Place management from Mike Granoff, February 1, 2008.

113 *"a good friend ... and an immediate convert":* ibid.

113 *At the Department of Energy, Granoff met with chief of staff Jeff Kupner and with David Strickland:* ibid.

113 *"We were in the West Wing, just like in the TV show":* Author's interview with Mike Granoff.

113 *Agassi and Granoff met with presidential advisor Pete Rouse:* ibid.

113 *"Dramatic things were happening every day in that period":* ibid.

113 *"The political climate in Washington is very much in our favor":* internal status update to Better Place management from Mike Granoff.

114 *the Presidential Task Force on the Auto Industry:* "Obama to Announce Task Force for Auto Industry Recovery," *The Guardian*, February 16, 2009.

114 *Agassi and Granoff saw the Presidential Task Force as their last chance:* Author's interview with Mike Granoff.

114 *Steven Rattner, who had co-founded the private equity firm Quadrangle Capital Partners:* Steven Rattner, "The Auto Bailout: How We Did It," *Fortune*, October 21, 2009.

114 *with Joshua Steiner:* "Quadrangle Co-Founder Joshua Steiner Joins Bloomberg," *AltAssets*, January 17, 2013.

114 *Agassi and Granoff met with the Task Force four times:* Author's interview with Mike Granoff.

114 *"The relationship between the automotive companies and the oil makers is like an abusive marriage":* ibid.

114 *"Give us one battery switchable car from GM and we'll take care of the rest":* ibid.

114 *The car Agassi had in mind was the Saturn:* ibid.

114 *"a different kind of car company":* Jerry Garrett, "Saturn: A Different Kind of Car Company, Indeed," *The New York Times,* September 5, 2007.

114 *But the Saturn division had been losing money for years:* Lindsay Chappell, "Saturn was a Loser for Years—But Who Knew?" *Automotive News,* June 8, 2015.

114 *GM made the decision to discontinue the car:* Bill Vlasic and David M. Herszenhorn, "Pursuing U.S. Aid, GM Accepts Need for Drastic Cuts," *The New York Times,* December 2, 2008.

115 *the Penske Automotive Group announced it would be buying the brand:* Tim Higgins, "Penske to Buy Saturn; GM Will Make Cars for Brand for 2 Years," *ABC News,* June 6, 2009.

115 *Penske had a partner in mind:* Jesse Snyder, "If Penske Buys Saturn, Could Renault-Nissan Be His Partner?" *Automotive News,* May 11, 2009.

115 *Agassi's idea was that Better Place would "buy one of the factories GM was shutting down":* Author's interview with a former Better Place executive.

115 *"No one said anything. So I spoke up":* ibid.

115 *"It was fun to float the idea":* ibid.

115 *Renault got cold feet, and Penske withdrew its offer:* "Renault Says Saturn Supply Deal 'Just Didn't Add Up,'" *AutoWeek,* October 1, 2009.

115 *Agassi was also in the dark about the fate of the Presidential Task Force:* Author's interview with Mike Granoff.

115 *His tour de force in Washington took place just days before the Task Force was abruptly shut down:* ibid.

115 *GM had declared bankruptcy:* David Welch, "GM Files for Bankruptcy," *Bloomberg,* June 2, 2009.

115 *Chrysler would soon be saved by the Italians:* Steve Schaefer, "Treasury Sells Chrysler Stake to Fiat, Sees $1.3 Billion Loss on Bailout," *Forbes,* July 21, 2011.

115 *The officials who had held all those meetings with Agassi and Granoff:* Author's interview with Mike Granoff.

116 *The American Recovery and Reinvestment Act ... was being finalized:* "Recovery Act," U.S. Department of the Treasury website.

116 *a $200 million line item for reseeding the National Mall:* "So What is All This Tea Party Hoo-Ha?" *Stand Up for America,* March 28, 2009.

116 *The idea of spending so much money on a lawn didn't sit right:* Author's interview with Mike Granoff.

116 *In its place was $400 million for vehicle electrification programs:* Kevin Bullis, "Stimulus Big Winner: Battery Manufacturing," *MIT Technology Review,* February 17, 2009.

116 *This was the chance they were waiting for:* Author's interview with Mike Granoff.

116 *the Pacific Electrification Program:* ibid.

117 *"if you lived in any of the cities on that corridor":* ibid.

117 *The price: $100 million—only a quarter of the $400 million budget:* ibid.

117 *Better Place's head of global alliances Lawrence Seeff wrote an email:* email from Lawrence Seeff to all Better Place staff, May 14, 2009.

117 *"Our application comes with over 90 letters of support":* ibid.

117 *"We never had a doubt that we'd get at least some of that money":* Author's interview with Mike Granoff.

117 *Better Place lost its bid for PEP:* ibid.

117 *"we asked them to give us the money now and then we'd find the cars":* ibid.

117 *"I was about to give a talk":* ibid.

117 *Granoff arranged an emergency conference call:* ibid.

117 *"It's just a minor setback":* ibid.

117 *"Who was that guy?":* ibid.

Chapter 10 - Two Scoops of Rocky Renault

119 *In January 2011, a spy scandal erupted:* David Jolly, "Fired Renault Executive Blames Tricks by a Rival," *The New York Times,* January 20, 2011.

119 *Renault filed a criminal complaint:* ibid.

119 *"factual proof":* John Lichfield, "Renault Security Chief Arrested Over 'Fake Spy Scandal' Allegations," *Independent,* March 15, 2011.

119 *"Of course we are sure":* Hugh Schofield, "Renault Spy Scandal Risks Denting Carmaker's Reputation," *BBC News,* March 15, 2011.

119 *"an organized international network":* Jennifer Thompson and John Reed, "Paris Warns Renault Apology Will Not End Scandal," *Financial Times,* March 15, 2011.

119 *Beijing vociferously denied any links to the spying accusations:* Jolly, "Fired Renault Executive Blames Tricks by a Rival."

119 *money had been deposited into three foreign bank accounts:* Thompson and Reed, "Paris Warns Renault Apology Will Not End Scandal."

119 *The three alleged bribe-taking executives were identified:* ibid.

120 *Tenenbaum had joined Renault at age 19:* Author's interview with Matthieu Tenenbaum, July 8, 2014.

120 *appointed deputy program director of the electric car program:* ibid.

120 *"a plum job":* Jolly, "Fired Renault Executive Blames Tricks by a Rival."

120 *investigators at Renault discovered Tenenbaum had received 500,000 Euros:* ibid.

120 *"his image fit the description":* Author's interview with Yoav Heichal.

120 *"I want to be totally clean with French justice":* Jolly, "Fired Renault Executive Blames Tricks by a Rival."

120 *France's domestic intelligence agency DCRI determined:* Schofield, "Renault Spy Scandal Risks Denting Carmaker's Reputation."

120 *there were in fact no bank accounts:* Thompson and Reed, "Paris Warns Renault Apology Will Not End Scandal."

120 *was a single anonymous informer:* Schofield, "Renault Spy Scandal Risks Denting Carmaker's Reputation."

120 *the anonymous caller had been paid 250,000 Euros by Renault:* ibid.

121 *Patrick Pelata had believed the rumors and authorized the initial transfer:* Author's interview with Yoav Heichal.

121 *"We are in the presence of a possible intelligence fraud":* Thompson and Reed, "Paris Warns Renault Apology Will Not End Scandal."

121 *Renault said it would press charges and was filing a civil suit:* ibid.

121 *Gevrey, who had previously worked as a French military intelligence agent:* Schofield, "Renault Spy Scandal Risks Denting Carmaker's Reputation."

121 *"deep throat":* Lichfield, "Renault Security Chief Arrested Over 'Fake Spy Scandal' Allegations."

121 *sincere apologies and regrets:* Thompson and Reed, "Paris Warns Renault Apology Will Not End Scandal."

121 *Carlos Ghosn was forced to take a pay cut:* ibid.

121 *he would "consider the consequences":* Lichfield, "Renault Security Chief Arrested Over 'Fake Spy Scandal' Allegations."

121 *"Working again in that atmosphere":* Schofield, "Renault Spy Scandal Risks Denting Carmaker's Reputation."

121 *"I need to find work very soon":* Jolly, "Fired Renault Executive Blames Tricks by a Rival."

121 *"I'd been gone already three or four months and it was difficult to come back":* Author's interview with Matthieu Tenenbaum.

121 *"special advisor to the president":* ibid.

122 *Pelata had been "our key guy at Renault":* Author's interview with Yoav Heichal.

122 *He resigned the following year:* Mark Rechtin, "Renault Spy Scandal: Former COO 'Had to Leave,'" *AutoWeek*, April 29, 2013.

122 *"We don't know the implications yet, but suffice to say it isn't a positive move for us":* email from Sidney Goodman to Mike Granoff, Dan Cohen and Joe Paluska, April 11, 2011.

122 *"This will blow over":* Author's interview with Dan Cohen.

122 *Carlos Tavares was a long-standing Better Place skeptic:* Author's interview with Eitan Hon.

122 *who had already been at Renault for 30 years:* Executive Profile—Carlos Tavares, *Bloomberg*.

122 *his loyalties were clearly with his first love:* Author's interview with Eitan Hon.

122 *"Tavares was a very straight person":* Author's interview with Yoav Heichal.

122 *Tavares was "a conservative guy":* ibid.

123 *"When Tavares came into the project, he had many urgent matters":* ibid.

123 *Renault announced it had signed an agreement with the Portuguese utility Energias de Portugal SA:* Author's interview with Matthieu Tenenbaum.

123 *"we'll make you this awesome car":* ibid.

123 *The battery switch stations, the centerpiece to the Better Place offering:* ibid.

123 *Better Place had in fact been working in parallel:* ibid.

123 *Agassi was "really upset with Tavares for cutting him out of the deal":* ibid.

123 *"At the time, we were working together on the specifications for the Fluence Z.E":* ibid.

124 *"There will be no more exchanges":* ibid.

124 *"We used to develop things together":* ibid.

124 *"there wasn't a lot of IP":* ibid.

124 *Agassi "went a bit paranoid on the IP stuff":* ibid.

124 *"For OSCAR, this might have been OK":* ibid.

124 *"Check this out":* Clive Thompson, "Batteries Not Included."

124 *hardware and software inside the car itself would unscrew the fasteners:* Author's interview with Dan Cohen.

125 *"It was a fantastic design":* Author's interview with Idan Ofer.

125 *which moved the hardware and software for unscrewing the battery from the car to the robotic arm:* Author's interview with Dan Cohen.

125 *A single screw could push costs up too high:* ibid.

125 *Each "smart screw" was estimated to cost up to $250:* Author's interview with Guy Tzur, March 13, 2014.

125 *"Look at how a car manufacturer designs the door-locking mechanism":* Author's interview with Yoav Heichal.

125 *a flat panel to "catch" the battery:* Author's interview with Dan Cohen.

125 *then the switch station was essentially hard-wired to the specific battery:* Author's interview with Evan Thornley.

126 *Renault's plan for the Fluence Z.E. also added complexity:* Author's interviews with Yoav Heichal and Daniel Campbell.

126 *whopping three-and-a-half minutes:* Author's experience driving a Better Place Renault Fluence Z.E.

126 *"They just didn't want to be dependent on Better Place":* Author's interview with Dan Cohen.

126 *"Renault didn't want to be stuck working only with Better Place":* Author's interview with Matthieu Tenenbaum.

126 *"It was the biggest mistake I've made in my life":* Author's interview with Robby Bearman.

126 *Letting Renault "win the argument" about the switch stations:* ibid.

126 *In Agassi's retelling of the story:* ibid.

127 *"I should have said to Renault, if we're going your way, we're not going anywhere":* ibid.

127 *"We let them win," Agassi said. "And Renault killed us":* ibid.

127 *Agassi "was admitting to losing an argument, not that he was making an error":* ibid.

127 *"Shai saying that he let Carlos Ghosn win, it never happened":* Author's interview with Matthieu Tenenbaum.

127 *"I think Better Place loomed very small for Ghosn":* Author's interview with Mike Granoff.

127 *Renault held a separate press conference with RWE:* Author's interview with Matthieu Tenenbaum.

127 *"it was on the front pages of every German newspaper":* ibid.

127 *Tavares admitted to Granoff that "he didn't think that switch wouldn't work":* email from Mike Granoff to Shai Agassi, Sidney Goodman, Lawrence Self, Mirko Kershbaum and Jeff Miller, June 11, 2009.

127 *"Now we know how he thinks":* email from Shai Agassi in response, June 12, 2009.

128 *retrofitting a station with new robots:* Author's interview with Guy Tzur.

128 *"ambassador to connect Better Place's software mentality with the old school hardware of a car company":* Author's interview with Yoav Heichal.

128 *"Better Place was filled with these really smart guys":* Author's interview with Matthieu Tenenbaum.

128 *"There's no real prototype":* ibid.

129 *"One time they left me waiting outside in the snow for two hours":* Author's interview with Yoav Heichal.

129 *It also helped that Heichal could speak French:* ibid.

129 *"Sidney was a good project manager":* ibid.

129 *"We needed a former CEO of an automotive company in that role":* Author's interview with Amit Yudan.

129 *"I had nothing against him":* Author's interview with Brian Goldstein.

129 *The disagreements got so intense:* Author's interview with Yoav Heichal.

129 *"I remember at least four times when this happened":* ibid.

129 *"It's so un-auto-like and there's no precedent in the industry":* Author's interview with Emek Sadot.

130 *"We had a discussion with Sidney about Better Place being able to service all cars from Renault":* Author's interview with Matthieu Tenenbaum.

130 *"All right, I understand":* ibid.

130 *Even Better Place CTO Barak Hershkovitz came around:* ibid.

130 *"Barak would come back to us and say, 'Shai vetoed it'":* ibid.

130 *creating a new car from concept to the time the first models roll off the production line:* Author's interview with Yoav Heichal.

130 *It was a slightly larger successor to Renault's popular Mégane:* Author's interview with Quin Garcia.

130 *In fact, the aim was to release two models of the Fluence almost simultaneously:* Author's interview with Dan Cohen.

131 *"a classic three-box sedan":* Reed, "Electric Cars are All the Rage in Israel."

131 *This was a big mistake:* Author's interview with Mike Granoff.

131 *"I used to drive a Honda Civic hybrid":* ibid.

131 *But the battery is much larger and, as a result, took up half the trunk:* Author's experience driving a Better Place Renault Fluence Z.E.

131 *we could understand why the car was built this way":* Author's interview with Yoav Heichal.

131 *The car Better Place really wanted from Renault was called the Zoe:* ibid.
132 *"They already had an engagement from Better Place to sell 100,000 Fluence Z.E.s":* Author's interview with Daniel Campbell.
132 *"All it involved was changing four screws":* ibid.
132 *"the new Zoe electric car could be switch-friendly":* Jim Motavalli, "Wiring the World," *Car Talk,* May 15, 2012.
132 *The bill was $5 million: Author's interview with Yoav Heichal.*
132 *"Renault's position was that if we build this car with a switchable battery":* ibid.
132 *"You're going to be the ones selling and earning from this car":* ibid.

Chapter 11 - A Startup in Pinstripes

134 *its infrastructure couldn't cope:* Victor Luckerson, "How Twitter Stayed the Fail Whale," *Time,* November 6, 2013.
134 *the MacWorld conference in 2008:* ibid.
134 *the death of Michael Jackson:* Maggie Shiels, "Web Slows After Jackson's Death," *BBC News,* June 26, 2009.
134 *the increasingly ubiquitous "Fail Whale":* Luckerson, "How Twitter Stayed the Fail Whale."
134 *"a time when I don't think we lived up to what the world needed Twitter to be":* Mat Honan, "Killing the Fail Whale with Twitter's Christopher Fry," *Wired,* March 25, 2013.
134 *having trouble keeping up with that demand in the core service:* Evan Williams, "IM Not Coming Soon," Twitter Status website, October 10, 2009.
135 *Better Place would soon have the bigger market capitalization:* Author's interview with Mike Granoff.
135 *in a drab industrial park in the outskirts of Madrid, Spain:* Author's interview with Ariel Tikotsky.
135 *Operating Better Place's core computing systems in a secure location in Europe:* ibid.
135 *"We're building a network on Day One that can serve 100,000-plus cars":* Reed, "Electric Cars are All the Rage in Israel."
136 *"the market leader in customer experience software solutions and services":* "Customer Experience Solutions," Amdocs website.
136 *Amdocs would build both the billing system and the customer relationship management backend:* Author's interview with Ariel Tikotsky.
136 *"We wanted Better Place to provide a mass solution, not just a niche":* Author's interview with Eitan Hon.
136 *Amdocs had plenty of experience with billing systems for the cellular phone business:* ibid.
136 *It had started off creating digital versions of the yellow pages:* "The Yellow Pages Years," Amdocs website.
136 *yet with global clients Better Place could tap into as it grew:* "Customers," Amdocs website.

136 *"Amdocs was great for billing and their revenues attest to that"*: Author's interview with Ariel Tikotsky, which also includes Tikotsky's description of how the knowledge management system at Better Place worked and Amdocs' lack of flexibility.

137 *"Amdocs was like a big ship"*: Author's interview with Motty Cohen.

138 *"We were building a battleship for a dinghy race"*: Author's interview with Evan Thornley.

138 *"to be nimble and flexible in the early years"*: ibid.

138 *"building for scale in a single step is simply not possible"*: Alan Finkel, "Anatomy of a Start-up's Failure—What Went Wrong at Better Place," *Cosmos*, December 16, 2015.

138 *"Yes, we built a platform that was way too big for the initial years"*: Author's interview with Dan Cohen.

138 *"Everyone hated it"*: Author's interview with Tal Bar, June 1, 2014.

138 *IBM won the tender to build and manage the Madrid data center*: Author's interview with Ariel Tikotsky.

138 *Alan Finkel questioned the move to Madrid in the first place*: Finkel, "Anatomy of a Start-up's Failure—What Went Wrong at Better Place."

139 *"Today you can run everything on the cloud"*: Author's interview with Motty Cohen.

139 *"Our guys weren't allowed to touch the system in Madrid"*: Author's interview with Ariel Tikotsky.

139 *"For long periods of time, no one could tell us anything about what was going on"*: ibid.

139 *"We want to build a slim, mean machine"*: Author's interview with Shelly Silverstein.

140 *"It developed like a geometric function"*: ibid.

140 *"It was like telling an artist to build the Sistine Chapel"*: ibid.

140 *"The luxury in the global office was amazing"*: Chafkin, "A Broken Place: The Spectacular Failure of the Startup that Was Going to Change the World."

140 *"I asked her 'Where did you get that from'"*: Author's interview with Shelly Silverstein.

140 *Silicon Valley startups have long been famous for their over-the-top perks and benefits*: perks described in this section from Nancy Messiah, "12 Tech Companies That Offer Their Employees the Coolest Perks," *The Next Web*, April 9, 2012; and Lauren Drell, "6 Companies with Awesome Employee Perks," *Mashable*, August 7, 2011.

140 *"being run like the IDF, with a different culture"*: Author's interview with Debbie Kaye, August 24, 2014.

141 *In Paris, Better Place opened a tres jolie office on the Champs-Élysées*: Author's interview with Yishai Horn, April 7, 2014.

141 *"We committed over a million dollars to this space"*: Author's interview with a former Better Place executive.

141 *"Paris was going to be our European headquarters and it was close to Renault"*: ibid.

141 *"Why were we opening an office in Paris when we didn't have an operation in France?"*: Author's interview with a different former Better Place executive.

141 *"You don't see the wasted money when you're in the middle of it"*: Author's interview with Shelly Silverstein.

141 *That wasn't unexpected*: Author's interview with Charles Stonehill, March 11, 2014.

141 *"It was hard to imagine Better Place as a small company just growing incrementally":* ibid.

141 *Better Place's finance team began making the rounds:* Author's interview with Mike Granoff.

142 *Dan Cohen made the introduction:* Author's interview with Dan Cohen, which also includes the rest of Cohen and Agassi's interaction with John Thornton.

142 *"Go for it":* ibid.

142 *Thornton introduced Cohen and the Better Place team to Kevin Adeson:* ibid.

142 *"Shai had an extraordinary ability to bring people with him":* Author's interview with Macgregor Duncan.

143 *"He'd say, you don't understand the company, the vision":* ibid.

143 *You could become the next Google:* ibid.

143 *"We will dwarf Google as a company":* ibid.

143 *"We all knew what the company was worth, and it wasn't that":* Author's interview with Jeff Johnson, June 30, 2014.

143 *"It takes a certain amount of chutzpah":* Author's interview with Macgregor Duncan.

143 *The Series B round closed on January 25, 2010:* Nelson D. Schwartz, "Sites to Refuel Electric Cars Gain a Big Dose of Funds," *The New York Times,* January 25, 2010.

143 *"one of the largest financial investments of its kind by HSBC":* ibid.

144 *Kevin Adeson joined Better Place's board of directors as part of the deal:* ibid.

144 *HSBC wanted to invest at $2.25 a share:* Author's interview with Mike Granoff.

144 *"Shai was insistent":* ibid.

144 *"Listen, we have to make it $2.50":* ibid.

144 *Among the milestones was setting up a full Better Place operation in France and raising another $500 million:* ibid.

144 *"We didn't even come close":* ibid.

144 *"We are confident":* Jonathan Shapira, "Better Place Secures $350 Million Series B Round Led by HSBC Group; Electric Car Start-up Valued at $1.25 Billion," *Cleantech Investing in Israel,* January 25, 2010.

144 *"Our technology and solutions, together with our strong partnership with Renault":* "Better Place Secures $350 Million Series B Round Led by HSBC," press release, *Bloomberg,* January 25, 2010.

Chapter 12 - Plugged in at the Great Wall

146 *China is the world's deadliest country in terms of outdoor air pollution:* Adam Vaughan, "China Tops WHO List for Deadly Outdoor Air Pollution," *The Guardian,* September 27, 2016.

146 *More than a million people died from dirty air in China in 2012:* ibid.

146 *China's pollution deaths are due primarily to a tiny particulate matter called PM2.5:* ibid.

146 *1/30th the size of a human hair:* "Region 4: Laboratory and Field Operations - PM 2.5," EPA Web Archive, *U.S. Environmental Protection Agency.*

146 *coughing, chest tightness and shortness of breath:* "Extremely High Levels of PM2.5: Steps to Reduce Your Exposure," Embassy of the United States, Beijing China website.

146 *motor vehicles and power plants to wood-burning:* "Particulate Matter Primer," Air Pollution: What's the Solution? website.

146 *"Beijing cough":* Li Jing, "Pollution-Free Days of Beijing Olympics Now Just a Happy Memory," *South China Morning Post,* August 10, 2013.

146 *several U.S. cyclists arrived at Beijing Capital International Airport:* ibid.

146 *China banned some 300,000 trucks and 1.7 million private vehicles:* ibid.

146 *"The whole of northern China was making sacrifices for Beijing":* ibid.

147 *less than 40 percent of days:* ibid.

147 *It's hit tourism to Beijing, too, which was down 14.3 percent:* ibid.

147 *Expats are leaving as well:* ibid.

147 *The Chinese Academy of Sciences ranked Beijing:* "Beijing Ranked as China's Least Livable City," *GB Times Beijing,* June 15, 2016.

147 *"like a smoker who needs to quit smoking at once":* Sophie Yeo, "China's Air Pollution Compared to a Smoker at 'Risk of Lung Cancer,'" *Climate Home,* February 24, 2014.

147 *Idan Ofer made the initial introductions for Better Place in China:* Author's interview with Idan Ofer.

147 *Ofer had lived in Hong Kong during the 1980s:* Todd Woody, "How Two Billionaires Are Supercharging The Electric Car To Upend Big Oil," *Forbes,* December 10, 2012.

147 *as part of a joint manufacturing deal with the Chinese auto manufacturer Chery:* Author's interview with Idan Ofer.

147 *Ofer wanted to diversify his operations:* ibid.

147 *"That was the reason I went into Better Place with so much weight":* ibid.

147 *"marry my car-making business in China with Better Place's ability to build infrastructure":* ibid.

148 *"we would have gone straight to China":* ibid.

148 *"China was quickly becoming the biggest automotive market in the world":* Author's interview with Dan Cohen.

148 *China "could end up doing electric so big that it creates a global industry":* Author's interview with Mike Granoff.

148 *China had just set a goal to get 5 million electric cars on the road by 2020:* Motavalli, "Wiring the World."

148 *the Chinese government had "made a clear policy":* Rebecca Zeffert, "Why China Will be Tipping Point for EVs," *Green Prophet,* August 17, 2010.

148 *a discount worth nearly $9,000:* Jim Motavalli, "China to Subsidize Electric Cars and Hybrids," *The New York Times,* June 2, 2010.

148 *Within a couple of years, that incentive would jump to as much as $19,000 per car:* Motavalli, "Wiring the World."

148 *a third party made a connection:* Author's interview with Dan Cohen, which also includes Cohen's description of the discussions with State Grid Shanghai.

149 *Garcia flew to Beijing in November 2009:* Author's interview with Quin Garcia.

149 *Forbes reported that the state-owned Beijing Automotive collaborated with Better Place:* Woody, "How Two Billionaires Are Supercharging The Electric Car To Upend Big Oil."

150 *That is, until Shai Agassi stepped in:* Author's interview with Dan Cohen.

150 *in China he felt out of his comfort zone:* ibid.

150 *all but irrelevant when working with a translator:* ibid.

150 *"The back-and-forth goes slower":* ibid.

150 *"Shai's a very effective communicator and negotiator in English":* Author's interview with Kiyotaka Fujii.

150 *"We were in a beautiful conference room":* Author's interview with Quin Garcia.

150 *"At the head of the table were two seats at an angle":* Author's interview with Dan Cohen.

150 *"Israelis are loud and aggressive in meetings while the Chinese are much more subtle":* Author's interview with Quin Garcia.

151 *Garcia bounced back and forth between the two sides:* ibid.

151 *"I was trying to show I was on their side, too":* ibid.

151 *"He'd heard all kinds of war stories about China":* Author's interview with Dan Cohen.

151 *"He did everything he could to put spokes in that wheel":* ibid.

151 *"Shai resisted China from Day One":* Author's interview with Idan Ofer.

151 *Better Place had a standard clause in the contracts it wrote to work:* Author's interview with Dan Cohen.

151 *"We had a couple of clauses":* ibid.

152 *China State Grid had joined a multi-country consortium:* "Two Groups Vie for Multi-billion Dollar Manila Power Deal," *Reuters,* December 12, 2007.

152 *China State Grid insisted that it be given the rights:* Author's interview with Dan Cohen.

152 *"it was a red line for us":* ibid.

152 *"They were already being perceived as being too much of a monopoly in the energy sector":* ibid.

152 *"it was still early days for electric vehicles in general":* ibid.

152 *Better Place signed a Memorandum of Agreement with Chery Automotive:* Chuck Squatriglia, "Better Place Brings its EVs to China and Tokyo," *Wired,* April 26, 2010.

152 *A picture of an electric car plugged into one of Better Place's already iconic blue-and-gray charge spots:* ibid.

153 *"The two companies say the partnership offers the potential":* ibid.

153 *"With only two percent of China's population owning cars":* ibid.

153 *Chery was China's largest private automotive maker and its top automotive exporter in 2009:* ibid.

153 *It built about 500,000 cars:* ibid.

153 *"China never developed a globally competitive automobile industry"*: Zeffert, "Why China Will be Tipping Point for EVs."

153 *"Just as they are doing cars much faster than the United States ever did"*: ibid.

153 *"China is what's going to make this revolution happen faster than anyone thinks"*: ibid.

154 *"We want to create a brand with Western levels of quality"*: Motavalli, "Wiring the World."

154 *Ofer hired former Volkswagen head honcho Volker Steinwascher:* Sabine Gusbeth, "Ex-Volkswagen Manager: 'We are Taken Seriously,'" *Finanzen.net*, April 26, 2014.

154 *Ofer instructed his Qoros managers to cooperate fully with Better Place's engineers:* Author's interview with Idan Ofer.

154 *Qoros worked up a detailed specification:* ibid.

154 *"You should be building this car for 8,000 Euros"*: ibid.

154 *"Come to China and see for yourself"*: ibid.

154 *"He was undermining the viability of Qoros as a company"*: ibid.

154 *"Qoros was always a hedge for me against Better Place"*: ibid.

154 *"I told Shai that from this day onward, you are no longer allowed to speak to one another"*: ibid.

154 *Qoros began selling its first model in 2013:* "New Qoros 3 Hatch to Debut in Geneva, 3 Sedan Starts Sales in Europe," *The Truth About Cars,* January 16, 2014.

154 *"It was all designed"*: Author's interview with Idan Ofer.

155 *Cohen and Garcia turned their attention south:* Author's interview with Dan Cohen.

155 *China Southern Power covered only 12 percent of the country:* ibid.

155 *It was the eighth-largest utility in the world at the time:* Viva Sarah Press, "Better Place China Southern Grid Sign Deal," *Israel21c,* May 3, 2011.

155 *"The conversation was much friendlier"*: Author's interview with Dan Cohen.

155 *It signed its first solid contract in the People's Republic with China Souther Power:* Press, "Better Place China Southern Grid Sign Deal."

155 *"Electric cars present a great opportunity for China"*: ibid.

155 *"China Southern Grid is an important partner"*: ibid.

155 *The deal also called for the creation of a 1,900-square-meter Demonstration Center:* Qui Quanlin, "Helping Drivers Make Switch to Electric Cars," *China Daily,* December 15, 2011.

155 *The operation occupied the downstairs of what would now be Better Place's official Chinese headquarters:* Author's interview with Quin Garcia.

156 *The Guangzhou center opened to the public in December 2011:* Quanlin, "Helping Drivers Make Switch to Electric Cars."

156 *"We found a mouse living in the space between the battery and the car"*: Author's interview with Carlo Tursi.

156 *"We never caught him"*: ibid.

156 *"We had some strange voltage readings on the battery"*: ibid.

156 *By 4 a.m., the battery cells were finally charging:* ibid.

156 *"Most Chinese are new buyers who don't have a history of car ownership":* Quanlin, "Helping Drivers Make Switch to Electric Cars."

157 *China Southern Power had agreed to build 14 charging stations:* ibid.

Chapter 13 - U-Turn

158 *he would be taking a "sabbatical" from Palo Alto for the year:* email from Shai Agassi to Better Place staff, August 12, 2009.

158 *A few months later, he made it permanent:* Chafkin, "A Broken Place: The Spectacular Failure of the Startup that Was Going to Change the World."

158 *a common tax-saving practice:* Leslie Wayne, "How Delaware Thrives as a Corporate Tax Haven," *The New York Times,* June 30, 2012.

158 *Agassi assembled his staff in Palo Alto to share the news:* Author's interview with a former Better Place executive.

158 *"You can expect to see me at least twenty-five percent of my time":* email from Shai Agassi to Better Place staff, August 12, 2009.

158 *"he degraded into a kind of calm but very nasty rant on the global operation":* Author's interview with a former Better Place executive.

159 *"You guys don't deliver value to the rest of the operation":* ibid.

159 *"OK, if you don't think we're important, then shut it down":* ibid.

159 *"At first Shai tried to maintain a routine of coming to Palo Alto regularly":* Author's interview with Dan Cohen.

159 *"We thought we'd lose that Silicon Valley edge":* ibid.

159 *The main action in Better Place at that point was happening in Israel:* email from Shai Agassi to Better Place staff, August 12, 2009.

160 *an equally plausible explanation:* Author's interview with Mike Granoff and Amit Nisenbaum, February 19, 2014.

160 *"He was bitter about the whole American situation":* Author's interview with Dan Cohen.

160 *Tesla was so broke that its founder Elon Musk was pouring his personal fortune:* Owen Thomas, "Tesla's Elon Musk: 'I Ran Out of Cash,'" *VentureBeat,* May 27, 2010.

160 *In October 2009, Musk claimed to be out of cash:* ibid.

160 *offered Tesla a loan for $465 million:* Erick Schonfeld, "The Government Comes Through for Tesla with a $465 Million Loan for its Electric Sedan," *TechCrunch,* June 23, 2009.

160 *the company was able to pay back the loan by May 2013:* Ashlee Vance, "Tesla Pays Off its $465 Million 'Loser' Loan," *Bloomberg,* May 23 2013.

160 *"the only American car company to have fully repaid the government":* ibid.

160 *Agassi hired Tami Chotoveli as his personal coach:* Chafkin, "A Broken Place: The Spectacular Failure of the Startup that Was Going to Change the World."

160 *Chotoveli ran a luxury watch company:* Eleanor Fox, "Electric Shock," *Mako,* May 30, 2013.

161 *"The company had become huge, with hundreds of employees"*: Author's interview with Nir Gilad, April 17, 2014.

161 *after a vacation in Thailand*: ibid.

161 *"He told us he had consulted with an organizational behavior expert to create it"*: ibid.

161 *Mike Granoff met Chotoveli with Agassi a few months later*: Author's interview with Mike Granoff.

161 *Agassi referred to Chotoveli not as his advisor but as his girlfriend*: ibid.

161 *"I didn't know she existed before that moment"*: ibid.

161 *"She's the first person I've met who's smarter than me"*: ibid.

161 *"fancy Louis Vuitton bag that cost seven or eight thousand dollars"*: Author's interview with Idan Ofer.

161 *"From that moment on, I didn't trust her"*: ibid.

161 *she was at his side in meetings with prospective investors*: Author's interview with Macgregor Duncan.

161 *"She would write notes to him in meetings"*: Author's interview with Idan Ofer.

161 *"This is a guy who never read from paper"*: Author's interview with Nir Gilad.

161 *Chotoveli was eroding Agassi's confidence*: ibid.

162 *"I forbade Shai from taking her to any more meetings"*: Author's interview with Idan Ofer.

162 *"It was just the three of us for two days"*: Author's interview with Macgregor Duncan.

162 *Agassi's marriage was already in trouble*: Author's interview with Mike Granoff.

162 *"I'm on some thin ice at home"*: ibid.

162 *Agassi's father was not happy with his son's behavior*: Author's interview with Nir Gilad.

162 *"I cannot even approach Shai with these rumors"*: ibid.

162 *Chotoveli's Facebook and Twitter feed filled up with pictures of her and Agassi*: Tami Chotoveli Facebook and Twitter pages.

162 *"a very tight guy, stingy"*: Author's interview with Idan Ofer.

163 *"We have no tangible facts to back up this theory"*: ibid.

163 *he created a highly irregular stock option program*: Author's interview with Dimitri Dadiomov.

163 *the final tranche of options wouldn't vest until Better Place had a million people driving*: Author's interview with Mike Granoff.

163 *"four years is already more than you can predict in business"*: Author's interview with Dimitri Dadiomov.

163 *"The stock option program was a motivational disaster"*: Author's interview with a former Better Place executive.

164 *"But the option program kept us from attracting top executives"*: ibid.

164 *"The Israelis didn't quite get it"*: Author's interview with a former Better Place executive.

164 *"Shai thought that four-year stock option programs were bad plans"*: ibid.

164 *"Shai would say that Better Place is going to be the biggest company in the world"*: Author's interview with Mike Granoff.

164 *to determine whether there was a business case:* Author's interview with Kiyotaka Fujii.

165 *But they are responsible for 20 percent of vehicle CO2 emissions:* John O'Dell "Better Place's Tokyo Taxi Battery Exchange Program Ends Without a Glitch," *Edmunds Auto Observer,* August 6, 2010.

165 *half the taxis in the fleet are circulating the city's streets looking for customers:* ibid.

165 *"A single internal-combustion taxi produces twenty-nine tons of CO2 a year":* ibid.

165 *"Tokyo's taxis define the face of the city":* Author's interview with Kiyotaka Fujii, which also includes Fujii's comments on why battery switchable taxis were ideal for Tokyo.

166 *The main pickup station for passengers:* O'Dell, "Better Place's Tokyo Taxi Battery Exchange Program Ends Without a Glitch."

166 *"This is the equivalent to Rockefeller Center in Manhattan":* Author's interview with Kiyotaka Fujii.

166 *The taxi trial began on April 26, 2010, and lasted for three months:* O'Dell "Better Place's Tokyo Taxi Battery Exchange Program Ends Without a Glitch."

166 *Three taxis were put into service with real taxi drivers:* ibid.

166 *The base model for the taxis was a modified Nissan Dualis:* ibid.

166 *Most of the financing came from the Japanese Ministry of Economy, Trade and Industry:* ibid.

166 *The batteries were provided by American battery maker A123 Systems:* ibid.

166 *they could range as far as Haneda Airport:* ibid.

166 *"It means 'cool'":* Author's interview with Quin Garcia.

166 *"Compared to the other taxis I've driven, it's a very good ride, and easy to drive":* O'Dell "Better Place's Tokyo Taxi Battery Exchange Program Ends Without a Glitch."

166 *"Yes, you have to do it frequently, but it goes by very fast":* ibid.

167 *"you must be very careful coming up on pedestrians from behind":* ibid.

167 *200 stations, each serving approximately 200 cabs:* ibid.

167 *only one cabbie pushed his luck and ran out of juice:* ibid.

167 *"If you have a taxi driver going to Tokyo every day":* "Better Place launches switchable-battery electric taxi project in Tokyo," video, April 27, 2010.

167 *Huge empty drums punctuate the landscape:* Author's visit to Visitor Center.

167 *Five million dollars later:* Chafkin, "A Broken Place: The Spectacular Failure of the Startup that Was Going to Change the World."

168 *opened on February 8, 2010:* Author's interview with Lilach Gon Carfas, April 2, 2014.

168 *Mike Granoff brought dozens of visiting politicians:* Author's interview with Mike Granoff.

168 *The Visitor Center included three main components:* Author's interview with Lilach Gon Carfas and author's visit to Visitor Center.

168 *Enthusiastic drivers would triple or quadruple up in the cars:* Author's visit to Visitor Center.

168 *Amos Shapira … was paralyzed by the silence:* Author's interview with Tal Bar.

168 *"Now I can drive":* ibid.

169 *"We will allow every citizen of Israel to experience driving the electric car":* Karin Kloosterman, "Better Place Launches Test Drive and Electric Car Education Facility in Israel," *Green Prophet,* February 14, 2010.

169 *more than 80,000 people were exposed to Better Place through the Pi Glilot Visitor Center:* Amy Teibel, "Electric Car Network Gets First Test in Israel," *Associated Press,* May 19, 2012.

169 *Visitors would enter from the rear of the theater:* Author's visit to Visitor Center.

169 *"begins with images of carefree people relaxing on a beach":* Reed, "Electric Cars are All the Rage in Israel."

169 *"We've all become slaves to the price of oil":* ibid.

169 *"This is a new era of transportation":* ibid.

169 *he was holographically projected:* Author's interviews with Tal Bar and Lilach Gon Carfas.

169 *the screen slid to the side to expose a model of a Renault electric car:* Reed, "Electric Cars are All the Rage in Israel."

169 *the screen slid to the side:* Author's interview with Lilach Gon Carfas.

169 *Visitors exited the screening room into a second rounded chamber called the "Vision Room":* ibid.

170 *Visitors' names would magically appear in the middle of the map:* ibid.

170 *Leonardo DiCaprio ... Bar Refaeli ... Ashton Kutcher ... Demi Moore:* ibid.

170 *"we had to clear the entire building":* ibid.

170 *"Only three or four people were allowed to stay":* ibid.

170 *Mitt Romney ... Chris Christie:* Author's interview with Mike Granoff.

170 *Agassi initially didn't think it was worth his time to meet Christie:* ibid.

171 *bluntly asked for $200 million:* ibid.

171 *"That's doable":* ibid.

171 *Better Place inventory was sold out for two years:* Chafkin, "A Broken Place: The Spectacular Failure of the Startup that Was Going to Change the World."

171 *Better Place reservations were not binding:* ibid.

171 *"He would sometimes humiliate people":* Author's interview with a former Better Place executive.

171 *"Shai was finding it harder and harder to accept contradictory views":* Author's interview with Charles Stonehill.

171 *"They shook hands and would smile around one another":* Author's interview with Shelly Silverstein.

171 *"If you were painted with Kaplan's colors, you couldn't be faithful to anyone else in the company":* ibid.

172 *"The esprit de corps that was present in the first years of the company was quickly going away":* Author's interview with Mike Granoff.

172 *"He was going through a difficult personal period":* Author's interview with Yoav Heichal.

172 *The night before the meeting, the Executive Committee had dinner without Agassi:* Author's interview with Mike Granoff.

172 *"We wanted to have a discussion about Shai without Shai being there":* Author's interview with Idan Ofer.

172 *the board hoped to cover overall strategy:* Author's interview with Mike Granoff.

172 *"I have made some of the best friends I ever had in the company":* email from Mike Granoff to Shai Agassi, June 22, 2010.

173 *"In the middle of dinner, I got this long email from Shai":* Author's interview with Idan Ofer.

173 *"How dare you do this thing!":* ibid.

173 *"He felt like people were stabbing him in the back":* Author's interview with Dan Cohen.

173 *"Listen, Shai, I can have a conversation with anyone I want to":* Author's interview with Idan Ofer.

173 *stormed out of the room:* Author's interview with Mike Granoff.

173 *"This is over. I'm finished with him":* Author's interview with Idan Ofer.

173 *"We can't fire someone after he's just raised three hundred and fifty million dollars":* Author's interview with Mike Granoff.

173 *"The cemetery is full of people who couldn't be replaced":* Author's interview with Dan Cohen.

173 *Cohen believed Agassi had realized that "he'd overplayed his hand":* ibid.

173 *Granoff wondered whether what he was witnessing was just a game:* Author's interview with Mike Granoff.

174 *Half an hour after Agassi had walked out, he was reinstated:* ibid.

174 *"That day defined all of Shai's relationships going forward":* Author's interview with Dan Cohen.

174 *"We bowed to peer pressure and didn't make the right decision":* Author's interview with Idan Ofer.

174 *"Everything changed after this":* Author's interview with Mike Granoff.

174 *Macgregor Duncan ... joined a staff retreat at Evan Thornley's huge colonial-era private farm:* Author's interview with Macgregor Duncan.

174 *It was 11 at night and Duncan and Thornley were sharing a bottle of wine:* ibid.

174 *"I was telling Evan about some of my reservations":* ibid.

174 *"Shai has tremendous talents":* ibid.

175 *"We talked for another two to three hours":* ibid.

175 *"He was happy running his Better Place business in Australia":* ibid.

175 *"I'm flattered by your confidence in my ability":* Author's interview with Evan Thornley.

175 *Agassi penned a detailed email to the members of the Better Place board:* all quotes taken from Agassi's email to the board, June 21, 2010.

Chapter 14 - Bait and Switch

177 *it even included an official sticker inside the car attesting to that:* Author's interview with Dan Cohen.

177 *The car's true range was no more than 85 miles:* ibid.

177 *the Fluence Z.E. would be lucky to get as far as 60 miles:* Author's experience driving a Renault Fluence Z.E.

177 *New European Driving Cycle:* Romain Nicolas, "The Different Driving Cycles," *Car Engineer,* January 5, 2013.

177 *driven on a flat road in the absence of wind:* Tom Denton, *Advanced Automotive Fault Diagnosis (Automotive Technology: Vehicle Maintenance and Repair, 4th Edition),* Institute of the Motor Industry, Routledge, 2017.

177 *"roller bench":* "11 Legal Cheats Car Makers Get Away with Across the Pond," *Mobopreneur,* April 21, 2016.

177 *All "ancillary loads":* ibid.

177 *"homologated range of 185 km":* Fluence Z.E. product page, Renault website.

178 *"Regenerative braking":* White Paper, "Electric Vehicles for Israel."

178 *it feels like the car is facing down a strong wind:* Author's experience driving a Renault Fluence Z.E.

178 *If you resist your instinct to brake, the car does it for you:* ibid.

178 *"If not, you won't be able to drive from Tel Aviv to Haifa and back without a switch in-between":* Author's interview with Dan Cohen.

179 *"When you have just five percent left on your battery, you feel a little bit afraid":* Author's interview with Eitan Hon.

179 *"was never designed to squeeze out the last five kilometers before getting home":* Author's interview with Daniel Campbell.

179 *"You couldn't drive from Yotvata to Mitzpe Ramon in the winter":* ibid.

179 *"We would drive to the hotels near Masada":* Author's interview with a Renault Fluence Z.E. owner.

179 *"They always said just that 'we'll try to get there'":* Author's interview with Eitan Hon.

179 *"If you look at our press release from 2008":* Author's interview with Matthieu Tenenbaum.

180 *the Fluence Z.E "would offer a range about a hundred kilometers in 'Israeli' conditions":* Nathalie Brafman, "Renault Launches Electric Car in Israel," *Le Monde,* January 21, 2008.

180 *Renault CEO Carlos Ghosn said the same:* "Project Better Place & Renault-Nissan to Electrify Israel," video.

180 *Israel "is a small country where ninety percent of the population drives less than seventy kilometers a day":* Nathalie Brafman, "Renault Launches Electric Car in Israel."

180 *"We knew that in tests the car could reach a hundred and eighty kilometers":* Author's interview with Matthieu Tenenbaum.

180 *"It was Shai who was saying it had to be two hundred kilometers":* ibid.

180 *"A billboard for the business":* Author's interview with Hugh McDermott.

180 *he wouldn't feel comfortable having his wife pull in for a switch alone after dark:* Author's interview with Ariel Tikotsky.

181 *the station wasn't even close to the main commuter highway:* Author's interview with Yoav Heichal.

181 *One switch station was on the grounds of a cement factory:* Author's experience driving a Renault Fluence Z.E.

181 *outskirts of Jerusalem, adjacent to the city's recycling center:* ibid.

181 *Nearly all along well-traveled highways:* Author's interview with Susanne Tolstrup.

181 *Australia had plans to build … next to gas stations:* Author's interview with Geoff Zippel.

181 *Most of Israel's gas stations were built illegally:* Author's interview with Yoav Heichal, which also includes Heichal's description of why gas stations didn't work out and the extent to which Better Place tried to classify the switch stations as industrial facilities.

182 *A second batch of stations could always be built later in the "right" locations:* ibid.

182 *"We needed the prime minister himself to say, 'This is a national project'":* Author's interview with Guy Pross.

183 *could have taken 10 years:* Author's interview with Eitan Hon.

183 *"So we built the stations off an exit":* ibid.

183 *"The fact that the battery switch stations got built at all is something amazing":* ibid.

183 *Zippel brought his 20 years of experience:* Author's interview with Geoff Zippel, which also includes Zippel's description of how Better Place planned to work with gas stations in Australia.

184 *"We didn't know anything four years ago":* Nadav Shemer, "Better Place Unveils Battery Swap Network," *The Jerusalem Post,* February 13, 2012.

184 *"Imagine what it is like to do this simultaneously in dozens of locations":* ibid.

185 *It will take "less time than it takes to fill your gasoline tank":* Thompson, "Batteries Not Included."

185 *scaled back its switch stations in Israel from 120 to just 40:* Author's interview with Eitan Hon.

185 *the most convenient switch station on the Jerusalem-Tel Aviv route:* Author's experience driving a Renault Fluence Z.E.

185 *But there was no switch station anywhere near Highway 443:* ibid.

185 *If there were two cars ahead of you, tack on another 10 minutes of waiting time:* ibid.

186 *right off the street. "But who cares?":* Author's interview with Rebecca Shliselberg, February 24, 2014.

186 *"wasted money":* ibid.

186 *"It would have been cheaper to let you rent a gasoline-powered car":* ibid.

186 *a voucher to rent "a petrol or diesel car, free of charge, for up to 14 days":* "Nissan Leaf: Our Promise, Your Experience" Nissan UK website.

186 *the IAA will conduct a survey of the area:* Yehuda Dagan, "Archaeological Survey of Israel," Israel Antiquities Authority website.

186 *Tel Hadid—an ordinary looking mound of dirt:* "Tel Hadid," Hadashot Arkheologiyot website, Volume 122, Year 2010.

186 *in the days of the biblical Joshua:* Israel Finkelstein and Neil Asher Silberman, *David and Solomon*, Free Press, Simon & Schuster, 2006.

186 *A half-kilometer long tunnel under the site:* "About Highway 6," Kvish 6 website.

187 *is at the forefront of the battle to prevent desecration of Jewish bones:* Jeremy Sharon, "Haredim Spar Over Construction, Grave Desecration," *The Jerusalem Post*, August 12, 2012.

187 *when burial remains were found at the proposed location of a new hospital emergency room:* Donald Macintyre, "Ultra-Orthodox Fury at Removal of Ancient Remains from Israel Hospital," *Independent*, May 17, 2010.

187 *"the land of Israel to go to war":* ibid.

187 *"Digging is not just the process of bringing a machine":* Author's interview with Guy Tzur.

188 *"the mapping of underground cables and pipes is not complete":* ibid.

188 *Better Place's battery switch stations eventually reached a depth of 13 feet:* ibid.

188 *"Gas stations don't want a big and imposing structure on their forecourt":* Author's interview with Geoff Zippel.

188 *"The rent for a regular battery switch station in the center of the country":* Author's interview with Efi Shahak, April 9, 2014.

188 *"I talked to an employee who told me that people assumed that Better Place was rich":* ibid.

188 *A big chunk of the rest went to the electricity:* ibid.

189 *But if the battery is fast charged under extremely cold conditions:* Author's interview with Guy Zzur.

189 *The cost of 24/7 air conditioning, spare parts, taxes and maintenance:* Author's interview with Efi Shahak.

189 *Seventy percent of the money was fronted to Better Place as a four-year loan:* Aviv Levy, "Baran Worried About Better Place Debt," *Globes*, November 28, 2012.

189 *Baran reported in a public earnings statement:* ibid.

189 *"They looked at us as a milking cow":* Author's interview with Yoav Heichal.

189 *"They didn't ask for cash up front but they padded the bills by huge amounts":* ibid.

189 *"I used to come to make fixes on the stations":* ibid.

189 *"A guy would come, drill a hole to hang a sign and bill us for five hundred dollars":* ibid.

190 *separating ownership of the battery—the most expensive "extra" for electric cars:* "Q&A with Sidney Goodman of Better Place."

190 *At up to $15,000 a battery:* Author's interview with Ben Keneally, April 25, 2014.

190 *Better Place planned to charge customers upwards of $300 a month:* Author's interview with Zohar Bali, March 9, 2014.

190 *drivers would discover that their batteries would degrade to an unacceptable level:* Author's experience driving a Renault Fluence Z.E.

191 *They were to be financed, like a mortgage:* Author's interview with Mike Granoff.

191 *The pooled assets could then be sold to investors:* ibid.

191 *"No one wanted to take the risk":* ibid.

191   *"Financing the batteries would only generate a seven to eight percent return"*: Author's interview with Ben Keneally.

191   *"These are bullshit numbers by someone who has no understanding in finance"*: email from Shai Agassi to Mike Granoff, September 4, 2010.

191   *finance a total of 10,000 batteries:* Candace Lombardi, "Better Place Recharges Business Model with GE," *CNET,* September 22, 2010.

192   *GE also committed to making sure its own WattStation home charging spot would be compatible:* Katie Fehrenbacher, "GE & Better Place Buddy Up Over Electric Vehicles," *GigaOm,* September 22, 2010.

192   *"solid, strong vision about how the EV will evolve"*: Jim Motovalli, "G.E. and Better Place to Partner on E.V. Charging," *The New York Times,* September 24, 2010.

192   *"not any better than what we could have gotten from the bank"*: Author's interview with Amit Nisenbaum.

192   *"He'd say, 'This is just small change'"*: Author's interview with a former Better Place executive.

192   *That $20 million wound up as a general investment in Better Place:* ibid.

192   *which made a deal:* Author's interview with Mike Granoff.

192   *Shortly after the Better Place board meeting in London:* Author's interview with Charles Stonehill.

192   *"I left because of some private disagreements with Shai"*: ibid.

192   *"Could we vary the business model to be more inclusive of other electric vehicles"*: ibid.

193   *The individual OpCos and Barak Hershkovitz's Better Place Labs all had their own financial teams and internal CFOs:* ibid.

193   *"We were originally supposed to go to market in 2010"*: Author's interview with Hugh McDermott.

193   *"Every time I came to visit Israel, it seemed like another floor had been built"*: ibid.

193   *"The size of the staff was ridiculous and entirely unnecessary"*: Author's interview with Macgregor Duncan.

193   *the decision to relocate the company headquarters from Palo Alto to Israel:* Author's interview with Charles Stonehill.

194   *"every time an American quit, he or she was replaced by an Israeli"*: Author's interview with David Shlachter, February 23, 2014.

194   *"The management became more provincial at that time"*: Author's interview with David Kennedy.

194   *"We've got three candidates. I like this guy"*: Author's interview with Andrey Zarur.

194   *"Shai didn't want to have a CFO who would ask too many questions"*: Author's interview with Idan Ofer.

194   *"We have to get someone who was formerly the CFO of General Motors or Microsoft"*: Author's interview with Mike Granoff.

194   *"Basically, the 'ungettables'"*: ibid.

194   *"The entire governance by the board was exceedingly poor"*: Author's interview with Geoff Zippel.

195 *an attitude that "we can always raise more money":* Author's interview with Mike Granoff.

195 *"It was like, we've already done the impossible":* Author's interview with Dan Cohen.

195 *The Series B money—$350 million:* Author's interview with Mike Granoff, which also includes Granoff's comments on why the price Agassi wanted for the Series B was too high, and sources for funds.

196 *Agassi's pitch resonated with the company's existing investors:* Chafkin, "A Broken Place: The Spectacular Failure of the Startup that Was Going to Change the World."

196 *committing $130 million:* Author's interview with Mike Granoff.

196 *"We needed a fig leaf":* ibid.

196 *If he could get Baron on board, Better Place would have a "new" investor:* ibid.

196 *"as a personal favor to Umansky":* ibid.

196 *"The way you're spending, you don't need $200 million, you need $400 million":* ibid.

196 *"No problem":* ibid.

196 *"And what if you don't?":* ibid.

196 *Elon Musk pushed himself to the verge of personal bankruptcy:* "Elon Musk, of PayPal and Tesla Fame, is Broke," *The New York Times,* June 22, 2010.

196 *"My father kept complaining, why isn't he putting any money of his own into this?":* Author's interview with Idan Ofer.

196 *While Agassi agreed to Baron's end-of-the-year demand:* Author's interview with Mike Granoff.

197 *"The valuation was excessive":* Author's interview with Macgregor Duncan.

197 *only large investment banks and institutional money managers could justify that price:* ibid.

197 *"I had many conversations with Shai, saying 'Why are you pressing for such a large valuation?'":* ibid.

197 *"The price today is irrelevant because we'll be so big in the end":* ibid.

197 *"Shai thought that the massively inflated valuation was part of the story":* ibid.

197 *which became increasingly erratic:* ibid.

197 *"We were having a due diligence discussion about the financial model":* ibid.

197 *"Sorry, can you repeat that?":* ibid.

197 *"OK, so your financial models are predicting you'll have 2,000 customers in 2012":* ibid.

198 *"Yes," he said, without missing a beat:* ibid.

198 *"The whole thing had veered into the absurd":* ibid.

198 *Perhaps that's because of who Agassi's fictional hero was:* ibid.

198 *"Shai was in this kind of ruminative mood":* ibid.

198 *"Not bad for a startup that has yet to launch its networks":* Todd Woody, "Better Place Raises Another $200 Million to Roll Out Electric Car Charging Networks," *Forbes,* November 11, 2011.

198 *the entire finance team resigned:* Author's interview with Macgregor Duncan.

198 *"None of us wanted to be involved in a company we believed was going south":* ibid.

198 *because they were offered significant cash bonuses to stay:* ibid.

198 *"If I had left three months earlier, the Series C may not have been signed":* ibid.

198 *"I thought there was a possibility":* ibid.

199 *"He had to keep going through the motions":* ibid.

199 *Better Place always felt like a political campaign:* ibid.

Chapter 15 - How to Lose Money Without Really Trying

200 *The price announcement came at a news conference:* Maurice Picow, "Better Place EVs Priced at $35,623 USD for Summer Delivery," *Green Prophet,* May 17, 2011.

200 *at the tony David InterContinental hotel:* Author's interview with Zohar Bali.

200 *Murmuring turned into ill will:* ibid.

200 *The basic five-door sedan was given a sticker price of $35,623:* Picow, "Better Place EVs Priced at $35,623 USD for Summer Delivery."

200 *The price in Denmark was roughly equivalent:* Maurice Picow, "Better Place Reveals Danish Car Prices," *Green Prophet,* March 6, 2011.

200 *The "premium" model … was $2,000 more:* Picow, "Better Place EVs Priced at $35,623 USD for Summer Delivery."

201 *"The media just killed us":* Author's interview with Zohar Bali.

201 *"People thought they'd get the car for free":* Author's interview with Lilach Gon Carfas.

201 *The actual price of the Fluence Z.E. from Renault to Better Place:* Author's interview with Zohar Bali.

201 *How did Renault come up with that price?:* Discussion on Renault's pricing calculations from author's interview with Zohar Bali.

201 *"A carmaker doesn't have a specific set price list":* ibid.

201 *Renault "wanted to compare it with other electric cars or plug-in premium vehicles like the Toyota Prius":* ibid.

202 *"the price from Renault to Better Place for the Fluence Z.E.":* Author's interview with Eitan Hon.

202 *"If you look at our first discussions, you'll see that the target price of the car we gave":* Author's interview with Matthieu Tenenbaum.

202 *"It was an argument we didn't win":* Author's interview with Dan Cohen.

202 *"In the entire time it's operated in Israel":* Author's interview with Zohar Bali.

203 *"In Israel, Mazda sells ten thousand to twelve thousand Mazda 3s a year":* ibid.

203 *"We couldn't point to an example from another market":* ibid.

203 *"would be a good score for the Fluence Z.E.:* "The Electric Car Aims at the Mass Market," *Les Echos,* May 15, 2012.

203 *"I thought, maybe this is so new, maybe Shai knew better":* Author's interview with Zohar Bali, which also includes Bali's description of Carasso's objections to distributing the Fluence Z.E. in Israel and the need to set up Better Place Motors.

204 *Bank Igud was given a prominent office in the Visitor Center:* Author's experience at the Visitor Center.

204 *"not because it is an electric vehicle, but because it is a great car":* Shai Agassi, "Tesla's a Threat to the Auto Industry, But Detroit's Reacting All Wrong," *LinkedIn,* August 19, 2013.

204 *If that wasn't possible, then NIS 99,000 instead of NIS 120,000:* Author's interview with Yishai Horn.

204 *Tal Bar ... thought the total price should be even lower:* Author's interview with Tal Bar.

204 *"What Shai had in mind":* Chafkin, "A Broken Place: The Spectacular Failure of the Startup that Was Going to Change the World."

205 *"That's HP's business model":* Author's interview with Yishai Horn.

205 *"The pain of adoption should have been balanced with a super attractive car price":* ibid.

205 *Better Place created a guerrilla-marketing program:* Author's interview with Zohar Bali.

205 *There were two tiers:* Eric Loveday, "Better Place Announces Pricing for Renault Fluence Z.E. in Israel," *AutoBlog,* May 16, 2011.

205 *"are actually showing up for financial reasons":* Kalman, "Baby You Can Drive My Car."

206 *The packages were too expensive; they didn't show a big enough savings:* Author's interview with Tal Bar.

206 *Zohar Bali convened a meeting at the Visitor Center for a group of 15 Champions:* Author's interview with Zohar Bali.

206 *"I didn't have any other idea at the time":* ibid.

206 *"They wanted something much simpler, like pay as you drive":* ibid.

206 *The original package pricing "was not a good business offering":* Author's interview with Tal Bar.

206 *"We struggled for the full four hours":* Author's interview with Zohar Bali.

206 *"I understood now that Better Place had made a mistake":* ibid.

206 *"I can't keep going with this offering":* ibid.

207 *"No way—this is crazy":* ibid.

207 *Bali went on the sly to one of Better Place's sales managers:* ibid.

207 *The revised proposal:* ibid.

207 *"It was very simple: Pay only for what you drive":* ibid.

207 *a new option where drivers could "lock in" a lower per-kilometer price:* ibid.

207 *Dafna was afraid of her brother's reaction:* ibid.

207 *"You're right, that's the way to deliver it":* ibid.

207 *"How is it that he said this was the pricing he had wanted from the beginning":* ibid.

207 *"From that point on, the packages became a lot easier to sell":* Author's interview with Tal Bar.

207 *"Thank you":* Author's interview with Zohar Bali.

207 *The initial pricing for a Better Place subscription package in Denmark was also high:* Michael Kanellos, "Better Place Releases Prices: Not Bad at All," *Greentech Media,* March 3, 2011.

208 *analyzed the total cost of owning a Fluence Z.E. in Denmark:* ibid.

208 *"The Fluence Z.E. in Denmark with all these factors looks like a good deal":* ibid.

208 *"oh, this is a car only for rich people"*: Author's interview with Tal Bar.

Chapter 16 - "Who Trusts Shai?"

209 *An "investor's day" was convened:* Author's interview with Andrey Zarur.

209 *"someone external to the organization who could help identify gaps"*: Mike Granoff email to Shai Agassi, June 22, 2010.

209 *Agassi started the meeting by showing a chart on which colorful bubbles:* Author's interview with Mike Granoff.

209 *"So you see we have two hundred and fifty million coming in"*: ibid.

210 *"We went through all the ancillary products that the team was cooking up"*: ibid.

210 *"Everyone left in high spirits"*: Author's interview with Andrey Zarur.

210 *Agassi invited him to join:* ibid.

210 *"I immediately sensed a high level of discord"*: ibid.

210 *"No way ... I'm not signing up for those. Forget it"*: ibid.

210 *"Tough luck"*: ibid.

210 *"Hold on a minute"*: ibid.

210 *"People were yelling"*: ibid.

210 *"Trust is the most important thing in a company"*: ibid.

211 *"There were only ten people in this room"*: ibid.

211 *"Who feels Shai doesn't trust them ... OK, guys, this is a problem"*: ibid.

211 *"Shai was beaming laser shots out of his face at me"*: ibid.

211 *Several managers approached Zarur afterward to thank him:* ibid.

211 *"What you did in that meeting was out of bounds"*: ibid.

211 *"What are you talking about?"*: ibid.

211 *"That meeting was very negative to the CEO... you're giving them an excuse"*: ibid.

211 *"Were they really not doing their jobs?"*: ibid.

212 *"Like everybody, you have strengths and weaknesses"*: email from Mike Granoff to Shai Agassi, June 22, 2010.

212 *"It was gradual"*: Author's interview with Andrey Zarur.

212 *"I never had Shai on a pedestal like the rest of the company"*: ibid.

212 *"I would say, 'Guys, I don't like this plan, it's overly aggressive"*: ibid.

212 *Not knowing ... "scared the shit out of me"*: ibid.

212 *"We had all this information being put forth by a fragmented finance group"*: ibid.

213 *Better Place's burn rate ... had reached a staggering $1 million a day:* ibid.

213 *the $200 million Series C would run out by October:* ibid.

213 *"By May, I was now screaming, yelling at the top of my lungs"*: ibid.

213 *"By my calculations, you'll run out of money by October"*: Author's interview with Mike Granoff.

213 *"We're done building the switch stations, that's the biggest burn"*: ibid.

213 *now converted into a full-fledged sales facility:* Author's interview with Lilach Gon Carfas.

214 *Better Place's PR team organized a three-day press "event":* Author's interview with Julie Mullins, March 5, 2014.

214 *Julie Mullins … divided the journalists into small groups:* ibid.

214 *The OSCAR unit in each car had been pre-programmed with a driving route to Jerusalem:* ibid.

214 *Every itinerary included a stop at a switching station:* ibid.

214 *at the city's swanky Mamilla Hotel:* ibid.

214 *the journalists had the opportunity to meet and mingle with Better Place's executive team:* ibid.

214 *"Will there be enough time to buy potato chips":* Mette Winkler, "Electric Cars with Brain Capacity," *Borsen,* May 11, 2012.

214 *"Will my neighbor's child get electrified":* ibid.

215 *"Will OSCAR reveal your latest route to your mistress":* ibid.

215 *"the ophthalmologist who doubles as Better Place's chief technical officer":* Jim Motavalli, "Car Battery Swapping in Israel," *The New York Times,* May 9, 2012.

215 *"It's a well-appointed and finished five-passenger sedan":* ibid.

215 *"in line with similarly equipped gas cars in Israel":* ibid.

215 *"if not an assured future, at least a bright vision":* ibid.

215 *"I do not know if this system holds a future":* Simon Rozendaal, "Recharging an Electric Car is Complicated," *Elsevier,* May 14, 2012.

215 *by 2016, Better Place expected that half of all cars sold in Israel will be electric:* Rolf Bos, "Thumbs Up to 100% Electric," *Volkskrant,* May 12, 2012.

215 *"Is that too optimistic?":* ibid.

215 *"will swap a petrol car for an electric":* ibid.

215 *there's no station attendant "to clean the windshield":* ibid.

216 *"accurate range predictions based on each person's individual driving style and history":* Nikki Gordon-Bloomfield, "Better Place Battery Swapping: The Technology Behind the Idea," *Green Car Reports,* May 15, 2012.

216 *compared OSCAR favorably to KITT:* Winkler, "Electric Cars with Brain Capacity."

216 *"it is impossible to say if the car is 'on' at all":* ibid.

216 *"a well-respected car journalist who had been really hard on us":* Author's interview with Julie Mullins.

216 *"113 people who decided to lead the change":* Shai Agassi, tweet, June 4, 2012.

216 *Here's what actually was involved:* description of the process to install home charge spots and dealing with the *va'ad habayit* from the author's interviews with Zohar Bali and Eitan Hon, and the author's experience driving a Renault Fluence Z.E.

218 *"We convinced the va'ad habayit that we'd provide what they needed":* Author's interview with Zohar Bali.

218 *Better Place had promised free installation of the home charge spot:* Author's interview with Eitan Hon.

218 *one-time fee of $1,868:* Kanellos, "Better Place Releases Prices: Not Bad at All."

218 *an off-the-shelf charge spot:* Brad Berman, "Buying Your First Home EV Charger," *PluginCars* May 26, 2016.

219 *The average installation cost is $1,350:* Mark Kane, "Installation Costs of Electric Car Charging Stations By Type," *Inside EVs,* February 15, 2016.

219 *the total cost to Better Place for installation:* Author's interview with Eitan Hon.

219 *The more cars Better Place sold, the more money it would lose:* Author's interview with Andrey Zarur.

220 *perhaps just in a few-mile corridor between Herzliya and Ra'anana:* Author's interview with Idan Ofer.

220 *A turn to China and departure from Israel:* ibid.

220 *a long enough runway:* Author's interviews with Zohar Bali, Debbie Kaye, Susanne Tolstrup and Geoff Zippel.

220 *"It is true that we needed a little bit longer than we thought at the beginning":* Matthias Lambrecht, "Charge Inhibition," *German Financial Times,* May 15, 2012.

221 *"We invited all our customers who'd already received their Fluence Z.E":* Author's interview with Susanne Tolstrup, which also includes Tolstrup's description of the parade of Fluence Z.E.s across Copenhagen.

221 *so-called"Janteloven" was partly to blame:* ibid.

221 *"Janteloven is an integral part of Danish culture":* ibid.

221 *It began a list of ten rules created in 1933 by Danish author Aksel Sandemose:* David Nikel, "What Exactly is Janteloven?" Life in Norway website, June 2015.

222 *"When Better Place was first established, its ambitions were outrageously high":* Author's interview with Susanne Tolstrup.

222 *"Better Place is a small company in an ocean of big car manufacturers":* Winkler, "Electric Cars with Brain Capacity."

222 *"People here were surprised that a state-owned energy company would invest in a project":* Author's interview with Susanne Tolstrup.

222 *Anders Eldrup was ousted as CEO of DONG:* James Quilter, "DONG CEO Eldrup Resigns Amid Legal Enquiry," *WindPower Monthly,* March 12, 2012.

222 *hired four individuals with huge bonuses:* "DONG's CEO Acted 'Disloyally,' Report Concludes," *CPH Post Online,* March 28, 2012.

222 *"The media blamed Eldrup for using Better Place as a sort of greenwashing project":* Author's interview with Susanne Tolstrup.

222 *Hansen replaced Jens Moberg as CEO of Better Place Denmark:* email from Shai Agassi to Better Place staff, March 1, 2011.

222 *after Moberg had had a heart attack:* email from Shai Agassi to Alex Umansky, August 22, 2010.

222 *Hansen had been the CEO of transportation giant Arriva Scandinavia:* "Better Place Denmark Names Johnny Hansen as CEO," *Reve—Wind Energy and Electric Vehicle Review,* March 5, 2011.

223 *"DONG was doing all sorts of investments":* Author's interview with Johnny Hansen.

223 *"If the CEO hadn't been kicked out, we probably would have gotten that money":* ibid.

Chapter 17 - "Not for Everyone"

224 *"She's not for everyone"*: text and description of visuals from Better Place television commercial, July 2012.

224 *it was filmed in Prague:* Author's interview with Ariel Tikotsky.

225 *"We still think we're selling to them"*: Roth, "Driven: Shai Agassi's Audacious Plan to Put Electric Cars on the Road."

225 *"They're going to be zealots"*: ibid.

225 *They even get free gas:* ibid.

225 *The vast majority:* Author's interview with Zohar Bali.

225 *A system known as a "Dalkan"*: "Promoting Competition and Efficiency in the Fuel Economy," website of the Israeli Ministry of National Infrastructure, Energy and Water Resources.

226 *but unless you were a "greenie"*: Author's interview with Zohar Bali.

226 *it saw it as inconvenient:* ibid.

226 *Employees who receive a car from their job have to pay a "usage tax"*: ibid.

226 *Determined petitioning:* Author's interview with Ziva Patir.

226 *"Everyone was against us"*: ibid.

226 *"We asked the government to make an exception for the Fluence Z.E"*: ibid.

227 *"We want more efficient small cars on the road"*: ibid.

227 *"The government didn't want to lose the income it made from taxing gasoline"*: Author's interview with Dubi Ben-Gedalyahu, June 16, 2014.

227 *Usage tax is considered to be on employees' "enjoyment" of their vehicles:* Author's interview with Ziva Patir.

227 *"If you use that argument, we'll never sell the car to individual buyers"*: ibid.

227 *only discounts available to Better Place drivers:* Author's interview with Zohar Bali.

227 *"Israel Chemicals employees travel long distances"*: Lan and Magen, "Can Better Place Get Better?"

227 *In 2008, the average car in Denmark sold for about $30,000:* Author's interview with Johnny Hansen.

227 *Danes were going for two tiny, two-door "A" class cars:* ibid.

228 *Leasing companies make money:* Author's interview with Zohar Bali.

228 *"it would sign its 'main agreements'"*: Dubi Ben-Gedalyhu, "Better Place in Wrong Place at Wrong Time," *Globes*, May 26, 2013.

228 *Their business model is heavily based on the "residual value" of the car:* Author's interview with Zohar Bali.

228 *"The leasing companies would say to us, 'It sounds great, but let's wait a year'"*: ibid.

228 *"Renault doesn't have a very good image in Israel"*: Author's interview with Dubi Ben-Gedalyhu.

228 *Fleet operators like Hertz and Avis generally expect to receive:* Author's interview with Zohar Bali.

228 *"we always came in 10 percent less than everyone else"*: ibid.

229 *"The objective is to keep Shai as CEO":* Author's interview with Andrey Zarur, which also includes Zarur's description of his "shpiel" at the London board meeting.

230 *"You're taking my company away from me!":* ibid.

230 *"It was very clear that he was going to fight this tooth and nail":* ibid.

230 *Agassi tried to assure the board that money was not going to be a problem:* ibid.

230 *"No, Shai … It has maybe a three percent probability":* ibid.

230 *The $50 million that was missing from the Series C "was in progress":* ibid.

230 *Agassi had started quietly meeting with investors without informing the board:* ibid.

230 *"New investors don't want to put money into a company":* ibid.

230 *"This is what's known as the 'don't throw good money after bad' rule":* ibid.

230 *a week to review the resolutions:* Author's interview with Mike Granoff.

231 *"We came to a decision that, although Shai may kick and scream":* Author's interview with Andrey Zarur.

231 *"I was conflicted by the loyalty that I had to my friend":* ibid.

231 *"try to salvage whatever relationship I could with Shai":* ibid.

231 *No committees were formed:* ibid.

231 *Shai was very smart about it":* Author's interview with Mike Granoff.

231 *Board member Alan Salzman quit in frustration:* Author's interview with Andrey Zarur.

231 *"I didn't invest in an Israeli company; I invested in an American one":* Author's interview with Dan Cohen.

231 *"I didn't quit, but I wish I had":* Author's interview with Mike Granoff.

231 *Agassi summoned Granoff into his office in Rosh HaAyin:* ibid.

232 *"Where's the fifty million dollars you promised me?":* ibid.

232 *"Horrible things were being said about me":* Author's interview with Andrey Zarur.

232 *"I have zero tolerance for back stabbers!!!":* Tami Chotoveli, tweet, June 9, 2012.

232 *"Sometimes, the person you'd take a bullet for ends up being the one behind the gun":* Tami Chotoveli, tweet, July 9, 2012.

232 *"Nobody likes a liar":* ibid.

232 *Those who disappoint, cheat themselves…I am easily fooled, ONCE!":* Shai Agassi, tweet, May 31, 2012.

232 *"Friends are either True or not friends":* Shai Agassi, tweet, June 16, 2012.

232 *Zarur's founding role as Agassi's partner:* Chafkin, "A Broken Place: The Spectacular Failure of the Startup that Was Going to Change the World."

232 *"Being loved by the right person allows you to move forward":* Tami Chotoveli, tweet, February 15, 2012.

232 *"When you find your ONE … you become someone different, someone better":* Tami Chotoveli, tweet, April 8, 2012.

232 *"What did Andrey do?":* Author's interview with Mike Granoff.

233 *While the country is only 9.3 miles wide at its most narrow point:* Daniel Greenfield, "How Small is Israel? So Small You Can Run it in 9 Days," *Front Page Mag,* March 14, 2013.

233 *it is nearly 300 miles from northern Metula:* "Israel in Brief," Israel Ministry of Foreign Affairs website.

233 *as he set out August 19, 2012:* Brian Thomas, "Better Place Distance Dash," *IsraellyCool*, August 20, 2012.

233 *Agassi took to Twitter to document his trip:* quotes and description in this section come directly from Shai Agassi's tweets, August 19, 2012.

234 *we drove fast (sometimes really fast...):* email from Shai Agassi to Better Place staff, August 20, 2012.

234 *"No other electric car in the world with any other fast charging technology could do that":* Thomas, "Better Place Distance Dash."

235 *"I was more convinced than ever that the company would be out of cash then":* Author's interview with Andrey Zarur.

235 *"You're wrong about this, Andrey":* ibid.

235 *"Thank you for having raised the alarm so enthusiastically in the past":* ibid.

235 *"My reputation had been dragged through the mud":* ibid.

235 *The board meeting in Copenhagen lasted 12 hours:* Author's interview with Mike Granoff.

235 *[Agassi] emphatically assured the board:* ibid.

235 *There could be a gap between when we need the money and when we get the loan":* ibid.

235 *"No one said 'yes' loudly, but no one said no loudly either":* ibid.

235 *Idan Ofer decamped to his private yacht:* ibid.

236 *He had named his yacht the Better Place:* ibid.

236 *Built by the Monegasque yacht maker Wally, at a cost of $10 million:* Dubi Ben-Gedalyahu, "The Better Place Chairman's $10 Million 50-meter Yacht Carries the Electric Car Venture's Logo on its Sails," *Globes*, November 5, 2012.

236 *Ofer sailed the Better Place to nearby Greece:* Author's interview with Idan Ofer.

236 *The report, written by Michael Maccoby for the Review's January 2000 issue:* Michael Maccoby, "Narcissistic Leaders: The Incredible Pros, the Inevitable Cons," *Harvard Business Review*, January-February issue 2000.

236 *won a Harvard Business Review McKinsey Award:* ibid.

236 *"I saw all the prerequisites, all the data points":* Author's interview with Idan Ofer.

237 *Maccoby began his analysis by noting that today's CEO superstars have embraced the limelight:* quotes taken from Maccoby's paper on Narcissistic Leaders and the author's interview with Idan Ofer.

237 *The Mayo Clinic defines narcissistic personality disorder:* "Narcissistic Personality Disorder," Mayo Clinic website.

239 *Dan Cohen had also read the Harvard Business Review article:* Author's interview with Dan Cohen.

239 *"There was no one event that sparked and finished it":* Author's interview with Dan Cohen.

239 *"I felt like it was describing Shai":* ibid.

239 *"If you have any illusions that Better Place can succeed without Shai, you'd better think again":* ibid.

239   *"Could someone else take Shai's role?":* ibid.

240   *Better Place opened a new battery switch station at Schiphol airport:* "Better Place Consortium Delivers EU Showcase in Amsterdam," press release, *BusinessWire*, September 3, 2012.

240   *The station was intended to serve a fleet of 10 taxis:* ibid.

240   *Three local taxi providers signed on:* ibid.

240   *more than 700,000 taxi trips originate from Schiphol each year:* ibid.

240   *plans for 28 more across the Netherlands in the coming years:* "Better Place Launches Battery Switch Station in Amsterdam," Netherlands Embassy in Tel Aviv website, September 3, 2012.

240   *Maxime Verhagen, Olivier Onidi, Jean-Paul Renaux:* "Better Place Consortium Delivers EU Showcase in Amsterdam."

240   *Paul Harms, who came to the company from Dutch car-leasing leader Athlon:* ibid.

240   *Agassi continued on to New York:* Author's interview with Mike Granoff.

240   *a quick lunch at Frank's Express Pizza:* ibid.

240   *"Tell me about the next meeting":* ibid.

241   *"If you can't move them, Mike, how do you think I can do it?":* ibid.

241   *"This wasn't the Shai Agassi I knew … Shai was defeated":* ibid.

241   *Who will die at his predestined time and who before his time?:* traditional text of *Unetanneh Tokef* prayer, this version from Steven Kepnes, *The Future of Jewish Theology*, Wiley-Blackwell, John Wiley and Sons, 2013.

242   *Agassi asked the board members to step up with the bridge loan:* Chafkin, "A Broken Place: The Spectacular Failure of the Startup that Was Going to Change the World."

242   *Better Place would be out of cash in a matter of weeks:* Author's interview with Andrey Zarur.

Chapter 18 - The End of the Road

243   *only 457 cars had been sold so far in Israel:* Daniel Schmil and Yoram Gabison, "Better Place Founder and CEO Shai Agassi Ousted by Board," *Haaretz*, October 2, 2012.

243   *"We said that before we'd deployed the entire network, we cannot sell more than 500 cars":* Daniel Schmil and Yoram Gabison, "Take the Keys: Better Place Founder and CEO Shai Agassi Dismissed," *The Marker*, October 2, 2012.

244   *For NIS 9,900 down and NIS 1,990 a month for 36 months:* ibid.

244   *the Better Place booth was packed:* Author's interview with Zohar Bali.

244   *Forty-eight consumers signed lease deals with Albar during the show:* "Albar sells 48 Better Place cars in Sukkot fair," *Globes*, October 9, 2012.

244   *"You made me so happy today. I'm so proud of you":* Author's interview with Zohar Bali.

244   *Agassi came prepared with the latest spreadsheets:* Author's interview with Mike Granoff.

244   *He brought a flower for Ofer's wife, Batya:* Author's interview with Idan Ofer.

244   *"It was like a peace offering":* ibid.

244   *"he started to explain how the budget he conjured up was actually doable":* ibid.

245 *"The board has lost confidence in you"*: Author's interview with Mike Granoff.

245 *"I don't want you to work for me anymore"*: Author's interview with Idan Ofer.

245 *"You will fail without me"*: ibid.

245 *"That's OK," Ofer responded. "I will take the consequences"*: ibid.

245 *He called on the other members of the board*: ibid.

245 *"I had told the board already"*: ibid.

245 *The news dropped on the second day of the Automania car show*: Schmil and Gabison, "Better Place Founder and CEO Shai Agassi Ousted by Board."

245 *From that moment, sales stopped short*: Author's interview with Zohar Bali.

245 *Buyers who had purchased vehicles in the previous days*: Tomer Hadar, "Better Place Hit by Order Cancelations," *Ynet*, November 6, 2012.

245 *"It felt like a big hammer came from above"*: Author's interview with Tal Bar.

246 *"Everyone was in disbelief that this can happen"*: ibid.

246 *"Why haven't you cleaned out Shai's office yet?"*: dialogue between Kaye and Ofer from author's interview with Debbie Kaye.

246 *he quit in solidarity with his brother*: Tomer Hadar, "Better Place Changing Direction," *Ynet*, November 16, 2012.

246 *Agassi's sister, Dafna, left a month later, in November*: Dubi Ben-Gedalyahu, "Among the Latest Departures is VP Marketing Dafna Agassi, the Sister of Ousted Founder and CEO Shai Agassi," *Globes*, November 15, 2012.

246 *CTO Barak Hershkovitz stuck around for another couple of months*: Barak Hershkovitz, LinkedIn profile.

246 *loyalists had created a graffiti wall*: Author's interview with Johnny Hansen.

246 *"Shai, we love you"*: photograph of graffiti wall posted to Barak Hershkovitz's Facebook.

246 *"Whoever makes a deal with the devil pays the price"*: Hadas Magen and Shlomit Lan, "Idan Ofer Not Willing to Lose Money as the CEO Travels the World," *Globes*, October 11, 2012.

246 *"Everyone knows who Shai Agassi is"*: ibid.

246 *"It's very difficult to get fired from any role"*: Author's interview with Debbie Kaye.

247 *"Under Shai's leadership, we've successfully achieved our goals"*: Schmil and Gabison, "Better Place Founder and CEO Shai Agassi Ousted by Board."

247 *"joint decision"*: ibid.

247 *"Shai Agassi is a smart man and I like him and his idea"*: "Idan Ofer Justifies Firing Shai Agassi," *Globes*, December 24, 2012.

247 *"I'm honest and always hope that others will be as honest as I am"*: ibid.

247 *"I also never give up"*: ibid.

247 *"successfully positioned the company's goals in the first chapter of its life"*: Schmil and Gabison, "Better Place Founder and CEO Shai Agassi Ousted by Board."

248 *"As far as I'm concerned, Better Place has proven what it set out to do successfully"*: Todd Woody, "What's Behind Better Place's Ouster of Shai Agassi?" *Forbes*, October 2, 2012.

248 *Evan Thornley got the call at midnight:* Author's interview with Evan Thornley.

248 *"We want you to be the CEO of all of Better Place":* ibid.

248 *Thornley was on a plane at 10 that same morning:* ibid.

248 *"I didn't know how I was going to work it out with my family":* ibid.

248 *"Evan has built an impressive track record":* Schmil and Gabison, "Better Place Founder and CEO Shai Agassi Ousted by Board."

248 *"Four years ago, Shai asked me to join the Better Place mission":* ibid.

248 *"Was I the right guy?":* Author's interview with Evan Thornley.

249 *"It is not uncommon for a startup to replace a visionary founder":* Woody, "What's Behind Better Place's Ouster of Shai Agassi?"

249 *"It's part of the business school literature":* Joshua Mitnick, "CEO of Electric Car Network Better Place Steps Down." *The Wall Street Journal,* October 2, 2012.

249 *"The press is calling the resignation of Shai Agassi a surprise":* Brian Dumaine, "Shai Agassi's Ouster No Surprise," *Fortune,* October 3, 2012.

249 *Agassi "did what entrepreneurs are supposed to do":* ibid.

249 *"for taking a radical notion and getting to the proof of concept stage":* ibid.

249 *Better Place had blown through an estimated "$477 million since the beginning of 2010":* Schmil and Gabison, "Take the Keys: Better Place Founder and CEO Shai Agassi Dismissed."

249 *Idan Ofer "could absorb a lot":* Magen and Lan, "Idan Ofer Not Willing to Lose Money as the CEO Travels the World."

250 *Agassi's "dealings were extravagant and arrogant":* ibid.

250 *Agassi had "a thousand tons of charisma":* ibid.

250 *"There's a lot of black humor running around the corridors of Better Place":* Lan and Magen, "Can Better Place Get Better?"

250 *The 120-page full-color book was stuffed with pictures and stories:* Shai Agassi and Mike Granoff, *Chapter One: The Start of the Story.*

250 *Not "Chapter 1" but "Chapter 11":* Lan and Magen, "Can Better Place Get Better?"

250 *"When all over the world the brand is associated with you":* ibid.

251 *"This whole thing reminds me of how Apple ousted Steve Jobs":* Schmil and Gabison, "Take the Keys: Better Place Founder and CEO Shai Agassi Dismissed."

251 *"Five years ago, I followed the vision of weaning the world from oil":* ibid.

251 *"someone would pick up the local assets at a discount price":* Brian Thomas, "Shai Agassi Out of Better Place (Or Is He?), *IsraellyCool,* October 3, 2012.

251 *"Knowing what I know today I'd still buy my car":* ibid.

251 *Shai Agassi sent an email:* email from Shai Agassi to Better Place staff, October 2, 2012.

Chapter 19 - Saving Private Better Place

253 *the number of people on the payroll:* Author's interview with Evan Thornley.

253 *set up a makeshift office in the lobby of the West Hotel:* Author's interview with Osnat Tirosh.

253 *radically cutting staff, projects and locations:* Author's interview with Evan Thornley.

253 *Thornley spent the next two days in interviews:* Author's interview with Osnat Tirosh.

253 *with OpCo staff scouting out the TopCo floor and its fancy equipment:* ibid.

253 *The assumption had been that Kaplan ... would take over:* ibid.

253 *Instead, Kaplan was promoted to deputy chief operating officer:* Daniel Schmil, "Things Getting Worse at Better Place as Israeli CEO Quits," *Haaretz,* November 14, 2012.

254 *"Evidently, it wasn't enough":* ibid.

254 *Kaplan abruptly quit on November 14, 2012:* ibid.

254 *[Ofer] pledged an additional $100 million for Better Place:* Ela Levy-Weinrib, "Israel Corp sued over last Better Place investment," *Globes,* April 27, 2014.

254 *Mike Granoff raised another $100,000:* Author's interview with Mike Granoff.

254 *Ofer offered Agassi a newly created position:* Golan Hazani, "Shai Agassi Quits Better Place Board," *Ynet,* October 9, 2012.

254 *"The decision is said to be personal and has not been explained":* ibid.

254 *And sales did pick up:* Author's interview with Zohar Bali.

254 *half the orders for the 48 cars sold through Albar at Automania:* Hadar, "Better Place Hit by Order Cancelations."

254 *were moving dozens of cars per month:* Author's interview with Zohar Bali.

254 *January saw an unprecedented 102 cars sold:* John Reed, "Better Place toils in electric car market," *Financial Times,* February 22, 2013.

255 *Better Place started its own direct leasing program:* Author's interview with Zohar Bali, which also includes how Better Place solved the "residual value" problem and convinced Carasso to sell the Fluence Z.E.

256 *all 40 stations were operational:* Author's experience driving a Renault Fluence Z.E.

256 *"Better Place had three silos":* Author's interview with Evan Thornley, which also includes what Thornley discovered once he became CEO.

256 *He merged the three silos:* ibid.

257 *the company had its long missing chief financial officer:* Yossi Nissan, "Better Place Appoints Alan Gelman as CFO," *Globes,* November 1, 2012.

257 *Up to 200 people would be fired:* Golan Hazani, "Better Place to Sack 150 R&D Workers," *Ynet,* October 28, 2012.

257 *now that the company had completed the development of most of its infrastructure:* ibid.

257 *Thornley and his team would eventually lay off 500 people:* Author's interview with Evan Thornley, which also includes the process of layoffs and Sidney Goodman's surprise at being kept on.

257 *Renault sent a delegation to Israel:* Author's interview with Evan Thornley, which also includes Thornley's description of and quotes from the meeting with Renault in Paris.

258 *"We started with the usual five minutes of diplomatic posturing":* ibid.

258 *"Enough of the bullshit":* ibid.

258 *"He then launched into a two-hour monologue":* ibid.

258   *the Renault executive was under pressure to make a call before the end of the year:* ibid.

258   *If Renault declared the project a loss, it would stop producing the Fluence Z.E:* ibid.

258   *"What do you have to say for yourselves?":* ibid.

258   *"I agree with you":* ibid.

258   *why the business was not a bust:* ibid.

258   *"We showed him how many miles people were driving each day":* Author's interview with Ben Keneally.

258   *"Yes, you're right":* Author's interview with Evan Thornley.

258   *"Look, we're not disguising the fact that we messed up":* ibid.

259   *The group reconvened over dinner:* Author's interview with Ben Keneally.

259   *"We came into the meeting fully planning to shut this whole thing down today":* Author's interview with Evan Thornley.

259   *"The Israeli business is hemorrhaging money":* ibid.

259   *Thornley had put together a 160-page PowerPoint presentation:* PowerPoint presentation, Better Place Board Meeting, December 2012.

259   *the company had sold only 330 cars to non-employees in Israel:* ibid.

259   *"There isn't a snowball's chance in hell we can get to positive cash flow in Israel":* Chafkin, "A Broken Place: The Spectacular Failure of the Startup that Was Going to Change the World."

259   *shifting the company's "center of gravity" to Western Europe:* PowerPoint presentation, Better Place Board Meeting, December 2012.

259   *A Better Place-led consortium, called EV Engineering:* Barry Park, "EV Engineering Adds Range-Extending Hybrid Commodore to Project Wishlist," *GoAuto.com.au,* July 23, 2013.

259   *the Australian government got behind it as well:* Author's interview with Alison Terry.

259   *"GM's top-selling car in Australia":* Author's interview with Evan Thornley.

260   *Detroit "would never let GM in Australia do that kind of experimentation":* ibid.

260   *"They were without a doubt some of the finest prototype electric vehicles":* ibid.

260   *"the Australian market represented a proof of concept":* Author's interview with Geoff Zippel.

260   *expensive agreements the company had with third party vendors:* PowerPoint presentation, Better Place Board Meeting, December 2012.

260   *"provided Better Place with a system worth $50 to $60 million":* ibid.

260   *Amdocs investment in Better Place was "only" about $12 million:* ibid.

260   *Better Place needed to raise an additional $300 million:* ibid.

260   *"We need to prove the concept with a growth story":* Author's interview with Evan Thornley, which also includes his description of winning backing from the board, making plans to take some time off, and unexpected corporate intrigue and politics.

261   *Ofer had become overly focused on small issues:* ibid.

261   *Ofer demanded they drive the Fluence Z.E:* ibid.

261   *"What I say goes!":* Author's interview with Mike Granoff.

262   *"A bunch of locals kept stealing the diesel":* Author's interview with Evan Thornley.

262   *"We had to deal with things costing us $300,000 a day":* ibid.

262   *"Idan, I don't want to belittle your concerns":* ibid.

262   *"It's my money, and my company":* ibid.

262   *"I know what it's like being a leader who's being undermined":* ibid.

262   *calling in by video conference from his home:* Author's interview with Mike Granoff.

262   *Thornley suffered what he thought was a heart attack:* Author's interview with Evan Thornley.

262   *"It turned out to be not life-threatening, but it was quite scary":* ibid.

262   *Mike Granoff and Dan Cohen ran interference:* Author's interview with Mike Granoff.

262   *"Dan and I went to Evan's room to talk to him":* ibid.

262   *"To be fair, I wasn't very forthcoming about it":* Author's interview with Evan Thornley.

262   *It was clear to Granoff and Cohen that Ofer was about to fire Better Place's second CEO:* Author's interview with Mike Granoff.

263   *"We won't be able to survive another CEO shift so soon":* ibid.

263   *"we still only had six months left of cash":* ibid.

263   *Thornley's departure was announced on January 16, 2013:* John Reed, "Better Place Loses Second Chief in Months," *Financial Times,* January 16, 2013.

263   *"Evan Thornley felt that he had reached the end of his road":* Shahar Haselkorn, "Better Place CEO Quits After 3 Months," *Ynet,* January 16, 2013.

263   *Stepping into Thornley's shoes was Dan Cohen:* Guy Katsovitch, "Dan Cohen Appointed Better Place Acting CEO," *Globes,* January 23, 2013.

263   *"It was a clear conflict of interest":* Author's interview with Debbie Kaye.

263   *Cohen continued the cutting Thornley had begun:* Author's interview with Dan Cohen.

263   *Thornley's dismissal meant bad news for Better Place Australia:* Todd Woody, "Better Place to Shut Down U.S., Australian Operations," *Forbes,* February 5, 2013.

263   *Thornley's final job at Better Place was to lay off his own management team:* Author's interview with Evan Thornley.

263   *Cohen also moved quickly to shutter the U.S. office:* Woody, "Better Place to Shut Down U.S., Australian Operations."

264   *All these moves led journalist Daniel Roth to tweet:* Chafkin, "A Broken Place: The Spectacular Failure of the Startup that Was Going to Change the World."

264   *"When you look at the overall trends":* Soren Spring Borg, "Renault Boss Weakens the Better Place Model," *EnergiWatch,* May 1, 2013.

264   *the Fluence Z.E. would be the last battery-switchable car made by Renault:* Nikki Gordon-Bloomfield, "Renault-Nissan CEO Rejects Battery Swapping, Leaving Better Place Stranded," *PluginCars,* May 6, 2013.

264   *a switchable-battery version of the Zoe:* ibid.

264   *"Swappable batteries are no longer the central part of [our] business model:* Soren Spring Borg, "Renault Boss Weakens the Better Place Model."

264   *"We're in a very serious situation here":* Author's interview with Dan Cohen.

264   *"I'm sure he didn't really mean it":* ibid.

264   *Cohen implored Tavares to ask Ghosn to issue a "corrective statement":* ibid.

264 *"I'll relay your concerns"*: ibid.

265 *(there were just 100 people left in the company at this point)*: Author's interview with Efi Shahak.

265 *indicated the company would need an additional $500 million*: Author's interview with Dan Cohen.

265 *Another $70 million was needed immediately*: ibid.

265 *Idan Ofer was unable to invest any more*: Author's interview with Mike Granoff.

265 *The company's $2.25 billion valuation was too high for them*: Author's interview with Macgregor Duncan.

265 *"They liked what Idan was doing in China"*: Author's interview with Dan Cohen.

265 *But an investment from China would take at least six months*: ibid.

265 *the board of directors of Better Place voted to formally file for bankruptcy*: Edmund Sanders, "Electric Car Start-up Better Place Files for Bankruptcy," *Los Angeles Times*, May 26, 2013.

265 *"Unfortunately, after a year's commercial operation, it was clear to us"*: ibid.

266 *"This is a very sad day for all of us"*: Karin Kloosterman, "Israel's Better Place EV Company Declares Bankruptcy," *Israel21c*, May 27, 2013.

266 *"always envisioned and required great scale"*: Mike Granoff letter to Better Place investors, May 28, 2013.

266 *"Crossing the chasm to that scale"*: ibid.

266 *who went by the nickname "Captain Sunshine"*: Emily Harris, "Can Captain Sunshine Save the Israeli Electric Car Dream?" *NPR*, June 14, 2013.

266 *teamed up with up the Association for the Advancement of Electric Transport in Israel*: Daniella Cheslow, "Electric-Car Company 'Better Place' Fails to Make it in the Start-up Nation," *Tablet*, June 25, 2013.

266 *But when government bureaucracy kept some 350 Fluence Z.E.s he intended to sell*: Author's interview with Yosef Abramowitz, May 16, 2014.

266 *planned to rebrand the company as "DRiiVZ"*: Hillel Fusk, "Better Place with DRiiVZ: Will the Next Incarnation Survive?" *Ynet*, September 24, 2013.

266 *caught trying to pass a $500,000 check drawn on a fictitious foreign account*: Ela Levy-Weinrib," Better Place Again for Sale," *Globes*, October 17, 2013.

266 *Within a few months, all the switch stations were padlocked*: Author's experience driving a Renault Fluence Z.E.

266 *The clock on the dashboard of the Fluence Z.E. was stuck in perpetual Standard Time*: ibid.

267 *Carasso promised to honor its agreement with Renault*: ibid.

267 *closed its Turkish production line for the Fluence Z.E*: Sebastian Blanco, "Renault Moves All Fluence Z.E. Production to Korea," *AutoBlog*, February 4, 2014.

267 *known as the Renault-Samsung SM3 Z.E.*: Joey Wang, Dongfeng Fengnuo E300 EV is a Renault Fluence Z.E. on the Beijing Auto Show," *CarNewsChina*, May 3, 2016.

267 *A version of the all-electric Fluence Z.E. also appeared at the 2016 Beijing Auto Show*: ibid.

267 *fewer than a thousand Fluence Z.E.s were sold or leased:* Cheslow, "Electric-Car Company 'Better Place' Fails to Make it in the Start-up Nation."

267 *would eventually be so damaged by the sea air:* Efrat Peretz and Dubi Ben-Gedalyahu, "Importer Destroys Hundreds of Better Place Cars," *Globes*, August 26, 2013.

267 *Renault quietly "bought back" the few cars tooling around Copenhagen:* Author's interview with Johnny Hansen.

267 *adapted its charging cable for two-wheelers to work with the Fluence Z.E:* Author's experience driving a Renault Fluence Z.E.

267 *adopted several mobile apps:* one of the leading apps used was Plugshare.com.

267 *"We're a band of brothers":* Nir Ben-Zaken, "Shai Agassi's Car—How it Drives Today," *Ynet*, May 24, 2015.

267 *"Electric car owners are a special population":* ibid.

268 *"We love to tackle big problems":* Author's interview with Saul Singer, March 3, 2014.

268 *TEN-T consortium:* Author's interview with Amit Yudan.

268 *EZ-Batt and Green eMotion:* Author's interviews with Guy Zzur and Yariv Nornberg, June 24, 2014.

268 *there was no awareness that electric vehicles were a viable option:* Author's interview with Amit Yudan.

268 *"Better Place created huge attention with heads of state":* ibid.

268 *it was reincarnated as Taxi Electric:* TaxiElectric.nl website.

268 *Madrid's La Ciudad del Taxi:* Steve Hanley, "Madrid Going All In on Electric Taxi Fleet," *Gas2*, May 19, 2016.

268 *Gogoro has built a network of switchable battery motor scooters:* Aaron Tilley, "The Tesla of Scooters is Driving Asia's Two-Wheel Revolution," *Forbes*, April 15, 2015.

269 *Greenway in Slovakia proposed developing switchable battery delivery vans:* Laurent J. Mason, "Another Try at Battery Swap, from Slovakia," *PluginCars*, November 7, 2012.

269 *Tesla announced that its high end Model S would have a switchable battery option:* Niv Ellis, "Tesla Unveils Switchable Battery, Filling Better Place Void," *The Jerusalem Post*, June 21, 2013.

269 *"We've invited all the Model S owners in the area to try it out":* Benjamin Zhang, "Tesla's Battery-Swapping Plan has a Mere Shadow of the Promise it Once Showed," *Business Insider*, June 27, 2015.

269 *"Being willing to take risks is essential":* Author's interview with Saul Singer.

269 *"Israel was home to the world's first full-service network":* Author's interview with Mike Granoff.

269 *'In investing you can be really right, but temporarily quite wrong":* Mamta Badkar, "22 Brilliant Quotes from Legendary Short-Seller Jim Chanos, *Business Insider*, November 16, 2013.

269 *" I have no regrets for having tried":* ibid.

ABOUT THE AUTHOR

Business and technology journalist Brian Blum tells the stories of the world's most fascinating entrepreneurs and the companies they create. A high-tech startup veteran, his work has appeared in The Jerusalem Post, Haaretz and Israel21c. He is a senior analyst for the Advanced Interactive Media Group and its "Classified Intelligence Report."

Blum's own Internet publishing startup Neta4 raised $3.2 million, in 1998. He served as entrepreneur-in-residence for Jerusalem Global Ventures and was an assistant vice president of marketing for telecommunications provider Comverse.

Blum has spoken at conferences and universities worldwide and was international president of the IICS multimedia professional association. He holds a B.A. in Creative Writing from Oberlin College and a master's in Instructional Technology from San Jose State University. His first book, *Interactive Media: Essentials for Success,* was published by Ziff-Davis Press.

Originally from the San Francisco Bay Area, Blum lives in Jerusalem with his wife and three children. He has published his blog "This Normal Life" weekly since 2002.

GET YOUR FREE PASS TO
EXCLUSIVE ONLINE EXTRAS AND MORE

Receive insider insights on electric vehicles, stories from the marketing trenches and curated links and downloads of new thinking on global tech startups. For access to special bonus content, visit brianblum.com/bonus

Liked *TOTALED*?

Please **leave a review** at your favorite bookseller

Free discussion points available for entrepreneur groups, incubators, high-tech companies, book clubs, and classes:

Contact the author at brianblum.com

Made in the USA
San Bernardino, CA
23 October 2017